"... not only to be a temporary structure but to continue for ages and for laudable purposes, ..." Henry Winemiller, 1836

A SALUTARY INFLUENCE:

GETTYSBURG COLLEGE, 1832-1985

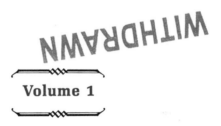

Volume 1

Charles H. Glatfelter

Gettysburg College
Gettysburg, Pennsylvania
1987

Printed in the United States of America by W & M Printing, Inc.
Design and typography by C & J Enterprises,
Mechanicsburg, Pennsylvania

The College Seal, 1832-1921
From an 1850 deed

Contents

Illustrations and Maps	viii
Tables	ix
Preface	xi

1. The Background of Gettysburg College (1776-1832) — 3

July 4, 1832	3
Two Colleges for Southcentral Pennsylvania	6
Lutheran Ministerial Training	13
Samuel Simon Schmucker	16
Gettysburg and the Lutheran Theological Seminary	22
Classical School and Gymnasium (1827-1832)	26
Pennsylvania College of Gettysburg (1831-1832)	32

2. Acquiring a Proper College Edifice (1832-1837) — 41

Getting the Money	41
Building	58

3. After the Manner of a Well-Regulated Family (1832-1868) — 73

Trustees	75
Finances	81
Presidents and Faculty	92
The Campus	104
Preparatory Department	119
Curriculum	122
Library	135
Equipment	139
The Medical Department	141
Students	146
Student Organizations	159
Alumni Association	167
Town and Gown	169
The College and the Lutheran Church	173
In the World of Higher Education	180
The Civil War	181
Changing the Guard	190

4. A Wider Place for a Greater Work (1868-1904) — 193

Trustees	195
Finances	207
Presidents and Faculty	222
The Campus	242
Preparatory Department	270
The Curriculum	276
From Admission to Commencement	297
Library	313
Equipment	315
Students	318
Student Organizations	331
College Publications	343

Athletic Activity   348
College Spirit   362
Alumni   367
Town and Gown   377
The College and the Lutheran Church   383
In the World of Higher Education   404
Toll No More the Bell   406

Illustrations and Maps

Cupola of Pennsylvania Hall   ii
Order of Exercises for July 4, 1832   2
Benjamin Rush (1745-1813)   10
Samuel Simon Schmucker (1799-1873)   17
Pennsylvania Colleges and Universities in 1832   21
Gettysburg Academy   24
Gettysburg Gymnasium, Prospectus   30-31
Seminary Building   33
To the Public   37
Elevation Drawing and Floor Plan, College Edifice   40
Letter Favoring the College Appropriation Bill   49
Thaddeus Stevens (1792-1868)   56
John Cresson Trautwine (1810-1883)   60
Soliciting Proposals for the College Edifice   64
John George Schmucker Casts a Negative Vote   66
College Edifice, about 1843   69
College Campus, about 1862   72
The First Twenty-One Trustees   76
Four Early Resident Trustees   77
Four Early Nonresident Trustees   79
Charles P. Krauth (1797-1867)   94
Henry L. Baugher (1804-1868)   97
Four Early Faculty Members   100
College Edifice, 1882   105
Linnaean Hall   110
Stevens Hall   113
Christ Lutheran Church   117
Course of Instruction, 1832   123
Page from the Matriculation Book, 1840-1841   130
Student Grade Report, 1854   132
Announcement of the 1850 Commencement Exercises   134
Medical Department Building   144
John Hopkins (1806-1868)   150
"We are heartily sorry for these, our offenses"   155
Program for Philomathaean Celebration, 1848   162
Class of 1868   167
Samuel Simon Schmucker in old age   177
New Recitation Building   192
Four Trustees   197
Four Trustees   200

Receipt and Check, 1887-1888 209
Milton Valentine (1825-1906) 223
Harvey W. McKnight (1843-1914) 228
Four Faculty Members 235
Four Faculty Members 238
The Campus between 1868 and the Late 1880s 243
McCreary Gymnasium 247
Observatory 249
Cornerstone Laying, New Recitation Building 255
Brua Chapel 259
South College 264
Adam Foutz (1841-1911) 266
Panoramic View of the Campus, 1897 268-269
Charles H. Huber (1871-1951) 273
The Curriculum as Described in the 1887 Catalogue 282-283
Page from the Matriculation Book, 1883-1884 301
Women Students, 1902-1903 303
Student Grade Report, 1885 306
Program for the 1886 Commencement 308
General View of College Libraries, 1897 314
Biology Laboratory, 1897 316
Museum, 1903 318
Burlesque, 1872 327
"A Typical College Room," 1903 330
Philo Hall 333
Phrena Hall 333
Fraternities Introduced, 1899 *Spectrum* 338
Miller Hall 340
William L. Glatfelter Hall 341
College Musical Clubs 342
First Page of the First *Gettysburgian,* 1897 346
First College Football Team, 1890 352
1891 College Baseball Team 352
Nixon Field 355
Sons of Hercules 360
Gymnasium, Interior View 362
"The Orange and the Blue" 366
"Our Alma Mater" 367
View of Gettysburg, about 1890 378
Monument, Company A, Twenty-Sixth Regiment 381
Seminary Faculty and Students, 1904 391
Eli Huber (1834-1911) 393
H. Louis Baugher (1840-1899) 393

Tables

Students in College and Degrees Granted, 1832-1868 127
Students in College and Degrees Granted, 1868-1904 310

Preface

The main purpose of this work, commissioned to be part of the observance of its 150th anniversary, has been to stress the history of Gettysburg College as an educational institution endowed by its charter with a continuing existence. Its trustees, administrators, faculty, and students have gained their places by election, appointment, or admission. For a longer or shorter period of time they have helped shape College policies and programs. Presumably they have benefited from the experience. Eventually, all have yielded (or will yield) their seats to successors. For more than a century and a half, Gettysburg College has survived as the generations of all those who have given it life have come and gone.

Another major purpose of this work has been to stress the history of the College as an educational institution whose policies and programs have been influenced in various ways and in varying degrees by the surrounding community (since 1863 one nationally, even internationally, known), by its long continuing relationships with the Lutheran church, and by its consistent awareness that it is an integral part of the large and growing American enterprise in higher education.

A third major purpose has been to present the historical facts of the College's past in such a way as to leave to the reader ample (although not complete) opportunity to decide for himself or herself whether or not the policies and programs pursued by the men and women responsible for its welfare since 1832 were wise and proper. Ultimately, those who read this account seriously should evaluate the evidence presented and then decide for themselves how salutary an influence Gettysburg College has exercised in advancing the cause of liberal education.

No person can write an account which completely recreates the past. The best one can do is search for as many surviving primary sources as possible, use every available means to determine their credibility, and then construct an account characterized by what historians sometimes call verisimilitude. That is what I have tried to do. As a former student, alumnus, faculty member, former administrator, and a Lutheran, my association with Gettysburg College spans almost 30 percent of its existence to date. This is at once an advantage and a disadvantage for one who assumes the responsibility for writing about its past.

Many members of the College faculty and staff have responded, both patiently and willingly, to my numerous requests for information and assistance. Among them are Richard P. Allen, Bruce Bigelow, Robert L. Bloom, Kim S. Breighner, Jay P. Brown, G. Ronald Couchman, Daniel A. Dundon, Ruth S. Groft, Roland E. Hansen, Barbara J. Herman, Dwight A. Huseman, Robert D. Kenworthy, Linda Lagle, Gary Lowe, Robert D. Smith, Janet M. Upton, and Frank B. Williams. Separate mention must be given to two special collections librarians: Nancy C. Scott and David T. Hedrick.

I have benefited from the counsel of Bernadine Dorich, Edwin D. Freed, Carol Kefalas, and Anna Jane Moyer, members of the editorial board. Several students with whom I worked either in individualized study or in a January term course on the history of the College, especially Gregory J. Landrey, have made their contribution to my understanding of the subject. I am deeply indebted to the late President C. Arnold Hanson, who first asked me to undertake the task, and also to President Charles E. Glassick, who encouraged me in a number of important ways and who kindly agreed to read and comment on the final chapter of the work.

There were persons in several other institutions who went out of their way to search for and send information which was subsequently used. Among the institutions were Allegheny College, Easton Area Public Library, Evangelical and Reformed Historical Society, Franklin and Marshall College, Hamilton College, The Johns Hopkins University, Lafayette College, Lutheran Theological Seminary at Gettysburg, Ursinus College, and Washington and Jefferson College.

Staff members at the following state, regional, and national educational agencies responded promptly and helpfully to requests for information: American Association of University Professors, Association of American Colleges, Association of Governing Boards of Universities and Colleges, Board of Regents of the University of the State of New York, and the Middle States Association of Colleges and Schools.

Few, if any, lists of the debts one incurs in a major piece of research and writing are ever complete. This one certainly is not among them, but it should not be closed without mention of Walter B. Lane, the Gettysburg photographer who was always most cooperative, and Jane Adams Clarke, who found several key sources for me among the voluminous Philadelphia county estate papers. My son, Philip H. Glatfelter, compiled the lists included in the appendices and helped in other ways. My wife, Miriam G. Glatfelter, assisted in the task of proofreading.

Since no one else decided what was to be included in this work, the responsibility for it is entirely mine.

Charles H. Glatfelter

Gettysburg, Pennsylvania
September 17, 1986

Pennsylvania College.

ORDER OF THE PROCESSION,
July 4th, 1832.

The Patrons, Clergy, Students of the Gymnasium and Seminary, the Orator of the day, Citizens, and Strangers, are requested to assemble at the Academy, July 4th, at 10 o'clock, A. M. At the ringing of the two bells in the German Church, at half past 10 o'clock, the procession will move to the English Presbyterian Church, in this borough, under the direction of Gen. T. C. Miller and Col. M. C. Clarkson. Marshals, in the following order, viz.

1. The Strangers and Citizens, two and two;
2. The Invited Strangers,   do.
3. The Students,   do.
4. The Teachers and Professors,   do.
5. The Clergy,   do.
6. The Patrons,   do.
7. The Orator of the Day, accompanied by the officiating Clergyman.

Having arrived at the Church doors, the Marshals will order a halt, and separate the procession into two files, through which the Orator and officiating Clergyman will pass, followed by the Patrons, &c. in inverted order. All being seated in the respective places assigned them by the Marshals, the following Hymn will be sung by the Choir:

PRAISE, happy land! Jehovah's name ;
His goodness, and thy bliss proclaim ;
For thee each blessing largely flows,
That Freedom's lib'ral hand bestows.

Thy children are secure and blest;
Thy shores have peace, thy cities rest ;
He feeds thy sons with finest wheat,
And adds his blessing to their meat.

Thy changing seasons he ordains,
Thine early and thy latter rains ;
His flakes of snow like wool he sends,
And well the springing corn defends.

But he hath nobler works and ways,
To call his people to his praise :
To all our land his laws are shown ;
His gospel's through the nation known.

After which a Prayer will be offered up by the Rev. WM. PAXTON, D. D.

THEN WILL FOLLOW AN

Oration, by the *Hon. C. Blythe.*

After which the following HYMN will be sung by the Choir :—

SAY, should we search the globe around,
Where can such happiness be found,
  As dwells in this much favor'd land ?
Here plenty reigns ; here freedom sheds
Her choicest blessings on our heads :
  By God supported still we stand.

Here commerce spreads the wealthy store,
Which comes from every foreign shore ;
  Science and art their charms display ;
Religion teacheth us to raise
Our voices in our Maker's praise,
  As truth and conscience point the way.

These are thy gifts, Almighty King !
From thee our matchless blessings spring;
  Th' extended shade, the fruitful skies,
The raptures liberty bestows,
The eternal joys the gospel shows,
  All from thy boundless goodness rise.

With grateful hearts, with cheerful tongues,
To God we raise united songs ;
  His power and mercy we proclaim ;
And still, through ev'ry age, shall own,
Jehovah here hath fix'd his throne,
  And triumph in his mighty name.

Long as the moon her course shall run,
Or man behold the circling sun,
  May'st thou o'er fair Columbia reign;
Still crown her counsels with success,
With peace and joy her borders bless,
  And all her sacred rights maintain.

The ceremonies will be closed by the Benediction ; and the Procession will return in the above order.

Committee of Arrangement.

Order of Exercises for July 4, 1832
This program recalls the details of the formal organization of what is now Gettysburg College, which occurred on July 4, 1832. The English Presbyterian church was located on the west side of the first block of North Washington street. Courtesy Adams County Historical Society.

1.

THE BACKGROUND OF GETTYSBURG COLLEGE (1776-1832)

July 4, 1832

Wednesday, July 4, 1832, was the date chosen for the formal organization of the newly chartered Pennsylvania College of Gettysburg. At 10:30 A.M. on that day a procession began moving northward from the academy building located at the corner of South Washington and High streets to the Presbyterian church three blocks away, in the first block of North Washington street. Since the nationally known public figure who was the first choice as orator of the day had declined the invitation to speak, those planning the events had invited Calvin Blythe (1790-1849) in his stead. A native of the area, former Secretary of the Commonwealth and Attorney General, and now president judge of the Twelfth Judicial District of Pennsylvania, Blythe quickly directed the attention of his audience to the very beginnings of the American Republic.

"The day on which we are assembled," he began, "makes it not only proper, but indispensable, that we should recur to the scenes of the revolution." Recalling Lexington, Bunker Hill, and Saratoga, Blythe praised the common soldiers, "their invincible chief," the other "prominent actors" in the struggle, as well as the "great body of the people" to whom we are "indebted for our revolution." It was they who had refused to submit to "taxation without their consent, because they held that the right to govern them was founded on consent." With probably a few veterans of the American Revolution in his audience, he noted with pride that one signer of the Declaration of Independence still survived, a man whom he ranked among the "most illustrious of the human family." That last survivor, Charles Carroll, died in Baltimore on November 14, 1832.

Calvin Blythe believed that "the transition from contemplating the men and principles of the Revolution, to the subject of Education, is not difficult." We must rely on the latter to preserve the former. Pennsylvania, he declared, while "so distinguished for its wealth, its improvements, and the understanding of its people," had not "given to Education that attention which, I think, her best interests demand." To be more specific, "intelligence is not diffused among her people, in proportion to their wealth and their means of acquiring it." He was convinced that "the age in which we live, the form of our institutions, the political position we occupy and our best interests, all require, that the great mass of the people should be elevated by a higher grade of intelligence." This was needed because to the people "belongs as well the right to decide, as the consequences of decision, on questions of the last importance."

Realizing that he was discussing a standard of public education which should be, "as near as possible, universal," Blythe hastened to add that colleges were needed in Pennsylvania to provide its people with "the benefits of a systematic education, that will enable us to keep pace with the progress of knowledge, and to maintain our rank in the civilized world." He regretted that there appeared to be in America an "indifference, which seems even to approach to a dislike or distrust of what is called a liberal education, among the great mass of our people." In his opinion, there was "no profession, rank, order, or condition of men, in our commonwealth, to whom a liberal education is not suitable." Experience having shown that learning can lead to a life of "happiness and contentment," it should not be limited "to the few destined for the professions." Pennsylvania College of Gettysburg, he concluded,

> there is every reason to believe, will prove a valuable auxiliary in the great cause of Education. Located in a healthy country, in the midst of an active and intelligent people, under the direction of men of approved learning and ability, it may with confidence be predicted, that it will receive, as it assuredly will deserve, the public patronage.[1]

A fitting place to begin this sesquicentennial history of Gettysburg College - since 1921 the corporate name of the institution chartered in 1832 - is with the American Revolution to which Calvin Blythe turned his attention and with the state whose name the college legally bore for almost ninety years.

In 1776 Pennsylvania had a population of about 300,000 and ranked second in numbers of people to the oldest colony, Virginia. Its capital, Philadelphia, was the largest city in the colonies and the second largest in the British Empire. Its central location between New England and the South helps explain why the First Continental Congress met in Pennsylvania in 1774 and why the Second Continental Congress returned to Philadelphia in the following spring. As it had been for a generation or more, Pennsylvania in

---

[1]C. Blythe, *Oration Delivered at the Organization of Pennsylvania College of Gettysburg* (Gettysburg, 1832). This publication became a promotional piece. It listed the trustees and faculty, and reported that the first session of the new college would begin on November 7, 1832.

1776 was the most heterogeneous of the thirteen colonies in British North America. About one-third of its residents were English or Welsh, a significantly smaller percentage than was the case in any other province. About one-third were Scotch-Irish, or Scots-Irish; these were Scots who moved to Ireland in the seventeenth century and to America in the eighteenth. Finally, about one-third of all Pennsylvanians in 1776 were Germans or Swiss.

The Scotch-Irish took the leadership in prosecuting the revolution in Pennsylvania, not only against the British, but also against the Quakers and their supporters who had controlled the provincial government, either directly or indirectly, since it was established in 1682. After chafing for about twenty years under an arrangement which gave the three original counties (Philadelphia, Bucks, and Chester) three-fourths of the seats in the legislature, even though they had less than one-half of the taxables in the province, the Scotch-Irish inserted into the Pennsylvania Constitution of 1776 a provision which gave every one of the eleven counties equal representation until such time as the apportionment of seats could be based on the actual number of taxables in each county. In 1779 they moved against the Penn proprietors, divesting them of almost all of their remaining lands in Pennsylvania - they were, after all, the original landlords of the entire province - and voting them a monetary compensation only in recognition of what they called the "enterprising spirit" of the long-gone founder, William Penn. Also in 1779, during one of the dark periods of the war, the leaders of the revolutionary government revoked the charter of the College of Philadelphia (one of the nine colonial colleges), took away its properties, and established in its place the University of the State of Pennsylvania. Convinced that the trustees and faculty of the college, many of whom were Anglicans, were not genuine supporters of the revolution, they provided the new university with a board of directors which included some from their own ranks and the senior pastors of six Philadelphia churches.

After the war had ended and Great Britain had formally recognized the independence of the United States, Benjamin Franklin in 1784 acknowledged what had happened in Pennsylvania when he wrote to an old friend in England that "the Irish emigrants and their children are now in possession of the government of Pennsylvania, by their majority in the Assembly, as well as of a great part of the territory."[2]

---

[2]Benjamin Franklin to William Strahan, Passy, August 19, 1784, in *The Works of Benjamin Franklin; . . .,* ed. Jared Sparks 10 (Boston, 1856): 131.

Two Colleges for Southcentral Pennsylvania

One of the persons most interested in the Irish emigrants to whom Benjamin Franklin was referring was Benjamin Rush (1745-1813), a Philadelphia physician and teacher in the College of Philadelphia, who in 1776 was elected to the Second Continental Congress. Along with Charles Carroll one of the signers of the Declaration of Independence, he never wavered in his support of the American cause. In the decade after the Treaty of Paris in 1783, Rush worked assiduously in an effort to reform American behavior in ways which, he believed, would bring it into harmony with his vision of what a republican society should be. In an often-quoted essay which he published in 1787, Rush asserted that "the American War is over: but this is far from being the case with the American Revolution." We have seen but the first act in that drama, he told his readers. "It remains yet to establish and perfect our new forms of government; and to prepare the principles, morals, and manners of our citizens, for these forms of government, after they are established and brought to perfection."[3] To advance these ends, he wrote against war, slavery, and the use of alcoholic beverages and tobacco. At the same time, he wrote and acted in favor of education.

Benjamin Rush believed that one of the requirements for unity and stability in a heterogeneous republican Pennsylvania was a system of education which extended from the elementary school to the university. An essay which he published in 1787 sketched such a system, which envisaged public support of elementary education, four colleges in different parts of the state, and one university in Philadelphia, where law, medicine, divinity, and other subjects would be taught.[4]

In 1782 Rush began promoting the founding of a college which he proposed to locate west of the Susquehanna river, at Carlisle. By now strongly opposed to the leadership which had controlled the state government since 1776, whose policies he believed were too radical to unite the peoples of Pennsylvania and to make possible the reform of its society, Rush saw his projected college as an institution which would appeal first and foremost to Presbyterians. Since their major strength was in the central and western parts of the state, many of their young men might never attend a university in Philadelphia. As Rush began to solicit the support necessary for making the college a reality, he encountered opposition from at least two quarters. Some argued that there were scarcely enough students

---

[3]Benjamin Rush, "On the Defects of the Confederation," in *The Selected Writings of Benjamin Rush,* ed. Dagobert D. Runes (New York, 1947), p. 26.

[4]Benjamin Rush, "Education Agreeable to a Republican Form of Government," in ibid., pp. 98-99.

to enable the university to function properly; what need was there for a second such institution? Others, especially his political and personal opponents, some of whom still controlled the university, saw his proposed college as an act of vengeance against them. But Rush had done the necessary preliminary work with such skill that on September 9, 1783 the legislature passed an act chartering Dickinson College. The new institution was named for John Dickinson, who was president of the Supreme Executive Council (the officer closest to a governor in Pennsylvania at the time). Although much work had already been done in securing subscriptions to the new college and in arranging for a library and some equipment, it was not until 1786 that the college was able to open for instruction.[5]

Benjamin Rush's major concern in promoting Dickinson College may have been to secure an institution for the education of Scotch-Irish Presbyterian youth, but almost from the very beginning of his campaign he solicited the support of the German inhabitants of Pennsylvania. Included among the first trustees were four German pastors and four prominent German laymen, one each from Northampton, Berks, York, and Adams counties. Rush worked to obtain for the new college the blessing of both German Lutheran and Reformed church bodies and urged his fellow-trustees to engage the services of a German faculty member.[6]

In the 1780s, about one-third of the residents of Pennsylvania were still of German or Swiss birth or extraction. Between 1727 and 1775 about 65,000 of them had entered the province through the port of Philadelphia. They had come from many areas of southwestern Germany and Switzerland, each with its own customs and traditions. Although they settled in all parts of the province, and although many went into western Maryland, the Shenandoah valley of Virginia, and New Jersey, most lived in the present Pennsylvania counties of Montgomery, Northampton, Lehigh, Berks, Lebanon, Lancaster, and York. The vast majority were farmers, and contemporaries (including Benjamin Rush) praised them as being excellent husbandmen. Among these Germans were Mennonites, Dunkards, Moravians, and some Roman Catholics, but perhaps as many as nine-tenths of them claimed some attachment to the

---

[5]Legislative acts are identified in this work by the date on which they became law. The Pennsylvania legislature has long published the laws passed during each session. Copies are available in county law libraries and elsewhere. For information on Dickinson College, see Charles Coleman Sellers, *Dickinson College: A History* (Middletown, Connecticut, 1973). Hereafter cited as Sellers, *Dickinson College*.

[6]For information on Rush's activity on behalf of Dickinson and Franklin Colleges, see *Letters of Benjamin Rush*, ed. L. H. Butterfield 1(Princeton, 1951): 290-453.

Lutheran or Reformed churches. In 1776, measured by the numbers of congregations, these were the two largest churches in Pennsylvania. The Lutherans had 126 congregations and the Reformed had 123. In addition, there were 67 Lutheran and Reformed congregations in Maryland, Virginia, and West Virginia, as well as 32 in New York and New Jersey which had some affiliation with those in Pennsylvania. These churches were still growing. By 1793 more than one hundred new congregations were begun in Pennsylvania alone.[7]

From the beginning of their settlement in America, most Germans, whether Lutheran, Mennonite, or whatever, were determined to preserve their own culture, and particularly their own language. At the time of the French and Indian War, which ended the five-year period of greatest German immigration (1749-1754), some provincial leaders, including Benjamin Franklin, were fearful that these newcomers with their different political traditions and strange ways might prove disloyal in the event of war. When the French and Indians began attacking along the extended Pennsylvania frontier in 1755, killing and carrying off people without first asking from where in Europe they had come, the question of German loyalty was answered. Twenty years later, when the revolution began, few Germans were in positions of political leadership; but when the time came for them to decide whether to obey the many laws passed in an effort to win British recognition of American independence, most German Lutherans and Reformed elected to pay their taxes, accept the increasingly worthless Continental money, participate in the militia, and take the controversial required oath of allegiance. During the war the Scotch-Irish courted the Germans, if only because of the large block of votes which they commanded in any election. The Lutherans and Reformed emerged from the revolution with good reputations. If anything, their performance reinforced their privilege, or right, to use the German language and retain their treasured customs. The first published Lutheran liturgy in 1786 included a pastoral prayer which declared that the Lord had used chiefly the Germans in transforming Pennsylvania into a blooming garden and an airy pasture. This being the case, Lutherans using this liturgy prayed that God would help them not to deny their Germanness and assist them in preserving their German churches and schools.[8]

---

[7]While there were important differences in belief and practice between the German Lutheran and Reformed churches, there were many more similarities. Perhaps the strongest tie between their members in Pennsylvania resulted from the many marriages in which one spouse was Lutheran and the other Reformed. At least in the eighteenth and nineteenth centuries, the two churches should be studied together.

[8]*Kirchen-Agende der Evangelisch-Lutherischen Vereinigten Gemeinen in Nord-America* (Philadelphia, 1786), p. 7.

In spite of the several gestures which the founders of Dickinson College made in an effort to secure the support of German Lutherans and Reformed, it became increasingly clear during the year 1785 that the latters' response was, at best, going to be lukewarm. Assisting this college "might tend to suppress the German language, and even our nationality, and might be to the disadvantage of our religion," wrote the secretary of the Reformed church body after its 1785 meeting.[9] Aware of what was happening, during the early summer of that year Benjamin Rush decided to change his approach to the Germans. If they were unwilling to support a college under Scotch-Irish and Presbyterian auspices, he would urge them to organize a college of their own. In August an "Address to the Citizens of Pennsylvania, of German birth and extraction," appeared in the leading German newspaper, the *Philadelphische Correspondenz*, and also in the influential *Pennsylvania Gazette*. The "friend to equal liberty and learning in Pennsylvania" who signed the address was certainly Benjamin Rush.[10]

"Harmony and Christian friendship between the different religious societies" in Pennsylvania, the author now believed, "is best promoted by their educating their youth in separate schools." Several denominations had already realized this truth and had acted accordingly, but not the Germans:

> When we consider the number and wealth of the Germans in Pennsylvania, we are at a loss to account for their having so long neglected to establish a College for the education of their youth. They compose nearly one third of the inhabitants of the state. They fill the treasury with their taxes, and their blood was shed liberally in the establishment of the independence of the state. But what advantages do they derive from their numbers, their wealth, or their patriotism? How few of their sons, born and educated in Pennsylvania, fill the learned professions, or possess offices in the state! Instead of this, are not the Germans at the mercy of the lawyers of other societies, and of the quacks of their own nation? . . .
> All this is entirely owing to their want of learning, which would defend them from mistakes, deceptions, and abuses, in law, physic and in government.

Rush then proceeded to answer several possible objections to a German college. Admitting that it would tend to preserve the German language in Pennsylvania, he argued that such a college would nevertheless "open the eyes of the Germans to a sense of the importance and utility of the English language, and become perhaps the only possible means, consistent with their liberty, of spreading a

---

[9]*Minutes and Letters of the Coetus of the German Reformed Congregations in Pennsylvania, 1747-1792* . . . (Philadelphia, 1903), p. 404.

[10]This address appeared in the *Correspondenz* on August 9 and in the *Gazette* on August 31.

Benjamin Rush (1745-1813)
Rush's championing of a successful college for the German inhabitants of Pennsylvania bore its earliest actual fruit in Gettysburg College, which awarded its first baccalaureate degrees in 1834. Courtesy Independence National Historical Park Collection.

knowledge of the English language among them." He had a ready answer for a second objection: that a college of their own would make the Germans a people apart from the rest of the citizens. Not learning, he insisted, but rather "ignorance and prejudice" keep people apart. "A German College, by removing these, will prepare the way for the Germans to unite more intimately with their British and Irish fellow-citizens, and thus to form, with them, one homogeneous mass of people." Nor did he give much credence to a third objection, that society would lose because a German college would convert "some of our best farmers into scholars." He cited Great Britain as an example of a society in which improvements in arts, sciences, and agriculture went hand in hand. The same could happen in Pennsylvania. Equally important to him was the fact that the "business of government is incompatible with the duties of the three learned professions," and thus "our rulers must be taken . . . from the cultivators of the earth." Rush foresaw "a revolution in our state, high with human happiness, when the farmer and the scholar shall be blended together, and when the same men who have been competitors for fame at our Colleges, shall be competitors for honor in the Councils of the State." This had already happened in Massachusettes and Connecticut, he noted, and it should also happen in Pennsylvania.

Having answered the objections and sketched the possibilities, Rush urged his German fellow-citizens, if they concurred in his sentiments, to begin immediately to seek funds and ask the legislature for a charter. He suggested Reading, Lebanon, Lancaster, or Manheim as possible locations for a German college. "A village should be preferred to the city of Philadelphia," he advised, "not only because education will be cheaper, but because the youth will be kept out of the way of those vices which always prevail in large towns."

Those who might choose to accept Rush's challenge would need to take at least four steps before a German college could become a reality. First, they would have to persuade enough other Germans to join with them to demonstrate to the public that a sizable body of German opinion favored a college. Second, they would need to win the support of enough influential non-Germans to convince the public that their intended college had broad backing. Third, they would have to secure monetary subscriptions from as many sources as possible, to demonstrate that they were capable of generating more than good will. Fourth, they would need to use the results of these steps in an effort to persuade the legislature to grant them a charter of incorporation. In addition, since even more funds would probably be required, they would have to ask for public financial support.

There were four prime movers who responded to Rush's call for a German college. Henry Helmuth (1745-1825) and Casper Weyberg (1734-1790) were Lutheran and Reformed pastors in Philadelphia. Henry Muhlenberg (1753-1815) and William Hendel (1740-1798) were Lutheran and Reformed pastors in Lancaster. Since most of those whose support was essential for success lived in the southeastern part of the state, the two Philadelphia pastors took the lead in persuading such men as Peter Muhlenberg, then a member of the Supreme Executive Council; Chief Justice Thomas McKean; Speaker of the General Assembly Thomas Mifflin; Robert Morris, financier of the revolution; and Benjamin Rush to lend their names to the undertaking. On December 11, 1786 the four pastors and six of their associates petitioned the legislature for a charter. Five days later, its proposed text was introduced in the form of a bill. After it was read for a second time and debated, the legislature, according to the practice of the time, ordered the bill printed and published in the newspapers, where it would be available for public consideration and comment. The prime movers had done their work so well that the bill was passed without opposition.

The act of March 10, 1787 chartered a college in Lancaster "for the instruction of youth in the German, English, Latin, Greek and other learned languages, in theology and in the useful arts sciences and literature." It was named Franklin College "from a profound respect for the talents, virtues and services to mankind in general, but more especially to this country," of Benjamin Franklin. At the age of eighty-one, he was president of the Supreme Executive Council, the post John Dickinson held when Dickinson College was named in his honor in 1783. The government of the new college was vested in a board of trustees, not to exceed forty-five in number, fifteen of whom had to be members of the Lutheran church, fifteen of the Reformed church, and the remaining fifteen of "any other society of Christians." Unless the trustees agreed unanimously otherwise, the presidents of the college were to be chosen alternately from the Lutheran and Reformed churches. The charters granted the trustees and faculty the authority to enact and enforce rules and regulations within the college and to grant "such degrees in the liberal arts and sciences . . . as are usually granted and conferred in other colleges in America or Europe." Finally, the act awarded the college ten thousand acres of unappropriated state land and directed the land office to confer a proper title to it.

The charter set June 5, 1787 and Lancaster as the time and place for the first meeting of the trustees. The more than thirty who attended elected Henry Muhlenberg president and William Hendel vice president of Franklin College. They also chose three faculty members. Frederick Melsheimer, a Lutheran pastor, became professor of Latin, Greek, and German. Joseph Hutchins, Episcopal rector in Lancaster, took the chair of English and the Belles Lettres. William Reichenbach, a recent immigrant, became professor of Mathematics. On the following day the formal opening of the college took place, complete with a procession from the courthouse to the Lutheran church, sermons, prayers, hymns, and odes. Both German and English were used in the exercises.

Unfortunately, the high hopes which were much in evidence in Lancaster on June 6, 1787 were not to be realized. Benjamin Rush greatly overestimated the ability, willingness, or both of German youth in his time to attend a college, even one of their own. Few came; those who did brought little tuition money for the treasury. Not all of those persons who had made pledges to the college paid when they became due. The ten thousand acres of land which the state had given were located in the present Bradford, Tioga, and Lycoming counties. While they might have been valuable as a long-term investment, these acres were worthless in meeting the pressing immediate needs of the college. Hutchins left the faculty in 1788 and Melsheimer in 1789, both with back salary already due them. No one of comparable attainments ever replaced them.

Franklin College maintained its separate corporate existence until 1850, but it never granted a baccalaureate degree. The trustees continued to meet, replenished their numbers, and authorized the use of their facilities for a series of different educational ventures of less-than-college grade.[11]

Lutheran Ministerial Training

It is evident that Benjamin Rush saw Franklin College as an institution which would bring the German residents of Pennsylvania into a closer community with their English and Scotch-Irish fellow-citizens. While the four prime movers of the college and their German associates were neither oblivious nor opposed to this purpose, they acted from different motives. Both Lutheran and Reformed churches had strong traditions of a learned clergy, of men trained first in the arts and sciences, and then in theology and those other subjects long associated with it. Beginning in the 1740s, the theological faculty of the University of Halle had sent a total of twelve Lutheran pastors to Pennsylvania, while authorities of the Dutch Reformed church sent thirty-eight Reformed pastors. All of these men were regularly trained and ordained. It was their vanguard which organized the first German church bodies in America: the Reformed coetus in 1747 and the Lutheran ministerium in 1748. Their members introduced the established principles and practices of the European churches and adapted them to American conditions. At no time were there enough of these men to fill nearly all of the pulpits being fashioned either in Pennsylvania or in the adjacent provinces into which the German settlers went. To meet the incessant demand for pastors, their ranks were supplemented in part by ordained men who came from Europe without a regular call from congregations. While some of these men became useful American pastors, others, having left Europe because of their own ineptitude or moral lapses, were scarcely more successful here than they had been at home. Lutheran and Reformed pastoral ranks were also supplemented by men, often schoolmasters, who took it upon themselves to act as pastors without the benefits of the customary formal training, examination, and ordination. Almost one-third of the Lutheran and Reformed pastors who began their ministry before 1776 fall into this category of what are called irregular ministers.

In the 1780s the leaders of both German church bodies in America knew that they could not hope to continue much longer supplying their congregations with pastors who were prepared for the ministry

---

[11]For the history of Franklin College, see Joseph Henry Dubbs, *History of Franklin and Marshall College* (Lancaster, 1903), pp. 3-147.

in Europe. Not only were the religious authorities in Halle and Holland recruiting fewer and fewer men - the last of them arrived in 1786 and 1788, respectively - but also they were sending less qualified pastors. Even before the revolution, Lutheran and Reformed leaders in Pennsylvania were fully convinced that their churches needed a native ministry, one which was properly trained and, as some of them expressed it, well-adapted to the customs of the country. The experiences of the revolution only reinforced this conviction. The prime movers of Franklin College hoped that it would offer instruction in the arts and sciences for American-born ministerial candidates, who would then be able to study theology and the associated subjects either in Lancaster or under the instruction of an experienced parish pastor. The almost immediate failure of the college forced Lutheran and Reformed leaders to devise alternate ways of supplying their churches with pastors, while at the same time preserving as best they could the tradition and reality of a learned clergy.

Long before the revolution a few pastors, including the Lutheran leader, Henry Melchior Muhlenberg (1711-1787), had begun to train some promising young men for the ministry in their homes and parishes, offering them a combination of formal study and practical experience. When these candidates were able to pass an examination conducted by several experienced pastors, they were recommended for a call to a parish and ordained, in the hope that they would be a credit to the profession. With the failure of Franklin College, this procedure seemed to offer the greatest promise for both German churches until such time as institutions of higher learning under their influence and control could be established and sustained. In 1792, when it adopted a new constitution, the Lutheran ministerium, or synod, tacitly recognized that such institutions were not about to be formed. One of the provisions of the new organic law authorized "every ordained minister possessing the requisite qualifications" to take "young men, desirous of devoting themselves to the ministry, and by oral instruction, the recommendation of good books and practical directions, to prepare them for the service of the Lord." Whenever such a student "obtained a systematic knowledge of the doctrines of salvation, the gift of speaking, an unblemished character and evidences of experimental religion," he could be permitted to preach. If a student, having reached this stage, wished to advance to the ordained ministry through the ranks of catechist and licensed candidate, he was required to be at least twenty years old, "have acquired a systematic knowledge of Christian doctrine and ethics; . . . possess some knowledge of human nature, manifest a gift of speaking, and above all things [have] a practical knowledge of experimental religion."[12] There was, of course, nothing to prevent a prospective ministerial candidate from attending the University of Pennsylvania (where Henry Helmuth was professor of the German and Oriental Languages until 1796), Dickinson College, or some other college within or without Pennsylvania. Nevertheless, most of the men who entered the Lutheran and Reformed ministries during the first quarter of the nineteenth century bypassed both colleges and universities, electing instead to devote their entire period of preparation (beyond possible time spent in an academy) to an apprenticeship with an ordained parish pastor.

Soon after 1800 major changes began to occur in the pattern of American ministerial training. Roman Catholics, Moravians, Congregationalists, Dutch Reformed, Presbyterians, Episcopalians, and Baptists all established separate educational institutions, called theological seminaries, designed specifically to train men for the ministry. The founders of these schools intended that applicants for admission would have completed a college-level course of study in the liberal arts and sciences.

The first Lutheran theological seminary, Hartwick, began operations in Otsego county, New York, in 1815. Few of its students either came from Pennsylvania or later went into parishes there. Two years after Hartwick opened, in 1817, the Reformed synod approached its Lutheran counterpart in Pennsylvania with a proposal that the two churches join in organizing a theological seminary. The Lutherans responded favorably, and during the next several years leaders in both denominations discussed how this goal might be achieved. They gave serious consideration to how the nearly defunct Franklin College, in which there was still a Lutheran and a Reformed interest, might be used for that purpose. Several suggested that the two churches should first unite and then begin a theological seminary. Nothing came of these proposals and discussions.[13] Eventually the Reformed accepted the offer of Dickinson College to provide them with classroom and library facilities for faculty and students if, in return, their theological professor would join the faculty and offer instruction in the college. In March 1825 the first German Reformed theological seminary opened in Carlisle. Four years later the institution moved to York and in 1837 it relocated in Mercersburg.

---

[12]*Documentary History of the Evangelical Lutheran Ministerium of Pennsylvania and Adjacent States . . .* (Philadelphia, 1898), pp. 250-252. Hereafter cited as *Documentary History.*
[13]Ibid., pp. 513f.

Within a year after he took charge of the Reformed seminary, Professor Lewis Mayer wrote about

> how difficult it is to deal with unprepared students . . . , especially if the professor is called upon to teach all branches of learning. It is not only desirable and fitting, but is absolutely necessary that those who would pursue theological studies, first learn to read the Latin and Greek languages and be well grounded in the essential sciences.[14]

On several occasions he urged the Reformed synod to authorize organization of a "scientific and literary" institution in which theological students could be properly prepared to do the work expected of them. By 1832 there was a classical institute, or academy, associated with the seminary. Four years later, on March 31, 1836, the legislature granted a charter transforming what it called "the high school of the German Reformed church, located at Mercersburg," into Marshall College. By this time, the spring of 1836, the Lutherans also had their own theological seminary and college.

Samuel Simon Schmucker

The chief founder of the Lutheran theological seminary and college was Samuel Simon Schmucker (1799-1873). Born in Hagerstown, Maryland, he was the son of John George Schmucker (1771-1854), who had come from Germany with his family in the 1780s. After having studied under several pastors, John George was licensed as a catechist in 1792 and ordained into the ministry in 1800. Nine years later he resigned his Hagerstown parish in order to become pastor in York, where he remained until he retired from the active ministry in 1836. Young Samuel was a student in the York County Academy from 1812 to 1814 and in the University of Pennsylvania from 1814 to 1816. He spent the next year in York as a teacher in the academy, after which he enrolled in the theological seminary at Princeton. While he was a student there, from 1818 to 1820, the University of Pennsylvania conferred upon him the degree of bachelor of arts (1819). Years later, Schmucker recalled that when he left Princeton there were three career goals in his mind: translating some German theological work into English, founding a Lutheran theological seminary, and establishing a college under Lutheran auspices.[15]

---

[14]Quoted in H. M. J. Klein, *The History of the Eastern Synod of the Reformed Church in the United States* (Lancaster, 1943), p. 140.

[15]The most recent biography is Abdel Ross Wentz, *Pioneer in Christian Unity: Samuel Simon Schmucker* (Philadelphia, 1967). Hereafter cited as Wentz, *Schmucker*. Schmucker's translation of a German theological work was published in two volumes in 1826, the year in which the theological seminary in Gettysburg began operating. The college opened six years later.

16

Samuel Simon Schmucker (1799-1873)
An engraving by Sartain from an early daguerreotype. Courtesy Abdel
Ross Wentz Library, Lutheran Theological Seminary, Gettysburg.

In May 1820 Schmucker appeared before the Lutheran synod and asked to be received into membership. The committee assigned to examine him reported that they "were entirely satisfied with his examination, and that they have no hesitation in proposing him as a candidate."[16] Given a license, in December 1820 he took charge of four small congregations in Rockingham and Shenandoah counties, Virginia. He lived at New Market and conducted his ministry in the English language. The synod which ordained him in 1821 also approved him as an instructor of candidates for the ministry. Within a year or two there were six students under his care. They lived in the parsonage, pursuing a regular program of instruction and, when their teacher believed them ready, assisting him with his pastoral duties.

The Lutheran synodical body organized in 1748 adopted its first constitution in 1778. Its framers chose a most ambitious name for the new body: Ministerium of the Evangelical Lutheran Church of North America. As this church grew in numbers and continued to expand geographically, it became increasingly impractical to expect that all pastors and lay delegates from each parish would be able to attend the annual meetings. A second constitution adopted in 1792 recognized as much by creating The German Evangelical Lutheran Ministerium in Pennsylvania and Adjacent States.[17] When Samuel Simon Schmucker appeared before this body in 1820, there were already four other regional Lutheran synods in existence: New York, North Carolina, Ohio, and Tennessee. Several months after the Pennsylvania Synod licensed him as a candidate for the ministry he became a member of the Synod of Maryland and Virginia when it was organized in Winchester, Virginia, in October 1820. It was this synod which ordained him in 1821.

Young Schmucker entered the ministry at the very time when some Lutheran church leaders were convinced that, given the size of the country and the continuing increase in the number of congregations, more regional synods would need to be formed. That being the case, they believed, there should be a general body, to which each regional synod would send delegates to deal with the larger concerns of the church. The first meeting of the Evangelical Lutheran General Synod of the United States of North America convened in Hagerstown in October 1820. Four regional synods sent delegates: Pennsylvania, New York, North Carolina, and Maryland and Virginia. Samuel Simon Schmucker was in attendance.

The constitution which the General Synod adopted in 1820

---

[16]*Documentary History*, p. 566.
[17]Subsequent references to this body identify it as the Pennsylvania Synod.

declared that one of the purposes of the new body was to plan for "seminaries of education" and, "with the help of God, to carry them into effect." Accordingly, the president appointed a committee of five, all of them (including John George Schmucker) chosen from the Pennsylvania Synod, to draw up a plan for a Lutheran theological seminary.[18] However, before the General Synod could accomplish this purpose, it had to survive a major crisis: the defection of the Pennsylvania and New York Synods. In numbers of congregations and members, the former was by far the largest regional synod in the country. In breaking away, its leaders were responding to the strong belief among their parishioners that the General Synod, and any theological seminary it might establish, represented threats to their continued use of the German language and to the prized autonomy of their congregations. Understandably, when the General Synod held its first business meeting in 1821, the committee of five recommended that the plan for a seminary be deferred for several years. In the meantime, all pastors in member synods were urged to inform and remind their congregations of the pressing need for such an institution.

The revival of momentum for a seminary can be traced, at least in part, to a sermon which Schmucker preached before the Synod of Maryland and Virginia in October 1824. Four months later, four of his pastoral colleagues met in Martinsburg, West Virginia, and resolved to "engage in the important work of founding a theological seminary to be under the direction and for the benefit of the Evangelical Lutheran Church, and . . . [to] begin the work at once."[19] They informed Schmucker of their decision and quickly enlisted his support. When the Synod of Maryland and Virginia met in Hagerstown in October 1825, the five pastors persuaded it to name a committee to bring in a plan for a seminary to be organized as promptly as possible. Since Schmucker had already prepared the draft of a plan, it could be presented and adopted on the same day. The next step was to convince the General Synod that the time had come to act.

The General Synod met in Frederick in November 1825. Only three regional synods sent delegates: North Carolina; Maryland and Virginia; and West Pennsylvania, newly formed by congregations located in the western part of the territory of the old Pennsylvania

[18]*Minutes of the General Synod* (1820). The minutes of this and other Lutheran synods were published under various titles. The title used here is a simplified form which gives the essential information necessary to locate the source.

[19]Quoted in Wentz, *Schmucker,* p. 127. The four pastors were Charles Philip Krauth (1797-1867) of Martinsburg; Benjamin Kurtz (1795-1865) of Hagerstown; Frederick Ruthrauff (1796-1859) of Williamsport, Maryland; and John Winter (1799-1854) of Gerrardstown, West Virginia.

Synod.[20] The General Synod named a committee of six pastors (including Samuel Simon Schmucker and Benjamin Kurtz) and laymen to propose a plan for a seminary. On the same day it presented, and the synod adopted, a slightly altered version of the plan which had originated in the Synod of Maryland and Virginia several weeks earlier.

The plan called upon the General Synod to establish a theological seminary to be governed by directors elected by member synods and responsible to them. The General Synod undertook to select the members of the first board and the first professor. Instruction was to be conducted in both English and German. Without delay, the synod then elected fifteen persons to the board of directors and chose Schmucker professor. It instructed the board to hold its first meeting in Hagerstown on March 2, 1826; at that time to locate the seminary "in such place as shall, at the close of three months, offer the greatest advantages"; and to arrange for prompt opening of the new school. The synod also designated agents to solicit the necessary funds in many places in the United States and Europe. It ordered preparation of a pastoral letter urging members of affiliated congregations to be especially generous in their contributions. Finally, as though to place on record an expression of their confidence in what they were doing, the members of the General Synod decided to hold their next biennial meeting, scheduled for October 1827, "at such place where the Seminary shall be located."[21]

As scheduled, the seminary board of directors held their first meeting in Hagerstown on March 2, 1826. They elected John George Schmucker president; Charles Philip Krauth secretary; and Charles A. Barnitz, one of Schmucker's York parishioners, treasurer. It was a foregone conclusion that the nine persons present at this meeting would choose to locate the seminary somewhere near the center of the territory of the then-member synods of the General Synod. They had before them offers from three towns: Carlisle, Hagerstown, and Gettysburg. The proposal from Carlisle was similar to the one recently made to and accepted by the German Reformed synod: use of the classroom and library facilities of Dickinson College if, in return, the theological professor would be willing to join the faculty and teach Hebrew and Oriental literature. In addition, Carlisle offered a residence for the professor for five years and $5,000 in

---

[20]The West Pennsylvania Synod was organized in September 1825. Its eastern boundary was the Susquehanna river and its southern boundary the Maryland-Pennsylvania line. Pastoral members were present in 1825 from as far north as Centre county and from as far west as the state of Ohio. John George Schmucker was elected president. Gettysburg has always been on the territory of this and its successor synod: the Central Pennsylvania Synod, which was formed in 1938.

[21]*Minutes of the General Synod* (1825), pp. 5-8.

cash, $3,000 of which was committed for a building to be erected on a lot of ground which the college would make available from its campus. Citizens of Hagerstown offered $6,635 in cash. The offer from Gettysburg was $7,000 from its citizens and the use of the Gettysburg Academy building until such time as the seminary had its own quarters. After the nine members present considered the three offers, they took a vote. No location received the required majority on the first ballot, but on the second Gettysburg received six votes and Hagerstown, three. Thus the directors decided to locate the seminary at Gettysburg, the county seat of Adams county, Pennsylvania.[22]

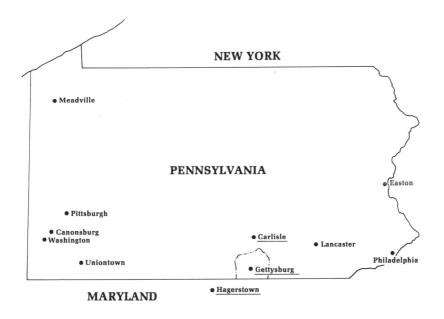

Pennsylvania Colleges and Universities in 1832
This map shows the location of colleges and universities in Pennsylvania at the close of the year 1832. The three towns whose names are underlined – Carlisle and Gettysburg in Pennsylvania and Hagerstown in Maryland – were those considered for the location of the Lutheran theological seminary in 1826.

---

[22]The minutes of the seminary board of directors, beginning with those of the first meeting, are in the Abdel Ross Wentz Library, Lutheran Theological Seminary. The secretary made a full record of the offers presented by Carlisle, Hagerstown, and Gettysburg.

Gettysburg and the Lutheran Theological Seminary

Over the years much has been written about why the seminary directors chose Gettysburg as the site of their new institution. Some of the explanation has been based upon factual evidence; much has been speculation.

The first Europeans who established themselves in the vicinity of the present Gettysburg were, almost without exception, Scotch-Irish Presbyterians. They began coming in the late 1730s and early 1740s. The area in which they lived was known as the Marsh Creek settlement. Until 1800 it and the rest of the present Adams county were part of York county. The Marsh Creek and neighboring Scotch-Irish settlements contributed more than their fair share of the political leadership of colonial York county. They sent assembly-men to Philadelphia and sheriffs, commissioners, justices of the peace, and other officers to the county seat in York. Benjamin Rush and his associates in planning Dickinson College in the 1780s recognized the importance of these settlements by naming four of their prominent Presbyterian residents to its first board of trustees: Rev. John Black, Rev. Alexander Dobbin, Rev. John McKnight, and Robert McPherson.[23]

In the early 1760s Samuel Gettys, Scotch-Irish and Presbyterian, was licensed to keep a tavern along the Marsh Creek road which ran from York through the settlement and into the South mountain. His establishment soon became one of the best-known in the western part of York county. Its location was enhanced about ten years later when a road from Shippensburg to Baltimore passed close by his tavern door. In 1786 Samuel's son, James Gettys (1759-1815), laid out a town at the crossroads on land acquired from his father. The inducements which he and several other citizens of the new town offered led the legislature to designate Gettysburg as the seat of justice when it passed an act creating Adams county in 1800. The town became a borough in 1806 and acquired its first bank, one of the earliest west of the Susquehanna river, in 1814. By 1826 state roads and privately constructed turnpikes made it easily possible to reach the town from north, east, south, and west. The population of Gettysburg in 1820 was 1,102 and in 1830, 1,473.

A few years after he became pastor of the Rock Creek Presby-terian church in 1774, Alexander Dobbin (1742-1809), already identified as a charter trustee of Dickinson College a decade later, began conducting an academy in the sturdy stone house which he built in 1776 and which is still standing (1982). It is now within the borough limits of Gettysburg. His academy was one of the first of its

---

[23]Sellers, *Dickinson College,* p. 482.

kind west of the Susquehanna river. Few of its records survive, but Dobbin may have continued operating it until shortly before his death in 1809. A year later, on March 19, 1810, eight residents of Gettysburg, all of them Scotch-Irish and Presbyterian, secured a charter incorporating the Gettysburg Academy.[24] The measure included authorization for a grant of $2,000, half of which was to be used for operating expenses and half toward the construction of a building. Two lots were purchased at the corner of High and Washington streets, on which a two-story brick building was built in 1813-1814. Although the trustees announced early in 1814 that they were receiving applications for teachers of Latin, Greek, and mathematics, it was not until May 1815 that they could report that they had "at length the satisfaction of stating to the Public, that the Institution is now in full and complete operation." There were then three faculty members, one each in Latin and Greek; mathematics; and English language and penmanship.[25] Unfortunately, the academy did not prosper. Its building had been erected during a period of severe wartime inflation, the worst since the revolution, and in 1817 the legislature permitted the trustees to use the $1,000 reserved for operating expenses to help reduce the building debt. The academy continued to function into the 1820s, but, when the trustees offered its facilities for the use of the proposed Lutheran seminary in 1826, a troublesome debt still remained and the future of the institution was in doubt.

Before the American Revolution, the Germans living in what is now Adams county had their homes and farms in the eastern townships. One indication of their presence was the existence of three Lutheran and three Reformed congregations close to the York county line. Then, beginning in the 1770s and accelerating in the 1780s, many other Germans from counties to the east began purchasing farms located in the central and western parts of the county from Scotch-Irish families who were moving west and south. By 1832 a remarkable change in the ethnic composition of Adams county had taken place. There were then no fewer than twenty-six Lutheran and Reformed congregations in the county. In his gazetteer of Pennsylvania which was published in 1832, Thomas F. Gordon wrote that the population of Adams county is "principally composed of the descendants of Germans" and that "the prevailing religion of the county is Lutheran."[26]

[24]To govern the academy, the act empowered the voters of Adams county to elect eight trustees: two each year to serve four-year terms.
[25]Gettysburg *Sentinel*, May 10, 1815. This newspaper appeared under different titles; the most common one is used in this work.
[26]Thomas F. Gordon, *A Gazetteer of the State of Pennsylvania* (Philadelphia, 1832; reprint ed., 1975), p. 3.

Gettysburg Academy

Built in 1813-1814, this building housed the seminary (1826-1832), classical school and Gymnasium (1827-1832), and College and its preparatory department (1832-1838). For much of the time between 1838 and 1871, it sheltered an academy for young women. Since 1871, it has been used for private residences. This picture appeared in the 1882 history of the College.

In the town of Gettysburg, as at many other places in Pennsylvania, the Lutherans and Reformed united to build and then share the use of one church edifice. Each congregation was entitled to use the church every other Sunday. Dedicated in 1814, the German church, as it was called, stood at the corner of High and Stratton streets. The first resident Lutheran pastor was a young man named John Herbst (1791-1834), who came to Gettysburg from York county in 1819. A friend of both Samuel Simon Schmucker and his father, Herbst assisted them in numerous ways during the discussions and plans which preceded the decision to establish a seminary. It is probable that he played a major role in preparing the offer which the town of Gettysburg presented to the board of directors in 1826. One of Herbst's parishioners was Samuel H. Buehler (1783-1856), who in 1819 moved to Gettysburg from York, where he was a parishioner of John George Schmucker. In Gettysburg, Buehler operated a general store which specialized in drugs, medicines, and paint. In the obituary which he wrote for a local newspaper in 1856, Samuel Simon Schmucker praised Buehler as "an ardent and active friend and benefactor" of both seminary and college, declaring that "he took a prominent part in securing to our borough the location of the Theological Seminary, and thus of the College which grew out of it."[27]

The formal opening exercises of the Lutheran theological seminary occurred on September 5, 1826 in the German church. Although this was a distinctly Lutheran occasion, with a German sermon by John George Schmucker and an English sermon by Charles Philip Krauth, the two prayers were delivered by local Presbyterian ministers, William Paxton and David McConaughy. Samuel Simon Schmucker was inaugurated as professor of Christian theology and delivered an address on the subject of "the theological education of ministers." The announcements of the forthcoming opening which had begun appearing in newspapers in July urged prospective students to confer in advance with the professor concerning their entrance. By September 5 seven men had responded to this call, and during the first year a total of fifteen students were matriculated.[28]

---

[27]Gettysburg *Star and Banner,* September 12, 1856. This newspaper appeared under different titles; the most common one is used here.

[28]A letter to the editor of the *Evangelical Lutheran Intelligencer* which appeared in the July 1826 issue (p. 120) named eighteen theological seminaries then in existence in the United States: five Presbyterian, three Baptist, three Episcopal, two Roman Catholic, and one each Congregational, Dutch Reformed, Moravian, German Reformed, and Lutheran (Hartwick). The seminary at Gettysburg was the nineteenth. For further information on the latter, see Abdel Ross Wentz, *Gettysburg Lutheran Theological Seminary,* 2 vols. (Harrisburg, 1964-1965).

Although some members of the first year's student body at the seminary were college graduates, it did not take long for Schmucker to reach the same conclusion regarding the qualifications of most of them as that being reached by his Reformed counterpart and contemporary, Lewis Mayer, in similar circumstances. Reporting to the General Synod in the fall of 1827, the seminary board stated that "in determining the course of instruction . . . [it] thought it best at once to assume an elevated ground, and presuppose in the applicants for admission as many preparatory attainments, as are required in any other similar institution in our country." However, given "the present imperfect state of education in the Middle and Southern sections" of the United States, there will always be some applicants who cannot afford a college course and older men whose age makes it impractical for them " to spend so many years in the pursuit of secular learning."[29] There was no reason to believe that the situation would soon improve, unless something were done about it.

Classical School and Gymnasium (1827-1832)

When the seminary directors met in May 1827, at the close of their first year of operation, they decided to accept Schmucker's proposal for action. According to their minutes, they resolved that "a well conducted Classical School would not only promote the cause of education in this place, but also be highly conducive to the welfare of the Seminary." Schmucker and John Herbst were named to a committee on organization; they were authorized to proceed "if it shall appear that the income of such a school would defray the expenses attendant on it."[30]

The two committee members had few doubts about the prospects for the new venture. Securing the necessary consent of the trustees of the academy for this further use of their facilities, on June 5 they issued an advertisement for the newspapers, announcing the opening of the Gettysburg Classical School on June 25. The instructor was to be David Jacobs (1805-1830), a graduate of Jefferson College and one of the first-year seminary students. The stated purpose of the classical school was to "qualify young gentlemen for admission into any College in the Union, and to give to others, who may wish it, the higher branches of an English and Scientific Education." Jacobs' instructional talents were assumed to be limitless. He was expected to teach Latin, Greek, English grammar, arithmetic, mathematics, geography, astronomy, history,

---

[29]Minutes of the General Synod (1827), pp. 14-15.
[30]Quoted in the Sentinel, May 23, 1827.

composition, elocution, political economy, chemistry, as well as natural, political, and moral philosophy. The announcement proclaimed that a "prominent feature" of the classical school would be the "peculiar attention" to be given "to the morals and the religious instruction of youth, whilst every thing of a sectarian nature shall be entirely avoided." Parents were assured that students coming from a distance would be responsible to the instructor for their conduct at all times. The Gettysburg Classical School went into operation in late June 1827, nine months after the opening of the seminary.[31]

The peaceful progress of these two new schools in Gettysburg was soon threatened by the debt of more than $1,100 which the academy still owed to the Bank of Gettysburg. As long as the academy was in operation, there was at least some prospect that it would earn enough to meet the interest payments on this obligation and make a small reduction in the principal, but since the seminary enjoyed the use of the building rent free, the academy had no income. In the fall of 1828, the Bank of Gettysburg informed the trustees that, unless the debt were paid soon, it would appeal to the courts to order the sheriff to sell the property. At a town meeting held in the courthouse on December 26, Thaddeus Stevens (1792-1868), a local attorney, presented, and the body adopted, a motion "that it is expedient for the Borough of Gettysburg to raise, by Tax, as for other Borough purposes, a sum sufficient to pay the debt charged on the Gettysburg Academy, and to purchase said Academy for the use of said Borough - to be applied to Literary purposes only." Committees were named to obtain the written approval of borough taxables for the town council to levy the necessary taxes and to obtain whatever legislation might be needed to permit the change in ownership.[32]

In the months that followed, whatever momentary enthusiasm there might have been for an increase in borough taxes vanished, and at the end of July the sheriff announced that, as directed by the courts, he would sell the academy property on August 15, 1829. Since one of the strongest assets of the seminary and classical school was their access to rent-free quarters until such time as they had their own, this impending sale presented Schmucker with a major threat to their continuing existence. He responded by entering into

---

[31]Ibid., June 6, 1827. In their 1827 report to the General Synod, the seminary directors publicly thanked the academy trustees for permitting the classical school to use their facilities and also "the citizens of Gettysburg in general, for the promptness and cordiality with which they have uniformly co-operated with the Board in promoting the prosperity of the Seminary." *Minutes of the General Synod* (1827), p. 15.

[32]*Sentinel,* December 31, 1828.

discussions with men he described as some of the "principal citizens" of the borough, as a result of which they agreed not to bid against him when the sheriff sold the property. In return, he made the following promises, which were committed to writing. First, the building would be used only for purposes of a "literary and scientific institution," but for a "reasonable rent" the seminary could continue to occupy it until such time as its own quarters could be built. Second, neither Schmucker nor anyone to whom he might sell the building could use it for any other purpose than the one agreed upon without first giving the citizens of Gettysburg the opportunity of purchasing it at a fair price. Third, in the event such a sale were contemplated, the citizens would have three months after due notice had been given in which to make a decision on purchasing it. On August 15 Schmucker bought the academy property for $1,160.[33]

The next step for the young professor was to find some practical way to manage the debt which he had transferred from the academy trustees onto his own shoulders. One thing was certain. He did not have $1,160 of his own funds. Always resourceful, he soon devised a plan designed to permit expansion of the classical school while at the same time raising money to liquidate the indebtedness. He announced his intention of forming an unincorporated group whose members would purchase stock valued at $50 per share. The original issue amounted to $1,100. These stockholders were empowered to elect five trustees to manage the business affairs of the classical school, but matters relating to curriculum, instruction, and discipline were entirely the responsibility of a committee consisting of the professor and directors of the seminary. Original stockholders could send their children to the school without paying tuition; all stockholders were promised dividends if the venture proved to be a financial success. The heading which Schmucker gave to his statement of these stipulations explains succinctly what his purposes were: "Articles of agreement for the establishment of a Classical and Scientific department in subservience to the objects of the Theological Seminary at Gettysburg, and for the establishment of a fund for the purchase of the Adams County Academy."[34]

In October 1829 some of Schmucker's pastoral colleagues in Pennsylvania, Maryland, and Virginia began subscribing to his stock offering. No one took more than one share. If the record can be

[33]Record Book of Board of Patrons of Pennsyl'a College, Gettysburg College Archives. Latter hereafter cited as GCA. The price paid for the academy building was $1,160 and not $1,100, as most accounts have it. Sheriff's Deeds, Insolvent Debtors, Naturalization Docket, 1819-1833, p. 372. Office of the Prothonotary, Adams County.
[34]Record Book of Board of Patrons of Pennsyl'a College, GCA.

trusted, some of the twenty who committed themselves never paid the $50 which they had promised, but enough money was received to liquidate about half of what Schmucker had paid for the academy. Meanwhile, the reorganization of the classical school occurred. Michael Jacobs (1808-1871), brother of David and an 1828 graduate of Jefferson College, agreed to offer the mathematical and scientific instruction in what was now called the Gettysburg Gymnasium. Several months after Michael began his duties, David Jacobs took a leave of absence in the hope of recovering his health, but he died in November 1830. In the spring of 1831 Henry L. Baugher (1804-1868), an 1826 graduate of Dickinson College, took his place.

An undated prospectus of the Gymnasium, issued over Schmucker's signature in late 1829 or early 1830, described its purpose as follows:

> It is designed to prepare young gentlemen for admission into any class of College, and to give such as desire it, an acquaintance with the higher branches of a College course. Parents are permitted to select the Studies, to which they wish their Children to attend; and, when it is desired, the Student may be permitted to pursue the whole circle of the Sciences, and, without attending to the Learned Languages, to complete a finished English and Scientific Education.

The announced course of studies was divided into five "classes," the last several of which resembled a college curriculum of the time. The prospectus promised that "Globes, an Electrical Machine, and an increasing Chymical and Philosophical Apparatus, have been provided," and noted that a library was being formed. In the meantime, students attending the Gymnasium who were interested in theology had access to the seminary library of more than 6,000 volumes. The new school continued its predecessor's emphasis on "strict morality" and "true piety," while promising that "every thing sectarian is absolutely avoided." Unless parents directed otherwise, students were still held "responsible to the Teachers for their conduct out of school" and were required to attend weekly worship services. Both Gettysburg institutions prospered. "We believe there are now 33 students of Theology, or preparing to enter the Theological department," wrote David F. Schaeffer in June 1830, "and, perhaps about 50 pupils in the Classical and Mathematical departments."[35]

---

[35]Gettysburg Gymnasium. Copy in the Adams County Historical Society, Gettysburg. *Evangelical Lutheran Intelligencer* 5 (June 1830): 119. Schaeffer was vice president of the seminary board and editor of the *Intelligencer*.

Gettysburg Gymnasium.

THIS Institution, having recently been enlarged, and established on a permanent basis, may be confidently recommended to Parents and Guardians, who wish to send their Children or Wards abroad to receive an Education. It is under the immediate care of several very excellent and well qualified Teachers, and under the general superintendence of Professor SCHMUCKER. Additional Teachers will be added, as occasion may require. It is designed to prepare young gentlemen for admission into any class of College, and to give such as desire it, an acquaintance with the higher branches of a College course. Parents are permitted to select the Studies, to which they wish their Children to attend ; and, when it is desired, the Student may be permitted to pursue the whole circle of the Sciences, and, without attending to the Learned Languages, to complete a finished English and Scientific Education.

The Edifice, recently purchased for the Institution, is large, and situated on a commanding eminence. Globes, an Electrical Machine, and an increasing Chymical and Philosophical Apparatus, have been provided. Students of any denomination, destined for the Ministry of the Gospel, have gratuitous access to the very valuable Library of the Theological Seminary, containing upwards of Six Thousand Volumes ; and, for the accommodation of others, a separate Library is forming.

Strict morality is required of every Student ; and, whilst true piety is studiously promoted, every thing sectarian is absolutely avoided. Students from a distance, unless placed by their Parents under the particular charge of some citizen of this Town, are also responsible to the Teachers for their conduct out of school ; and, on the Lord's day, they are required to attend the Public Worship of such one of the several Churches, as their Parents may prefer. No applicant known to be vicious, will be admitted ; and, if the mild, but decisive discipline and instructions of the Institution, be disregarded by any Student, he shall be advised to withdraw. A semi-annual Report of the conduct, scholarship, &c. of each Student, will be made to Parents and Guardians. Those Scholars, whose Parents wish it, are boarded in the same apartment with one of the Teachers, are constantly under his eye, and subject to all the regulations of good Boarding-schools.

The year is divided into two sessions, ending on the last Wednesday of April and September. Each session is succeeded by a Public Examination; and by a vacation of three weeks' continuance. Punctuality in returning, at the beginning of each session, cannot be neglected, without much injury to the Student.

The terms of tuition are Twenty-four Dollars per annum, payable quarterly ; and no allowance is made for vacations, or loss of time of the Student, cases of sickness alone excepted. Price of Board &c; One Dollar and Fifty Cents per week.

On behalf of the Trustees of the Institution,

S. S. SCHMUCKER.

Gettysburg Gymnasium
This prospectus for the reorganized classical school was published in 1829 or 1830.
Courtesy Adams County Historical Society.

REV. DAVID JACOBS, *Teacher of the Languages.*

MR. M. JACOBS, *Teacher of the Sciences.*

—◦◦◦●◦◦◦—

COURSE OF STUDIES.

FIRST CLASS.

Latin and Greek Grammar, Jacob's Latin Reader, Cæsar's Commentaries, Adams' Roman Antiquities, Mair's Introduction to Latin Syntax, and Greek Testament.

English Grammar and Arithmetic.

SECOND CLASS.

Sallust, Virgil's Bucolics and Æneid, Roman Antiquities and Mair's Introduction continued, Jacob's Greek Reader, Neilson's Greek Exercises, and Potter's Grecian Antiquities.

Woodbridge and Willard's Ancient and Modern Geography, Keith on the use of the Globes, and Bonnycastle's Algebra, as far as Simple Equations.

THIRD CLASS.

Virgil's Georgics, Cicero's Select Orations, Livy, Odes of Horace, Homer's Iliad, Greek Exercises and Antiquities continued.

Algebra concluded, Elements of Geometry by Playfair, Gummere's Surveying, Chemistry, and Tytler's General History.

FOURTH CLASS.

Horace's Satires, Epistles and Art of Poetry, Cicero de Senectute et de Amicitia, and Græca Majora.

Lacroix's Plane and Spherical Trigonometry, Conic Sections, Differential and Integral Calculus, and Blair's Rhetoric.

FIFTH CLASS.

Cicero de Oratore, Tàcitus, Græca Majora 2d vol. and Hebrew and German Languages.

Cavallo's Natural Philosophy, Gummere's Astronomy, Say's Political Economy, Moral Philosophy, and Stewart's & Brown's Philosophy of the Mind.

—◦◦●◦◦◦—

REFERENCES.

Rev. Dr. Schæffer, Philadelphia.
" C. P. Krauth, do.
" C. R Demme, do.
" E. S. Ely, do.
Robert Ralston, Esq. do.
Rev. Dr. Kurtz, Baltimore.
" J. G. Morris, do.
" —— Nevins, do.
Professor Miller, do.
Rev. Dr. Schmucker, York, Pa.
Hon. H. A. Muhlenberg, Reading, Pa.

Rev. Mr. Ernst. Lebanon, Pa.
" B. Kurtz, Hagerstown, Md.
" D. F. Schæffer, Frederick, Md.
" L. Eichelberger, Winchester, Va.
" A. Reck, Middletown, Md.
" M. Meyerheffer, Augusta, Va.
" J. P. Cline, Newmarket, Va.
" G. Shober, Salem, N. Carolina.
" C. A G. Storch, do. do.
" J Reck, Salisbury, do.
" J. Bachman, Charleston, S. Carolina.

Pennsylvania College of Gettysburg (1831-1832)

Although, as its curriculum testifies, the Gettysburg Gymnasium was obviously a step in the direction of realizing the third of Samuel Simon Schmucker's goals, he recognized that it was no more than that. Before he could have a recognized and accepted college, the legislature would have to grant a charter authorizing it to confer baccalaureate degrees and vesting it with the other corporate powers associated with institutions of liberal learning. Schmucker knew that he needed major help in securing such a charter and also that the assistance which his Lutheran pastoral colleagues might be able to lend was inadequate to the task. Some of them had already contributed to the Gymnasium; all of them could expect to be asked to help pay for the new seminary building then under construction on the ridge in the western end of town. The cornerstone of the seminary edifice, as it was called, was laid on May 26, 1831; the building was under roof by the end of the year.

It is evident from the rules which Schmucker prescribed for both the Classical School and the Gymnasium that he believed such educational institutions should be nonsectarian in character, even though they were in fact under the control of the seminary board of directors. That being the case, he was not at all reluctant in seeking a broader base of support when, sometime late in 1831, he decided that the time had come to make an effort to organize a college.[36]

More than thirty years later, in an account in which he used the third person to describe himself, Schmucker recalled what happened next:

> As the number of students had rapidly increased, and it had long been the desire of Prof. Schmucker and of many other friends of the Lutheran Church, to have not only a Theological Seminary, but also a literary institution of the highest class, he resolved on making the effort to elevate the Gymnasium into a College by legislative action. Accordingly, he called a meeting of a half-dozen of the principal citizens of different denominations at the Bank in town, and invited their co-operation in the effort to obtain a charter from the Legislature for a college. He informed them that the college he aimed at was to be un-sectarian in its instruction, but at the same time to be prevailingly under Lutheran influence and control.[37]

---

[36]Schmucker was a trustee of Dickinson College from 1828 to 1833. There appears to be no evidence to indicate that he ever considered supporting Dickinson instead of establishing a new college at Gettysburg. In any event, internal squabbles and declining enrollment led the Dickinson trustees in February 1832 to announce that the school would close at the end of the session then in progress. Sellers, *Dickinson College*, pp. 487, 181-193.

[37]"Early History of Pennsylvania College," *College Mercury* (March 1895), p. 4.

Seminary Building
This engraving of the edifice of the theological seminary appeared in Sherman Day's Historical Collections of the State of Pennsylvania, which was published in 1843.

Nowhere does Schmucker identify these "principal citizens" with whom he conferred, but it is quite possible that they were six men who were not stockholders of the Gymnasium but who became members of the first board of trustees of the College. If so, they were Thomas J. Cooper (1797-1875), merchant; Samuel Fahnestock (1796-1861), merchant; Robert G. Harper (1799-1870), editor of the *Sentinel*; John F. Macfarlane (1789-1851), farmer; John B. McPherson (1789-1858), cashier of the Bank of Gettysburg; and Thomas C. Miller (1789-1860), public official and militia officer. Three of these men had served as trustees of the now-defunct Gettysburg Academy. Several had been members of the borough council, bank directors, or militia officers. Miller had been county sheriff. Several were financially interested in local turnpike companies and would soon be involved in efforts to bring the railroad into Adams county.

Whatever their identity, these "principal citizens" recommended that Miller accompany Schmucker to Harrisburg once the legislature met in December 1831 and that both men lobby vigorously for a charter of incorporation. Even before they left Gettysburg, Schmucker wrote to acquaintances in some thirty counties of the state, asking them to obtain signatures on the form petition which he enclosed and then to forward them to their legislators. Schmucker stated that he spent several weeks in Harrisburg, talking to individual legislators. He also claimed that Governor George Wolf arranged for him to address legislators in the chamber of the lower house, on which occasion he discussed "the claims of the Germans in Pennsylvania to legislative sanction in the establishment of a college for the education of their Anglicised descendants." Many legislators, the governor, and heads of departments crowded into the hall, where they were joined by "others of the most intelligent citizens of Harrisburg."[38]

Having done his best to convince legislators individually and as a group that it would be sound public policy to grant him a charter, Schmucker learned that it was his responsibility to draft the bill which, if passed, would be the document which he desired. Securing copies of earlier college charters which the legislature had approved, he sat in a room in the Capitol building and prepared a draft. In some instances, particularly where he was defining the legal powers of and limitations upon the proposed corporation, he lifted sentences or whole paragraphs from existing charters. But the document he was crafting was intended to be the organic law of a particular college, and therefore it contained distinctive features.

To begin with, the draft proposed, not to create an entirely new institution, but to "erect" an already existing "literary and scientific institution in Gettysburg, Adams county, in this Commonwealth, known by the name of Gettysburg Gymnasium" into a college "for the education of youth in the learned languages, the arts, sciences, and useful literature." Second, the draft recognized the cultural heritage as well as the obligation of the prime movers of the Gymnasium by stating that, not only was it "resorted to by a large number of young men from different portions of this state," but also it "promises to exert a salutary influence in advancing the cause of liberal education, particularly among the German portion of our fellow citizens." Third, the draft assigned a name to the college. The practice of naming colleges after presidents of the Supreme Executive Council had ceased with the disappearance of that body in 1790. There already were Pennsylvania colleges named after such heroes of the revolution and early republic as Washington, Jefferson, Madison, and Lafayette. There was a university which carried the name of the state itself, but no college. Accordingly, Schmucker wrote that the "style and title" of his proposed school "shall be 'Pennsylvania College of Gettysburg.' "[39]

---

[38]Ibid., pp. 4-5. The journals of the Pennsylvania House of Representatives make no reference to this occasion, nor do any Harrisburg papers consulted.

[39]Pennsylvania College of Gettysburg was the tenth such institution chartered in the state. Its predecessors were the University of Pennsylvania (1779); Dickinson (1783); Franklin (1787); Jefferson (1802); Washington (1806); Allegheny (1817); Western University of Pennsylvania, now the University of Pittsburgh (1819); Lafayette (1826); and Madison (1827). The last named, located at Uniontown, Fayette county, had a short life.

Fourth, the draft bill called for a method of governing the college which no previous Pennsylvania charter had contained. Because Schmucker was proposing that the legislature alter the standing of an existing, although unchartered, institution, the Gettysburg Gymnasium, he felt obligated to recognize in some way the claims of its stockholders. He did so by placing the college "under the management, direction and government of all the subscribers to the funds of said institution, by whose private contributions the said funds have been raised, and its present edifice purchased." Schmucker's draft named twenty-seven of these subscribers.[40] Twenty were Lutheran pastors who had purchased one share of the original stock issue; one of them was the recently elected second seminary professor (Ernest L. Hazelius); and the remaining six were "prominent citizens" of Gettysburg, only one of whom (Samuel Fahnestock) was Lutheran. These twenty-seven persons, and their successors, constituted the "Patrons of Pennsylvania College" and were empowered to elect twenty-one trustees "to transact all business, and be liable to all the responsibilities of bodies politic." Schmucker defined the trustees "as a committee of the patrons" and made the latter "in law responsible for all their acts." Fifth, either now or after further consultation with legislators, Schmucker added a section - it came at the very end of the charter proper - calling for a professorship of German, the incumbent of which was to offer instruction in German and English to prospective teachers in certain schools authorized by the previous session of the legislature.[41]

Some provisions of Schmucker's proposed charter were routine. The trustees were authorized to "hold, enjoy and exercise all such powers, authorities and jurisdictions as are customary in other colleges within this commonwealth." The faculty were empowered "to enforce the rules and regulations enacted by the trustees for the government and discipline of the students" and, with the consent of the trustees, to award "such degrees in the liberal arts and sciences . . . as have usually been granted in other colleges." Also routine was

---

[40]In transcribing the bill, a clerk omitted the names of two original stockholders. There were only twenty-five names mentioned in the act as finally approved.

[41]The act of April 2, 1831 established a common school fund and allotted to it certain proceeds from the operations of the state land office. When the annual income from this fund amounted to $100,000, it was to be "applied to the support of common schools" in Pennsylvania, in a manner yet to be determined. Some people believed that the legislature passed this measure in an effort to delay as long as possible beginning a practical program of public education in Pennsylvania.

In 1823 Allegheny College published an address to the German inhabitants in Pennsylvania and elsewhere in America, announcing a proposed German professorship in the college and asking for German support of the undertaking. Gettysburg *Compiler*, November 5, 1823. The act of March 9, 1826, which chartered Lafayette College, required it to maintain "forever" a professorship in the German language.

the provision that "at elections either for patrons, or trustees, or teachers, or other officers, and in the reception of pupils, no person shall be rejected on account of his conscientious persuasion in matters of religion, provided he shall demean himself in a sober manner, and conform to the rules and regulations of the college.[42]

The bill for erecting the Gettysburg Gymnasium into a college was introduced into the lower house of the legislature in February 1832. Petitions supporting the measure came from Adams, York, Lancaster, Somerset, and Franklin counties. At the end of the month, the editor of the local *Star and Banner* wrote (February 28) that "there appears to be no doubt of the passage of the bill." Schmucker and Miller had done their work so skillfully that when the roll was called on March 29, only twenty of the eighty-one votes cast were in the negative. They were scattered among twelve districts extending from the city of Philadelphia to Venango and Warren counties and from Lehigh to Fayette counties. The bill was then presented to the Senate, which passed it without amendment or roll call vote on April 6. Governor George Wolf signed the measure into law on Saturday, April 7, 1832.[43]

Before he and General Miller went to Harrisburg, Schmucker had informed some of the stockholders of the Gymnasium of what he was trying to accomplish, but he had yet to obtain the formal approval of at least a majority of that group. Now that he had a charter, he had to meet with them and persuade them to accept it. The meeting took place in Gettysburg on May 16, but only eight stockholders, including himself, attended. After extended sessions, and two adjournments, those present agreed that they would accept the charter and persuade the others to do likewise, but only under certain conditions. First, they retained the right of free tuition for their children. Second, they insisted that each of the seven persons added to the list of patrons by the charter be required to pay $25 for the privileges which it conferred upon them. Third, they requested that two original stockholders whose names were omitted in transcribing the charter should be elected patrons when the first two vacancies occurred. Fourth, they reserved the right, by a three-

---

[42]The charters of the following institutions had similar provisions: Dickinson, Jefferson, Washington, Allegheny, Western University, and Lafayette.

[43]The progress of the bill can be traced in the published journals of the 1831-1832 legislature, available in the Pennsylvania State Library, Harrisburg, and elsewhere. Act 142, approved on April 7, 1832, is the charter of the College; the state issued no separate document. Sections 12 and 13 are riders applying to two Clearfield county academies and having nothing to do with Gettysburg College. On April 6, 1832 the governor signed a bill incorporating the Adams County Railroad Company. Among its nine commissioners were Thomas J. Cooper, John B. McPherson, and Thomas C. Miller.

ours he was
correct hab-
elons a few
heir unusual
f them. As
l, he was at-
l died.
ur. of Com.

can of Tues-
een received
ie unpleasant
:d population
: counties, on
suffering se-
ort says that
lve, and Mr.
l people."

y, postmaster
t two female
, 4th auditor,
gnant typhus
iry, printer,
d died of the
irs. He had
evious days.

ave had cases
y this fearful
ilitulate them.
iink, that the
s through the
reater or less
causes. So
orming an o-
d—it seems
wful severity
; not because
e disease, but
carelessness
Niles.

ORTER, well
ig world, and
of fine imagi-
ay be said to
as Mrs. Rad-
ar Bristol on

Current.

irday last,
          34
rseed,   5 75
eed,   1 50
key,   29
er,   4 25

D,

. S. Gutelius,
nover, to Miss
y.
ev. C. G. M'-
s *Susan Cane*,

G Schmucker

of the Gettysburg Water Company.
By order,   R. SMITH, *Sec'y.*
Aug. 21.   te

Pennsylvania College.

TO THE PUBLIC.

THE Trustees of Pennsylvania College, recently organized and located at Gettysburg, would respectfully inform the Public, that the Institution will be opened for the reception of Students on the *7th of November next.* The following gentlemen have already been elected Professors, but an additional number of Instructors will be engaged as soon as the number of Students renders it necessary :

S. S. SCHMUCKER, A. M. *Professor of Intellectual Philosophy & Moral Science.*

E. L. HAZELIUS, D. D. *Professor of the Latin Language & German Literature.*

H. BAUGHER, A. M. *Professor of the Greek Language & Belles-Lettres.*

M. JACOBS, A. M. *Professor of Mathematics, Chemistry, & Natural Philosophy.*

J. H. MARSDEN, A. M. *Professor of Mineralogy & Botany.*

It has been the aim of the Trustees to adapt this Institution to the wants of the German population of our country, a Professorship of that language having already been established, and other measures adopted which will render it singularly advantageous to that respectable class of the community. Provision will be made for instruction in the other modern languages by competent teachers, and no pains will be spared to render this department highly efficient.

The proximity of Gettysburg to Baltimore and Philadelphia, the healthiness of the place, the morality of its inhabitants, its being the location of a flourishing theological seminary, the cheapness of living, and the high qualifications of the Professors, all recommend the institution to the patronage of parents.

Good boarding may be had in the village at $1 50 per week—the price of tuition is $24 per year.

There being no other collegiate institution in central Pennsylvania, this College will afford uncommon advantages to parents, who do not wish to send their sons to a great distance from home.

CALVIN BLYTHE,
President of the Board.

JNO. G. MORRIS. *Secretary*

☞Editors in Pennsylvania and elsewhere, friendly to the Institution, are requested to give the above one or more insertions.

To the Public

This advertisement, which began appearing in newspapers in August 1832, announced the forthcoming opening of a new college in Pennsylvania. Gettysburg Sentinel, August 21, 1832.

fourths vote, to reject the charter and resume their earlier organization if they should become dissatisfied with the new arrangement. It was agreed that the absent patrons would have three weeks in which to express their approval or disapproval of what had been done. Assuming that it would not be rejected, the stockholders then ratified the choice of July 4, 1832 as the date for the formal organization of the college. Daniel Webster having turned down an invitation to speak, Schmucker was authorized to invite President Judge Calvin Blythe of the Twelfth Judicial District (Dauphin, Lebanon, and Schuylkill counties) to deliver the oration of the day. Hearing of these plans, the editor of the *Star and Banner* observed (May 22) that the new college "promises to be highly useful, especially to our German population, who feel a deep interest in its success. It cannot be denied, that that portion of our citizens have, heretofore, too lightly valued the advantages of education."

At 10:30 A.M. on July 4, 1832, the bells in the German church began ringing. This was the signal for a procession to begin moving from the academy building to the Presbyterian church on North Washington street. Under the direction of two marshals, General Thomas C. Miller and Colonel Michael C. Clarkson (1799-1871), the Gettysburg Guards, the local militia unit; townspeople; "strangers"; students; faculty; the clergy; the patrons; and the orator of the day walked the three blocks and then entered the church, filling it to capacity. There were hymns, prayers by the Presbyterian William Paxton and the Lutheran John George Schmucker, and the address by Calvin Blythe already discussed. After the benediction, the procession re-formed and moved to the courthouse in the square, where it was dismissed. In his account of the exercises, the editor of the *Sentinel* wrote that he was "much pleased to see the order and harmony which reigned throughout the whole proceedings - nothing having occurred with which even the most fastidious could find fault."[44]

Following a public dinner in the Franklin House (years later the site of the Hotel Gettysburg), the patrons withdrew in midafternoon to conduct some necessary business. The charter requiring that three-fourths of the trustees be chosen from their own ranks, they elected sixteen patron and five nonpatron trustees. Since the charter assigned to them the authority to determine the length of trustee terms, they decided upon three years and divided the newly elected trustees into three classes, so that the terms of seven would expire each year. That evening, the board of trustees held its first meeting, elected officers, chose the first faculty, and announced that the rules of the Gymnasium would continue in force until superseded. It was, indeed, a busy and eventful day.

[44]*Sentinel,* July 3 and 10, 1832.

By mid-August, over the signatures of the newly elected board president and secretary, Pennsylvania College was announcing to the public, both in and out of state, that it would open for the reception of students on November 7, 1832. The names of the first five faculty members were given and the promise was made to employ more teachers whenever enrollment required it. The announcement stressed the desire of the trustees "to adapt this Institution to the wants of the German population of our country," by means of a German professorship "and by other measures adopted which will render it singularly advantageous to that respectable class of the community." Since at the time Dickinson College was not in operation, the trustees could truthfully say that "there being no other collegiate institution in central Pennsylvania, this College will afford uncommon advantages to parents, who do not wish to send their sons to a great distance from home."[45]

The last session of the Gettysburg Gymnasium began on May 23, 1832. Soon after it was concluded four months later, the seminary moved to its new home on the ridge and Pennsylvania College of Gettysburg took its place in the old academy building. Both institutions began their fall terms on November 7, 1832.

[45]This announcement first appeared in the *Lutheran Observer* on August 15, 1832 and in the *Sentinel* six days later. Editors "in Pennsylvania and elsewhere, friendly to the Institution," were asked to give the notice "one or more insertions." According to the custom of the time, the announcement would not have been complete if it had not stressed the advantages of the place chosen for the location of the College: proximity to cities, healthfulness of the town, "the morality of its inhabitants," and "the cheapness of living."

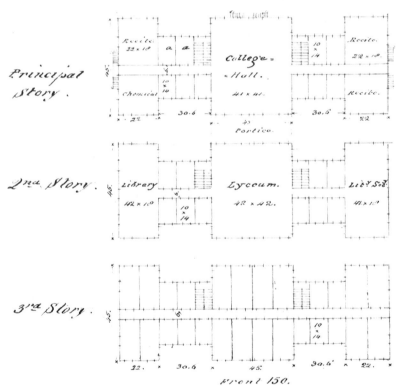

Elevation Drawing and Floor Plan

Undated and uninscribed, this drawing of the College edifice was probably one of the earliest papers which the architect John C. Trautwine submitted to the building committee in 1835. Many changes were made before actual construction began in the spring of 1836.

2.

ACQUIRING A PROPER COLLEGE EDIFICE

(1832-1837)

Getting the Money

From the moment of their election in July 1832, the first trustees of Pennsylvania College decided that the four rooms in the academy building at the corner of High and Washington streets could never adequately accommodate the two new enterprises for which they were now responsible: the College and the preparatory department which quickly replaced the Gymnasium.[1] What they needed and wanted, as quickly as possible, was a facility large enough to room and board the students as well as to contain the necessary classrooms, library, and chapel. The pressing question before them in the summer of 1832 was where to find the money to construct such a facility.

The trustees could not hope to charge their students much, if any, more than the going rates at such sister institutions as Jefferson College or the University of Pennsylvania. Nor could they expect private gifts to yield the large sums that were urgently needed. There were as yet no John D. Rockefellers or Andrew Carnegies to visit and solicit. Citizens of Gettysburg had already contributed generously to attract the seminary. Lutherans were being asked to support that school, which now had its own large building to be paid for and maintained. The trustees could not expect to be able to borrow heavily from either the Bank of Gettysburg or some other bank. Even if that were possible, the College required large gifts, not loans.

There was another possibility, the state treasury, and the trustees were not unaware of the precedents which they could cite if they decided to seek a grant from this source. In 1786 and 1787 the legislature had awarded ten thousand acres of public land each to Dickinson and Franklin Colleges. Between 1791 and 1819 it had

---

[1] See pp. 119-122 for a discussion of the preparatory department.

made a total of seven loans and grants to the former. Since 1820 it had given Allegheny College $9,000; Dickinson College $31,000; Jefferson College $17,000; Madison College $5,000; Washington College $11,500; and Western University $12,000.[2] It is not surprising then that, when they held their second meeting on September 26, 1832, six weeks before the formal opening of the College, the Gettysburg trustees voted to name a committee to apply to the legislature for an appropriation, if and when, in its judgment, there was "the probability of success." The committee consisted of two judges and one professor: Calvin Blythe; Daniel Sheffer, an associate judge in Adams county; and Samuel Simon Schmucker.[3]

The tentative character of the trustees' charge to their committee may have reflected a sensitivity to the unsettled political situation in Pennsylvania in the early fall of 1832. The state had just about completed construction of the main line of a system of internal improvements. The purpose of this system was to link together Pittsburgh and Philadelphia in an effort to recapture for Pennsylvania much of the western trade which since 1825 the Erie Canal was diverting to New York. Begun in 1826 with the high hope that revenues from use of the canals (and some railroads) in the system would eventually bring prosperity to the inhabitants and large surpluses to the state treasury, these public works had already cost much more than any previous peacetime venture in the history of the state. In the face of strong local pressure to construct expensive branch lines into sections far removed from the main route of the system, many residents were becoming convinced that retrenchment rather than further expenditure was the only way for the state to preserve its solvency.

In the fall of 1832, Pennsylvania still lacked a system of public elementary and secondary education, except for that which went into effect when parents or guardians were willing to give public testimony that they could not afford to educate the children in their care. Although there appeared to be insufficient public sentiment to warrant immediate passage of legislation beyond that enacted in 1831, there were many vocal residents who were convinced that Pennsylvania was falling behind her sister states and who wanted to move beyond the concept of pauper education, even though that meant inevitably an increase in taxes, both state and local.

The unsettled political situation in 1832 was not confined to Pennsylvania. The first national party system which developed

[2]See the several acts passed between 1791 and 1832 appropriating these sums.
[3]The original minutes of the trustees and faculty of Gettysburg College are in the GCA. Except in cases where no dates of meetings are given in the text or where there is some doubt as to clarity, there will be no further footnote references to these sources.

under the Constitution of 1787 and which had pitted Federalists against Jeffersonians had broken down soon after the War of 1812. Its successor was slow in emerging. By 1832 it was becoming evident that the new system was forming in response to the political and economic policies of the administration of Andrew Jackson, who was president from 1829 to 1837. However, while the Whigs and Democrats were beginning to take the place of the Federalists and Jeffersonians, a third party flourished for a time and attracted wide support. Begun after the 1826 disappearance of William Morgan, a New York Freemason who had begun to reveal the secrets of that order, the Antimasonic party attracted some people primarily because they had no other political affiliation at the moment. Many others joined because they thought they saw in Freemasonry unfair privilege, not only firmly entrenched in government, business, and society, but also taking full advantage of its opportunities to dominate everything in sight.

In 1828 Adams was one of only five Pennsylvania counties which failed to support Andrew Jackson for the presidency; four years later, it was one of only nine which opposed his reelection. In 1829 and again in 1832 the county gave the majority of its votes to the Antimasonic candidate for governor of Pennsylvania. In 1832 there were three newspapers in Gettysburg, each one of which, in common with most others of the time, was strongly partisan.[4] The oldest paper was the *Sentinel,* begun in 1800. Its editor was Robert G. Harper, a trustee of the College and a Mason. The *Sentinel* supported the Federalists in years past and now strongly favored the emerging Whigs. The second oldest paper was the *Compiler,* which first appeared in 1818 and was edited by Jacob Lefever, an ardent supporter of Andrew Jackson. The youngest paper was the *Star and Banner.* Begun in 1830 as the journal of the Antimasons in Adams county, it was edited by Robert W. Middleton, but its opponents claimed that the dominant force behind this paper was the county's leading opponent of Masonry, Thaddeus Stevens, and that he had established it primarily to advance his own political career.[5]

---

[4]All three were four-page, weekly newspapers.

[5]A native of Vermont and a graduate of Dartmouth College, Thaddeus Stevens began the practice of law in Gettysburg in 1816. Within a few years he was widely recognized in Adams county as a strong and unwavering supporter of education and as a bitter opponent of slavery, Andrew Jackson, and Freemasonry. Elected as an Antimason to the lower house of the legislature in 1833, he was reelected five times: 1834, 1835, 1837, 1838, and 1841. During the administration of the state's only Antimasonic governor, Joseph Ritner (1835-1839), he was one of the most powerful political figures in Pennsylvania. Stevens moved to Lancaster in 1842. The biography which pays most attention (but not always accurate attention) to this still controversial person while he resided in Adams county is Fawn M. Brodie, *Thaddeus Stevens: Scourge of the South* (New York, 1959).

Under the state constitution which was in effect in the fall of 1832, senators served four-year and representatives one-year terms in the General Assembly. The term of Senator Ezra Blythe had one year to run, but two representatives were to be elected by the voters of Adams county. At the October election, James Patterson and James Renshaw, the Antimasonic candidates, won resounding victories over their Democratic rivals. When they reached Harrisburg in December for the opening sessions of the General Assembly, all three county legislators learned that the committee from the College had decided to ask for an appropriation and were planning to support their request by means of the customary petitions from various parts of the state. In January 1833 the senate education committee reported favorably on a bill to aid both Pennsylvania and Lafayette Colleges, the former with a grant of $18,000. The full senate added to the bill grants for Washington and Jefferson Colleges and then passed it without a record vote.[6] Just before adjourning for the session, the lower house on April 4 rejected the measure by a 39-45 vote. James Renshaw voted for the bill, but James Patterson voted against it, after declaring to the house that the people of Adams county were opposed to an appropriation for the College located in his district.

The reaction to this unexpected development was immediate. What the *Star and Banner* described as "a very large meeting of the Citizens of Adams County" gathered in the courthouse on the evening of April 5. Thaddeus Stevens was elected chairman and presided over a heated discussion which led to the unanimous adoption of three resolutions. The first condemned Patterson and asserted that his reading of the sentiment of his constituents was "entirely destitute of truth." The second thanked Blythe, Renshaw, and others who had supported the appropriation bill. The third named a committee of seven men, including Thomas C. Miller, Robert G. Harper, and Daniel Sheffer, to proceed to Harrisburg in order to "correct the . . . misrepresentation of James Patterson, Esq." During their regular meeting on April 17, the College trustees voted to renew their request for an appropriation when the legislature met again in December. Before that occurred, however, the voters of Adams county would have to choose one senator and two representatives at the election scheduled for October 8, 1833.

As was the practice at the time, county party leaders met in September to name their candidates. The Antimasonic ticket included the names of James Patterson and Thaddeus Stevens for the

[6]The bill which the senate passed would have reduced the appropriation to $12,000 and required that a professorship of German be established. *Star and Banner,* February 5, 1833.

44

lower house. The opposition, calling itself the Democratic-Republican or Democratic party, presented two other names. During the short campaign which followed, there was little in the newspapers about the College, but a letter to the editor of the *Star and Banner* reminded its readers that both Patterson and Stevens had pledged themselves to oppose the "wasteful expenditure of public money" on internal improvements, an outlay which the writer believed was "about to overwhelm us." Letters to the *Compiler* were especially critical of Stevens, asking what he had ever done for the people of Adams county to warrant their support, accusing him of never having spoken "favorably of any living creature" and of making it his "daily purpose to abuse and slander every body," insinuating that he had taken advantage of his position as an attorney to cheat some of his clients, and charging finally that he had used devious tactics among his fellow-Antimasons in order to secure his own nomination for the legislature. One writer accused Stevens of trying to win votes by taking two positions on the College appropriation question. "When in town (Gettysburg) he is a whole hog College man," the writer claimed, but "if in Reading or Conewago township, he goes the whole swine against it."[7]

On the day of the election, the editor of the *Star and Banner* charged that the political opponents of Stevens, among whom were most of the resident trustees of the College, were trying to secure his defeat by taking "advantage of the prejudice existing in the minds of many against Literary Institutions." They were telling Antimasons, many of whom opposed public aid for the College, that Stevens was one of the latter's supporters and favored the aid bill. The editor insisted that "not a single Anti-Mason has any thing to do with, or interest in, the management of that Institution! Whatever interest, as members of one common community, some Anti-Masons may feel in it, care has been taken to exclude them from its direction." Middleton identified five of the resident trustees and every member of the committee named in April to go to Harrisburg as a Mason or pro-Mason. The tactics of his political opponents drove Stevens to issue a handbill, copies of which were distributed on election day in those parts of the county where opposition to the College appropriation was strongest. "I will now give no pledge [to oppose aid for the College]," he stated. "It would appear like sacrificing my own views for the sake of office: But I will say, that the College is under the control of the Masonic party; and they have now forfeited the last claim upon my services."[8]

---

[7]*Star and Banner* and *Compiler*, September 24, 1833. The latter newspaper appeared under different titles; the most common one is used here.

[8]*Star and Banner*, October 8, 1833 and January 28, 1834.

On election day 1833 the turnout of voters in Adams county was more than ten percent greater than in any of the two preceding or two following years. As editors Harper and Lefever claimed, it was probably a record poll. Patterson and Stevens were easily elected to the lower house, but David Middlecoff, the opposition candidate, won the state senate seat.[9]

In preparation for the legislative battle which was about to begin in Harrisburg, eight resident patrons and trustees of the College prepared a lengthy letter "to the citizens of Adams County." Dated November 8, it was published a few days later in all three of the local newspapers.[10] In presenting their case for the College, the authors made six points. First, they reminded their readers that the seminary and College were two distinct institutions. The former belongs to one denomination and is designed for one purpose. The latter "is the property of all denominations, receives students designed for any and every future pursuit in life, and its Trustees and Patrons belong to five different religious denominations, the Lutheran, the Presbyterian, the German Reformed, the Associate Reformed, and the Baptists." Second, in answering the charge that "Colleges are only beneficial to the rich," they declared that, in company with most other Pennsylvania colleges, the trustees at Gettysburg had set student charges so low that, "emphatically . . . , it is the poor man's institution." Most of the nearly ninety students were described as being "in limited circumstances." More than three-fourths were said to be the sons of farmers and mechanics. Third, the "moderate aid" sought from the state treasury would permit the College to place itself on a firm basis, enabling it to continue to serve "persons of very moderate circumstances" and, in fact, grow into an even more useful institution in the future. Fourth, a strong college in Gettysburg would help in the campaign to "abolish the aristocracy of wealth, and counteract the tendency to inequality incident to all governments."

The fifth argument was that the College already "scatters, every year, at least $10,000 among the surrounding populace." Operators of stages, storekeepers, tailors, shoemakers, printers, butchers, farmers, widows who keep boarders, and others, all benefit from having a college in their midst. "This is not money which passes from one pocket in Adams county to another," the readers were told, "but it is almost entirely brought from distant parts of this and other

[9]The Antimasonic candidate for the senate, James Renshaw, carried Adams county by a wide margin, but not the rest of the district of which it was a part.

[10]The *Compiler*, for example, printed the address on November 12, 1833. The eight signers were, in order, J. F. Macfarlane, J. B. McPherson, Thomas J. Cooper, S. S. Schmucker, Samuel Fahnestock, R. G. Harper, Daniel Sheffer, and Thomas C. Miller.

States, and expended here." One might well ask "what other public object is there, which annually brings an equal sum of money into Adams County, and distributes it so extensively among so large a portion of her inhabitants." Sixth and finally, since each county in the state should participate "equally in the benefits of public appropriations," and since "the public improvements of the State have hitherto, from the peculiar location of our county, been prejudicial to our interests," an appropriation to the College would only return to Adams county a share of what most legislators in the last session believed she could justly claim, and indeed would have granted, "had not a diversity of opinion existed among our representatives as to the real wishes of their constituents." Having thus expressed "their views and motives in desiring the prosperity of Pennsylvania College," the eight signers closed by expressing "the pleasing hope, that their efforts will meet the continued and increasing approbation and aid of an enlightened public."

If the framers of this letter believed that their carefully expressed arguments would terminate the county debate over the College appropriation, they were sadly mistaken. Instead, it only served to inaugurate a campaign of letter writing to the editors which was unprecedented in the history of the county. Over a period of ten weeks between mid-November and the end of January, more than thirty letters appeared in the *Compiler* and the *Star*. The editor of the *Sentinel* declined to cooperate in this unusual expression of reader sentiment. The authors of the letters identified themselves by such names as Farmer, Mechanic, One of the People, a Friend to Learning, Menallen, Darius, and Junius.

Nine of the letters, appearing in the *Compiler* beginning on November 19, were signed by Work. In language which sometimes bordered on the sarcastic, he chose to answer the arguments of the College patrons and trustees point by point. It might be commendable for five denominations to be included among their number, he thought, but why should not Catholics, Methodists, and Quakers also be among the recipients of public funds? One could indeed call the College a poor man's institution whose students have limited means and many of whose parents are farmers and mechanics. However, it is a fact that all persons have limited means and there are many wealthy farmers and mechanics. Truly poor people, he insisted, cannot afford to send their children to college even if no charge is made for instruction.

There were six major arguments advanced by the letter writers who opposed the College appropriation. First, the majority of the people of the county were said to be against it, and they had registered their sentiments by electing legislators known or believed at the time to share their opinion. Second, in proper response to the large and growing state expenditures, economy must start some-where, and soon. The people had been told that the canals were going to cost two, three, then five million dollars, wrote A Citizen of Adams, but the cost was already more than twenty million and was still growing. If we receive an appropriation, he pointed out, we cannot deny similar grants to other counties whose support would be needed in obtaining ours. "The 'log rolling' system, (that is, 'help me and I'll help you') has led us into the 'Banking System;' and the 'Canalling System,' and now commences the 'College System.'" All of this must stop somewhere. The government will soon come to a halt, warned One of the People, "if the axe be not laid at the very root of the system."[11]

Third, several writers urged that, if the legislature wanted to give money to Adams county, it should be used to support a system of common schools. "The people are resolved to do not much longer without public schools," wrote A Farmer. "They are fully sensible that a certain portion of education is requisite for the maintainance of their rights, and the continuance of their republican institu-tions."[12] Instead of one new college building, the county could build as many as fifty or even eighty one-room schoolhouses to replace the few unsatisfactory log cabins then in use. These writers rejected the argument that colleges were needed to train the teachers required for these schoolhouses, arguing that most college graduates go into the traditional professions of ministry, law, and medicine. Few would ever be content to be common school teachers; these would have to be trained in some other, as yet undetermined, way. At one point the *Star and Banner* quoted approvingly from the Philadelphia *Sun*:

> Let us take things in their natural order. Let us begin with the school-house and end with the college. Let us have the necessaries and afterwards the luxuries of education. Let us adopt a general system of common schools, instead of dotting our state with ricketty colleges, which are held up awhile by the legislature, turn off a few batches of petty-foggers and [then] tumble down.[13]

Fourth, some writers, in opposing the College appropriation, claimed that it was wrong under any circumstances to use public money to help an institution which would benefit directly only a few. They were not impressed by the arguments that the College

---

[11]*Star and Banner*, January 7 and 14, 1834.

[12]*Compiler*, January 7, 1834.

[13]This excerpt from the *Sun* appeared in the *Star and Banner* for February 11, 1834, shortly after the issue had been decided. The argument is similar to one advanced by Work in the *Compiler* for December 17, 1833: "if the 'populace' must continue to build, as they have always built, their own schoolhouses at their own expense, then let the 'aristocracy' build their colleges and academies with their own money; and let them no longer expect, that you will build splendid palaces, for their children, whilst your own children are seeking instruction in Log Cabins."

ocated at
neat cal-
llars and
I do not
he means
with the
'e to bear
I would
stance he
the prin-
governed
they are
ciple, the
neral ed-
ment of
necessary
squander
usands in
es, there-
ir wishes,
r of that,
e so fre-
.
hat with-
ild be im
iumber of
i success
of public
;s," may
iss of our
s and me-
by their
alculated
ier years.
us young
of a Col-
ine them-
compara-
eaching a
ir minds
d in sci-
rned pro-
or a vo
I at once
urdity of
quacy ,of
g class of
long im-
taxation,
submit to
ed to en-
e benefits
em of tax-
the opu-
erflowing,
them, as
of the in-
ind I ven-
e just as
ins of the
n, merely
they can
will sanc-
;es. The
ontestibly
ie citizens
an appro-

long as appropriations are granted for colleges, such a system can never be established. Do not suffer yourselves to be misled by the fine spun sophistry of the learned.

A Farmer.

COMMUNICATED.

PENNSYLVANIA COLLEGE.

The following circumstance took place a few days ago, a short distance from the Borough of Gettysburg:

An honest farmer called, one morning, on one of his neighbors, stating that he had a remonstrance against an appropriation to Pennsylvania College at Gettysburg, and wished him to sign the same. Why, friend, replied the neighbor, the thing is wrong—altogether wrong. Thee has been misled by some designing persons, I fear: thee is not aware what thee is doing. Why, friend, thee is opposing thine own interest and the welfare of the County. Take a seat and let us reason the matter together. Thee, and many of our neighbors, frequently take marketing to Gettysburg, and as the town increases in population, the more produce can be sold there, and the more money is circulating in that neighborhood the more ready our sales will be; and that, surely, is an advantage to us farmers. Now, thee must remember that a few years back large appropriations were made to Colleges in our neighboring counties—was there any remonstrance then? No: not one. Many people are perhaps not aware, that if an appropriation is made to any College in Pennsylvania, Adams County would have to pay its quota, the same as if it were made to one in Adams County. Now, let us simply take into consideration the advantage it would be to our County. That institution is in a very flourishing state; it has now nearly one hundred students, and, in all probability, in a few years there will be two hundred; and the appropriation is wanted to enlarge its buildings, which are now entirely too small. Now, friend, just make a calculation of the advantages: At the lowest calculation it would cost each student 150 dollars per year. Now, one hundred students would bring into the County annually Fifteen thousand dollars; and let any impartial man say, if that would not be an advantage to our county.

The man, fully convinced of his error, committed his remonstrance to the flames.

From the Trenton Emporium.
A Timely sentiment.—Mr. M'Duffie has concluded his speech for the Bank,

and thus o
cious unio
deliver up
which noth
tion can e

Misrepr
see in the I
of the pay
Fort Moni
nents raise
about the i
by paying
Virginia B
that no obj
ey, and th
could hav
kind of m
charge or
actually p
the Virgini
of the Unit
told that t
to lose 12½
not being
ter Bank.
that institi
cause, and
Truly they
engaged in
sort to des
port it.
schemes at
mighty and

Mr. M
pointed ou
of charging
subservien
tion to the
when it wa
long entert
ion that th
McDuffie f
that he ros
tion to ap
Taney. ?
whom he i
not Mr. T
McDuffie f
application
broken th
desires not
he did not
head.

Conduc
ington cor
Journal of
" the tone
the admini
sulting to t
language o
tration..
becomes a

Letter Favoring the College Appropriation Bill
This letter, which appeared in the Compiler for January 7, 1834, was one of more than thirty which were published in Gettysburg newspapers during the heated debate over whether the legislature should grant the College $18,000.

would grow and that its economic benefit to the county would increase at the same time. Nor were they moved by the argument that making grants to colleges was a well-established practice in Pennsylvania. In all probability the enrollment of the College at Gettysburg will never exceed two hundred, wrote Work in one of his first letters, informing his fellow-countians that at least twenty-nine of every thirty of their children "must be forever excluded from this College."[14] Fifth, a few writers insisted that, in spite of anything which their proponents might say to the contrary, colleges were incompatible with democratic institutions. Work, for example, quoted the Philadelphia *American Sentinel* to the effect that they "create a privileged and dangerous order of men, a monopoly of knowledge and power, claiming pre-eminence from superior intelligence, and exclusive privileges from superior ability and influence, and drawing a broad and offensive line of distinction between the educated and prosperous few and the ignorant and despised many."[15] Sixth and finally, several of the letters argued that if colleges were indeed the worthwhile institutions which their supporters claimed, they would find ways to support themselves. If colleges were thrown upon their own resources, wrote A Farmer, "a more rigid economy would doubtless be practised, the number would be less, consequently the number of students in each would be greater, and I venture to predict, their condition more prosperous and flourishing."[16]

The letters in favor of the College appropriation bill were in the minority, and most of them were more restrained in tone than those opposing it. The trustees, faculty, and students maintained a low profile during the debate. As already noted, Robert G. Harper printed no letters for or against the appropriation. When the trustees met in September 1833, before the election, they passed two resolutions, at least in part prompted by a desire to keep the College on the sidelines. One instructed the faculty "to see that nothing relating to party politics be admitted into the exercises of this Institution." The other prescribed that "no Student, during his connexion with the Institution, be permitted to attend any political party celebration."

In one of the strongest letters supporting the College bill, Menallen reminded its opponents that "it has always been a part of the settled policy of the State to grant aid to Colleges" and that this practice would continue, "notwithstanding your opposition." Indeed, he warned them that their determined stand might well result

[14]Ibid., November 26, 1833.
[15]Ibid., December 17, 1833.
[16]Ibid., January 7, 1834.

in an outcome "which you will ever have great cause to regret." Several other towns, including Chambersburg and York, were already "talking of raising sums sufficiently large to induce those who have charge of this College to move away from Gettysburg." It was obvious to Menallen that the College would continue to exist and that, wherever located, it would eventually get an appropriation from the state. The community had already raised $7,000 to obtain the seminary. "Shall we, the same people," he asked, "now oppose an appropriation from the State to an institution which in a business point of view is worth five times as much to us as the Seminary?" In closing, he asked his opponents: "Will you continue to fight against yourselves by banishing from our town an institution to which we owe a large portion of our present prosperity, and which promises more for our future welfare than any thing which could possibly be done?"[17] A Friend to Public Good was much more blunt in his assessment of the situation. After stating his own reasons for supporting the College bill, he concluded that

> we are paying every year a large sum into the State Treasury, and while other counties are receiving thousands upon thousands, we are receiving nothing at all! Why let others suck the marrow, and you stand looking on, not content even to "pick the bones?" . . . Let those then who have signed remonstrances against the College, without reflection, do as a large number already have done, petition the Legislature to grant the prayer of the Trustees. By so doing, they will confer a favor on the community which will be felt long after they shall have been numbered among those who have gone down to their silent graves.[18]

While the newspaper debate continued in Adams county, so did the progress of the appropriation through the legislature in Harrisburg. A bill to provide $18,000 for Pennsylvania College – this time there was no omnibus measure – was introduced into the lower house in December 1833. This was the signal for Patterson, Stevens, and representatives from other counties to submit many petitions either favoring or opposing the measure. As he had two years earlier, Samuel Simon Schmucker traveled to Harrisburg to lobby for the College. In January, the leaders of the house brought the bill to the floor for debate, which extended over a period of several days. Adams county's two members stated their cases and, as was to be

---

[17]Ibid. About this time, all three Gettysburg newspapers reprinted a letter which had appeared in a York paper, describing the opposition to an appropriation as a "suicidal policy" and urging the people of York to encourage the College to relocate, "bringing to our town an institution whose healthy influence would be felt throughout the whole community." The opponents of the College appropriation believed that this letter was an empty threat, possibly nothing more than a trick.

[18]*Star and Banner*, January 21, 1834.

expected, they took opposing sides.

James Patterson rose to speak on January 21, 1834:

> The people of Adams county, sir, are a poor people. They already bear sufficiently public burdens, and pay contributions for purposes which they do not approve, and in the results of which they have no interest. This, intended to be an addition to that burden, will be more onerous to their feelings at least; as it would seem to particularize them as objects for Legislative infliction. They have not, and will not approve of the schemes of internal improvement, and the state debt resulting therefrom, for it retards instead of advancing their interests. Their consistency in opposition to the state debt, is shown by their remonstrances against the passage of this bill.

If the members of the legislature are determined to force a bounty of some sort upon the citizens of Adams county, he suggested, they should do so by exempting them from taxation. "That would be a gratuity consistent with every principle of justice," he argued, "for they are receiving injuries by the construction of the Pennsylvania canal, for which a court of equity should decree relief." In the absence of such an order, a compromise solution would be an appropriation for the support of common schools in the county. In any event, not one dollar of public money should be spent for universities, colleges, or academies anywhere in Pennsylvania "until ample provision shall have been made previously for the equal and efficient education of all the children of the commonwealth."[19]

In spite of the fact that Thaddeus Stevens had been elected to the legislature on the Antimasonic ticket, there was, or should have been, no question of his position on the College bill. As the debate and vote approached, several of his close political friends from different parts of the county wrote to him, asking that he consider their personal embarrassment and the political consequences for himself if he supported the measure. Consistent in his support of education at all levels, on January 13 he replied in a friendly but uncompromising manner. He confessed to his friends his "mortification" that an organized political party, "the one to which it was my pride to belong," would take a formal stand against a college aid bill, and informed them that "I have already resolved that the weight of my name shall never again burthen your ticket." He concluded by telling his friends that, if necessary, "I will withdraw from your county to some place, where the advocates of Anti-Masonry may

---

[19]Patterson's speech, as reported in a Harrisburg newspaper, appears in the *Sentinel*, February 3, 1834.

still be the advocates of Knowledge."[20]

Eight days later, when Stevens rose to speak in the house, he directed his initial remarks to his Adams county colleague, comparing him to the Roman father who, "in stern and cold integrity," sat in judgment and pronounced the sentence of death upon his own son. He criticized Patterson's economy as a threat to the barest operations of good government, and wondered whether he might decline to accept the pay due him as a legislator. Noting that Patterson had voted for appropriations for repairing canals, roads, and bridges, Stevens concluded that

> he, and those who think with him, deem it of much more importance, that the mud holes in their roads should be filled up, that their horses may go dryshod to mill, than that the rubbish of ignorance should be cleared away from the intellects of their children.

Regrettably, it was true that if one were to

> bring in a bill to improve the breed of hogs, to discover some mode of fattening them with less corn, . . . these worthy gentlemen would be enthusiastic in its favor. But attempt to improve the race of men, and it costs too much!

Stevens then presented this description of the "conditions and prospects" of the College which was at the center of the debate:

> It has been chartered two years; and organized about eighteen months. It has now ninety-eight students, without a house to put them in; a library or an apparatus. It is under the peculiar patronage of the German portion of our population. The intelligent men among them feel a deep interest in it. And if this legislature should deem it worthy of their countenance, it is not difficult to forsee its complete success, under the industry and talent, and national pride, which will be brought to its aid.

After repeating the argument that Adams county was entitled to a share of the large sums of money which the state was spending and reaffirming his own lifelong faith in the value of education, Stevens addressed himself to the counsel that a representative should obey the instructions of his constituents and the warning of the conse-

---

[20]*Star and Banner,* January 21, 1834. Stevens told his friends that he believed their opposition to the College bill was based, not in "real hostility to the Institution," but rather primarily "in the detestation which every honest man feels at the base conduct of our opponents immediately preceding the election." But, he asked, will you then "sacrifice the interests of Science, and of posterity, for the sake of inflicting vengeance on a few political knaves?" Obviously, Stevens would not follow such a course. He told his friends that, soon after the election, when one of the College trustees visited him to ask whether he would support an appropriation bill, he replied in the affirmative, because "my politics should never interfere with general legislation."

quences if he did not. Where one's constituents have "formed their opinions under mistaken impression of facts, or through an imperfect knowledge of the subject, and under the influence of such opinions were to order their own destruction," Stevens insisted, it was the "duty of their representatives to resist their will, and do them good, however unthankful they may be for it." Nor should legislators fear the consequences. "It was the opinion of the ancients that it was necessary to the success of any great enterprize that some victim should be offered up on their altars," he said, "and it may be, that the great cause of education in Pennsylvania, requires that some victim should be offered up on the altar of ignorance and avarice." Without hesitating, he volunteered to be sacrificed and hurled his challenge to all who would hear:

> Let demagogues note it for future use, and send it on the wings of the wind to the ears of every one of my constituents, in matters of this kind, I would rather hear the approving voice of one judicious, intelligent, and enlightened mind, than to be greeted by the loud huzzas of the whole host of ignorance.[21]

What more was there to be said on the subject then before the legislators? They had other business to conduct; they were ready to make their decision. On January 23, 1834 the lower house passed the College appropriation bill by a vote of 64 to 25. On February 3 the senate also acted favorably; the vote on second reading was 24 to 8. Three days later Governor George Wolf signed the bill into law. The act "for the endowment of Pennsylvania College at Gettysburg" appropriated $18,000 over a six-year period, with the following stipulations. First, the initial grant of $3,000 had to be applied to the purchase of land and the erection of a building. Second, no money would be paid until the trustees satisfied the governor that they had raised $3,000 from other sources and to be used for the same purposes. Third, the College was required to offer free instruction to "fifteen young men annually, (if that number apply from this Commonwealth), in the elementary branches of an English education, in such manner as the said trustees shall deem best calculated to qualify them for teachers of common schools." Fourth, the maximum annual room rent to be charged students living in the proposed building was set at $5.

Samuel Simon Schmucker left Harrisburg after the senate passed the aid bill and before the governor signed it. Before departing the

---

[21]Stevens' speech, as reported in a Harrisburg newspaper, appears in the *Sentinel*, February 10, 1834. Stevens doubted that many who said they opposed aid to higher education but favored common schools were sincere. "It is too late now to attack education at large," he said, "and therefore its enemies confine their assaults to literary institutions of the highest order, while they profess to favor common schools."

capital, he wrote to the editor of the *Lutheran Observer* in Baltimore that it was "with feelings of no ordinary pleasure" that he was able to report "the final accomplishment of our most sanguine expectations by the Legislature of our state." Convinced that "this event will form a new era in the history of education among our German population," he expressed his hope that the future performance of the College would demonstrate "that no appropriation in behalf of education was ever entrusted to more willing, enterprising, and diligent hands." He paid tribute to all of those in Adams county and elsewhere who had supported the cause, either by signing petitions or in other ways. He thanked Senator David Middlecoff for his "persevering and faithful efforts," but his warmest praise was reserved for "our highly talented representative in the lower house," Thaddeus Stevens, who, Schmucker wrote, "in a speech of consummate legislative tact and most commanding eloquence, beat down before him the combined forces of ignorance and prejudice." It was a contented founder who penned the last paragraph of his letter:

> To-morrow morning I expect to return to my duties at Gettysburg, with a heart not a little cheered by the fact, that after three years of persevering effort we have not only obtained a charter for a College, but succeeded by the divine blessing in placing that College on a permanent and most respectable basis.[22]

The residents of Gettysburg were prompt in responding to the good news from Harrisburg. They rang the bells in the German church. Faculty and students brightly illuminated the academy building and built a bonfire in the front yard. Owners of some of the boarding houses in which students lived joined in the celebration by placing candles in their windows. The students met in the College chapel and named a committee to thank Middlecoff and Stevens for their efforts.

In supporting the College appropriation bill, David Middlecoff and Thaddeus Stevens were representing the sentiments of the 1833-1834 legislature far better than James Patterson. On February 27 the governor signed a recently passed bill chartering another new college in Pennsylvania: Bristol, in Bucks county. Over the next six weeks he approved grants of $12,000 to Lafayette College (March 11), $5,500 to Washington College (March 11), and $8,000 to Allegheny College (April 5). Then, on April 1, 1834, he signed into law "an Act to establish a General System of Education by Common Schools." Under the terms of this measure every city ward, borough, and township in the state (there were 987 of them) was constituted a school district. On September 19 the voters in each district were to be summoned to determine whether they wished to have public

---

[22]*Lutheran Observer*, February 8, 1834.

Thaddeus Stevens (1792-1868)
In 1838 Jacob Eichholtz made this painting, which recognized Stevens' recent contributions to secondary and higher education in Pennsylvania. Other evidence suggests that Eichholtz presented his subject as a more benign and friendly person than he actually was. The original of the painting was given to Gettysburg College in 1886.

schools. If their decision was affirmative, local and state taxes were to be used to support these free, or common, schools, as they were called. If it was negative, the district would continue as before, and the only education at public expense would be that provided for children of paupers.

When the patrons of Pennsylvania College met on April 16, 1834, they elected Thaddeus Stevens to the board of trustees, a position which he continued to hold until his death thirty-four years later. On September 19, along with Robert G. Harper, he was elected one of the first six school directors of the borough of Gettysburg. Swallowing hard, the Antimasons renominated Stevens for the legislature. He and his running mate defeated the Democratic slate, which included James Patterson, when the election was held in October.

Although there was almost no opposition in the legislature to the free school law when it was passed in April – only four negative votes were cast – the measure became highly controversial when the general public was at last confronted with a law which, if accepted by a particular district, meant elementary education in the English language and at public expense. In September only about half of the 987 districts voted to accept common schools. Most of the opposition came from persons who opposed paying taxes to support education and from those of German descent who wanted to retain their own privately maintained schools, in which their ancestral language was taught and used. In heavily German Berks and Lehigh counties, for example, only five of the forty-eight districts voted for free schools in September. When the legislature reconvened three months later, it was deluged with more than five hundred petitions bearing more than 30,000 signatures and calling for repeal of the law. As candidates in the fall campaign, some of its members in both houses had promised that they would so vote when the matter came before them. The senate passed the repeal measure and sent it to the lower house which, by a vote of 57 to 30, refused to concur. Instead, it sent the senate a measure making a few desired changes in the act of 1834 and to which, in the closing days of the session, the senate agreed. During the debate in the lower house, on April 11, Thaddeus Stevens delivered one of the most effective speeches of his long public career. It did not rescue free schools from repeal, as has often been claimed, since there were always enough votes in the house to accomplish that, but it was an able and forceful defense of the merits of public education.[23]

---

[23]Louise Gilchriese and Matthew John Walsh, *History and Organization of Education in Pennsylvania* (Indiana, 1930), pp. 120-131. Stevens' speech can be found in the *Star and Banner* for May 4, 1835 and in many other places.

Building

After passage of the College appropriation bill, the trustees wasted little time in making their next moves. At a meeting on April 15, 1834 they laid plans for raising the $3,000 which the act required of them in order to qualify for the state grant. Ten weeks later they were able to furnish Governor Wolf with satisfactory evidence of their success, and on July 11 he ordered the first payment from the state treasury. When the trustees met again on September 17, Thaddeus Stevens, attending his first meeting as a board member, moved and his colleagues adopted a resolution that "Nine Thousand Dollars of the State appropriation, together with the Three Thousand to be otherwise provided, be applied to the erection of a College Edifice."[24]

The matter of selecting a site was delayed until the following year. When the board met on April 23, 1835, it adopted Thaddeus Stevens' suggestion that the nonresident trustees view several possible sites and make recommendations to their colleagues. Three locations were then considered by the full board. One was the academy property at the corner of South Washington and High streets, where an additional town lot had been purchased the year before. A second was George Shryock's field, south of town, on what is now known as Cemetery Hill. The third was described as being along the west side of the Newville road; it is now the west side of the 300-block of Carlisle street. On the first ballot, the academy property received one vote and each of the two other locations, six votes. On a second ballot, the third site was chosen by a vote of seven to six for the Shryock property. Stevens, John B. McPherson, and David Gilbert (1803-1868) – three resident trustees – were named to make the purchase from the three owners of the Newville road property, at prices which the board determined. When the trustees met again in September, they learned that one of the three owners was now unwilling to sell on terms to which Stevens believed he had earlier agreed. That being the case, the trustees looked at several alternate sites and, over the recorded protest of Robert G. Harper, then decided to reopen the question of location. They now considered three parcels: one was the Newville road site; one was land belonging to Thaddeus Stevens; and the third was land belonging to Thomas C. Miller in the south end of town. On the third ballot, the second tract of six acres gained the required majority of votes. Stevens having asked the board to set the price, it was decided to use

---

[24]Stevens withdrew two other motions which he made at this meeting. One called for purchase of a tract of not less than four acres. The other authorized a committee of three (nonresidents of Gettysburg, nonpatrons, and nontrustees) to select a site for the new building.

the average of the figures given by each trustee present at the meeting: $88 per acre.

Earlier, at the meeting in April, the trustees named a committee to solicit and receive plans for the new building. The members of this committee were Charles P. Krauth, newly elected president of the College; John B. McPherson, treasurer; David Gilbert; Samuel Simon Schmucker; and Thaddeus Stevens. Obviously, further progress had to wait the outcome of the efforts of these five men.

No evidence has come to light to indicate how the plans committee made its choice of an architect to recommend the form which the new building should follow. It was not a foregone conclusion that the services of a trained architect would be secured. In 1835 the function of architect was still in the process of being separated from that of builder. Many large projects were yet being undertaken using plans which the builders themselves devised. There is no known evidence, for example, that a professional architect prepared the plans for the building into which the seminary moved in the fall of 1832.

Without a doubt, one of the three or four best known and most highly respected architects in the United States in 1835 was William Strickland (1788-1854). Reared in Philadelphia, he was apprenticed at the age of fifteen to Benjamin Latrobe (1764-1820), who is considered to be the father of the profession of architecture in the United States. Latrobe is best known for work done while he was architect of the United States Capitol, but his first major design in this country was the Bank of Pennsylvania building (1798) in Philadelphia. Closer to Adams county, he designed the Dickinson College building (1804-1805) and the Baltimore Cathedral (1805-1818).

After working for five years with the master, William Strickland started out on his own. Although he could accurately call himself an engineer, surveyor, engraver, or artist, it was as an architect that he did his best work. He designed so many halls, churches, theaters, and houses in the Philadelphia area that he became known as the "city architect." Among his most memorable projects here were the Second United States Bank building (1818-1824); the United States Naval Asylum (1826-1833); the Delaware Breakwater (1828-1841); the tower for Independence Hall (1828); the United States Mint (1829); and what many considered his masterpiece, the Philadelphia Exchange (1832-1834). During the course of his long and successful career Strickland drew from a number of traditions for the buildings which he designed, but he is best known as a highly talented and imaginative promoter of what is often called the Greek Revival movement in American architecture. Its first monument was Latrobe's Bank of Pennsylvania in 1798, but almost a generation

John Cresson Trautwine (1810-1883)
Architect and engineer. Courtesy Historical Society of Pennsylvania.

passed before Strickland and other students of Latrobe began popularizing this design. American sympathy with the Greek revolution against the Turks in the 1820s made their task much easier. From then until the 1840s or 1850s, the Greek revival was the dominant force in American architecture, and Philadelphia was its major center.[25]

The letter which David Gilbert of the plans committee of Pennsylvania College sent on August 7, 1835 was addressed, not to William Strickland, but to one of his recent students, John Cresson Trautwine (1810-1883). A native of Philadelphia, at the age of eighteen he had begun studying architecture and engineering with Strickland and had assisted him with the Delaware Breakwater and the United States Mint. Now on his own, he had just prepared the plans for and helped erect the new building at Bristol College, the institution which the legislature chartered three weeks after it

---

[25]Talbot Hamlin, *Greek Revival Architecture in America: . . .* (Dover edition; New York, 1964), pp. 62-63, 73-81, and Agnes Addison Gilchrist, *William Strickland: Architect and Engineer, 1788-1854* (Philadelphia, 1950).

granted $18,000 to Pennsylvania College. Closer to Adams county, Trautwine had designed the Second Presbyterian church in Carlisle, which was built in 1834. David Gilbert's letter reached him at Wilmington, Delaware, where he was temporarily located while serving as principal assistant engineer for a projected Philadelphia-Baltimore railroad. In agreeing to Gilbert's request for plans (August 23), the young architect wrote that, as soon as his immediate pressing obligations had been completed, he would "as you suggest send at first merely crude outlines from which you may make a selection and will afterwards prepare a set of working drawings."[26] Gilbert made it quite clear to Trautwine that cost was a key factor in any plans which his committee would recommend to the other trustees. Trautwine immediately understood and accepted this as a firm imperative. "My design for the church at Carlisle," he wrote, "was executed at an expense . . . vastly inferior to what I thought possible." But before proceeding, he told Gilbert, he needed to know two things: the number of students to be accommodated in the building and the "size and situation" of the lot on which it was to be built.

During the next several weeks the young engineer-architect was on his own. He was free to draw upon whatever he had learned directly from Strickland and from his own experience, as well as indirectly from Latrobe, in designing a building which, according to his best judgment, would be both useful and in good taste. Having decided, as he had in previous instances, to follow in the tradition which we call the Greek Revival, he did not thereby limit himself to a narrow range of choices. Most of the men who worked in that tradition were bent upon developing an architecture which would give expression to what they took to be the distinctive characteristics of the American people and their republic. The classical Greek buildings or their Roman modifications, both of which most of them knew largely through books of reproductions, were not to be duplicated exactly upon some American hill or plain. Rather, they were the models used to provide the initial inspiration which the architect sought in his efforts to break away from the long-established and increasingly elaborate British forms. In the sense that these men were trying to create a genuine American architecture, the word "revival" is scarcely accurate in describing their work.[27]

In his correspondence with Dr. Gilbert during the fall and early winter of 1835, Trautwine explained what he was trying to accomplish for Pennsylvania College and what personal expectations

---

[26]There are nine Trautwine letters to David Gilbert in the GCA. All were written between August 23, 1835 and July 25, 1836. They are identified in the text by date.

[27]Talbot Hamlin, *Greek Revival Architecture,* pp. 61-62, 88.

he entertained for the outcome of his plans. "I consider the front the cheapest that can be devised," he explained in his letter of October 20, "while at the same time, its effect, if properly executed, according to the detail drawings, will be exceedingly good." As for the portico, it "is of the same order of architecture as the Bank of U. S. in Philadelphia." Seven weeks later, on December 9, as he was about to send his plans to Gettysburg, he told Gilbert that "the order is the Grecian Doric; and based on one of the most chaste remains of Athens." In the context in which he and his contemporaries in the Greek Revival used the word "chaste," it meant plain, simple, or unadorned. These were adjectives which described their conception of an ideal architecture for the American republic. Trautwine did not further identify the source of his inspiration, but it is possible that he had in mind what was left of an Athenian agora, or market place, which was known as the new market. Trautwine and his contemporaries were all quite familiar with the pioneer effort of the English painter, James Stuart, and the architect, Nicholas Revett, both of whom visited Athens in the early 1750s and had drawings prepared of all of the architectural remains of Classical Greece which they could find. The very first specimen discussed in the first volume of their work, *The Antiquities of Athens*, is the Doric portico of the new market, with its four fluted columns. These could have been the "chaste remains" to which the young engineer-architect referred.[28]

In his letter of December 5, Trautwine revealed that he had "shown the drawings to Mr. Strickland, who approves of them entirely." Not content with this statement, he underscored the point in a letter written four days later: "I stated in a note which I sent you a few days ago . . . that Mr. Strickland approves entirely of the plans, and facade of the building. It may be satisfactory to the board to be aware of that fact." Undoubtedly, it was.

Trautwine's willingness to accommodate himself to the particular situation in which the College found itself is evident from his statement (December 9) that "there are some ornaments peculiar to the order of architecture which I have selected which I judged it expedient to omit, from considerations of expense." At the same time, he explained that he had placed question marks at several places in the plans, "intimating that those points had better be decided on by the Board, as I was not certain that my views might (in those respects) coincide with theirs." Nevertheless, he had the craftsman's pride in his work and asked repeatedly that no changes be made without his approval in the exterior of the building, with which he was much more concerned than with the interior. "Let me

---

[28]5 vols. (London, 1762-1830) 1(1762):1-6 and plates I-III.

again request," he wrote on December 9, "that no *external* alterations be made without first acquainting me of them; as a very slight deviation in some parts would entirely destroy the effect of the building." He was not averse to approving changes when he was consulted, as the correspondence clearly shows. For example, he had no objection to altering the size of the glass panes. "An inch one way or the other is of no importance," he wrote on January 5, 1836, but he "should like that of the windows to be retained as nearly as possible." Finally, it is evident from his entire correspondence that Trautwine was pleased with the plan which he had presented to Pennsylvania College. "It cannot fail to please you," he wrote on December 9, if *carefully* and *accurately* executed."

When the trustees met on September 16, 1835, in addition to changing the site of their proposed building they examined the initial plan which Trautwine, acting most promptly, had sent. Then they adopted Thaddeus Stevens' motion to authorize the construction of a building about 150 feet by 40 feet, finishing as much of it as they could for $12,000. The committee on plans was authorized to select a final design. The trustees also named a building committee and empowered it to enter into a contract. Its members were all resident trustees: McPherson, Schmucker, Gilbert, Thomas C. Miller, and Thomas J. Cooper. They elected McPherson chairman and Gilbert secretary.

Impatient to get under way, the building committee began in late November running advertisements in Gettysburg, Harrisburg, York, and Chambersburg newspapers, soliciting proposals, first by December 18, and then, since the drawings and specifications were not ready when the committee expected them, by December 31. The ten bids received ranged from $13,800 to $21,400, with lesser amounts quoted if the fourth story were left unfinished. When the low bidder asked a few days later to be withdrawn from further consideration, since he had made an error in calculating and could not get sufficient security for finishing the project, the committee decided to ask the nine remaining bidders to resubmit proposals, with the understanding that specified changes would be made in the plans in order to reduce costs, it was hoped to an amount below $12,000. This time five bids were received, one of which contained sentiments which must have attracted the immediate attention of the committee:

> I know the importance of the trust placed in your Committee and in consequence thereof would have the completion of the work done well, as well for the honour of the Committee as myself, as this not only to be a temporary structure but to continue for ages and for laudable purposes, should you consider no applicant of your place, then please let me have a preference.[29]

---

[29]Henry Winemiller to J. B. McPherson, Chambersburg, January 9, 1836, GCA. The letter is quoted as it was written.

College Edifice.

Sealed Proposals

WILL be received by JOHN B. M'
PHERSON, Chairman of the Building Committee, on or before the 18*th
day of December next*, for the erection (and furnishing all the materials) of an Edifice for PENNSYLVANIA COLLEGE, at Gettysburg. The Edifice to be 150 feet front, 42 feet back, and four stories high, with a cupola on the centre building. The drawings and specifications of said Building may be seen on or after the 5th day of December next, by calling upon

D. GILBERT,
Sec'y Building Committee.
Gettysburg, Nov. 23.   td

☞The Editors of the Repository, Chambersburg, Reporter, Harrisburg, and Republican, York, will give the above three insertions, and charge this Office.

REGISTER'S ACCOUNT.

Notice is hereby Given,

TO all Legatees and other persons

Soliciting Proposals for the College Edifice

This notice appeared in the Sentinel for November 30, 1835. Much to the discomfiture of the building committee, all of the ten contractors who presented bids quoted figures far higher than the $12,000 which it was authorized to spend.

The author of these words, Henry Winemiller, a Chambersburg contractor, happened to be the low bidder. Unfortunately, even leaving the fourth story and one entire wing unfinished, and with the other changes being made, his price was $13,350. The members of the building committee, aware that they lacked authority to commit themselves for more than $12,000, decided on January 9, 1836 that they had no alternative to placing the matter before each trustee in a letter. Describing what had been done since the last board meeting in September, the notice stated that the committee had adopted a plan "drawn by a distinguished architect, which gives universal satisfaction." Now they had a low bid presented by "an excellent mechanic, and responsible man." Even though it exceeded $12,000, the members of the committee were "anxious to accept" it. Both they and the faculty were convinced of the urgent need to proceed and, moreover, "every body admits that the price is low."[30] Unless a majority of the trustees objected within two weeks, the committee would enter into a contract. Since only three did object, the articles of agreement with Winemiller were signed on February 9, 1836. By their action, the committee rejected the pleas contained in a "Memorial of the Mechanics and other Citizens of the Borough of Gettysburg." Containing sixty-seven signatures, the memorial reminded the committee that local persons had supported the College appropriation and made financial contributions, believing that the contract would be awarded to a local builder, rather than one from a "foreign" county.[31] When the trustees met in April, there was considerable discussion of whether to accept the report of the building committee and thereby sanction the larger financial commitment which had been made. It was considered a matter of such consequence that a roll-call vote was taken, and the five yeas and three nays were identified in the minutes. The members of the building committee, having already voted decisively by entering into a contract, abstained on this occasion.

In mid-March 1836, Henry Winemiller began advertising in local newspapers his need for 400 cords of wood, 1500 to 2000 bushels of lime, 400 bundles of straw, and scaffold poles, all "to be used in the erection of the College Edifice." On March 22 he wrote to David Gilbert that he was coming to Gettysburg on the following Monday "for the purpose that you may fix on the precise spot where you intend to locate the College at your place (of which you confered the honour on me to complete)." He reminded Gilbert that "the time is drawing near to commence work and I am making every possible arrangement to engage in the undertaking such as procuring materials, carpenters, stone masons, Brick layers etc. and would be willing to commence as early as the season may permit."[32] April 1 was the traditional day for people to move from one place to another, to begin working in the soil after the long winter, and to commence building operations for the season. Accordingly, Henry Winemiller began fulfilling his contract early in April 1836. By the time the board of trustees met on the twentieth of that month, the foundation had been dug.

As work on the College building began and progressed, the correspondence between John C. Trautwine and David Gilbert came to an end. There was no longer any need for it. The committee had acted on the architect's suggestion that it consider as early as possible changes it might want to make in the design, before construction actually began.

---

[30]Copy of letter sent to all trustees, January 9, 1836, GCA.

[31]Undated memorial, sometime in January 1836, GCA. A Chambersburg builder told David Gilbert he could not see why local men "should be any more intitled to a Job of that Nature then a man from any other part of this free Country." Silas Harry to D. Gilbert, Chambersburg, January 23, 1836, GCA.

[32]Henry Winemiller to David Gilbert, Chambersburg, March 22, 1836, GCA.

John George Schmucker Casts a Negative Vote
In haste, and forgetting that he was ten days into the new year (1836), this firm supporter of the seminary and College registers his opposition to spending more than $12,000 for the College building. Other opinions, however, prevailed.

Many alterations were agreed upon even before the committee found itself at the end of December in the quandary already referred to. It did submit to Trautwine changes which it proposed at that time in order to reduce the costs of building.

The engineer-architect was opposed to less sturdy walls and inside timbers than he had first recommended, but most other suggestions met with his approval. When the committee proposed a change in the portico columns which would actually increase costs, he heartily concurred (December 19): "I recommended wood instead of brick for the columns of the portico as being cheaper," he wrote, "although in the end brick is incomparably superior." But, he warned, fluted brick columns are difficult to construct and, he insisted, "I would not like to dispense with the Flutes *on any consideration.*" He had no objection to painting the building instead of roughcasting it, as he first proposed, "provided the brickwork be done *smoothly.*" After all, he explained, "the U.S. Capitol at Washington is painted outside." As for the College building, he wrote, "the Colour will of course be white." Quick and decisive was his reaction (January 5, 1836) to the suggestion that, to save money, it not be painted at all:

> Respecting the leaving of the exterior red instead of white, it would entirely destroy all architectural beauty – you say a new coat would be required every 3 or 4 years – but I think one every 10 or 12 years would be too frequent – I know houses that have been painted 16 years, and to all apearances they will not require another coat for 16 more.

In his very first letter to David Gilbert, Trautwine answered the question of the costs of his services by writing (August 23, 1835) that "I cannot exactly tell at present, but they shall at all events be agreeable to the Trustees." The figure eventually agreed upon was $100, which included some free advice to Gilbert on at least two other subjects: the pillars of Christ Lutheran church, then under construction in Gettysburg, and railroads. In May 1836, by an act of the legislature, six of the active supporters of the College, including three members of the building committee (Cooper, McPherson, and Miller) were named commissioners to organize the newly chartered Wrightsville to Gettysburg Railroad Company. Apparently the railroad fever had also overtaken David Gilbert, who broached the subject to engineer Trautwine. There came this pointed reply in a letter written on July 25, 1836: "Respecting your question, as to meddling with Rail-road matters, I would not advise it, unless in company with some good practical man, of considerable experience."

Although David Gilbert made at least one trip to Wilmington, there is no evidence that John C. Trautwine ever came to Gettysburg, either when the building was under construction or later, when he could have determined for himself whether, indeed, his plans had been "carefully and accurately executed." His failure was not caused by lack of interest. "It would have afforded me great pleasure to have been present, to assist in laying the corner stone," he told Gilbert on July 10, 1836, after he learned that construction had already begun. "But business would not permit it."[33] After 1836 Trautwine's energies were devoted entirely to engineering, and his many commissions took him to such places as Tennessee, Georgia, Colombia, Panama, Honduras, and Canada. In 1871 he published the first of many editions of The Civil Engineer's Pocket-book. Carried on by his son and grandson, this work eventually reached more than twenty editions and 150,000 copies. Many called it the engineer's Bible.[34]

---

[33]There is no evidence either of a formal laying of a cornerstone for the College building or of a dedication after it was completed. In this letter, Trautwine cautioned again: "I hope you will make no alterations in the exterior, without consulting me."

[34]Joseph Jackson, Early Philadelphia Architects and Engineers (Philadelphia, 1923), p. 169. For a good, brief sketch of Trautwine's career, see the obituary written by Thomas U. Walter, Joseph M. Wilson, and Frederick Graff and published in the Journal of the Franklin Institute, Third Series, 116 (November 1883): 390-396.

The contract with Henry Winemiller called for the completion of his work by September 1, 1837 and for a schedule of payments determined by the progress of his workmen. In addition to serving as secretary of the building committee, David Gilbert was its superintendent of construction. In that capacity, he visited the site once or twice a day and made certain that the plans were being executed to the committee's satisfaction. By early December 1836 the building was under roof. Whether because of the national economic downturn which began in 1837 or for other reasons, Henry Winemiller was forced in July of that year into bankruptcy. While this was happening, progress on the building slowed. "The disappointment to the institution will be very great," Gilbert told the assignees of Winemiller in July, "were the house not ready by the time specified in the contract."[35] By September 1 it was clear that the most important goal – the opening of the winter session in the building – would be met. "The new and splendid edifice erected by the Trustees of the College," according to the brief notice in the Sentinel for September 25, 1837, "will be occupied next session, which will commence on the 2nd of November." And it was.[36]

Unfortunately, it was not Henry Winemiller, but his assignees, who turned over the keys to the new College edifice near the end of October. Even more unfortunately, they were keys to a structure whose interior was still far from completed. With ten rooms ready for the steward and his family, two rooms for chapel and library, and six classrooms, there were but fourteen rooms for students. This explains why, when the trustees met on April 19, 1838, they adopted a resolution "that the college edifice be finished immediately." On May 4 the building committee entered into a contract with Samuel Hunter of Gettysburg, whose low bid was $2,400. "The new College edifice will be entirely completed before the Commencement of the session" on November 1, ran the College advertisement in the Sentinel for September 10, 1838, "and will conveniently room and lodge 100 students."

It is difficult to determine from the records which have survived what the exact total cost of the College building was. To the $15,750 paid on the Winemiller and Hunter contracts one must add amounts for land, wells, outbuildings, fill, grading, trees, furniture, and other items, all of which came to about $3,000 more. On the other hand, it is not difficult to determine from the surviving records that this building program stretched the College close to its financial limits. It is true that the state was paying its grant of $18,000 according to the schedule

---

[35]D. Gilbert to Messrs. Radebaugh and Berlin, Gettysburg, July 24, 1837, GCA.

[36]Winemiller and his sureties were released from any further liability for the building on October 20, 1837, "the same being fully finished and completed according to contract and the workmanship of the same fully approved . . . without exception or reservation." Addendum to articles of agreement between the building committee and Henry Winemiller, February 9, 1836, GCA.

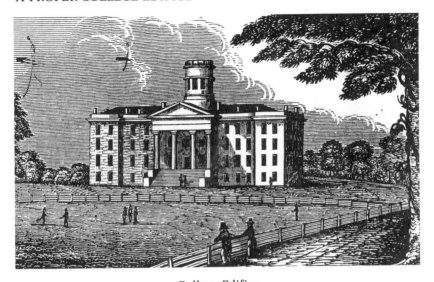

College Edifice
This engraving appeared in Sherman Day's Historical Collections of the State of Pennsylvania, which was published in 1843.

included in the act of 1834 and that the College had secured private pledges of at least $3,000 more. In addition, it could still count the academy building as an asset, although it was clearly one not easily converted into cash. On the other side of the ledger, not all of the pledges were ever paid and some of the state money was used to meet current expenses.

An attempt to get a second grant from the legislature was made in the spring of 1837. In March of that year the state senate approved a measure appropriating $5,000 for Pennsylvania College, "to be applied in the payment of debts contracted in the erection of a college edifice, now in the progress of completion." The house of representatives referred the bill to a committee which had just recommended that all state aid to colleges and academies should cease. There the measure died.[37] When the College trustees met in April 1838, they learned that

---

[37]Pennsylvania *Senate Journal,* 1836-1837 session, 1:616. The senate bill also included grants to Allegheny, Dickinson, and Lafayette Colleges. The report of the house education committee recalls the debate in Adams county in 1833-1834. The argument went as follows: It is difficult to decide between colleges truly entitled to public aid and those "leeches upon the body politic" which depend "entirely upon legislative beneficence." Truly good colleges should sustain themselves, especially since they are "in themselves, aristocratic." It is wrong to take "the substance from the poor for the advantage and promotion of the rich." Thus far, colleges and academies have received large sums of public money. What benefit has the public received in return? The state should stop supporting colleges and academies and increase its support of common schools. Pennsylvania *House Journal,* 1836-1837 session, 2:739-740.

three members of the building committee had borrowed $3,750 over their own signatures in order to meet the final payments on the Winemiller contract.[38]

In spite of these financial problems, a new era in the history of Pennsylvania College opened when the faculty began its sixth academic year on November 2, 1837. For the very first time, the educational program could now be conducted in a facility designed especially to accommodate it. As Thaddeus Stevens might have said it, the Gettysburg College now had a house in which to put its students. For that accomplishment, its supporters owed an expression of thanks to many persons, not the least of whom were the majority of the members of the 1833-1834 legislature of the Commonwealth of Pennsylvania.

---

[38]The last payment on the Winemiller contract was made in December 1837, at which time the state had paid the College only $12,000. The last two state payments, of $3,000 each, were made in June 1838 and June 1839.

College Campus, About 1862

Charles J. and Isaac G. Tyson, early Gettysburg photographers, took this picture for inclusion in the album which Frank E. Beltzhoover (1862) prepared for himself at the end of his senior year. It may be the earliest photograph of the College campus.

3.

AFTER THE MANNER OF A
WELL-REGULATED FAMILY (1832-1868)

Promoters of educational institutions in 1832 were in general agreement about what a good college should have and what it should be. Certainly there had to be faculty and students and, as Thaddeus Stevens put it, library and apparatus. In addition, there needed to be a "house" in which the students lived, in company with each other and with one or more of the faculty. Here, under the watchful eye of men charged with acting in the place of their parents while they were away from home, the students would eat, sleep, study, recite, and take their recreation. Here, also, as they passed into manhood, they would develop both intellectually and morally along desirable lines. These houses were to be located preferably in a rural area, and for at least three good reasons. First, it was held to be cheaper than living in the city. Second, rural air was thought to be cleaner and more healthful. Third, a location in the country was considered to be removed from those temptations of the city which young men should avoid. Parents ought to be able to send their sons to a good college with only the slightest concern for their health, welfare, and safety.

This, then, was the model which the founders of Pennsylvania College of Gettysburg had before them, and which they shared with the founders of most similar institutions, as they moved quickly to the tasks of getting the College into operation.[1] In their first announcement to the public, which began appearing in the newspapers in August 1832, they pointed to five advantages which their chosen location offered: "the proximity of Gettysburg to Baltimore and Philadelphia, the healthiness of the place, the morality of its inhabitants, its being the location of a flourishing theological seminary, the cheapness of living, and the high qualifications of the Professors."

When the statutes of the College were first published in 1834, they contained the statement, placed under the section dealing with the

---

[1]As noted in the first chapter, the corporate name of Pennsylvania College was changed to Gettysburg College in 1921. In the text which follows, the present name is used except where the context suggests that the older name would be more appropriate.

faculty, that "the government of the College shall be administered as nearly as possible after the manner of a well regulated family."[2] While the board and faculty attempted to realize this objective as soon as the first students entered and the first classes were held in November 1832, they could not function under what they considered to be the best possible conditions until they moved into their new building in the fall of 1837. Only after it had been completed in the following year did they insert this statement into the annual catalogue:

> The discipline of the Institution is, as nearly as possible, parental. The members of both departments [college and preparatory], except in special cases, are required to room in the College edifice. The President, under whose immediate supervision the building is placed, lives in it with his family, and together with the Tutors and Professors, exercises a constant guardianship over the whole establishment: so that parents from a distance have all the security they may desire for the proper government of their children.[3]

This chapter deals with the history of the College between the time of its founding in 1832 and 1868, the year in which its second president, one of its most colorful and controversial trustees, and its first janitor all died in office. Within five years of their deaths, almost all of the founders had also passed from the scene and the College was now in the hands of persons who, from their own experience, knew little or nothing of the frustrations and achievements of the first few years. In 1868, both the country and the state in which the College functioned were being transformed from an agricultural into an industrial society. The changes which accompanied this transformation extended sooner or later to every aspect of American life, including higher education. While in 1868 the College still formally embraced the ideal of the well-regulated family, it had abandoned some key parts of it and significantly altered others.

In this and subsequent chapters, we shall begin our treatment of the history of the College with an examination of the part played by those legally charged with the tasks of maintaining and advancing

---

[2]This same statement was included in the Dickinson College regulations adopted in 1826. Sellers, *Dickinson College,* p. 179.

[3]Except in a few instances, quotations from the College catalogue are identified in the text by date and there is no footnote reference to them. The first catalogue was published in February 1837. The faculty saw it as a valuable and inexpensive advertisement of the College. "This document has been extensively circulated," they told the board of trustees, "and has been noticed in most of the Newspapers in the State, and in a considerable number out of it. In this way at a low price, the institution has been extensively presented to the public, and on this point, nothing more can be desired." Report of the Faculty to the Board of Trustees, April 1837, GCA. Hereafter cited as Faculty Report.

the institution; then proceed to discuss the physical plant, curriculum, library, and equipment; then consider the students for whose benefit the College exists; and finally review a number of other important concerns, such as the relations between the College and the community as well as those between the College and the Lutheran church.

Trustees

The charter of Gettysburg College which Samuel Simon Schmucker wrote in 1832 differed from those of its sister institutions in that it vested "the management, direction and government" of the College in a group of twenty-seven patrons. Twenty of these men had subscribed for the purchase of the academy building and were the directors of the Gymnasium. Six were residents of Gettysburg who had agreed to support Schmucker's efforts to obtain a charter, in return for assurance of a voice in the affairs of the new institution. The remaining member was his colleague on the seminary faculty. Instead of giving the patrons direct control of the College, Schmucker specified that they should elect a board of twenty-one trustees, at least three-fourths from their own number, which board, "as a committee of the patrons," was given "power to transact all [College] business," although the patrons were "in law responsible for all their acts." As already noted, at their first meeting the trustees set their terms of service at three years, divided themselves into three classes so that the terms of seven would expire each year, and specified that they should serve until their successors were elected.[4]

The charter directed the patrons to meet annually in Gettysburg. Between 1832 and 1835 they complied faithfully with this requirement and promptly filled the vacancies on the board of trustees as they occurred. After that they met irregularly: in 1838, 1844, 1848, and 1851. On each of these latter occasions they chose twenty-one trustees, since the terms of the entire board had expired since their previous meeting.[5]

On April 19, 1850 the legislature passed an act which changed in a major way the governing bodies of Gettysburg College. The main purpose of this legislation was to consolidate Franklin College in Lancaster and Marshall College in Mercersburg into one institution, under the influence of the German Reformed church. The act dealt in part with the Lutheran interest in Franklin College, which had existed since 1787, by adding its fifteen Lutheran trustees to the Gettys-

[4]See Appendix 1 for a list of trustees from 1832 to 1985.
[5]Record Book of Board of Patrons of Pennsyl'a College, GCA.

THE FIRST TWENTY-ONE TRUSTEES

Calvin Blythe, Harrisburg
Alexander Thompson, Chambersburg
John G. Morris, Baltimore, Maryland
John George Schmucker, York
David F. Schaeffer, Frederick, Maryland
John C. Baker, Lancaster
Abraham Reck, Middletown, Maryland
Daniel Sheffer, York Springs
Christian Frederick Heyer, Somerset
Ernest L. Hazelius, Gettysburg
Samuel Simon Schmucker, Gettysburg
Thomas C. Miller, Gettysburg
John F. Macfarlane, Gettysburg
Robert G. Harper, Gettysburg
John B. McPherson, Gettysburg
Charles P. Krauth, Philadelphia
Jonathan Ruthrauff, Hanover
Jacob Medtart, Martinsburg, West Virginia
Benjamin Kurtz, Chambersburg
Emanuel Keller, Mechanicsburg
Augustus H. Lochman, Harrisburg

The names are listed in the order in which they appeared in the minutes of July 4, 1832.

burg board, thereby increasing the membership of the latter to thirty-six persons. At the same time, it made the Gettysburg board a self-perpetuating body and authorized its members to fill vacancies created by death, resignation, or failure to attend meetings for three successive years. By repealing "so much of the charter of Pennsylvania College at Gettysburg, as is inconsistent" with the act of 1850, the legislature brought to an end the board of patrons. They held their last meeting in 1851, and the fifteen new trustees were added to the board two years later. Beginning in 1853, therefore, there were thirty-six Gettysburg trustees. Their terms were indefinite, but their membership would lapse if they were absent from meetings for three consecutive years.

At first, the board of trustees met in Gettysburg, twice a year, in April and September (the latter meeting coincided with commencement). On several occasions, when the eleven members necessary for a quorum failed to appear, the scheduled meetings were simply not held. In 1861 the trustees decided that they could transact all of

Alexander D. Buehler (1814-1893)

Moses McClean (1804-1870)

David Gilbert (1803-1868)

John B. McPherson (1789-1858)

Four Early Resident Trustees

their business at one annual meeting. Beginning in 1862, they convened each August, at the time of commencement. However, they soon discovered that at least one special meeting in a year was often necessary.

Four men were presidents of the board during the years between 1832 and 1868: Judge Calvin Blythe (1832-1835, 1838-1843); Rev. Benjamin Kurtz (1835-1838); John B. McPherson (1843-1857); and Moses McClean (1857-1870), a Gettysburg attorney and member of Congress (1845-1847). Three men served as treasurer: John B. McPherson (1832-1839); Samuel H. Buehler (1839-1856); and Alexander D. Buehler (1856-1893), who was his father's partner and successor in business. Blythe's judicial and political careers kept him away from Gettysburg; he attended only one board meeting during his second term as president. Kurtz, who was editor of the *Lutheran Observer* from 1833 to 1858, and who lived in Baltimore, was a trustee for most of this period and continued to support the College in the columns of his journal, but he rarely attended meetings after he resigned as president in 1838, giving ill health as his reason. As local men, McPherson, McClean and the Buehlers were able to give the affairs of the College their close personal attention. Blythe, McPherson, and McClean were Presbyterian in background. Kurtz and the Buehlers were Lutherans.

Attendance at most board meetings scarcely exceeded a quorum. Some trustees came to only a few meetings during their entire tenure. Several, including most of the fifteen persons added by the act of 1850, attended none at all; they were dropped after three years. Among the Lutheran pastors who were dependable participants in board deliberations for a decade or more between 1832 and 1868 were John George Schmucker and Augustus H. Lochman (1802-1891), both of York; Benjamin Keller (1794-1864), of Gettysburg and later of Philadelphia; John Ulrich (1808-1862), of Adams county and later Shippensburg; and John G. Morris (1803-1895), of Baltimore. The latter's brother, Charles A. Morris (1792-1874), a York businessman and active churchman, was one of the few nonresident Lutheran laymen on the board during this period.[6] Thaddeus Stevens is a special case. Before he moved to Lancaster in 1842, he attended almost every board meeting and never hesitated to express his views or make motions. Although he came to only three meetings after 1842, his colleagues always reelected him when his membership lapsed; his name was still on the rolls when he died in 1868.

[6]This listing does not include a number of dependable trustees who joined the board during the last years of this period and who will be discussed in the following chapter.

Augustus H. Lochman (1802-1891)   John G. Morris (1803-1895)

Benjamin Kurtz (1795-1865)   John George Schmucker (1771-1854)
Four Early Nonresident Trustees
Schmucker and Kurtz pictures courtesy Abdel Ross Wentz Library,
Lutheran Theological Seminary, Gettysburg.

In the days before telephones, automobiles, and railroads (the latter reached Gettysburg from the east in 1858), much of the work of the board fell upon the resident trustees. They manned the committees named to repair and improve College property; they sometimes purchased land which they believed the College would need at some future time and then offered it to their colleagues at the next meeting; and they were the ones for the faculty to consult when something went wrong and required immediate trustee attention. During the time they were members of the board and lived in Gettysburg, John B. McPherson, Robert G. Harper, Thomas C. Miller, John C. Macfarlane, Thomas J. Cooper, Dr. David Gilbert, Samuel H. Buehler, Samuel Fahnestock (1796-1861), Dr. David Horner (1797-1858), Moses McClean (1804-1870), David A. Buehler (1821-1887), Dr. Henry S. Huber (1814-1873), and Alexander D. Buehler (1814-1893) carried more than their share of the burden which the trustees bore. Like Thaddeus Stevens, Samuel Simon Schmucker is a special case. During his forty-one years as a member of the board, he missed only five meetings.

Given the legal responsibilities for the well-being of the College which the charter imposed on the board of trustees, no problem was too small to claim its attention. Each time it met, the president of the College presented a report which the faculty had carefully scrutinized, perhaps amended, and finally approved. Committees reported on tasks assigned to them at previous meetings. Often there was little additional information available to the trustees to warrant their doing anything but accept the recommendations which their committees made to them. Most of the time their main consideration was the availability of funds which would permit new expenditures. The matter of financing the well-regulated family is so important that it will be discussed separately in the next section. But if the money was available, the trustees could be expected to authorize a needed additional tutor in the preparatory department, deepen or widen one of the wells, and authorize construction of a bathhouse on the campus. On the other hand, when persons unknown burned down one of the privies behind the College edifice, there was little or no alternative to rebuilding it.[7] As time passed, the trustees decided that they needed several regular standing committees to help in conducting their business. By 1868 they had such committees for finance and investment (1851), auditing (1856), buildings and grounds (1857), and repairs (1860).

[7]The treasurer dutifully entered in his ledger receipt on June 1, 1844 of $120 "from an unknown person, for damage sustained, in Burning privy." On July 8 he paid $28.74 to "sundry persons" for repairing the same.

In some colleges during these years, the boards of trustees often chose to exercise their legal authority in order to impose their will upon the educational enterprise, in spite of what either faculty or anyone else might believe was best for the institution.[8] There is little evidence of this attitude and behavior at Gettysburg, where the relations between faculty and trustees appear to have been, with very few exceptions, genuinely harmonious. One has only to read the minutes of a board meeting in close conjunction with the text of a faculty report to realize how often board action on a wide variety of matters was merely sanction for what the faculty had already recommended. Obviously this was not always the case. In 1837 the faculty disciplined a group of students who failed to obtain permission before joining a local military unit which was called out to deal with a threatened riot by Irish laborers on a railroad construction site near Gettysburg.[9] Some of the trustees, believing that the students had performed a patriotic duty, opposed the idea of censuring them. Although they disagreed with the faculty in this instance, they finally decided not to overrule the action taken. In the 1850s the faculty reached the conclusion that the practice of boarding students in the College building was not working and should be abandoned. It took some time and several recommendations before they were able to convince the trustees of the soundness of their position.

Finances

It is not difficult to understand why some state legislators in the 1830s opposed financial aid to colleges on the grounds that there seemed to be no end to their requests for more public money. Every one of the Pennsylvania colleges chartered before 1832 had experienced serious financial problems which, in most cases, required them to close their doors on at least one occasion and which drove them more often than that to Harrisburg seeking relief. Few colleges could hope to pay for their main building without a public

---

[8]Saul Sack, *History of Higher Education in Pennsylvania,* 2 vols. (Harrisburg, 1963) 2:667-670. Hereafter cited as Sack, *Higher Education.*

[9]A railroad projected to run from the Susquehanna to the Potomac rivers became part of the planned system of public works in the state in 1836. Thaddeus Stevens was one of its strongest advocates. The construction crews began in Gettysburg and moved west into the mountains. The route chosen followed such a circuitous path, one which brought it close to Stevens' iron interests, that the entire project was soon referred to as the tapeworm railroad. Many questioned whether the amount of business which this line could be expected to attract if completed would ever justify the extremely high per mile cost of construction already incurred. When the Antimasonic administration lost power in the state early in 1839, a legislative investigation soon led to abandonment of the project.

grant which, if obtained, was often not large enough to cover the entire costs of construction and furnishing.

Although it was never forced to close its doors, Gettysburg College had its share of financial difficulties in the period covered by this chapter. The economic downturns of the 1840s and 1850s and the Civil War in the early 1860s quickly resulted in a decline in enrollment and a consequent reduction of income. Payment of salaries due had to be delayed; plans for improvements, shelved; and loans, sought.

Between 1832 and 1868 the annual expenditures of the College averaged slightly less than $6,000.[10] About three-fourths of this amount was paid each year for faculty salaries. In 1833 the two professors brought into the College from the Gymnasium, Henry L. Baugher and Michael Jacobs, were promised up to $500 per year, depending on whether the money was available. A tutor in the preparatory department was promised up to $250. The salaries of Baugher and Jacobs were increased to $700 in 1838. On several occasions during the financially troubled 1840s the faculty asked for a further increase, which the board reluctantly turned down, explaining that the funds for it were simply not available. An annual advance of $100 voted in 1847 had to be postponed a year later because of what the secretary of the board called "pecuniary deficiencies." Beginning in 1853 the salary of a professor was $850 and of a tutor in the preparatory department, $300. During the early years of the Civil War a professor received $900. In 1865, following the wartime inflation, the board raised faculty salaries to $1,300 per year.[11]

Funds were also needed to purchase books for the library as well as equipment and supplies for the science course. From time to time the trustees appropriated $50 or $100 for each of these purposes, but never on a regular basis. In 1852-1853 the faculty asked the alumni to contribute at least $1,000 to a library endowment fund, the proceeds of which were to be used for the purchase of books. By a split vote early in 1854, the faculty agreed to invest the money received from this appeal in the name of the board of trustees, rather than in their own name. This fund was soon yielding $80 annually for its intended purpose. The trustees, for their part, were pleased

---

[10]Both expenditures and receipts increased rapidly between 1864 and 1868.

[11]All full-time faculty held the rank of professor during this period. The president of the College received $50 and then $100 more than the professors. In addition, President Charles P. Krauth was given room and board in the College building during his tenure (1834-1850). His successor, Henry L. Baugher (1850-1868), was paid $100 annually for maintaining his office in the building. In 1860 he gained rent-free quarters in the newly completed president's house on the campus.

when other donors came forward. For example, after they had refused several faculty requests for funds to purchase a telescope, on the grounds that no money was available for that purpose, Dr. Hiester H. Muhlenberg (1812-1886), a Reading physician and a trustee, gave one to the College in 1853. Muhlenberg also contributed many books to the library.

More money had to be spent on maintaining the physical plant in good condition than on the purchase of books and laboratory equipment. The treasurer's records show regular payments for sweeping chimneys, replacing broken windows, mending locks (there were ten separate charges for this purpose during the 1847-1848 fiscal year), repairing roofs, purchasing lightning rods, painting, whitewashing, building and repairing fences, repairing or adding outbuildings, and purchasing wood, which until about 1860 was a major item of expense. From the beginning, the trustees were careful to purchase insurance for the College buildings; in 1856 they secured a separate policy on the library. Before 1868 the College was often one, two, or three thousand dollars in debt, and interest was an important item of annual expenditure.

Between 1832 and 1868 the annual receipts of the College, like the expenditures, averaged slightly less than $6,000. About seventy percent of this amount came from tuition and room rent, the charges for which were, as they had to be, competitive with those of sister institutions. When the new building was first occupied in the fall of 1837, tuition was $30 per year and room rent was $10. Half way through the period under study, in 1852, tuition was $34, but room rent had been reduced to $5. The tuition for the year 1867-1868 was $39, while the room rent was $9. The trustees sometimes tried to gather some additional money by an assessment of 25¢ for repairs and a $5 fee for the diploma.[12]

In spite of the increasing sentiment against continuing state grants for higher education, in April 1838 the legislature, as part of a revision of legislation affecting common schools, voted to pay $1,000 annually for a period of ten years to every Pennsylvania college and university having four or more instructors and at least one hundred students.[13] Before this act was repealed in September

---

[12]The catalogue gave estimates of the total annual College costs, warning in 1838 that "of course a great deal will depend upon habits of economy." The estimates were $100 to $130 in 1838; $115 in 1852; and $211.50 in 1868.

[13]The fourth annual report of the Superintendent of Common Schools, presented to the 1837-1838 Pennsylvania legislature, listed eight colleges then in operation in the state and gave their enrollment as follows: Jefferson, 171; Dickinson, 128; Gettysburg, 118; University of Pennsylvania, 107; Washington, 107; Lafayette, 72; Marshall, 49; and Allegheny, 38. The total enrollment was 790. Pennsylvania House Journal, 1837-1838 session, 2:602.

1843, when the state was near bankruptcy, Gettysburg College had received $5,500 from this source. In the early 1840s the state grant was a welcome boon which amounted to about twenty percent of the College's total income. It made possible debt reduction and paying faculty salaries on time.

In 1833 and 1834 efforts were still being made to persuade delinquent patrons to meet their remaining financial obligations to the College. In the following year, the trustees decided to send out two collectors, one of whom was asked to exert his influence among the Germans, on whose behalf, as had been said so often, the College had been founded. These collectors could be expected to return with several hundred dollars, from which their own salaries would have to be taken. As early as 1835 the board began urging the president and faculty to use their vacation periods to make the rounds of potential donors. Presumably, they would expect to be paid nothing more than their actual out-of-pocket expenses. If one of these collectors returned to Gettysburg and reported that he had secured $500, that did not mean that he had cash and checks in hand. Perhaps most of what he had secured was in the form of written pledges to pay at some future date. When the time for redemption came, some of the donors were unable or unwilling to honor their commitment. Occasionally the College threatened to sue in an effort to collect, but then decided that such action might well make it more enemies than friends. Obviously, while this source of income did yield sums which were of significant and immediate help to the College in the 1830s and early 1840s, it did not produce the large amounts of money which could have inaugurated a reasonable endowment.

The first income which the College received in the form of a bequest came from Isaac Baugher (1786-1848), an Emmitsburg businessman, brother of Henry L. Baugher, active Lutheran layman, and a trustee from 1844 until his death. Baugher willed the College $500. The only other bequest received before 1868 was that of Mrs. Mary Doll, Frederick, Maryland. Paid in 1851, it amounted to $250.[14]

---

[14]Baugher also made bequests to the seminary, the Parent Education Society, the American Tract Society, and the Board of Foreign Missions. Mrs. Doll willed $500 to the trustees "of the Lutheran Institution at Getysburg for the use and benefit of said institution of learning." For which Gettysburg school did she intend her bequest? In the end, seminary and College divided it equally between them. The 1852 College catalogue suggested that "those of ample means" might remember the College "in making a testamentary disposition of their property at their decease." In that way "they might . . . very much contribute to its usefulness and render it more worthy of its position." For some reason this appeal was dropped after only a few years.

The 1840s were certainly one of the most financially threatening periods in the life of Gettysburg College. The same economic downturn which brought the state close to bankruptcy reduced tuition income from $4,720 in 1840-1841 to $3,242 in 1844-1845. It forced the College to abandon its plans to construct a needed separate building for the students of the preparatory department and, in 1843-1844, to borrow money in order to pay faculty salaries. A committee named to secure a long-term loan of $3,500 reported its inability to find anyone willing to extend it, although several countians did advance smaller sums. In an effort to obtain funds, the College sold the academy building in 1844 and also several lots between Carlisle and Washington streets, which were repurchased twenty years later. Somewhere, money was found for a second campus building (Linnaean Hall) in 1846-1847, as well as for a second and third land purchase from Thaddeus Stevens in 1848-1849. However, at this very time the trustees found it necessary to postpone paying the salary increases which they had only recently approved for the faculty. In a circular letter which they addressed in April 1849 to all Lutheran pastors within the constituency, asking for their support, the faculty gave this estimate of the gravity of the situation: "We have now arrived at a point in our history, in which the number of Students is inadequate to the support of the Institution. We cannot diminish the number of Teachers without serious injury to instruction."[15]

As early as 1844, the faculty strongly urged the trustees to adopt a method of raising money which many other institutions were then using.[16] The board agreed, and began offering scholarships for sale. In return for payment of a specified sum, the College would provide free tuition for a student of the holder's choosing. A permanent scholarship, which might sell for from $350 to $500, insured this privilege in perpetuity. A single, or transient, scholarship, whose price might be $100 to $150, guaranteed the privilege for one student through the College course, including the preparatory department. The proponents of this method of raising revenue claimed that the income from the invested funds would, in the long run, more than cover the actual cost of the services rendered in return. They assumed that not all owners of scholarships would begin to use them at once and that some would probably never use them. Although several of these scholarships were sold by Gettysburg College as early as 1845, the first concerted effort to offer them began in 1850. The following announcement appeared in the 1852 catalogue, under

[15]Faculty circular dated April 23, 1849, GCA. See pp. 172-178 for a discussion of the Lutheran constituency of the College.
[16]Sack, *Higher Education* 2:678-683.

the heading of Endowment:

> The trustees are desirous of placing the Institution on a permanent basis, and at the same time of offering the means of education, as cheaply as possible, to the great mass of the community. This they propose to accomplish by the sale of scholarships, transferable like other property. For $100, a single scholarship, or the tuition of one pupil through the entire course of studies, or six years of instruction, is secured; and for $350, a perpetual scholarship may be purchased.[17]

According to the records of the treasurer, which may be incomplete, between 1850 and 1863 a total of 113 scholarships were sold, 54 of which were permanent. Most of the purchasers were Lutheran congregations and individuals scattered through the College constituency, from Philadelphia in the east to Indiana county in the west, and south into Maryland. The amount realized from these sales was $22,396.62, most of which was used to create the first College endowment fund. The proceeds were invested in bank stock, Baltimore ground rents, and local notes and mortgages. Some of the moneys received were taken to reduce the existing indebtedness of the College, and more than $3,000 was allocated to pay for the president's house, built in 1860. The balance which the treasurer reported in August 1864 in what he called the Permanent Fund was $18,457.66. At that time the annual income from this source exceeded $1,000 and represented about twenty percent of the College's receipts.

It did not take long for the faculty to have serious second thoughts about the wisdom of selling scholarships as a way of building endowment. They were distressed by the large number of persons who, contrary to expectation, bought them with the intention of immediate use, and they warned the trustees that the resulting loss of current income could have disastrous consequences. At Jefferson College, scholarships presented between 1857 and 1863 reduced annual tuition income to less than $100.[18] The fact that nothing similar happened at Gettysburg, where receipts from tuition during those same years averaged about $4,000, did not restore the confidence of the faculty in this practice.

A second source of endowment for the College resulted from the act of April 19, 1850 which created Franklin and Marshall College.

---

[17]This announcement was repeated in the 1853 and 1854 catalogues, but was then dropped. The prices and conditions of these scholarships changed. For example, in September 1857 the board declared that single scholarships would sell for $100, would be nontransferrable, and would not become effective until the sum of $100,000 was secured. This latter was a provision which other colleges inserted in their regulations governing the sale and use of such scholarships.

[18]Sack, *Higher Education* 2:681.

According to the terms of this legislation, the assets of Franklin College were to be appraised and an amount equal to one-third of their value – considered to be the Lutheran interest in the institution – was then to be paid to Gettysburg College. Once invested, the income from this sum would be used to support a Franklin professorship. Early in 1853 the trustees of Franklin College paid over $17,169.61, at which time Frederick A. Muhlenberg (1818-1901) was designated Franklin Professor of Ancient Languages. The money received was invested in Lancaster and the income was handled separately from the general account of the College.[19]

There was a third source of College endowment in the 1850s. At the suggestion of the faculty, made early in 1851, the trustees proposed to the Pennsylvania Synod in June of that year that it endow a professorship of German Language and Literature in the College. This was in fact a faculty position called for by the charter of 1832. While the College had offered instruction in German from time to time since then, there never seemed to be enough money available to warrant adding another permanent position to the faculty. This had been especially true during the 1840s. The College was now directing its request to the Pennsylvania Synod because that body continued to represent the most German part of its constituency. Satisfied that the proposal was sound and desirable, similar to one it had itself considered a few years earlier, the synod unanimously accepted the request, and then named as its agent in raising the necessary funds Benjamin Keller, pastor of St. James Lutheran church in Gettysburg and a College trustee.[20] Keller resigned his parish and assumed his new duties in November 1851. During the next three years he made his appeal to more than one hundred congregations, with remarkable success. In 1855 the treasurer of the synod reported that a total of $16,010 was already drawing interest in the German Professorship Fund. According to the terms of its agreement with the College, the synod retained control of this fund and exercised the right to nominate candidates for the position. The first German professor under this arrangement, Charles F. Schaeffer (1807-1879), joined the Gettysburg faculty in

[19]The act of 1850 authorized the Lutheran trustees of Franklin College to elect the first Franklin professor, whose title was to be Professor of Ancient Languages. Subsequent incumbents were to be nominated by the Pennsylvania Synod and elected by the Gettysburg board of trustees. Frederick A. Muhlenberg became Professor of Greek Language and Literature at Gettysburg College in 1850; the Lutheran trustees of Franklin College elected him Franklin Professor of Ancient Languages three years later.

[20]In 1848 the Lutheran congregation which had worshiped with a Reformed congregation in the German church at the corner of High and Stratton streets built and dedicated its own church, St. James, at the corner of York and Stratton streets.

April 1856.[21]

The inaugurations of the Franklin and German professorships were events of great importance in the life of the College. Beginning in 1856, two of the five full-time faculty members were paid, not from the general treasury, but from endowment funds which yielded annual sums equal to or greater than the salaries then being paid to their colleagues. It is little wonder that the board of trustees in September 1855, acting upon the recommendation of the faculty, voted to "extend the right to any Evangelical Synod which endows a Professorship in Pennsylvania College to nominate the incumbent of that Professorship." No synods responded to this invitation, which in the long run was probably for the best. While this method of financing the educational enterprise was attractive at the time, as was the sale of scholarships, it invited potentially serious troubles whenever a vacant faculty position was to be filled from candidates selected by an agency outside the institution.

In spite of what had been accomplished since 1850, the faculty was satisfied neither with the progress that was being made nor with the role which they were being expected to play in endowing the College. On their behalf, the president told the board of trustees in September 1853 that "all the colleges of the state excepting our own have secured a sufficiency to elevate them above the point of fear . . . From the region whence we derive our support five colleges besides our own have been seeking endowment and they have secured it to the amount of nearly if not quite $400,000." The president identified Dickinson, Lafayette, Jefferson, and Washington Colleges as members of this group. Further endowment was a matter of great urgency for Gettysburg. "We lay it down as a first principle," he wrote, "that in an institution like ours the highest form of discipline and scholarship cannot be secured without adequate endowment."

Members of the faculty had done their best in trying to raise funds for the College during their vacation periods. Having had limited success, they were now asking the board "to take this work off of their hands," since they could not be both successful teachers and fund raisers at the same time. A year later, in September 1854, the faculty pointedly asked the board "why there is no progress made in the endowment of the institution," especially at a time when population and wealth in the country were increasing. Too many people in the constituency seemed to believe "that the institution is virtually a private enterprise of the Faculty and therefore that they should give instruction, secure endowment, exercise discipline,

[21]The synod paid Schaeffer a salary of $900, plus $100 toward rent of a house. Half of his time was to be given to theological instruction in the German language in the seminary, of which he was also a faculty member.

increase the library and philosophical apparatus and in short accomplish everything."[22]

A renewed attempt to increase the financial strength of the College finally began in September 1857, when the trustees chose a committee of seven members to frame an endowment plan, name an agent to make most of the necessary solicitations, and supervise "the whole business." Six months later, the seven reported that they had not been able to secure an agent, but in September 1858 they returned with a detailed plan for bringing the endowment fund total to $100,000. Reckoning the existing endowment at about $30,000 (the sum of the treasurer's Permanent Fund and the Franklin Professorship Fund), they proposed to raise the remaining $70,000 by securing traditional pledges or subscriptions and by the sale of 450 scholarships, ranging in amounts from $50 to $400. The committee estimated that it would take five years to realize their goal. The trustees approved this plan and began the campaign. Unfortunately, other urgent matters soon occupied the attention of the president of the College, who was chairman of the endowment committee, and only about $3,000 in gifts was received by the time the Civil War began in 1861.[23]

By far the most successful endowment campaign of this period was initiated in 1864 by several alumni and other friends of the College, including Frederick Benedict (1847), John E. Graeff (1843), and Charles A. Hay (1839). The editor of the *Lutheran Observer,* Frederick W. Conrad (1816-1898), began in June of that year running a series of articles designed to create public interest in the project. Noting that the friends of Wittenberg College were then holding a convention in Dayton, Ohio, in an effort to raise an endowment for that school, he pronounced this the best way to support a college. Tuition could never raise enough income; the scholarship system had failed wherever it was tried; and annual contributions, while helpful, were never sufficient. Recommending a minimum goal of $100,000, he believed that this would enable the College to establish two new professorships, improve the library, and increase the "apparatus." Conrad lamented the fact that not one Lutheran institution – neither the seminary, Gettysburg College, Wittenberg College, nor the Illinois State University – had been able to attain the standing of the schools of other denominations. The College at Gettysburg "is not now what it ought to be," he argued. "The time for

---

[22]Faculty Reports, September 1853 and September 1854; GCA.

[23]In 1859 the faculty took note of the suggestion of a sister college president that all of the colleges in the state unite in persuading the legislature to revive the practice of making annual grants to colleges. They urged Baugher to join this effort and lobby in its behalf in Harrisburg. If the proposal had a chance at this time, it too became a wartime casualty.

shifting along is past; the time for moving along in full vigor has come." Its faculty "must not be over-burdened with the mere lumber work of teaching, but should have time to prosecute their researches, and enrich the literature of the church by their productions."[24] Few weeks in June, July, and August passed without an article urging prompt action to endow Gettysburg College.

When the trustees met in August 1864, during commencement week, they accepted a recommendation by the faculty and called a convention to meet in Harrisburg on October 18. Fifteen pastors and laymen were named to organize the undertaking. The alumni association, which was also in session, named a committee to work with the organizers. Conrad presented four resolutions to the meeting of the West Pennsylvania Synod in September. When adopted, they committed that body to support the effort, urged each member pastor to interest his parishioners in it, and called upon other synods "on the territory of the institution" to cooperate. Speaking in favor of these resolutions, President Henry L. Baugher of the College expressed his regret that "the rich men of our church, with hardly an exception, had failed to make donations by thousands, and tens of thousands, to our institutions while they lived, and forgot them in their wills when they died." By comparison, "the rich men of the churches of New England had pursued the opposite course." The proper endowment of the College had been on his mind for so long, he stated, that, if it could be accomplished now, he was ready to "lie down satisfied and die in peace."[25] Meanwhile, circulars announcing the convention were distributed widely and Conrad continued using the editorial pages of the Lutheran Observer to inform his readers of what was approaching.

The endowment convention met on October 18, 1864 in Zion Lutheran church, Harrisburg, of which Charles A. Hay was pastor. Forty-three pastors and twenty-one laymen attended. There were many speeches, during which those present took time out to resolve unanimously to raise $100,000, "as speedily as possible, for the more perfect endowment of Pennsylvania College." When the time came for commitments to be made, John E. Graeff (1820-1898), alumnus, former pastor, and then a Philadelphia coal merchant, pledged $20,000 to endow a professorship of English Language and Literature, reserving the right to nominate the incumbent. Adolphus F. Ockershausen (1814-1877), a New York sugar refiner, Lutheran layman, and president of the convention, acting on his own behalf and also for his brother, George P. Ockershausen, pledged $20,000

---

[24]Lutheran Observer, August 5, 1864.
[25]Quoted in ibid., October 7, 1864.

90

for a second professorship.[26] Victor L. Conrad (1848), a New York businessman, committed himself for $10,000. Additional pledges, including one for $5,000 from residents of Gettysburg, brought the total amount subscribed to about $70,000. Since this was less than the goal which they had set for themselves, the members of the convention named an executive committee of five persons to continue and complete the effort. The secretary of the convention closed his minutes on a high and optimistic note:

> The session was short, spirited, and eminently successful. All present seemed to realize that this congregation ushered in a new era in the history of the Lutheran church in the United States – that the "day of small things," though not to be despised in its season, has now happily forever passed away – and that under the Divine blessing, her future operations will be conducted on a scale correspondent to the magnitude of her mission, to the immensity of her resources, and to the exalted rank she should of right occupy in the land, and in the world.[27]

Frederick W. Conrad, named chairman of the executive committee, lost no time in trying to sweep away "small things." In company with its other members, he undertook personal solicitations in Harrisburg, York, and western Pennsylvania. In addition to being editor of the *Lutheran Observer*, he was a parish pastor in Chambersburg. Hard hit by the Confederate burning of that town in July 1864, his congregation was unable to make a pledge of its own to the campaign, but it agreed to release part of Conrad's time to enable him to devote it to the interests of the College. In February 1865 he and his colleagues were able to announce that they had secured pledges bringing the total to $85,000.[28] In successive issues of the *Lutheran Observer*, Conrad tried to inspire his readers to contribute by telling them of one remarkable gift after another. Non-Lutherans were making contributions. Farmers were giving generously. Women were persuading their husbands to increase their proposed pledges. Nevertheless, while all of this effort was commendable, it did not measure up to the experience of many other colleges at the time. In February 1865 Conrad claimed that $2,500,000 had been contributed to American colleges during the preceding two years. Many institutions had received much more than the $100,000 Gettysburg was asking for.

When the board of trustees met in April 1865, it formally established the Graeff and Ockershausen professorships, effective

---

[26]In 1864 an investment of $20,000 at 6 percent yielded more than enough to pay the salary of a professor.

[27]The minutes of the "Convention to Promote the Better Endowment of Pennsylvania College" were published in ibid., October 28, 1864. The secretary of the convention was Rev. Edwin W. Hutter of Philadelphia, an erstwhile trustee.

[28]Ibid., February 10, 1865.

with the beginning of the new academic year. At its next meeting, in August, it named its own committee of five to complete what the endowment convention had started. The treasurer reported that he had actually received from the campaign thus far $74,938.05 in the form of stocks, bonds, notes, and cash. In the months that followed, little more came in. The effort had run its course.[29]

Presidents and Faculty

Gettysburg College was founded to provide earnest opportunities for teaching and learning to occur. While buildings, books, and equipment are essential for realizing this purpose, the two most important ingredients are the teachers and learners. The founders demonstrated that they realized this in their initial announcement to the public, in which they discussed the advantages of the new institution to prospective students. One of these advantages was "the high qualifications of the Professors," five of whom were identified:

S. S. Schmucker, A. M. Professor of Intellectual Philosophy and Moral Science.

E. L. Hazelius, D. D. Professor of the Latin Language and German Literature.

H. Baugher, A. M. Professor of the Greek Language and Belles-Lettres.

M. Jacobs, A. M. Professor of Mathematics, Chemistry, and Natural Philosophy.

J. H. Marsden, A. M. Professor of Mineralogy and Botany.

In other early announcements, a sixth instructor, E. Friederici, was identified as "Teacher of the French Language." Clearly, the two major figures in this first faculty were Baugher and Jacobs, who had taught in the Gymnasium since 1831 and 1829, respectively. Both Schmucker and Hazelius (1777-1853) were members of the seminary faculty who had agreed to teach, without compensation, for one year. Marsden (1803-1883) and Friederici were teachers in the Gettysburg Female Academy which was in operation early in 1832.

Unlike some nineteenth century colleges, this institution did not begin with one person who was founder-teacher-administrator, and who remained the towering figure in the school for a long time thereafter. It is evident that while Schmucker, the chief founder, wanted to retain his influence in the venture, he believed that his first commitment was to the seminary. John G. Morris used the columns of the *Lutheran Observer*, of which he was then editor, to

---

[29]According to the treasurer's report in August 1868, the endowment fund principal amounted to $92,876.66. This did not include the Franklin professorship fund. In 1873 the treasurer reported that the amount actually realized from the Harrisburg convention pledges was only $61,200. Two large subscriptions were never paid.

inform the public on July 1, 1832 that the board of trustees intended to elect a president of the College when they held their organizational meeting three days later. He predicted that the members might have difficulty in finding a good candidate on such short notice and that, until they did, a faculty member would probably act as chief executive officer. Never one reluctant to express his own opinions, Morris told his readers that he would prefer a distinguished layman as president rather than an equally distinguished pastor. July 4 came and went without an election. At the first faculty meeting in October 1832, Hazelius was chosen chairman. When he left Gettysburg in March 1833 to become teacher in a theological school in South Carolina, Schmucker briefly took his place, but soon yielded the chairmanship to his successor as Professor of Intellectual and Moral Science, Charles P. Krauth.[30]

In September 1833 the trustees appointed a committee to determine the interest of Edward Robinson (1794-1863) in the presidency of the College. A mutual friend on the faculty of the Andover Theological Seminary, Moses Stuart, may have recommended him to Schmucker.[31] A native of Southington, Connecticut, and a Congregationalist, Robinson was graduated by Hamilton College and from 1823 to 1826 taught Hebrew at Andover. He spent the next four years studying at the Universities of Goettingen, Halle, and Berlin, where he was strongly influenced by some of the world's leading philologists, theologians, historians, and geographers. In 1830 he returned to Andover as Professor of Biblical Literature and librarian. In April 1834 the committee of Gettysburg trustees reported that Robinson was not a candidate for the presidency of their College. Probably poor health was the major reason for his asking not to be considered; attacks of epilepsy had forced him to resign his Andover position in 1833. Several years later he did join the faculty of Union Theological Seminary in New York City. On two occasions he traveled to Palestine in order to conduct some of the earliest critical studies of the geography of the Biblical lands. Before his death in 1863, his work as an editor and author had firmly established his reputation as

---

[30]See Appendix 2 for a list of faculty and administration from 1832 to 1985. Charles Philip Krauth should not be confused with his son, Charles Porterfield Krauth (1823-1883).

[31]At one time Schmucker considered attending Andover Theological Seminary, a Congregationalist institution located in Andover, Massachusetts. Moses Stuart was a member of its faculty from 1810 to 1848. Schmucker was an admirer and correspondent of Stuart and consulted with him when he was deciding which German theological work to translate into English. The work which he chose was published in Andover. Wentz, *Schmucker*, pp. 107-113.

Charles P. Krauth (1797-1867)
Krauth was president of the College from 1834 to 1850. Courtesy Abdel
Ross Wentz Library, Lutheran Theological Seminary, Gettysburg.

the country's leading Biblical scholar.[32]

Unable to interest Edward Robinson in the presidency, the trustees then unanimously elected Charles P. Krauth to that position in April 1834. He was inaugurated at the beginning of the fall session, on October 30, 1834. Born in Montgomery county, the son of a Lutheran parochial schoolmaster, the new president grew up in Virginia and first chose medicine as a career. Running out of money before he completed his studies, Krauth gradually came to the conclusion that he was destined for the ministry. After the usual apprenticeship with two experienced pastors, he was ordained in

---

[32]*Dictionary of American Biography* 16(1935):39-40. William Foxwell Albright wrote the sketch. See also Jerry Wayne Brown, *The Rise of Biblical Criticism in America, 1800-1870: The New England Scholars* (Middletown, Connecticut, 1969), pp. 111-124. Brown describes Robinson as "the one American scholar to achieve an international reputation in biblical studies before the Civil War."

1821. While serving his first parish in Martinsburg and Shepherds-town, West Virginia, he became acquainted with Schmucker and was one of the small group of Lutheran pastors who assisted him in every stage of his efforts to organize a theological seminary. Although he took a parish in Philadelphia in 1827, Krauth's interest in the Gettysburg educational ventures continued. For example, he became a trustee of the seminary in 1826, a patron of the Gymnasium in 1831, and a trustee of the College in the following year. In September 1833 his colleagues on the College board named him to the faculty position which Schmucker had held: Professor of Intellectual and Moral Science. About the same time the seminary board elected him Professor of Biblical and Oriental Literature. The College set his salary as president at $500 per year, plus rent for a house, and required that he live in Gettysburg.

In defining Krauth's responsibilities as chief executive, the minutes of the board record that

> in addition to his duties as Professor the President shall have a general superintendence of the students, and of all matters connected with the instruction, discipline and general management of the institution, in accordance with the laws and regulations from time to time prescribed by the Board, and that he make a written report at every regular meeting of the Board, embodying such suggestions as the faculty may wish to make on the affairs of the institution.

Krauth was asked to devote seven half days each week to his College duties. In April 1839, in an attempt to end a misunderstanding which had arisen, the trustees declared that the president's powers and duties extended to the "Preparatory department, as well as . . . the College proper."

In the fall of 1837, as the College prepared to occupy its new building, everyone assumed that some member of the faculty would take up residence within its walls. The presence of such an officer was considered necessary for the proper management of a well-regulated family. In the absence of candidates, and with a marked lack of enthusiasm, Krauth set down for the consideration of the trustees (September 1837) a list of seven conditions for his own residence in the building. These remarks served as preface:

> The wish having been expressed that I should board at the College edifice, and believing it to be absolutely necessary that one of the professors should have the management of the house, I feel disposed, as no other one is willing to do it, to make the sacrifice of comfort, and to undergo the additional labour involved, on the following conditions –

The Krauths required sufficient family space, separate "necessary buildings" outside, no reduction in compensation, and several other concessions. "If the trustees can make another arrangement more advantageous than the above," the new president wrote, "it will be entirely agreeable to me."[33] Needless to say, the trustees quickly accepted the offer, without asking questions and before he had a chance to change his mind.

The Krauth family, consisting of the president, his second wife (whom he had married in 1834), and a fourteen-year old son by his first marriage, moved into their quarters in the western wing of the second floor of the College building. Once they were comfortably situated, the annual catalogue began to declare that

> the President, under whose immediate supervision the building is placed, lives in it with his family, and together with the Tutors and Professors, exercises a constant guardianship over the whole establishment: so that parents from a distance have all the security they may desire for the proper government of their children.

During the sixteen years that Charles and Harriet Krauth lived in the building, a son (1846) and a daughter (1849) were born to them.

Charles P. Krauth conscientiously carried out the duties of his office as the board of trustees defined them in 1834.[34] He served as chairman of the faculty, a body in which his role was definitely that of first among equals. He prepared the required written report for each meeting of the board, but his colleagues reviewed the document in detail and made their own suggestions for changes before he submitted it. Public announcements to one or more of the College's constituencies might come from Henry L. Baugher or Michael Jacobs as well as from the president. All of the available evidence points to the existence of a harmonious relationship among the faculty during these years. It also suggests that this harmony prevailed in the faculty's relations with the board of trustees, of which the patrons elected Krauth a member in 1844.[35]

It should be recalled that Krauth was elected to both seminary and College faculties in 1833. After becoming president of the College, he continued teaching in its sister institution. Soon after he moved into the building, the board in April 1838 asked him to devote his entire time to the College. Nevertheless, he soon resumed his

---

[33]Original dated September 1837, GCA.

[34]In a sketch of Krauth written for the 1882 history of the College, David A. Buehler (1843) wrote that "he possessed in a high degree the requisites for a successful college president – dignified bearing, suavity of manner, cool temperament, conservative judgment, enthusiasm for his work, and large sympathy with young men preparing for life's struggles . . . he was noted for his courtesy, high sense of honor, kind but firm administration, which compelled a return of respect and affectionate regard." *The Pennsylvania College Book, 1832-1882*, ed. E. S. Breidenbaugh (Philadelphia, 1882), p. 148. Hereafter cited as *1882 History*. Buehler was a local attorney, editor of the *Star and Sentinel* (a Gettysburg newspaper resulting from a merger of the *Sentinel* and *Star and Banner*), and long-time trustee of the College.

[35]Krauth's first term as a member of the board ended in 1834. In April 1838 the trustees invited him to attend their meetings, but they could not elect him to membership.

Henry L. Baugher (1804-1868)
Baugher was president of the College from 1850 to 1868. Photograph from
the Beltzhoover album.

seminary instruction and continued offering it during all or most of
the 1840s. Finally, in September 1850, he resigned the presidency in
order to become Professor of Biblical Philology and Ecclesiastical
History in the seminary, a position which he held until his death in
1867. Krauth continued as a trustee of the College for the remainder
of his life. He attended board meetings with great regularity and on
several occasions was present at faculty meetings as an advisory
member.

Krauth's successor as president of the College was Henry L.
Baugher, who was elected by a unanimous vote in September 1850,
at the meeting which accepted his predecessor's resignation. A
native of Abbottstown, Adams county, Baugher was the grandson of
one of the earliest resident Lutheran pastors west of the Susquehanna
river. He studied at the Gettysburg Academy and was graduated by

Dickinson College in 1826. Changing his career direction from law to ministry, he attended both Princeton Theological Seminary and the Lutheran Theological Seminary at Gettysburg. Licensed to preach by the West Pennsylvania Synod in 1828, Baugher became pastor of the Boonsboro, Maryland, parish, but in the spring of 1831 came to Gettysburg, at Schmucker's invitation, to take the place of the late David Jacobs on the faculty of the Gymnasium. In the following year he was ordained into the Lutheran ministry and was elected Professor of Greek Language and Literature in the College, a position which he filled for eighteen years. According to John G. Morris, when he and Robert G. Harper informed Baugher of his election as president and asked for an immediate answer which they could take back to their colleagues, who were still in session, Baugher insisted that he would not accept. Only after further reflection did he agree to change his mind.[36] He assumed his duties when the winter session began in October 1850. There is no evidence of a formal inauguration.

Perhaps one reason for Baugher's first response to the news of his election was his unwillingness to leave the spacious and comfortable home on the Harrisburg road which he and his family had enjoyed for many years. The trustees anticipated this, since in voting to offer him the same salary as his predecessor had received, "with residence and boarding in the house," they stipulated that "in the event of the President's declining residence in the house," a member of the faculty should be asked to take his place. Baugher did decline, and the trustees prevailed upon Martin L. Stoever (1820-1870), recently married, to move into the College edifice. This required a change in the 1851 catalogue, which read that "one of the Professors, under whose immediate supervision the building is placed, lives in it with his family, and together with the other officers, exercises a constant guardianship over the whole establishment." Stoever soon tired of the new quarters and claimed that his health required him to move out. The trustees attempted to solve the dilemma by directing that one of the tutors in the preparatory department take his place and later, in 1853, by making Baugher "resident officer of the College," in which capacity he was expected to spend as much time as possible in the building.[37] The catalogue reflected these changes in the arrangements for the well-regulated family. The 1858 edition informed the public that "the President,

[36]John G. Morris, *Life Reminiscences of an Old Lutheran Minister* (Philadelphia, 1896), p. 309. Hereafter cited as Morris, *Reminiscences.*

[37]For serving as resident officer, Baugher was paid $100 annually. In the September 1852 faculty report to the board, Baugher stated that he had "removed his study into the college edifice as a temporary arrangement."

under whose immediate supervision the building is placed, with the other officers, exercises a constant guardianship over the whole establishment." In 1860 the board built a house for the president on the campus; Baugher willingly occupied it. This time, no change in the wording of the catalogue was required.

Except for the inevitable differences in style traceable to differences in personality, which were considerable, the College presidency under Henry L. Baugher was a continuation of that established by his predecessor.[38] He too was first among equals in the faculty and enjoyed a good relationship with the board of trustees, of which he became a member upon election by the patrons at their last meeting in 1851. When he became president, he gave up his professorship of Greek in favor of that of Mental and Moral Science, which his predecessor had occupied. After about a year of failing health, Baugher died in office, unexpectedly, on April 14, 1868.

Between 1832 and 1865 there were usually five regular full-time faculty positions, each carrying the rank of professor. In the latter year, the board of trustees increased the number to seven, when it established the Graeff and Ockershausen professorships. Between 1832 and 1868 about twenty-five men held one or another of these positions.[39]

Of the original five professors of 1832, three soon retired from the faculty: Hazelius and Schmucker in 1833 and John H. Marsden in 1835.[40] Continuity in the teaching ranks during almost the entire period covered by this chapter was provided by the two remaining members of the original faculty: Henry L. Baugher and Michael

---

[38]Baugher was considerably more peppery in disposition than Krauth. In a sketch prepared for the 1882 history of the College, Frederick W. Conrad wrote: "Sanguine in temperament, he did everything with all his might; frank and candid, he uttered his sentiments without fear or favor; honest and courageous, he took his stand for the right, and rather courted than shrank from meeting difficulties and opposition. Possessed of strong points of character, he was not exempt from corresponding faults; but he strove earnestly to overcome them." Conrad characterized Baugher as a "rigid disciplinarian" who believed that "reverence for superiors, submission to authority, and obedience to the rules and regulations of the College, were indispensable to the formation of a good character." *1882 History*, pp. 150, 153. Conrad first learned to know Baugher in 1837 and was an intimate friend for thirty years thereafter.

[39]Under the terms of the charter, the board of trustees elected members of the teaching faculty, although the faculty as a body made necessary interim arrangements.

[40]Marsden studied in the Gettysburg Academy, was graduated by Jefferson College in 1825, and took work at the Theological Seminary of Virginia before entering the Episcopal ministry. After leaving the College faculty to take a parish, he entered Jefferson Medical College, by which he was graduated in 1847. He then practiced medicine in York Springs. *Star and Sentinel,* September 5, 1883. Ernest Friederici, engaged as a French teacher in 1832, left in the fall of 1833.

Michael Jacobs (1808-1871)   Martin L. Stoever (1820-1870)

Frederick A. Muhlenberg (1818-1901)   Charles F. Schaeffer (1807-1879)

Four Early Faculty Members
Photographs from the Beltzhoover album.

Jacobs. The career of the former has already been discussed. A native of Franklin county, Jacobs was graduated by Jefferson College in 1828. In the following year he came to Gettysburg to take over the instruction in science and mathematics in the classical school and later in the Gymnasium. In 1832 he was elected Professor of Mathematics, Chemistry, and Natural Philosophy in the College, which he continued to serve until his poor health led the trustees to prevail upon him to retire in the spring of 1866. The title of his appointment changed from time to time. When he became the first emeritus professor in the latter year, it was Emeritus Professor of Mathematics, Astronomy, and Mechanical Philosophy. The West Pennsylvania Synod ordained Jacobs to the Lutheran ministry in 1834.

A third long-time faculty member during this period was Martin L. Stoever. Born in Germantown, he was graduated by the College in 1838 and soon thereafter returned to Gettysburg, first (1839) as tutor and then (1841) as principal of the preparatory department, a position which he continued to hold until 1856. In 1843 he was elected Professor of History and seven years later became Professor of Latin Language and Literature, which was the title he held at the time of his death in 1870.

Several other faculty members, whose tenures were much shorter than those of Baugher, Jacobs, and Stoever, should be noted. One of these, William M. Reynolds (1812-1876), completed his work at the seminary in 1830 and was graduated by Jefferson College in 1832. With only a brief interruption, he was principal of the preparatory department from 1833 to 1841 and Stoever's predecessor as Professor of Latin Language and Literature from 1834 to 1850.[41] He left Gettysburg to become president of Capital University, Columbus, Ohio (1850-1853), and later served Illinois State University (1857-1860) in a similar capacity. Frederick A. Muhlenberg was graduated by Jefferson College (1836), studied at Princeton Theological Seminary, and taught at Franklin College (1840-1850) before becoming Professor of Greek Language and Literature in 1850. He served as Franklin Professor of Ancient Languages from 1853 to 1867, when he resigned to become the first president of Muhlenberg College. Charles F. Schaeffer, the first Professor of German Language and Literature under the Pennsylvania Synod endowment, was a graduate of the University of Pennsylvania and a parish pastor when he joined the faculties of the College and seminary in 1856. Eight years later he resigned these positions to become chairman of the faculty of the newly organized Lutheran theological seminary in

---

[41]In 1835-1836 Reynolds was engaged in collecting money for the College.

Philadelphia.[42]

The tenure of Herman Haupt (1817-1905) on the College faculty was brief but noteworthy. An 1835 graduate of the United States Military Academy at West Point, he resigned his army commission to serve as a railroad engineer in eastern Pennsylvania. In 1836 he came to Gettysburg in the employ of the state to assist in the construction of a railroad from there to the Potomac river.[43] In the following year the College elected him Instructor in Civil Engineering and Architecture; in 1838 – he was then twenty-one years of age – it changed the title to Professor. In December of that year he resigned, explaining that the railroad duties which he continued to perform (but no longer with the Gettysburg railroad) were now taking him away from Gettysburg for long periods of time. Between 1845 and 1847 he held the rank of Professor of Mathematics in the College, after which he took a position as engineer with the Pennsylvania Railroad. During much of the time he was associated with the Gettysburg community, he was engaged in other educational ventures, including an academy for young women and one in which he taught engineering to young men. Haupt's subsequent career as an engineer, inventor, and railroad administrator brought him national fame.[44]

Among the part-time faculty of this period was David Gilbert, local physician and trustee of the College, who held the rank of Lecturer on Anatomy and Physiology from 1838 until 1851, after which he moved to Philadelphia to devote his full time to one of the medical schools there. His successor was Henry S. Huber, another local physician, druggist, and College trustee. He served from 1852 until 1865. John G. Morris declined at least one opportunity to assume a full-time appointment, preferring instead to continue living in Baltimore and be Lecturer on Zoology (1844-1849) and Lecturer on Natural History (1868-1870). "The College could not afford to pay me any salary," he wrote years later, "and my services were gratuitous, excepting for one series of lectures," for which three friends raised a total of $300 and presented it to him.[45]

Before the Civil War there were no universities in the United States, at least none similar to those which were developed after

[42]The early incumbents of the Graeff and Ockershausen professorships, together with several other faculty whose tenure began in or after 1865, will be discussed in the next chapter.

[43]See pp. 80.

[44]William C. Darrah, *Engineering at Gettysburg College* (Gettysburg, 1974), pp. 3-5. See also James Arthur Ward, *That Man Haupt;* . . . (Baton Rouge, 1973). Haupt married a daughter of Benjamin Keller. He served as a College trustee from 1859 to 1873.

[45]Morris, *Reminiscences,* p. 353. The records of the treasurer indicate no payments to Gilbert or Huber, but Morris was occasionally paid traveling expenses.

1865 and which included, within one institution, a group of graduate and professional schools in which candidates for law, medicine, ministry, as well as for college and university teaching, could be trained. In the absence of such facilities, American college trustees who wanted to engage the most qualified faculty members had two choices. They could attempt to secure candidates educated abroad, especially in Germany, or they could search for persons with some of the best training available in this country who were improving themselves by continuing study and teaching experience.

In the early history of Gettysburg College, it is clear that those who were recruiting faculty looked for something more than academic preparation. They valued prior personal acquaintance with the candidates and also their affiliation with the Lutheran church. In the case of Edward Robinson, they were apparently willing to make an exception. If he had come to Gettysburg in 1833 or 1834, the first president of the College would have been a man none of the founders knew personally (assuming that Schmucker knew only about him) and who was not a Lutheran, but who was on his way to becoming a scholar of the first rank in his field. Charles P. Krauth, who did become president in 1834, was a man who never had a college education, but if we can believe John G. Morris, who knew him well, here "was a man of brilliant mind, and he had a wonderful faculty of acquiring knowledge." According to Morris, Krauth "was a most industrious reader,. . . and he remembered everything he read," but "it was only after he went to Gettysburg that he applied himself to those branches which he taught."[46]

Henry L. Baugher was salutatorian of his class at Dickinson College; Michael Jacobs was valedictorian of his class at Jefferson; and Martin L. Stoever was salutatorian at Gettysburg. Herman Haupt has already been identified as a graduate of the United States Military Academy – at the age of eighteen years.[47] The interests of John G. Morris in science were among the several avocations which this man vigorously pursued during an extremely active life. Concentrating on entomology, botany, and zoology, he acquired large collections of specimens by purchase and his own efforts; he bought many reference books and consulted others; he corresponded with amateurs and professionals in the fields of his interest; and he attended meetings of the American Association for the Advancement of Science.[48] Other colleges recognized the attainments of

---

[46]Ibid., p. 134.

[47]The 1838 catalogue noted specifically that "the gentleman who has charge of the department of Engineering, etc., has not only had the advantage of a regular course at West Point, but is still a practical Engineer in the employ of the State."

[48]Morris, Reminiscences, pp. 166-171.

some of the Gettysburg faculty. Dickinson conferred the D.D. degree on Baugher; Jefferson and Wittenberg Colleges conferred the same degree on Jacobs; Union conferred the LL. D. degree and Hamilton College the honorary Ph. D. on Stoever.

Between 1832 and 1868 the Gettysburg faculty met weekly. The members were few in number and they often changed the time of their meeting to suit present convenience. Charles P. Krauth became chairman of the body in December 1833, even before he was elected president of the College, and he continued to preside during its meetings until Henry L. Baugher succeeded him in 1850. Secretaries were retained for long periods: Baugher from 1834 to 1850 and Stoever from then until his·death in 1870. Sometimes many weeks went by with nothing more to be recorded than "met and adjourned," but occasionally the secretary noted that breaking up occurred only after much "interesting conversation." One of the most striking things about the early faculty minutes is the almost complete absence of references to the College curriculum. It is evident that the faculty was much concerned with general College matters, especially financial, and that many items which came before the board of trustees for action originated with the faculty in their meetings. But most of the time spent in these weekly sessions, in 1868 as well as in the early 1830s, was devoted to matters of student evaluation and discipline. Both individuals and groups of students were advised, exhorted, admonished, interrogated, and punished, as their situations seemed to warrant. One should not be surprised to find this preoccupation with scholarship and discipline, or discipline and scholarship, in men devoted to the ideal of the well-regulated family.

The Campus

The first campus of the College was located on the southeastern corner of High and Washington streets. It consisted of three town lots measuring 180 feet by 180 feet. In 1834 the College acquired this property when it assumed responsibility for the remaining part of the debt which Samuel Simon Schmucker had taken upon himself in 1829. The academy building had four large rooms, which were used for instructional purposes. The students roomed and boarded in private homes. As the trustees prepared to move into their new building in the fall of 1837, they named a committee to "attend to the preservation of the Building (old) and prosecute all they may find guilty of doing mischief," and to engage the borough constable to keep a nightly watch.

Meanwhile, the trustees considered what to do with the academy property, especially after the preparatory department moved into the new building in 1838. In view of the financial condition of the

College Edifice
This picture of what is now Pennsylvania Hall appeared in the 1882 College history.

The first seal of the College, as it appeared on the 1918 commencement program.

College at the time, the most desirable course of action was to sell it, but there were, unfortunately, no buyers in sight. The best available option, and the one used in 1838, appeared to be rental of the property for five years, at $75 per year, to the Gettysburg Female Academy, or Seminary. An act of April 14, 1838 chartered "a Female seminary or public school for the education of female youth in the English and other languages, and in the useful arts, sciences and literature, by the name, style, and title of the Gettysburg Female Academy." Among the nine charter trustees were Robert G. Harper, John F. Macfarlane, John B. McPherson, Samuel Simon Schmucker, and Thaddeus Stevens. By the time the term of the rental expired, during the hard times of the 1840s, the academy was in default of its annual payments and the College was eager to sell the property. A buyer appeared in 1844 and was promised a deed on completion of the agreed-upon schedule of payments. The deed which the College actually executed in the summer of 1848 was to Frederick A. M. Keller (1838), a Reading pastor and son of Benjamin Keller, who had purchased the rights of the earlier buyer. This deed was not given, however, until Schmucker, true to the promise which he had made to the community in 1829, called a town meeting for August 14, 1848, at which he offered the residents an opportunity to take the property before it was sold for private purposes. The price determined was $2,500, which included the original cost plus repairs made since 1829. The large number of citizens who attended the public meeting voted not to interfere with the sale.[49]

The 1838 catalogue informed the public that the new College building was located "a short distance from the village." This was an accurate statement. None of the town lots which James Gettys had laid out in 1785-1786 was located north of the present railroad tracks, and there were no houses close to the six acres which Thaddeus Stevens offered to the College in 1835.[50] Between that year

---

[49]*Sentinel,* August 21, 1848. For most of the time between 1838 and about 1870, the academy property was used for the education of young women. Since then, it has been a private residence.

[50]Most of the present College property is located on part of about 380 acres of land claimed by Samuel Gettys, father of James. In the 1780s the sheriff sold the real estate of Samuel Gettys in order to pay his debts. His son purchased the southern third, on which the family lived, and laid out the town which bears his name. James later bought the western half of the rest of his father's former property (it extended from the town limits north to Oak ridge) and developed it as a farm. In 1825, after his death, Thaddeus Stevens purchased the farm when the sheriff sold the assets of the James Gettys estate. For many years the land immediately surrounding the College consisted of small farms and town out-lots, the latter used for grazing, cultivation, or wood lots. When the College needed to expand, purchase of more land was much easier than would have been the case had the campus still been located in the middle of the town.

and 1849, the College purchased three lots from Stevens. These totaled twelve acres ninety-nine perches and constituted the pre-Civil War College campus. It extended west from North Washington street about 520 feet, with its northern limit about fifty feet south of West Lincoln avenue and its southern limit stopping short of the Tiber. In preparation for building Stevens Hall, between 1865 and 1868 the College purchased four tracts of land totaling about nine acres and located within the square bounded by Carlisle, Lincoln, North Washington, and Stevens streets. Thus, in 1868 the campus consisted of about twenty-one acres of land. [51]

Until long after 1868 the edifice which John C. Trautwine designed and Henry Winemiller built dominated the campus. Even after several other buildings appeared, it remained the center of College activities. The main entrance to the four stories was from the south portico; the north portico was not built until 1937. There were about fifty rooms for student use, most of them about ten by fourteen feet in size and located on the second, third, and fourth floors. These rooms could, and often did, accommodate as many as one hundred students. On the first or ground floor at the west end lived the steward and his family. The College dining hall was located under the portico. Rooms in which students of the preparatory department recited and studied occupied the east end. President Krauth and his family lived in the west end of the second floor, but their dining room was downstairs.

Six "recitation rooms," which also served as professors' offices, were located on the second and third floors. On the third floor the center section was divided into two large rooms, each forty-two by twenty feet, separated by a hallway running east and west through the building. The northern room was the library; the southern room, the chapel. On the fourth floor, space was reserved for the two literary societies.[52] Phrenakosmian Hall occupied the western end and Philomathaean Hall the eastern end; these rooms were nineteen by forty-two feet. In addition, each society had a library located on the north side of this floor, and later each was assigned space for its own reading rooms.[53]

On several occasions, the faculty reminded the trustees of the need for a College bell. When a hand bell proved to be inadequate, the trustees authorized (September 1847) the faculty "to purchase a

---

[51]Gregory J. Landrey, "A History of the Gettysburg Campus," (Gettysburg College paper, 1977), pp. 13-24. Much of the land purchased in 1865-1868 had been owned by the College between 1836 and 1850, when it was sold to raise money.

[52]See pp. 158-162 for a discussion of these societies.

[53]In September 1845 the trustees named a committee to arrange for care of sick students. Apparently no action was taken, since in January 1852 the faculty urged the trustees "to reserve a room in the College edifice for the use of the sick."

bell not to exceed 300 lbs. in weight." Cast in Philadelphia the following year, the bell was brought to Gettysburg by several faculty members on their way home from a meeting in New York City, and then placed in the cupola, or belfry.[54] The first of several schedules for ringing this bell was 7:55 and 10:55 A.M., and 1:45, 3:45, and 8:20 P.M. Fireplaces and then wood stoves were used to heat every room in the building until coal stoves began to replace them about 1860. Candles and sperm oil provided the lighting until kerosene and gas began to replace them about the same time.[55]

During the period covered by this chapter there were no major repairs or renovations to the College building. In 1852 the trustees did authorize cutting side windows into several rooms whose natural light was reduced by the portico. Eight years later, when the steward system was abandoned, the quarters which his family had occupied were converted into seven additional rooms for students.

Once construction of the College building was completed in 1837-1838, the task of creating a "college yard" or campus around it had to begin from the beginning. In 1838 workmen brought in about one thousand cubic feet of fill and graded the area. Trees were planted over and over again, more than five hundred of them between 1839 and 1853. What one student, writing years later, remembered as being "bare as your hand" in 1839, another student about a decade later called "a beautiful yard."[56] The transformation occurred after the faculty in February 1844 named Michael Jacobs and William M. Reynolds "to devise a plan for ornamenting the College grounds and interesting the students in it." Soon after College and seminary students organized the Linnaean Association in June of the same year, they voted to "take under its special care the improvement of the grounds around the College edifice." Their first project was to lay a walk from the portico to Washington street, to replace what one student thought was something in great need of attention. "A more stony, rough, shin-breaking path could not well be conceived,"

---

[54]The bell hangs in Christ Chapel.

[55]In 1850, responding to a faculty suggestion, the trustees prohibited the use of camphine or burning fluid in the building. This mixture of turpentine and alcohol or other ingredients was a fire hazard. "In the hands of careless persons," wrote Henry Eyster Jacobs (1862), son of Michael Jacobs, it was "very dangerous. In my memory a student [his name was Peter Hake] had been burned to death by it in the College." Nevertheless, he noted, his father used it in his study. Henry Eyster Jacobs, *Memoirs of Henry Eyster Jacobs: Notes on a Life of a Churchman,* ed. Henry E. Horn (1974), p. 215. Hereafter cited as Jacobs, *Memoirs.* The prohibition of 1850 not having accomplished its purpose, the board tried again in September 1860: "Resolved, that the students be not permitted to burn etherial oil or fluid in the College edifice, but that those not using gas, be advised to burn either candles, or Kerosene or Coal oil."

[56]*1882 History,* p. 443; William H. Cone to Messrs. Bell, Simington, and Gundy, Gettysburg, May 31, 1851, GCA.

he wrote, "particularly of a dark night."[57] The improvement was named Via Benedicta, in honor of Frederick Benedict (1847), who was in charge of the undertaking.

Subsequent Linnaean projects included replacing fences; planting about two hundred more trees; making flower beds on both sides of the Via Benedicta; and, under the direction of Herman Haupt, laying out what a student called "all sorts of roads and walks, circles and curves and ellipses, cutting each other in every direction, and making to the uninitiated a perfect labyrinth."[58] In 1847 the trustees remitted the tuition of one student "in view of services to the campus." In the late 1850s and early 1860s the faculty occasionally suspended some or all of the classes on a spring day so that students could work on the campus. In 1844 and again in 1856 the trustees took note of these efforts and formally thanked the students for what they were doing. Time and again fences were built around the campus, and occasionally they were taken away. After trying a wooden gate to keep cattle from entering and roaming through the property, the trustees in 1861 approved installing an iron gate, fastened to granite posts.

In the "back yard," north of the College building, several wells were dug and pumps installed. In fact, the very first facility on the campus was a well completed even before Henry Winemiller began construction in the spring of 1836. For the use of the steward, there were a garden and the needed outbuildings: a washhouse, smoke-house, oven, and stable, all constructed in 1837. A springhouse was added in 1840 and a cattleshed in 1851. There were also the inevitable privies, what was described as an "eight apartment" one for students and a "two apartment" one for the families of the president and steward. For some years the students, who were responsible for heating their rooms, had their own woodpiles in this area. Edward S. Breidenbaugh (1868) remembered being told that "the back yard was the general wood-yard."[59] In 1856 the College built a large woodhouse, from which the steward could then sell fuel at a fair price to keep the scholars warm. In 1857, using money the students had contributed, the College built a bathhouse northeast of the building, near one of the wells. When the steward system was discontinued in 1860, the trustees converted the washhouse into a residence for the janitor. Both faculty and trustees were sufficiently concerned about possible sources of income for the College to worry about renting part of the campus for agricultural purposes, to

---

[57]*Sketch of the Linnaean Association of Pennsylvania College,* . . . (Gettysburg, 1861), pp. 10-11. For information on the Linnaean Association, see pp. 162-163.
[58]Ibid., p. 12.
[59]Quoted in the *1882 History,* p. 443.

Linnaean Hall
From the 1882 College history.

consider using it for such purposes themselves, and to establish their ownership of the manure produced by the animals stabled "out back."

The second major building on the campus was Linnaean Hall, the impetus for which came from the Linnaean Association, organized in 1844. One of their first decisions was to attempt to construct a building to house their scientific collections. They resolved to begin as soon as they had in hand cash amounting to half of the estimated cost of the undertaking and subscriptions which exceeded the latter by $1,000. They persuaded the women of Gettysburg to assist them in conducting a fair at which they proposed to sell food, clothing, and related items contributed by friends and relatives from as far distant as Philadelphia, Baltimore, Hagerstown, and Chambersburg. The fair, which was held on July 1-4, 1845, was a decided success. It raised about $550.[60]

Upon the recommendation of the faculty, the trustees in September 1845 granted the petition of the Linnaean Association by authorizing it to build on the campus. The board reserved the right to determine the site and to set aside a classroom on the ground floor of the proposed building for the use of the preparatory department. It agreed to contribute $1,000 toward the cost of the building and designated several trustees to act with other persons chosen by the association as the building committee. Early in 1846 Joseph Clapsaddle, of near Gettysburg, entered into a contract to construct the building, which Herman Haupt had designed. The amount of the contract was $2,800; student members of the Linnaean Association agreed to provide some of the materials and contribute some of the labor required.

In the early spring of 1846, students began digging the foundations of Linnaean Hall. The site selected was due west of the College edifice. With appropriate ceremonies, including an address by state Representative James Cooper, the cornerstone was laid on July 23, 1846. Dedication took place on September 14, 1847, during the week of commencement. The main speaker was John G. Morris, who regarded himself as the founder of the Linnaean Association and was proud of what had been accomplished:

> It is the first time, that an edifice, devoted to Natural History, conceived, designed, erected and completed through the agency of Students has been dedicated in this country. Other prouder and more costly buildings have arisen in other places, which are depositories of more extensive collections than ours, but ours is the first, which the Students themselves undertook to erect, and for the existence of which, they alone deserve all the credit . . . I most heartily congratulate you, Linnaeans, on the auspicious event of this day. You can proudly say, our work is done, – all that we undertook is completed – we leave to our successors in College the farther prosecution of the work.[61]

Whatever the long-term legacy of the Linnaeans might have been, in the short run they left the College trustees with a sheaf of unpaid bills. In September 1848 the latter had to assume responsibility for what was still due the contractor. They borrowed some money and on several occasions called upon the Linnaean Association to help them in meeting the remaining obligations. Not all of the bills were paid until after the contractor died in 1850. The final transactions were complicated by the fact that some of the work was improperly

---

[60]*Sentinel*, July 7, 1845.
[61]*Sketch of the Linnaean Association of Pennsylvania College*, . . . (Gettysburg, 1861), pp. 9-10.

done and repairs were soon needed.[62] The Linnaeans used the building to display their growing collection of mineral, botanical, and other specimens, as well as for their small library. As planned, the College used the ground floor for the preparatory department.

The third major building on the campus was a residence for the president. Its completion and occupancy in 1860 provided the solution to a problem which Henry L. Baugher thrust upon the well-regulated family when he refused to move into the College edifice ten years earlier. As noted, no faculty member was willing to take his place, at least not on a permanent basis. The faculty and board might coerce a tutor in the preparatory department to accept residence in the building as a condition of employment, but no one expected any tutor to be as awesome as Baugher, Jacobs, or Stoever could be. In 1853, the same year in which the trustees tried to reach the best solution possible at the time by designating the president the resident officer in the building, they appointed a committee to investigate the possibility of constructing a house for the president on the campus. In April 1854 the committee reported that it had plans and an estimated cost, both of which it considered unsatisfactory. There the matter rested until September 1858, when the board named a new committee to study the matter and bring in its recommendations. A year later, in September 1859, after the faculty strongly recommended immediate action, the board named a committee to enter into a contract and supervise construction of a house, which was not to cost more than $3,500. In November the committee engaged George and Henry Chritzman, local builders, at a cost of $3,576. Construction was begun in the spring of 1860 and the Baugher family occupied the new house in December. It was one of the first private residences in Gettysburg to be illuminated by means of gas. The president's house "is a beautiful and much admired structure," insisted the building committee in its final report, "adding essentially to the appearance of the place as well as to the substantial value of the property of the Institution."[63] When the Baughers were comfortably settled in their new quarters near the College edifice, the faculty and trustees could breathe easier every time they read the statement in the catalogue that the "President, under whose immediate supervision the building is placed, with the other officers, exercises a constant guardianship over the whole establishment."

The completion of a fourth major campus building, Stevens Hall, in 1868 meant the achievement of a desire which faculty and trustees

---

[62]Between 1846 and 1851 the College treasurer paid out about $1,800 for the construction of Linnaean Hall.

[63]Report of the building committee, September 18, 1861, GCA. The treasurer's records show payments totaling $3,576 to the Chritzmans between 1859 and 1864.

Stevens Hall
From the 1882 College history

shared almost from the moment the College edifice was occupied in the fall of 1837. Those administering the College were in full agreement that a preparatory department was essential for its success. Their building was planned to accommodate about one hundred students, but in 1839 there were already about 140 in both departments and by 1841 there were about 190. The ideal of the College as a well-regulated family assumed that almost all of the students would be living in the one main building. Obviously, this was already quite impossible. In addition, the faculty were now becoming convinced that the different levels of maturity of preparatory and college students made it highly desirable that they not be living in the same building. Accordingly, the faculty began to urge the trustees to plan for a second structure, located nearby, to house the preparatory department.

Impressed with the strength of these arguments, the trustees voted in June 1841 to name a committee to select a site, buy the necessary land, and raise the needed money. In April 1842 they named a building committee and authorized it to choose a design, enter into a contract, and begin to build as soon as $3,000 in pledges was secured. The 1841 catalogue informed the public that

> the Board of Trustees are making active preparations to put up another building for the use of the Preparatory Department. It is intended to make it 80 feet long, 50 feet wide, and 4 stories high, and to arrange the whole interior with a view to the greatest convenience and comfort.

Although this statement was continued in the 1842 catalogue and the trustees reaffirmed their decision to proceed when they met in the fall of that year, it was soon evident that there was not nearly enough money, either in hand or in prospect, to spend $3,000 to $4,000 on a second building. In response to the economic downturn, enrollment by 1843 had dropped to about 130 students. In that year the catalogue statement about the proposed new building disappeared. Three years later, when the trustees approved the construction of Linnaean Hall, they allocated $1,000 from the subscriptions which they had received for a preparatory building as their share of its cost, with the understanding that they could use the ground floor for the preparatory department. There matters rested for almost twenty years.

During the Civil War (1861-1865), the College enrollment dropped about twenty percent from the level of the preceding four years. Although there were a number of reasons for what had happened, the trustees concluded in August 1864 that they needed to revitalize the preparatory department and appointed a committee to bring in its recommendations for achieving this end. One year later, after considering the committee's report, the trustees decided to propose revising the course of study, named a principal (the position had been in disuse for about ten years), and resolved to proceed with plans for a new building. At the same time, they named a committee to solicit contributions from the people of Adams county, in part at least because many of the students in the preparatory department were local boys. With the blessing of the trustees, Charles J. Ehrehart (1850), the new principal, made an addition to his residence on Carlisle street for the use of his students.[64]

Although the campaign to raise money was disappointing, the trustees decided in January 1867 to proceed and authorized the building committee to sign a mortgage, if necessary, in order to secure the required funds. Three months later they reaffirmed this action and resolved that, "in token of our appreciation of the valuable services rendered to the cause of Education by the Hon. Thaddeus Stevens, and of his constant and active interest in the

[64]The 1866 catalogue explained that "the Principal, who resides near the College, will receive into his family a limited number of the younger pupils, for whom temporary provision has been made by the Board of Trustees, in the erection of an addition to his residence." The Ehrehart residence was located at 227 Carlisle street.

growth of Pennsylvania College, the name of the Preparatory building be the Stevens Hall." The original plan submitted by John Frazer, a Philadelphia architect, called for construction of a building 63 by 55 feet, with a 50 by 46 feet wing. A structure of this size would accommodate about ninety students, the principal and his family, and the tutors. The contract later made with John R. Turner, of Carlisle, for $19,160, was for construction of the main building only, which was intended to accommodate sixty-five students and the tutors, but not the principal and his family.[65]

The cornerstone for the new structure was laid during commencement week, on August 8, 1867. After an address by M. Russell Thayer, Philadelphia, Samuel Simon Schmucker delivered what might be regarded as his valedictory, as far as Gettysburg College is concerned. Before he reviewed some of the events in the early history of the College, he paused to take note of the fact that, in the summer of 1867, Thaddeus Stevens was a highly controversial national figure. Since 1859 a member of the United States House of Representatives, he was one of the chief promoters of the Reconstruction Act passed in March 1867. Almost two years after the war was over, this measure divided the former Confederate states into military districts and required them to rewrite their constitutions according to certain federally prescribed guidelines which would insure that blacks could participate in the political process. Within a matter of months, Stevens would become one of the leading agitators for the impeachment of President Andrew Johnson, which occurred in February 1868. "As an attempt has been made by a portion of the public press to give a political aspect" to the naming of the new building, Schmucker told the gathering, "it seems proper to state, that this is an unqualified misapprehension." He assured his hearers that the board had acted entirely "on account of the eminent and life-long services of the Hon. Thaddeus Stevens to the cause of popular and collegiate education, throughout the State of Pennsylvania in general, and his services and liberality to Pennsylvania College, in particular." Recalling the rule adopted in 1833 excluding "all party politics from the exercises of the College," he noted that the faculty had always belonged to "different political schools" and "claim the right to form their opinions for themselves, on all the measures of government and interests of our beloved country, and out of the institution, in their intercourse with their fellow citizens,

---

[65]Report of the committee on the preparatory building [May 1867], GCA.

to express them."[66]

Responding to a faculty suggestion, the board of trustees in August 1867 directed the committee which was responsible for the new preparatory building to have two houses constructed on the campus for rental by members of the faculty. The committee chose the site now occupied by Schmucker Hall, where ground was broken in March 1868. About this time it was decided to build one two-story double frame house instead of two units, as originally planned. Construction work on Stevens Hall, halted during the winter months, was resumed in March. Two months later it was being roofed. By the fall of 1868 both buildings were ready for occupancy, although the work in and around Stevens Hall was far from completed.

The total costs attributed to this construction amounted to $37,352.93. Of this, $27,705.21 was chargeable to Stevens Hall, $8,692.72 to the professors' houses, and $955 to the temporary building added to the Ehrehart residence on Carlisle street.[67] Since this work had been completed with only $12,934.90, scarcely more than one-third of the cost, actually contributed, the College now faced a potentially serious financial problem, with which the board of trustees and a new president would have to deal.

A building which should be considered a functioning part of the College campus, beginning in 1836 and continuing for many years thereafter, was Christ Lutheran church, on Chambersburg street. When the College began operating in November 1832, it made frequent use of the so-called German church at the corner of High and Stratton streets. While seminary and College were permitted to use its facilities, and while both students and faculty were welcome to worship there, the facts that the services were conducted in German and that the Lutherans had use of the building only every other Sunday led some seminary and College faculty members to join with a number of Lutheran townspeople to plan a second

[66]*Addresses Delivered at the Laying of the Corner Stone of Stevens Hall . . .* (Gettysburg, 1867), pp. 30-31. Thaddeus Stevens was scheduled to give the main address on this occasion, but cancelled his appearance at the last minute. He did contribute $500 toward construction of the building named in his honor. At its August 1867 meeting, the board asked the faculty "to give increased attention to the rule requiring the exclusion of partizan politics from the public exercises of the Institution."

[67]John R. Turner, the contractor for Stevens Hall, was paid $19,856.30. John Frazer, the architect, received $600. Land purchased, equipment, furnishings, leveling the grounds, fencing, and other costs brought the total to $27,705.21. William C. Stallsmith, Gettysburg, the contractor for the faculty residences, was paid $7,500. Heating, a water supply, fencing, and other costs brought this total to $8,692.72. This information is taken from a financial statement presented to the board of trustees in June 1869.

Christ Lutheran Church
From the 1882 College history.

Lutheran congregation in Gettysburg. They purchased a lot in the first block of Chambersburg street and, on August 10, 1835, laid the cornerstone for what was then sometimes called the English Lutheran church. The completed building was dedicated on November 6, 1836.

Two days after the dedication the faculty accepted the congregation's invitation for them and the students to worship regularly with it. Unless they had written permission from their parents to go to some other church, all students were required to attend services every Sunday in this place, which was referred to as College church

117

as early as 1843.[68] College organizations met here. Baccalaureate and commencement exercises were held here. When the cornerstone of Linnaean Hall was laid in 1846, the procession moved from the campus to the church, where there was a prayer, an address, and music by a brass band. Then the procession returned to the campus, where the cornerstone was laid and the ceremonies were concluded.

Until long after 1868, Christ church had no regularly called full-time pastor. Members of the College and seminary faculties, one of whom was designated as pastor of the congregation, supplied most of the preaching, especially when these two schools were in session.[69] Relations between the College and the congregation were not always smooth, even though most, sometimes all, of the faculty were members of the latter. There were occasional disputes over what should be considered fair charges when the church was used for College events. Faculty tended to grow weary of preaching responsibilities when College was not in session.

Between 1832 and 1868, some colleges purchased farms, for which students could then supply the labor and use the wages in meeting their college expenses. In most cases this did not prove to be a satisfactory arrangement for very long.[70] Gettysburg never had such an extension of its campus, although the matter was once brought to the attention of the trustees. In September 1846, in the midst of financial stringencies, the semiannual faculty report discussed the "advantages which may be derived from the purchase of a farm in the immediate vicinity of the College upon which the Students may labour during the vacation and Sessions, so much as their health and comfort require." The student plan for the farm which accompanied the report maintained that "a judicious combination of mechanical and agricultural labour" would benefit everyone, especially if accompanied by "a course of instruction upon theoretical and practical agriculture."[71] The board voted to postpone the matter indefinitely. The proposal was not presented again.

The rules and regulations which the trustees adopted in September 1837, as the College was preparing to leave the academy

---

[68]Beginning in 1838 and for a number of years thereafter, the catalogue stated that students were "required to attend public worship on the Sabbath in a church of which the Institution has the use for the occasion, unless they bring written requests from their parents or guardians, specifying the particular congregation with which they wish them to worship." Only beginning in 1855 does the catalogue refer to it as the College church. Nowhere is it identified as a Lutheran church.

[69]Henry L. Baugher was pastor from 1841 to 1852 and from 1861 to 1866. As such, he was responsible for supplying pastoral services in addition to preaching.

[70]Sack, *Higher Education* 2:731-732.

[71]Faculty Report, September 1846, GCA.

building and occupy the present campus, contained a provision – expressed in rather obscure language – that "the lot adjoining that of the College shall be appropriated for a College campus for the purpose of exercise and play by the students in leisure hours." Another section of these rules prescribed fines and possible suspension for any student who "shall play at hand or foot ball in the College edifice or College yard, or throw anything which might damage the College building or property." The area set aside for "exercise and play" was that located north of Stevens and east of Washington streets, but there is no evidence that it was either much or long used for this purpose. In the spring of 1840 the students began to construct what was called a ball alley, which they located somewhere near the present site of Christ Chapel. At their meeting in April of that year, the trustees appropriated $50 "toward the erection of a battery to a ball alley, in aid to the effort now making by the students." Several months later, the treasurer paid George Chritzman, a local contractor, $50 for his work on this project. Many years later, Joseph B. Bittinger (1844) remembered that "our campus, in those days, was the field back of the present Preparatory building. There we played some 'corner-ball' and much 'long-ball,' till 'town-ball' drove those rustic games out of fashion."[72]

The ball alley, which was used for a form of bowling, was probably abandoned some time before 1850, when the College sold the land on which it was located. Convinced along with the faculty that more adequate facilities for "exercise and play" were needed, the board in 1866 directed that an "arrangement for Gymnastic exercises" be included in the preparatory building. Since this did not happen, it named a committee in May 1868 to bring in a plan for and estimated cost of a gymnasium for the use of all students in the College. Several years elapsed before this facility could be built.

Preparatory Department

Since there were at the time almost no public high schools and few academies located within the constituency of Gettysburg College, it is easy to understand why the trustees and faculty decided in 1832 to create an institution to replace the Gymnasium which the Pennsylvania legislature had recently transformed into a college of the liberal arts and sciences. A department to prepare young men for

---

[72]Quoted in 1882 History, p. 443. In its report to the trustees in September 1840, the faculty reported that the ball alley was being "made use of by the Citizens as well as the students and there is reason to fear improperly." Students built a ball alley at Dickinson. Sellers, Dickinson College, p. 180.

either that or some other school would be a service to the community; it might well attract students to Gettysburg College who would otherwise go elsewhere; it could train young men for the work required in the latter's classes; and it would be a welcome, perhaps necessary, source of income for the College. At its first meeting, on July 4, 1832, the board of trustees named a committee to select a teacher for what the minutes call "the preparatory department." At its second meeting, in September, it approved the committee's recommendation of Ernest Friederici to fill the post. At the end of October, the faculty adopted a "course of study and system of recitations" for the new department.

The purposes of "prep," as it was soon called, were clearly outlined in the 1838 catalogue and were then repeated with little change in subsequent issues as well as in other College literature. The statement in the 1838 catalogue is as follows:

> The Preparatory Department, under the supervision of the Faculty, is designed not only to qualify for entrance into the regular College Classes, but also to give thorough instruction in the higher branches of an English education. It is not merely a Latin Grammar School, but is intended to furnish a solid business education. The youth who enter it for the purpose of pursuing classical studies, are not permitted whilst doing so to neglect the every-day wants of business, or to forget their mother tongue.[73]

The course of study as it had developed by the 1850s included Latin, Greek, reading, writing, grammar, composition, orthoepy (pronunciation), arithmetic, algebra, bookkeeping, geography, and history. According to the 1855 catalogue, "throughout the whole course the students are required to attend to English Grammar, and particular attention is paid to Orthoepy and the use of grammatical language in common conversation." The curriculum was intended to be completed in three years, but a student's "attainments, abilities, and application" might result in a longer or shorter attendance.

The academic year of the preparatory department coincided with that of the College; the charge for tuition was the same. As soon as the prep students moved into the College building in the fall of 1838 (not 1837), the faculty adopted a set of rules and regulations designed especially for them. Their comings and goings were more circumscribed than were those of the College students. Exceptions to the rule requiring everyone to room in the building were more difficult for prep students to obtain, unless their parents lived in or near town. At first, their recitation and study rooms were located in the eastern end of the ground floor of the building. Beginning in

---

[73]By 1868 considerably more space in the catalogue was devoted to the preparatory department.

1847, they recited and studied on the ground floor of Linnaean Hall.[74] Prep students were permitted to enroll in College classes whenever the faculty deemed them qualified.

Ernest Friederici had a short tenure in the preparatory department. In April 1833 the trustees asked John George Schmucker to "tenderly admonish" him for "the alleged harshness of his deportment" as it related to students. At the next meeting, twelve of these students submitted a letter repeating the complaints. Advised by the board of his best course of action, Friederici now resigned. Between 1833 and 1841, with but a brief interruption, William M. Reynolds was principal of the preparatory department, in addition to performing his duties as Professor of Latin Language and Literature. In 1841 Martin L. Stoever became principal. Two years later, the College catalogue, the newspapers, and a printed brochure informed the public that Stoever

> devotes himself entirely to the duties of his station, in superintending and instructing his pupils, both during the regular hours of study and recitation, and at all other times. He boards in the building with the Students, visits them in their rooms, accompanies them to Church, and enjoying their regard and confidence, endeavors to occupy the position of a parent or friend in his government.[75]

This close care was apparently no more to Stoever's liking than it was to that of the students. In any event, after a few years the statement was dropped from the catalogue. In 1856, at his request, Stoever was relieved of the principal's duties and the position was eliminated. The one or two tutors who customarily provided much of the instruction in the preparatory department were now answerable directly to the president and faculty. Especially after the first few years of its operation, most of the tutors were recent graduates of the College who remained in Gettysburg for a year or two before leaving to pursue their intended careers. George Diehl (1837), Milton Valentine (1850), Eli Huber (1855), and Henry Eyster Jacobs (1862) were among the tutors who later served the College as trustees or faculty.

During the period under study, the preparatory department warranted all of the attention which the board of trustees and faculty devoted to it. Between 1837, when the College building was first occupied, and Stoever's resignation in 1856, its enrollment usually exceeded that of the College itself. For the entire twenty-year period, the annual average for prep was 86 students, while that for the College was 73. Each year, many of the students in the

---

[74] See pp. 112-113 for a discussion of the unsuccessful efforts in the early 1840s to get a separate building for this department.

[75] See, for example, the *Sentinel,* April 17, 1843.

department were from Gettysburg or other parts of Adams county.

After the office of principal was abandoned, enrollment in prep began to decline. By the early 1860s it was but half of what it had been a decade earlier, a condition which the faculty attributed to the competition being offered by an increasing number of preparatory schools in the area from which the College drew its students. Disturbed by what was happening, in 1864 the trustees named a committee to bring in recommendations designed to reverse the trend. A year later, in August 1865, after listening to the committee's report, the board declared that "the interests of the College demand the immediate resuscitation and improvement" of the preparatory department. To accomplish this end, they resolved to erect a separate building for its use; to revive the office of principal and give it the faculty status it formerly possessed; and, finally, to ask the faculty to revise the course of study in order to "adapt it to the present wants of the Institution."[76] The board then elected as principal Charles J. Ehrehart (1850), Lutheran pastor in Middletown and a man keenly interested in secondary education wherever he was serving a parish. Within a few months of his election Ehrehart joined the faculty which, as the board requested, revised the course of studies, in June 1866.

During the next two years, Ehrehart moved with great energy to resuscitate the preparatory department. As already noted, while the plans for constructing Stevens Hall moved to completion, he used a temporary addition to his house on Carlisle street to room and board some of his younger students. As the 1866 and 1867 catalogues advised, the new principal was prepared to receive these boys "into his family." Enrollment increased from 40 students in 1862 and 1863 to 87 in 1867 and 94 in 1868. By the time Stevens Hall was occupied in the fall of 1868, it appeared that the revival of the preparatory department was becoming an accomplished fact.

Curriculum

Among the fairly complete records of the organization of the College in 1832 there are none of any discussion of what should be included in the first curriculum, nor is there any notation either in the minutes of the faculty or of the board for that year that a course of

---

[76]The board also authorized a committee to visit schools within the College constituency to recruit students for prep and to determine whether additional preparatory departments could be established in urban areas "under the fostering care of the College as the Parent Institution." Nothing came of the latter proposal.

PENNSYLVANIA COLLEGE.

Course of Instruction.

S. S. Schmucker, A. M. Professorship of Intellectual & Moral Science.	E. L. Hazelius, D. D. Professorship of Lat. Lang.& Germ. Literature.	H. L. Baugher, A. M. Professorship of Greek Lang. & Belles-Lettres.	M. Jacobs, A. M. Professorship of Nat. Phil. Chem.& Mathemat.	J. H. Marsden, A. M. Professorship of Mineralogy & Botany.
SENIOR YEAR.	**SENIOR YEAR.**	**SENIOR YEAR.**	**SENIOR YEAR.**	**SENIOR YEAR.**
Session. II. { Moral and Political Philosophy.	II. { Tacitus and Hebrew.	II. { Græca Majora Vol. II. Elements of Criticism.	II. { Gummere's Astronomy. Say's Pol. Economy.	II. { Lectures on Botany.
Session. I. { Natural Theology and Evidences of Revelation.	I. { Tacitus German Literature.	I. { Græca Majora Vol. II. Philosophy of Rhetoric.	I. { Cavallo's Nat. Philosophy. Keith on the Globes.	I. { Lectures on Mineralogy.
JUNIOR YEAR.	**JUNIOR YEAR.**	**JUNIOR YEAR.**	**JUNIOR YEAR.**	**JUNIOR YEAR.**
II. { Hedge's Logic.	II. { Do. Do.	II. { Philos. of Rhetoric. Græca Majora Vol. I.	II. { Cambridge Calculus and Vince's Fluxions. Mensuration, Navigation.	II. { Nuttall's Botany.
I. { Lectures on Intellectual Philosophy.	I. { Cicero de Oratore and German.	I. { Blair's Rhetoric. Homer's Iliad.	I. { Turner's Chemistry with experiments. Conic Sections.	I. { Comstock's Mineralogy.
SOPHOMORE YEAR.	**SOPHOMORE YEAR.**	**SOPHOMORE YEAR.**	**SOPHOMORE YEAR.**	**SOPHOMORE YEAR.**
II. {	II. { Cicero de Officiis.	II. { Græca Majora Vol. I. Greek Exercises and Prosody.	II. { Gummere's Surveying. Lacroix's Algebra.	II. {
I. {	I. { Livy.	I. { Græca Majora Vol. I. Tytler's History.	I. { Locroix's Plane and Spherical Trigonometry.	I. {
FRESHMAN YEAR.	**FRESHMAN YEAR.**	**FRESHMAN YEAR.**	**FRESHMAN YEAR.**	**FRESHMAN YEAR.**
II. {	II. { Salust.	II. { Græca Majora Vol. I. Exercises.	II. { Playfair's Elem. &c. completed	II. {
I. {	I. { Orations of Cicero. Horace expurgated.	I. { Xenophon's Cyropedia. English Grammar. Greek Exercises. Composition and Declamation throughout the course.	I. { Colburns's Algebra. Playfair's Elem. of Geometry.	I. {

E. FRIEDERICI, Teacher of the French Language.

PREPARATORY DEPARTMENT.

The studies of the Preparatory Department are Latin Grammar, Latin Reader Part I & II, Cæsar, Latin Exercises, Virgil and Prosody ; Greek Grammar, Greek Reader Part I & II, Greek Exercises, English Grammar, Geography Ancient and Modern, and Arithmetic: together with the French Language.

N. B. The German, Hebrew and French Languages, together with Mineralogy, Botany and Navigation are optional studies.

Course of Instruction
On August 29, 1832, the faculty presented this course of study "to a number of gentlemen competent to judge of its merits" and asked for their "influence in recommending students to our Institution."

study was ever formally adopted.[77] Nevertheless, on August 29, 1832 the faculty issued a circular outlining the proposed course of instruction and sent it "to a number of gentlemen competent to judge of its merits," in the hope that they would recommend the new College to prospective students.[78]

Upon examination of the outline, it is immediately evident that the announced College course was the curriculum of the Gymnasium, with minor revisions and some additions. For example, much of the scheduled work for the senior year was that of the fifth class of the Gymnasium. Henry L. Baugher retained the instruction in Greek and turned over his Latin work to Ernest L. Hazelius. Michael Jacobs continued to be responsible for the offerings in mathematics, chemistry, astronomy, surveying, and political economy.[79] The courses in philosophy, logic, and theology which Samuel Simon Schmucker planned to teach for juniors and seniors represented an addition to the curriculum, as did those in botany and mineralogy assigned to John H. Marsden and those in French to be taught by Ernest Friederici.

The College required students to complete most of the work which it offered, although there were always some "optional studies."[80] The first catalogue, published in February 1837, identified these as German, Hebrew, navigation, botany, mineralogy, and geology, all of which were taught either during the second term of the senior year or "whenever the qualifications and convenience of the Students may best admit." In subsequent years French, zoology, anatomy, and physiology were added to the optional list, and were described as studies "attended to by the members of any Class having the necessary knowledge and leisure." As we shall see, German was eventually removed from the enumeration of optional studies.[81]

The early catalogues informed the interested public that the College offered "lectures on Chemistry with experiments," that the surveying included "field exercises with the instruments," and that

---

[77]The curriculum which the faculty approved at its second meeting, on October 31, was one for the preparatory department.

[78]Pennsylvania College. Course of Instruction. GCA.

[79]Later, Jacobs sometimes taught botany, mineralogy, and meteorology. In August 1856 his faculty colleagues urged him to publish his lectures on the last-named subject.

[80]There were no distribution requirements and no major or minor course of study.

[81]On several occasions (1846, 1852, 1854, and 1866) there are references to teachers of music, but these were not regular members of the faculty and tuition did not cover the cost of their services. Nor was occasional instruction in penmanship and drawing covered by the tuition fee. For a brief period in the 1840s the catalogue listed subjects on which the faculty delivered lectures from time to time, outside the classroom.

the anatomy instruction was "illustrated by an appropriate collection of Anatomical preparations." The engineering lectures were offered by a man who "has not only had the advantage of a regular course at West Point, but is still a practical Engineer in the employ of the State." Among the well-known texts which were used in the early College were the following: Andrew Dalzel, *Collectanea Graeca Majora. . .* (1802); John Playfair, *Elements of Geometry* (1795); Thomas Keith, *A New Treatise on the Use of the Globes* (1805), in astronomy; Alexander F. Tytler, *Elements of General History* (1801); and Jean Baptiste Say's work on political economy, or economics, the first of many editions of which was published in 1803.

The curriculum for the 1867-1868 academic year bore unmistakable traces of its close kinship with the one announced thirty-five years earlier.[82] The heavy concentrations in Latin, Greek, and mathematics remained. Of 122 topics or combinations of topics listed under "the studies of the several classes" for 1867-1868, 43 dealt with the Greek and Latin language, literature, and culture, while 13 dealt with mathematics. Philosophy, theology, history, chemistry, navigation, surveying, and economics were still being offered. New professors had changed some of the titles of the "studies" which they taught. Most of them had also adopted more up-to-date textbooks. Of those used in the 1830s, Thomas Keith's work on astronomy was probably the only one which remained. Among the newer texts being used were Asa Gray, *Botanical Textbook* (1842), François Guizot, *History of Civilization in Europe* (1828), Furman Sheppard, *The Constitutional Text-Book: A Practical and Familiar Exposition of the Constitution of the United States* (1855), Francis Wayland, *Elements of Moral Science* (1834), Edward L. Youmans, *A Class-Book of Chemistry* (1851), and several books by Elias Loomis, famous mathematician and astronomer.

Between 1832 and 1868 some important new work was added to the curriculum. As already noted, the College charter contained a provision that "in addition to the customary professorships in other colleges, there shall be in this institution a German Professorship," whose incumbent had the specific responsibility of giving instruction to young men preparing to be teachers in "those primary schools" in which both English and German were to be taught. This provision

---

[82]Frederick Rudolph concluded that widespread acceptance of the famous Yale Report of 1828, which advocated continuation of the long-established college course of study with but few changes, had the effect of stifling curricular reform in the United States for almost half a century. Frederick Rudolph, *The American College and University: A History* (New York, 1962), pp. 130-131. Hereafter cited as Rudolph, *American College.*

was an injunction which the College could not ignore, but it proved to be one which was difficult to obey. The first two catalogues in 1837 and 1838 indicated that there was a professorship of German Language and Literature, but in place of the name of the incumbent there were two conspicuous blanks. Henry I. Smith (1806-1889) was Professor of German and French Languages and Literature from 1838 until 1843, when the hard times of the decade led him to return to the parish ministry.[83] Neither of his two successors in German remained very long; by 1848 the position was again vacant. A few years later the board of trustees took the initiative, already described, which prompted the Pennsylvania Synod to endow the German professorship.

When Charles F. Schaeffer became its first incumbent in 1856, the study of German was optional. In the following year, the synod asked the College "to place the German language on the same footing with the Latin and Greek languages, in the regular course of studies, subject to like privileges and restraints."[84] After first rejecting the proposal, the board of trustees and faculty agreed in 1860 to accept it. Beginning with the 1860-1861 academic year, German became a required study. Exemptions were granted only upon written requests of parents or guardians. "Unsurpassed in its rich stores of literature, science, and theology," explained the 1868 catalogue, German is "a part of the regular College course" and is "continued throughout the entire course." Not all parents and guardians were convinced that their sons should be required to study this language. More than a few asked for exemptions, most of which were granted.

In addition to German, a second new area of study had been established in the curriculum by the end of the period covered by this chapter. In August 1862 the board of trustees named a committee "to revise the schedule of studies of the Institution, with a view to secure a larger attention to English Literature and Rhetoric." The committee was instructed to work with the faculty and to proceed with expedition, but at each succeeding meeting it asked for more time. Perhaps what it was really asking for was more money, since only after John E. Graeff contributed $20,000 during the 1864 Harrisburg convention could a new faculty position be created and proper attention be given to the subject. The faculty hastened to list the Graeff Professor of the English Language and Literature in the 1865 catalogue, but the first incumbent, Edsall Ferrier (1831-1903),

[83]Between 1839 and 1843 Smith was also a member of the seminary faculty. From 1848 to 1880 he was Professor of German Language and Literature at Columbia College, New York. Between 1832 and 1868 French was offered only infrequently at Gettysburg College.
[84]*Minutes of the Pennsylvania Synod* (1857), p. 29.

STUDENTS IN COLLEGE AND DEGREES GRANTED,
1832-1868

	Degree Candidates	Special Students	Preparatory Students	Total Students	Graduates
1832-33				96	
1833-34				86	3
1834-35				c.100	8
1835-36				95	0
1836-37	42	12	50	104	4
1837-38	51	8	64	123	6
1838-39	59	5	77	141	14
1839-40	66	4	88	158	6
1840-41	72	9	108	189	11
1841-42	65	13	96	174	13
1842-43	50	5	75	130	11
1843-44	60	11	71	142	12
1844-45	62	9	77	148	4
1845-46	74	11	108	193	14
1846-47	81	14	81	176	17
1847-48	73	9	62	144	13
1848-49	59	7	67	133	10
1849-50	67	9	66	142	18
1850-51	58	11	84	153	14
1851-52	50	5	109	164	7
1852-53	73	6	83	162	14
1853-54	71	10	83	164	12
1854-55	71	17	82	170	10
1855-56	71	10	83	164	21
1856-57	77	3	71	151	16
1857-58	76	3	55	134	11
1858-59	91	7	71	169	14
1859-60	93	4	54	151	19
1860-61	94	5	67	166	21
1861-62	86	5	40	131	18
1862-63	76	7	40	123	16
1863-64	62	4	48	114	12
1864-65	61	0	51	112	12
1865-66	70	0	86	156	9
1866-67	108	0	87	195	15
1867-68	101	0	94	195	13
					418

Sources: Faculty reports to the board of trustees and College catalogues. These figures do not include one student from each of the following classes whose degrees were withheld for disciplinary reasons and not awarded until after 1868: 1861, 1864, and 1865. In 1880, upon recommendation of the faculty, the board voted to award a degree to a member of the class of 1856 who was drowned during the senior vacation preceding commencement. According to the *Alumni Directory of Pennsylvania College of Gettysburg, 1832-1918* (Gettysburg, 1918), pp. 3-32, there were 595 students enrolled in the College between 1832 and 1868 who were not graduated.

did not assume his duties until January 1867. The courses which he then introduced included study of both language and literature. For example, students in 1868 were investigating the etymological, rhetorical, and poetical forms of the English language; its historical elements; Anglo Saxon; as well as Chaucer, Spenser, Shakespeare, and Milton.[85]

The 1868 catalogue noted that, in addition to all of the other topics included in the course of instruction, composition, declamations, written debates, or orations were assigned throughout the four years. It assured the public that professors "who have had the advantages of enlarged experience in their respective departments" were responsible for the instruction and that they used "both text books and lectures, as they find most efficient, in developing the minds of the pupils."

As the curriculum developed from 1832 to 1868, there is little evidence in the minutes of either the faculty or the board that it was the subject of extensive discussion or debate, or that the faculty was much influenced by what was happening in other colleges. On occasion, as in the case of the introduction of courses in the English language and literature, the board appears to have taken the initiative in curricular revision, but there is no indication that it intended to proceed without faculty cooperation and approval.

Between 1832 and 1861 the academic year consisted of two terms or sessions. The first term, or winter session, began late in October or early in November (the 1832 opening on November 7 was about a week later than usual) and extended into April. After a vacation of five or six weeks, the second term, or summer session, began in May and continued into September. Commencement occurred on the third Thursday in September. In April 1861 the board adopted a calendar of three thirteen-week terms, with vacations of six, three, and four weeks between them. Classes then began during the last week in September and commencement took place on the second Thursday in August. The adjustment in this calendar which was made in 1868 will be discussed in the next chapter.

The admissions requirements changed little between 1832 and 1868. In both years a prospective student needed to be able to pass an examination to determine the extent of his knowledge of Latin, Greek, English grammar, geography, and mathematics (in 1868 specifically arithmetic, algebra, and geometry). He also had to produce "satisfactory testimonials of good moral character." Students in the preparatory department could take the entrance examination before they left on vacation. Others who were willing

---

[85]For a discussion of the early history of the Ockershausen professorship, also established in 1865, see pp. 234-237.

to make a special trip to Gettysburg could come at the same time. More came at the beginning of the first term, anticipating that the professors would approve of their preparation in some academy or possibly in an early high school. A few appeared and qualified days, even weeks, after classes began.

The entire faculty voted upon every candidate. Well-prepared students were admitted unconditionally. Those whose command of Latin, Greek, or some other subject was marginal and who were admitted "on trial" were told that they had a term (or perhaps a year) in which to remove the conditions imposed upon their entrance. It was not unusual for applicants who fared well during their examinations to be admitted as sophomores or even juniors. Only rarely was anyone admitted as a senior. As early as 1838 the faculty required that a student wishing to transfer bring written evidence from the college which he last attended that he was in good standing in that institution and entitled to honorable dismissal.[86]

Although the faculty considered a student actually enrolled in College once he began to attend classes, the formal act of entry, called matriculation, did not take place until later. The first matriculation of students, for example, did not occur until December 15, 1832, when twenty-two young men signed their names to the following solemn promise:

> I solemnly promise, on my truth and honor, to observe and obey all the laws, rules and regulations of Pennsylvania College, and that I will abstain from the profanation of the Lord's day, from the use of profane language, from all kinds of gambling, from all indecent, disorderly behavior, and from disrespectful conduct towards my instructors and others.[87]

Most students had three classes, or recitations, each day except Wednesday and Saturday, when they had two. Wednesday afternoons were reserved for meetings of student organizations, while Saturday afternoons were free time. Classes lasted for an hour. In 1858-1859 they met at 8 A.M., 11 A.M., and 4 P.M. each day except Wednesday (when the times were 8 A.M. and 11 A.M.) and Saturday (when they were 8 A.M. and 9 A.M.) To meet their convenience and other obligations, at the beginning of a term members of the faculty often adjusted the times when they expected to meet their classes.

---

[86]In July 1861 the faculty approved admitting students of Northern Illinois University, a struggling Lutheran institution, if its president, William M. Reynolds, provided them with certificates evaluating their academic qualifications.

[87]The 1838 catalogue announced that "no student is matriculated until he is fifteen years of age and has been six weeks in the institution; until this he is merely a probationer." In addition to entering their own names, signers gave the name of their parent or guardian and their home address. Members of both preparatory and collegiate departments were required to sign the matriculation oath until after 1900.

Page from the Matriculation Book, 1840-1841

During the course of an academic year there were a number of days on which no classes were held. Twenty years before Abraham Lincoln issued the first proclamation calling for a national thanksgiving day (1863), the governor of Pennsylvania asked the residents of the state to set aside a day on which to give thanks. The College adjourned classes on this day and the days proclaimed by succeeding governors. Sometimes the Christmas-New Year recess included only those two days. If parents wanted to have their sons home for the holidays, they would have to send a written request to the faculty. At other times the recess included Christmas day, but ended before January 1. Occasionally it was long enough to allow students to be home on both holidays.

There were two February days without classes. One was George Washington's birthday and the other, first observed in 1839, occurred during the last week in the month. It was a day of prayer for all of the colleges of the country. Religious services were held in one of the churches in the town and students were expected to attend. Good Friday sometimes occurred during one of the vacations. If not, classes were suspended on that day and services were conducted in the church. There were never classes on July 4. These days without classes were not included in the published College calendar. The faculty early made July 4 a permanent holiday, but the students annually petitioned for some of the others. The one which gave rise to the most dissension was the Christmas-New Year break, which the students wanted to begin before December 25 and end after January 1. For a long time the faculty insisted that the calendar which the board had approved made impossible such a long interruption in classes. They did not admit that a change might easily be effected.

The faculty was greatly concerned about frequent evaluation of student performance. One of their earliest acts was to devise a "notation system" of grading and a "character bill," which included marks for both classroom work and general deportment. These reports were sent to parents twice each term until 1851 and once thereafter. According to custom, there were public examinations of students. The faculty tried to publicize these occasions in order to insure a proper attendance. To 1868 and beyond, a number of trustees (usually residents of Gettysburg) were delegated to participate in the examination of seniors and join in recommending them to the board for their bachelor's degrees.

Both faculty and board resisted the temptation experienced by most new colleges to graduate some students at the end of the first year of operation. The first Gettysburg commencement was held on September 18, 1834, when three students – Jacob B. Bacon, David G. Barnitz, and William H. Smith – were graduated.[88] Except for 1836,

---

[88] According to the list complied by Donald G. Tewksbury and published in 1932, as measured by the date of its charter Gettysburg College was then the fifty-sixth oldest functioning college or university in the United States. However, if measured by the date of its first baccalaureate degree, it was the forty-seventh oldest. Some colleges and universities did not grant their first degrees until ten or more years after they were chartered. In the case of Lafayette, it was ten years. In that of Mount St. Mary's, it was twenty-five years. Donald G. Tewksbury, *The Founding of American Colleges and Universities Before the Civil War* . . . (New York, 1932; reprint ed., 1965), pp. 32-39.

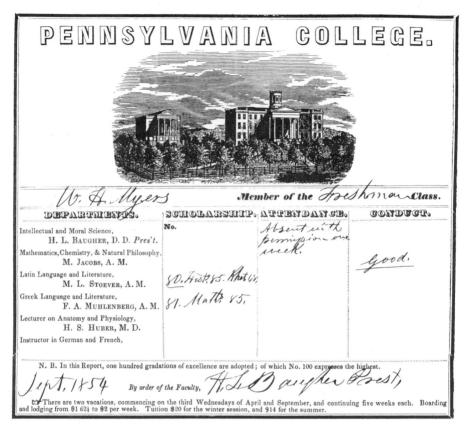

PENNSYLVANIA COLLEGE.

W. H. Myers ⸻ Member of the *Freshman* Class.

DEPARTMENTS.	SCHOLARSHIP.	ATTENDANCE.	CONDUCT.
Intellectual and Moral Science, H. L. BAUGHER, D. D. *Pres't.*	No.	*Absent with permission one week.*	
Mathematics, Chemistry, & Natural Philosophy, M. JACOBS, A. M.			*Good.*
Latin Language and Literature, M. L. STOEVER, A. M.	*80. Hist? 85. Rhet 68.*		
Greek Language and Literature, F. A. MUHLENBERG, A. M.	*81. Math 85.*		
Lecturer on Anatomy and Physiology, H. S. HUBER, M. D.			
Instructor in German and French,			

N. B. In this Report, one hundred gradations of excellence are adopted; of which No. 100 expresses the highest.

Sept, 1854   By order of the Faculty, *H. L. Baugher Prest,*

☞ There are two vacations, commencing on the third Wednesdays of April and September, and continuing five weeks each. Boarding and lodging from $1 62½ to $2 per week. Tuition $20 for the winter session, and $14 for the summer.

Student Grade Report, 1854

when there were no students qualified to receive degrees, there has been a commencement every year since.[89] As a means of advertising the College, almost every annual catalogue issued up to and beyond the year 1868 listed all of the alumni, with their addresses, giving them a prominent place in the front of the book, immediately after the lists of trustees and faculty. The 1869 catalogue, which listed the graduates through 1868, included the names and addresses of 418 persons, 357 of whom were still living. The average size of the thirty four classes which were graduated between 1834 and 1868 was twelve.

Commencement week in Gettysburg each September (beginning in 1862, each August) was a gala affair, with College and seminary coordinating their end-of-the-year activities. Most of the events

---

[89]On at least one occasion, in August 1863, one month after the battle of Gettysburg, the College graduated students without formal exercises.

were held in the College church. The week began with the president's baccalaureate sermon on Sunday. During the week the literary societies, the alumni association, and sometimes other organizations held their exercises. Occasionally there were special events, such as the dedication of Linnaean Hall in 1847 and the laying of the cornerstone of Stevens Hall twenty years later. Usually the College president gave a party, which was about the only formal event of the week which did not include at least one address. Always there was a meeting of the board of trustees.

Commencement exercises occurred on Thursday. Each senior was expected to give an address, the allotted time for which decreased from twenty minutes in 1837 to eight minutes thirty years later.[90] These talks were delivered in Latin, Greek, English, and sometimes also in German, on subjects which the faculty assigned. In 1853, for example, the topics ranged from Cardinal Wolsey and the Opium Trade to the Shady Side of our Country and the Sunny Side of our Country. Students could, and often did, ask to change the subjects which were assigned to them. All were required to submit either the outline or the full text of their orations to the president in advance of delivery. Participation in the commencement exercises was an obligation and students wishing to be exempted had to petition the faculty. In 1851 a student was excused and handed his diploma because the "morbid condition of his mind" required it. Three years later, a senior whose case was described as "peculiar" was given permission to read his speech instead of committing it to memory.

The College awarded the degree of bachelor of arts to all graduating seniors. In March 1838 the faculty decided henceforth to recommend each year to the board for the master of arts degree "those graduates who after the expiration of three years give evidence of good moral character and progress in intellectual attainment." The board agreed to participate in this practice and in September 1838, with its approval, the president conferred the master's degree on two members of the class of 1834. In succeeding years almost all graduates of three years' standing were recognized in this way. These degrees were considered to have been awarded in course.

Between 1835 and 1868 the College also awarded honorary degrees of bachelor of arts (1), master of arts (41), doctor of divinity or of sacred theology (33), doctor of laws (4), and doctor of philosophy (1). Most of the recipients of these degrees were Lutheran pastors who either had or would have some association

---

[90]The editor of the Sentinel wrote that the 1839 commencement lasted "for above four hours" and would have had his readers believe that the addresses were so absorbing that "there was not the least evidence of weariness amongst the large and attentive audience." Sentinel, September 18, 1839.

SIXTEENTH COMMENCEMENT OF
PENNSYLVANIA COLLEGE,
GETTYSBURG, PA.

YOU are respectfully invited to attend the Sixteenth Annual Commencement of Pennsylvania College, to be held on the 19th of September, 1850.

J. F. BAUGHER,	C. NITTERAUR,
J. F. CROCKER,	J. WORLEY,
J. M. EICHELBERGER,	*Committee*

GRADUATES, AND THEIR SUBJECTS.

Latin Salutatory.—HENRY RECK, of Adams Co., Pa.
Greek Oration.—MILTON VALENTINE, of Tancytown, Md.
Power of Example.—GEO. W. ANDERSON, of Harrisonburg, Va.
Man's Superiority.—DANIEL J. BARRICK, of Woodsboro', Md.
Empiric.—JOHN BAUGHER, of Frederick, Md.
Greek Drama.—WM. J. T. CARROLL, of Smithfield, Va.
Power of the Pen.—CHAS. JOHN EHREHART, of Adams Co., Pa.
Spanish and Anglo-Saxon Civilization in America.—JOHN M. EICHELBERGER, of Winchester, Va.
Mind upon Mind.—DANIEL GARVER, of Scotland, Franklin Co., Pa.
The Human Voice.—WILLIAM F. GREAVER, of Middlebrook, Va.
California.—ROBERT G. HARPER, JR., of Gettysburg, Pa.
Claims of the World upon the Young Men of America.—JACOB KELLER KAST, of Mechanicsburg, Pa.
True Glory.—SAMUEL O. KÆMPFFER, of Manchester, Md.
Popular Delusions—CORNELIUS NITTERRAUER, of Wadsworth, Ohio
Early Impressions.—DAVID STROH, of Mechanicsburg, Pa.
Claims of the Christian Ministry.—DANIEL WORLEY, of Harrisburg
Influence of Missions on Literature.—SAMUEL YINGLING, of York, Pa.
Valedictory.—JAMES F. CROCKER, of Smithfield, Va.

Announcement of the 1850 Commencement Exercises

with the College, but the list also included the names of Thomas H. Stockton, a Methodist pastor who was later chaplain of the United States Senate; Herman Haupt; two principals of the Gettysburg Female Academy; Oliver O. Howard, the Civil War general; and Edward McPherson (1848), then Clerk of the United States House of Representatives. The names of honorary degree candidates might originate with members of the board or with the faculty. In 1838 the trustees required that these names be submitted at a meeting previous to the one in which they acted on the nominations, thereby establishing a policy to which they made few exceptions. In 1859 the board resolved not to confer the divinity degree upon any who could not give evidence "of extensive theological learning by his writings or by his diligent studies." A candidate should be known "as a scholar, sedulously pursuing theological science and rising above his brethren around him in scholarly attainments." At the same time, the board agreed to vote by ballot, rather than by a show of hands, in choosing recipients of honorary degrees.[91]

Library

The first public announcement of the Gymnasium late in 1829 or early in 1830 contained the information that a library was being formed; in the meantime, students interested in theology had access to the seminary library, which then consisted of more than six thousand volumes. Apparently, the managers of the Gymnasium bought few books, since the trustees in April 1834 directed that Charles P. Krauth, Samuel Simon Schmucker, and John G. Morris purchase an "incipient College Library." These three men were authorized to spend $500 for that purpose, and to borrow the money if necessary. Their report, dated September 16, 1834, shows that they were prompt in carrying out the task assigned to them. Borrowing $500 from a Hanover bank, they traveled to Philadelphia and Baltimore, where they "selected the most important and valuable works in all departments of Literature and Science, suitable for a College library, to the amount of their means."[92] There being no adequate space for the collection in the academy building,

---

[91]Near the end of his life John G. Morris wrote that he opposed most nominations for the doctorate of divinity, including his own. He gave three reasons: he did not want to cheapen the title; he found most candidates falling short of his standards for the degree; and he did not believe in discriminating against many qualified persons who were never nominated. Morris, *Reminiscences*, p. 290.

[92]Report of the Library Committee, GCA. They spent $471 and, after paying interest on the note, had a balance of $21.62. They used some of the money received in the first installment of the state grant of $18,000 to repay the note.

the trustees rented one room in the house of Michael Jacobs, which was located one block away, at the northwest corner of Washington and Middle streets.

In June 1834 the faculty elected Michael Jacobs librarian and adopted the first regulations governing use of the collection. It was to be open for one hour in a week, from 11 A.M. to noon on Saturday. Each student could borrow one large or two small books for one week. There were fines for damaging a book or for returning it late. In 1834 it was not unusual for a college library to be operated on such a limited schedule. Course requirements were then based so heavily upon textbooks, lectures, and recitations that the need for student use of the library was minimal. As times and expectations changed, the hours of service were increased and the librarian was given more authority to alter the rules. In 1835 resident graduates were given access to the collection.

When the new College building was occupied in the fall of 1837, the library was moved to the large room on the north side of the center section of the third floor. Here it remained as the collection increased and outgrew these cramped quarters. While the two literary societies were attempting to erect their own building on campus in the late 1850s, as the Linnaean Association had done a decade earlier, the faculty proposed that it be built to accommodate the College library as well. Agents were sent out to collect funds, but the war dissipated these plans, and in 1868 the library still occupied the space allotted to it thirty years earlier. There was, however, now a separate reading room where students could use newspapers and journals. After Michael Jacobs, the following faculty members served as librarians: Martin L. Stoever, to 1850; Frederick A. Muhlenberg, from 1850 to 1866; and Luther H. Croll, beginning in 1866.

In 1834 the trustees agreed to allocate $100 each year to be used for augmenting the library collection. Two years later, they decided to charge each student $1 per year and assign the proceeds for the same purpose. In practice, neither of these resolves worked as intended. The small beginnings of sustained support for the library have already been described: the successful canvass of the alumni in 1852-1853 for a $1,000 endowment, the annual yield of which was used for the purchase of books.[93] Occasionally, outsiders contributed money for the library. James Buchanan, who gave $50 in 1853, is an example. More often, friends of the College gave books which, if they came from a personal collection, might be of limited use in a

---

[93]By 1868 the principal of the endowment fund amounted to $1,500, thanks to a special bank dividend during the 1865-1866 year. The fund was then yielding about $175 each year.

college library. Among the chief early donors were William G. Jones, of Baltimore; Hiester H. Muhlenberg, of Reading, a trustee whose gifts over an extended period of time approximated one thousand volumes; John G. Morris, whose interest in the library also extended over many years; and the heirs of Rev. John C. Baker, from whom the College received some 550 volumes, in addition to many pamphlets, in 1859. Both faculty and board made it a practice to thank these donors.

The estimated size of the library in 1840 was 1,050 volumes; in 1855, 2,500; and in 1868, 6,000. In the latter year the catalogue noted that the library holdings of the literary societies and other College organizations increased the total campus library collection to 16,500 volumes. The trustees indicated their estimate of the importance of these resources by having them separately insured, for $1,000, in 1857.

While the faculty may have spent little time in their weekly meetings discussing the curriculum and its development, the minutes show that they were greatly concerned about building a representative library collection appropriate for a liberal arts college. On many occasions they acted as a body to purchase specific works, and the secretary dutifully recorded the titles which they selected.[94] What follows is a sample of their orders, the date given being the date when the purchase was authorized:

Reference Works

Statesman's Manual, 1846
Poole's Index to Periodical Literature, 1853
Encyclopedia Britannica, 1859

Newspapers

Gettysburg, Philadelphia, New York, and Baltimore papers

Periodicals and Magazines

Silliman's Journal, 1834   The treasurer regularly paid for this subscription by sending money to the famous chemist and geologist, Benjamin Silliman (1779-1864)
Annals of Education, 1834
Edinburgh Review, 1835
Westminster Review, 1835
Transactions, American Philosophical Society, 1844
Blackwood's Review, 1847
American Journal of Education, 1856
Proceedings, Academy of Natural Sciences, 1860

---

[94]In 1838 they decided to purchase a "due proportion" of German works.

Government Documents

Complete or nearly complete set of United States government publications and publications from the states of Pennsylvania, New York, Massachusetts, and Rhode Island. Thaddeus Stevens, Simon Cameron, and other officeholders contributed many of these volumes.

Science

Edward Hitchcock, *Geology*, 1840
Charles Babbage, *Ninth Bridgewater Treatise*, 1841
Justus von Liebig, *Organic Chemistry*, 1841
Dionysius Lardner and Charles V. Walker, *Manual of Electricity, Magnetism, and Meteorology*, 1842
John Torrey and Asa Gray, *Flora of North America*, 1842
Isaac Newton, *Principia Mathematica*, 1843
Natural History of New York, 1852
Hugh Miller, *Popular Geology*, 1859
Charles Lyell, *Principles of Geology*, 1863

Language and Literature

Thomas Macaulay, *Essays and Reviews*, 1841
Henry Hallam, *Introduction to the Literature of Europe*, 1841
John Dunlop, *History of Prose Fiction*, 1842
Comparative Philology, 1854
Blaise Pascal, *Provincial Letters*, 1855
Andrew Comstock, *The Phonetic Reader*, 1857

Government

James Kent, *Commentaries on American Law*, 1841
Henry Wheaton, *Elements of International Law*, 1846
John Purdon, *A Digest of the Laws of Pennsylvania*, 1855
Decisions of Chief Justice John Marshall, 1855
Francis Lieber, *Manual of Political Ethics*, 1857

History

George Bancroft, *History of the United States*, 1839
Barthold Niebuhr, *History of Rome*, 1841
Alexis de Tocqueville, *Democracy in America*, 1841
William H. Prescott, *Conquest of Mexico*, 1844
John Lingard, *History of England*, 1855
Works of John Quincy Adams, 1856
Thomas Macaulay, *History of England*, 1858
John Lothrop Motley, *History of the United Netherlands*, 1861
Thomas Carlyle, *History of Frederick the Great*, 1865

Religion

Life and Works of John Wesley, 1843
John Calvin, *Institutes of the Christian Religion,* 1848
Robert Baird, *Religion in America,* 1856
William B. Sprague, *Annals of the American Pulpit,* 1856

Philosophy

Heinrich Ritter, *History of Philosophy,* 1841
William Whewell, *Philosophy of the Inductive Sciences,* 1858
William Hamilton, *Metaphysics,* 1859

Not all of the books in the College library were safe from the threat or the reality of a censoring authority. In September 1834, after the committee named to purchase the "incipient library" made its report to the trustees, Thomas J. Cooper moved "to remove certain Novels from the Library." During the ensuing debate, on the motion of Thaddeus Stevens, the matter was wisely dealt with by being postponed indefinitely. In 1843 the faculty transferred Walter Scott's Waverley novels to the president's study; nine years later it authorized the librarian to use his discretion in signing them out to students. In 1855 certain volumes of Thomas Jefferson's works, recently presented to the library and believed to contain "objectionable sentiments," were also consigned to the president's study.

Equipment

Along with information about student access to library facilities, the first public announcement of the Gymnasium contained the information that "globes, an Electrical Machine, and an increasing Chymical and Philosophical Apparatus" had been provided for use in the instructional program. While these pieces of apparatus, as they were called, may have been sufficient for a Gymnasium, they were certainly not for a college, and Michael Jacobs turned to the board for the funds necessary to obtain more and better equipment. In April 1834 the trustees appropriated $300 for his use, and at the next meeting they decided to spend $50 each year for "chemical and philosophical apparatus." Unfortunately, financial considerations led them to rescind this resolution in April 1836, when they repealed a similar authorization of annual support for the library. Beginning in 1840, the catalogue annually assured the public that the "apparatus for chemical and philosophical purposes is respectable, and increasing," but Jacobs never enjoyed the regular, although small, endowment income which was available to the library after 1854.[95] In 1835 the trustees authorized him to solicit funds for the purchase of a telescope. He was not successful in raising the money, and on several occasions during the 1840s the board postponed purchase of this piece of equipment because it did not have the funds. Finally, in 1853, trustee Hiester H. Muhlenberg, already identified as the most generous patron of the library, gave the College a telescope. About the same time Charles A. Hay contributed binoculars.

When Alfred M. Mayer (1835-1897) became the first Ockershausen Professor of Natural Science in 1865 and Michael Jacobs was made Professor of Astronomy, the trustees appropriated the unprecedented sum of $2,500 for the purchase of additional equipment, exclusive of a new telescope. The 1866 catalogue reported that during the preceding year the efficiency of Professor Mayer's department

> has been greatly increased by the addition of a complete collection of Philosophical Apparatus . . . specially constructed to bring before the students all the fundamentally important phenomena of Natural Philosophy and Chemistry, and thus cause Nature, as far as possible, to take the place of instructor, and give her own teachings in her own language. All the recent developments in reference to the correlation of the physical forces are thus experimentally illustrated and indelibly impressed upon the mind of the student.

The same catalogue announced the purchase of a "superior Telescope," made in Germany, with magnifying powers to 460 times. However, this acquisition was of no use to the students taking astronomy until an observatory could be built, which did not happen until after 1868.

Apart from the chemical and philosophical apparatus, the College from its early days had a collection of mineral and other specimens. The 1837 catalogue described it as "a respectable and increasing cabinet of minerals . . . designed to connect with it collections in Natural History and Antiquities." In April 1844 the trustees recognized the major contributions of time, effort, and specimens being made by John G. Morris to this collection by naming it the Morris Cabinet and appropriating $50 to defray the costs incurred in putting it into order. After Linnaean Hall was completed in 1847, the cabinet was moved onto its second floor. The 1856 catalogue described the collection as consisting of "minerals, shells, fossils, birds, quadrupeds, reptiles, insects, coins, paintings, engravings, medals, etc." In 1866 the College spent more than $2,500 to

---

[95]In 1882 Milton Valentine wrote that "in the hands of Prof. Jacobs,. . . who possessed rare skill, as well as industry, in utilizing and extemporizing instruments for illustrative experiments," the apparatus " was made to do very efficient service." *1882 History*, p. 47. In their regular reports to the board, the faculty often asked for more support of Jacobs' work.

purchase from E. Seymour, New York, a mineral collection which he had built up over a period of thirty years and which was reputed to be one of the best of its kind in the country.[96]

The Medical Department

Although the main business of Gettysburg College in the years before 1868 was to offer instruction in the customary liberal arts and sciences, leading to the degree of bachelor of arts, there were a number of occasions on which faculty and trustees demonstrated a willingness to consider the possibility of entering into additional educational ventures. In September 1839, on a motion by Thaddeus Stevens and David Gilbert, the trustees established a law department and named Judge Daniel Durkee of York as its professor. Stevens, Gilbert, and Samuel Simon Schmucker were delegated to inform Durkee of his appointment and urge him to accept. The professor-elect, who was president judge of the Nineteenth Judicial District, which included York and Adams counties, politely declined the invitation and thereby ended the law department before it was fairly begun.

Twenty-five years later, in January 1864, state Senator George W. Householder of Bedford reminded President Baugher that the Morrill Act of 1862 had awarded 810,000 acres of public land to the state of Pennsylvania, specifying that the proceeds were to be used for

> the endowment, support, and maintenance of at least one college where the leading object shall be, without excluding other scientific and classical studies, and including military tactics, to teach such branches of learning as are related to agriculture and mechanic arts, . . . in order to promote the liberal and practical education of the industrial classes in the several pursuits and professions in life.

Householder informed the president that Allegheny College had applied for the income from one-third of this grant and urged Baugher to consider making his request for a share of it. "Gettysburg, being the spot upon which one of the greatest battles of modern times was fought," the senator wrote, "would seem to present inducements at this time, over other institutions for the purposes named."[97]

---

[96]See ibid., pp. 47-49 for a good summary of the College "cabinet" as it existed in 1882. By 1840, the equipment of the College included blackboards, historical maps, and musical instruments.

[97]George W. Householder to Henry L. Baugher, Harrisburg, January 25, 1864, GCA. A copy of the printed letter from the president of Allegheny College to the members of the state legislature, dated January 4, 1864, is in the archives.

During the 1864 session of the legislature, which began in January and ended in April, Baugher joined other Pennsylvania college presidents in Harrisburg, where they discussed ways in which a number of institutions might share in the proceeds from the federal grant. Householder prepared a bill dividing the expected income among a number of colleges. In August the board of trustees named a committee to investigate the possibility of the College's being endowed as a land-grant college and authorized it to convene a special meeting if the prospects appeared favorable. In October the Harrisburg endowment convention voted its approval of the idea and named a committee to cooperate with the one appointed by the trustees to lobby for the pending legislation. Nothing came of these initiatives. In April 1865 the board committee reported that no bill acceptable to the College could be passed. As early as April 1863, the legislature had designated the Agricultural College of Pennsylvania (renamed Pennsylvania State College in 1874) as the provisional recipient of the benefits which the Morrill Act conferred upon the state. As it turned out, no other Pennsylvania college was to share in them.

In August 1867, as the construction on Stevens Hall was beginning, the faculty recommended to the board of trustees that it consider establishing a normal school for the training of teachers and housing it in the new building. An act of May 20, 1857 had divided the state into twelve districts, in each of which the Superintendent of Common Schools was authorized to recognize one privately owned normal school, which would then receive certain benefits from the state and be required to meet certain standards. By 1867 four such schools had been designated, but none in the district which included Adams county. The faculty was convinced that there were definite advantages for the College in owning the state normal school in its district:

> The effect of this arrangement will be to bring the Teachers of our Common schools into contact with a higher form of education and awaken the desire for a more enlarged preparation for their work. At the same time it will attract an additional number of Students to the College, will make the College more widely known, will constitute a desirable connection between the lower and higher forms of instruction. Above all, it will tend to dissipate the prejudice which exists against colleges amongst the masses of the people.[98]

---

[98]Faculty Report, August 1867, GCA. See Sack, *Higher Education* 2:528-539 for a discussion of the normal schools. During the period covered by this chapter, most Pennsylvania colleges, including Gettysburg, had no separate course of study designed for training teachers. Faculty reports to the board of trustees sometimes gave the numbers of students preparing for teaching who were taking advantage of the law requiring that the College offer free tuition to as many as fifteen persons, "if so many apply." The numbers in 1856 and 1857 were three.

The board named a committee to investigate the feasibility of this suggestion. It never reported, possibly because of the death of one of its members, the president of the College, before the next meeting of the trustees. In May 1867 the faculty went on record as approving the plan of the federal government to offer military instruction in colleges and later expressed its willingness to accept an army officer as a colleague.

Neither the law department, agricultural college, normal school, nor military courses became a reality before 1868, but for more than twenty years before the Civil War Gettysburg College did have a medical department, whose educational program was carried out in Philadelphia.

In April 1837 Thaddeus Stevens reported to the board of trustees that a number of Philadelphia physicians were beginning a new medical college in that city and wanted to establish an affiliation with the College at Gettysburg. The board named Samuel Simon Schmucker, Thaddeus Stevens, and John B. McPherson to investigate the character and standing of these men and to confer with them. A year later the committee reported that plans for the school had been suspended, at least for the moment. There matters stood until September 1839, when four physicians presented the board with a proposal, under the terms of which they could grant medical degrees, by virtue of the authority of the charter of Gettysburg College.

The leading figure among the petitioners was George McClellan (1796-1847), a graduate of the University of Pennsylvania medical school in 1819 and subsequently one of Philadelphia's most successful physicians. When the supporters of his alma mater blocked his attempts to found a second medical school in the city, he persuaded the trustees of Jefferson College in 1824 to establish a medical department in Philadelphia. McClellan became the leading professor in Jefferson Medical College when it opened the following year, teaching anatomy and surgery as well as pioneering in developing a clinic as part of the instructional program. An act of April 12, 1838 made the medical department a separate, independent college. A year later, after internal troubles prompted the trustees to dismiss the faculty, McClellan and three associates asked the Gettysburg trustees to do for them what the Jefferson College trustees had done on their behalf fifteen years earlier.

The same committee which had responded to the overture of 1837 was named to consider the proposal of 1839. It recommended that the board of trustees establish a medical department; name its first faculty of five men; authorize them to designate their successors, offer their instruction in Philadelphia, and confer the degree of doctor of medicine upon candidates who met certain specified requirements; and, finally, require the faculty to make an annual

Medical Department Building
This engraving of the medical department building on Ninth street in
Philadelphia appeared in the 1858 College catalogue.

report on the state of the department. The trustees accepted this recommendation as it was presented to them, at the same meeting at which they established a law department.

The Medical Department of Pennsylvania College went into operation in the fall of 1839. In order to remove any doubt about their ability to grant degrees, McClellan and his associates persuaded the legislature to pass the act of March 6, 1840, which specifically authorized the medical faculty to confer medical degrees in the name of Gettysburg College on candidates who met the same requirements as those used by the University of Pennsylvania medical school. At the same time, the legislators declared in this act that "hereafter it shall not be lawful for any College incorporated by the laws of this State, to establish any faculty for the purpose of conferring degrees, either in medicine or the arts, in any city or county of the commonwealth, other than that in which said college is or may be located." At first housed on Filbert street, near Eleventh, the medical school moved in 1849 to even more spacious quarters in a new building on Ninth street, between Walnut and Spruce. In order to make possible finance of the new quarters, the legislature passed an act on March 29, 1849, incorporating "the trustees of the medical department of Pennsylvania College," and authorizing them to raise up to $40,000 in order to purchase a lot and erect a suitable building.

Beginning in 1840, the College catalogue included information about the medical department, listing its faculty (and for several years its students) and stating the requirements for graduation: three years of study under a "respectable practicioner" of medicine; two full courses of lectures, one of which had to be in the department; and a thesis. As part of their clinical instruction, students observed and helped to treat patients in Pennsylvania Hospital and Blockley Almshouse as well as in other city hospitals and at the medical school itself. The adequacy of the physical facilities and the rigor of the instructional program brought high praise from contemporaries. Edgar Fahs Smith (1874), a graduate of Gettysburg College who later became provost of the University of Pennsylvania, believed that by 1860 the Medical Department of Pennsylvania College "was conceded to be the best medical school in the city."[99] During its lifetime, it awarded more than eight hundred degrees.

Except for the requirements that it make an annual report to the parent institution and pay it one-half of the $5 matriculation fee, and except for the fact that the president of Gettysburg College usually appeared in Philadelphia for its graduation exercises, the medical department functioned most of the time as though it were an independent entity. The act of 1849, which created a separate corporation for holding the school's real estate, only added to the anomaly of the entire arrangement. However, when dissensions within the faculty became serious, as they too frequently did, the Gettysburg trustees were called upon to assert their authority and give what limited help they could. On one such occasion, in 1843-1844, the original faculty was dismissed and an entirely new one, which included David Gilbert, was constituted. In 1854, after two of the leading faculty members attempted to replace their colleagues

---

[99]Quoted in Harold J. Abrahams, *Extinct Medical Schools of Nineteenth-Century Philadelphia* (Philadelphia, 1966), p. 560 n. Smith wrote this to Richard H. Shryock. Abrahams discusses the Medical Department of Pennsylvania College on pp. 29-110 and 549-560. See also Sack, *Higher Education* 2:385-390. For information on the early Jefferson Medical College, see Helen Turnbull Waite Coleman, *Banners in the Wilderness: Early Years of Washington and Jefferson College* (Pittsburgh, 1956), pp. 83-84. Hereafter cited as Coleman, *Banners in the Wilderness.*

and declared the school's independence, the Gettysburg board dismissed the two rebels and authorized the remaining members to fill the vacancies. A mass resignation occurred in April 1859, at which time the board appointed six men who had been faculty members of the Philadelphia College of Medicine, which then passed out of existence.

Another mass departure took place in July 1861. In a letter to President Baugher, the faculty explained that they had resigned because the outbreak of war robbed them of Southern students while the depression which accompanied it promised to reduce the number of Northern students attending in the fall. At this very time, they claimed, the trustees of the medical school building were insisting that the members of the faculty were personally responsible for real estate taxes and other obligations then due and payable. "In order to save ourselves from inevitable loss, which none of us can afford," they wrote, "we have no course left us but to resign our chairs." They did so regretfully and with appreciation for the previous cooperation of the Gettysburg board of trustees.[100]

In reconstituting the faculty on this occasion, the board reappointed two former members and David Gilbert, instructing him to attempt to secure a full faculty and open the school in the fall. He was not successful and the building was sold by the sheriff in the summer of 1862. Nevertheless, Gilbert remained hopeful. "The drain upon the ranks of the profession by the war," he told the president of the board on October 9, 1862, "will bring out a large number of medical students and another faculty can be sustained." The former building would still be available and could be rented.[101] His hopes were not to be realized. On August 7, 1863 the treasurer of the College wrote off as a bad debt the $1,478.50 from its endowment fund which it had invested in the new medical department building in the early 1850s.

Students

It is abundantly evident that the founders of Gettysburg College were convinced that education in the liberal arts and sciences was best carried on in a setting which resembled that of a well-regulated family. Such a family customarily lived under one roof, where it was thought both instruction and discipline could most easily occur. Thus, it is not surprising that, as early as September 1832, the board

[100]Lewis D. Harlow, lately Dean, to H. L. Baugher, Philadelphia, July 16, 1861, GCA.
[101]D. Gilbert to M. McClean, Philadelphia, October 9, 1862, GCA.

of trustees took the first steps toward acquiring a more adequate building for accomplishing these purposes than the academy could ever provide. Until such time as more suitable quarters were available, however, there needed to be rules and regulations which governed student conduct both in and out of class and which were adapted to the existing situation. At its very first meeting, on July 4, 1832, the board directed the faculty to prepare a draft and submit it for approval. Rules and regulations for the College were adopted in September 1832 and for the preparatory department in April 1833. Once these were printed in 1834, the faculty sent copies to the proprietor of every house in which students roomed and boarded, and professors undertook to visit these places every two weeks.

In April 1837, as the College edifice was nearing completion, the faculty reminded the trustees that it had now become "a matter of primary importance . . . to make such a disposition of the students of the whole institution as will secure for them the supervision and care which are necessary for their moral welfare." In the opinion of the faculty, "nothing will contribute more to the prosperity of the College than judicious arrangements for placing the students out of the way of vice, and the preservation of their moral purity."[102] Responding to this urgent initiative, the board appointed a committee to draft a "system of rules and regulations for the supervision of the students in the new edifice." In September, one month before the move to the new campus, it adopted the "system" which Samuel Simon Schmucker, Robert G. Harper, Thaddeus Stevens, and John F. Macfarlane proposed.

The very first "chapter" of the new rules and regulations requested the president of the College to reside in the building and gave him "the entire superintendance" of the people who lived there as well as of the College property within it. There were detailed provisions governing how the students were expected to conduct themselves in the building, on the campus, and beyond the campus. From time to time, the faculty amended or added to these rules and regulations. Every so often, with the concurrence of the board, they republished them.[103]

In September 1837 the trustees established the position of steward. The incumbent was directed, not only to "furnish good and sufficient boarding for all the students, and resident President or Professor and tutors," but also to serve as janitor of the new building. In the latter capacity, his duties were carefully defined.

---

[102]Faculty Report, April 1837, GCA.

[103]For example, in 1846, 1855, and 1865. The quotes from the latter used in the text are taken from *Regulations of Pennsylvania College, Gettysburg, PA.,* . . . (Gettysburg, 1865).

For example, he was responsible for keeping all of the rooms clean, maintaining the fires in all but student rooms, and "destroying vermin by touching them with corrosive sublimate every 4 weeks." He was enjoined, if at all possible, to engage "none but male servants to sweep and attend to the rooms of the students."

The ideal arrangement for the well-regulated family may indeed have been for all of its younger members (except possibly those from Gettysburg and its immediate vicinity) to eat, study, recite, and sleep under one roof. Needless to say, however much it might have been cherished, the College never realized this ideal. Since total enrollment in the two departments averaged about 150 between 1838 and 1868 and never dropped below 112, there were not enough dormitory rooms in the College edifice to accommodate every student. The catalogue and other publications often stated that all were required to live on campus, but the level of student occupancy of dormitory rooms was almost always sufficiently close to capacity that those who wished to live off campus could get the necessary faculty permission to do so. As it turned out, there was even less concern about requiring all students to board in the building, although here too faculty permission was required for those who wanted to eat elsewhere. For a number of years after 1838, the catalogue advised that pretheological students could take their meals at the seminary for $1.50 per week (twenty-five cents cheaper than the College rate) and in town at prices ranging from $1.50 to $2.50 per week.[104] In the later 1840s, when meals at the College cost $1.62½ each week, the catalogue informed prospective students that food could be obtained in a boarding house for much less and that, "if great self denial is exercised," a student might board himself for about $.50 per week. However, the faculty insisted that students were not permitted to board themselves in the College edifice.

In September 1837 the trustees engaged Peter Aughinbaugh (1778-1857), former steward at the Adams county home, as the first steward of the College. When he and his wife, Elizabeth (1780-1876), moved into the building, they were a couple in their late fifties. During their stay of more than a decade, they won the respect and affection of most students. The testimony in the *Lutheran Observer* for November 2, 1838 that Aughinbaugh was a man "of sober habits and good character" who "gives his undivided attention to the comfort and convenience of the College students who board in the Refectory" appears to have been truthful. There is evidence that

---

[104]One of the rules declared that students could not board in any house permitting "improper conduct, on the part of the Students."

Elizabeth Aughinbaugh endeared herself to students by her washing, mending, and general mothering.[105]

Peter Aughinbaugh resigned in 1847, was replaced, returned in 1848, and resigned for the second and last time in 1850. None of his four successors stayed longer than a year or two; at least two were discharged. The faculty warned one of them that he could not conduct a public boardinghouse in the building and later forbade him from holding public sale on the property at a time when it would disrupt instruction. There was no steward in the building in 1854 and 1855. The trustees were unsuccessful in their efforts to open their own boarding house in town, and in 1854 they were reduced to permitting students to eat at the McClellan House (later Hotel Gettysburg), a step which they took only because at the time its bar was closed.

As early as 1853, members of the faculty had reached the conclusion that the steward system was not working and should be abandoned. In September they told the board that

in comparing the difficulties and disadvantages connected with the stewardship in college and the character of the stewards whose services we have been enabled to obtain with the evils almost necessarily incident to it, the Faculty respectfully inquire of the Board whether it would not be better to abolish the office. The noise, the smell of the cookery, the evil of having girls about the establishment, and the frequent follies or vices of the steward seem to overweigh all the advantages which we can find in the office. Besides many of the rooms below may be rented to the students.[106]

In spite of this advice, and of the inability to secure a steward in 1854 and 1855, the board insisted on continuing the system. Conditions did not improve. Edward S. Breidenbaugh (1868) remembered being told that students made "complaints and serious violent protests against the system and against the quality of food."[107] In April 1859 the faculty repeated their earlier recommendation and urged the trustees to build some inexpensive facility on the campus, "as a club house so that boarding may be reduced to the minimum price for the benefit of the students of limited means." After all, they wrote, "good plain, wholesome and sufficient food

[105]Both Aughinbaughs recovered quickly from a minor crisis at the time of the move into the new building. The steward was not a paid employee of the College. He and his family were given rent-free quarters and were paid for meals served to the president's household. He charged students for their meals and also for his janitorial services. With the approval of the steward committee, Aughinbaugh set a price of $1.75 per week for boarding and $.25 for cleaning rooms. Since $2.00 per week was more than many of them had been paying in town, the students assembled and threatened not to move into the new building unless the charge was reduced. According to the catalogue, it was, to $1.75 per week.
[106]Faculty Report, September 1853, GCA.
[107]Quoted in the Spectrum (1913), p. 14.

John Hopkins (1806-1868)
This photograph of the janitor, taken from the Beltzhoover album, identified him as a vice president of the College.

for students ought not to cost more than from $1 to $1.25 a week."
Taking the course of action which they favored would not only
"relieve the pressure of anxiety for the future which disturbs so
many," but also it would increase enrollment.[108]

When the trustees took up this matter in September 1859, they
were more concerned about building a house for the president on the
campus than they were with relocating an eating establishment.
Consequently, they did no more than notify the steward that his
contract would not be renewed when it expired on April 1, 1860.
Gettysburg did not again maintain a dining hall for its College
students for three-quarters of a century. Although the faculty

[108]Faculty Report, April 1859, GCA.

continued to oppose use of the College building for eating purposes, Edward S. Breidenbaugh later wrote that, instead of going to boarding houses or clubs, some students made their own meals and that, for a time, "each morning the milkman and the baker came to the college building and their two articles of supply with molasses, in some instances, constituted the larger portion of the food supply. Others added dried fruit and boiled potatoes to the bill of fare." Fortunate indeed were those boarding students who lived near town and whose parents sent them a weekly basket of delicious food.[109]

In April 1847, when Peter Aughinbaugh resigned as steward for the first time, the trustees authorized the faculty to hire a janitor to carry out some of his former duties. They promptly engaged John Hopkins (1806-1868) at a salary of $15 per month. His duties were gradually increased to include care of the grounds as well as the building, and he moved onto the campus after the steward system was abandoned in 1860. The faculty were often displeased with the way in which Hopkins performed his duties. He did not ring the bell on time, his cleaning of the rooms did not suit them, and he sometimes left classroom fires go out. On one occasion they dismissed him; on another he resigned. But each time the differences were patched up, and Jack the Janitor, as he was called for most of his long tenure, died in office in 1868.

The conscientious student who lived in the College building before 1868 and who was determined to obey the rules and regulations which the faculty and board had adopted would follow this schedule:

5:30	A.M.	Rise when the bell rings
6:00	A.M.	Go to morning chapel
7-8	A.M.	Study
8-9	A.M.	Engage in recreation
9-12	Noon	Study and attend class
12-2	P.M.	Engage in recreation
2-5	P.M.	Study and attend class
5-8	P.M.	Engage in recreation
8-10	P.M.	Study and attend evening chapel
10	P.M.	Prepare for bed
10:30	P.M.	Lights out[110]

[109]Quoted in the Spectrum (1913), p. 14. Breidenbaugh wrote that some students who boarded themselves "laid the foundations of the dread dyspepsia to which some fatally yielded while students."

[110]This schedule is derived from the rules and regulations as included in the 1843 catalogue.

During the hours of study, the obedient student always remained either in his own room or in the recitation room. Not only would he not go to any other place either on or off campus, but also he would "abstain from all noise during study hours, in the College edifice and vicinity." He was free to leave the campus during the hours set aside for recreation, but there were many temptations in town which, in deference to the rules, he would studiously avoid. Smoking was not permitted "in the halls of the College, or in any of the public rooms, or on the porches of the building."

On Sunday morning our student joined his College and seminary colleagues in attending worship in Christ Lutheran church, unless his parent or guardian had asked in writing that he be permitted to attend some other church. It was apparently taken for granted none would ask that the young man be permitted to attend no Sunday services. Our student might or might not return to College church for evening worship, but he would surely attend the required Biblical recitation conducted on the campus by one of the professors. During the Sunday hours of recreation, he might walk on or near the campus, but never in company with more than one other person. Under no circumstances would he go to town on the Sabbath except to attend worship, nor would he "engage in any sport, or noisy exercise," or "ride either on horse back, or in any vehicle." On a weekday evening he might attend a prayer meeting at the church, but he would be sure to be in his room within fifteen minutes after it closed, suppressing any understandable urge he might have to visit a family in town, especially one with an attractive, eligible daughter.

Our conscientious student, desiring to go home during a term to visit his family and friends, would first ask the president for the necessary permission; if for some good reason he wished to be absent from one class, he would first secure the professor's approval. Over the years an increasing number of students asked for and received permission to leave College several weeks before the close of the term; in the language of the time they would "anticipate" their last assignments by completing them in advance. A fairly steady stream of requests came from those who wished to depart near the middle of the session to take a teaching position. The faculty almost always granted these requests, although it sometimes warned a student that, upon his return to the campus, he might have to repeat the entire work of the current term.

Given the carefully prescribed rules and regulations which were in force, there were many ways in which a student might get himself into trouble. One of the promises which he made in his matriculation oath was to abstain "from disrespectful conduct towards my instructors and others." The honor, if such it be, of having been the first recorded College discipline case belongs to Josiah V. Hoshour

(1814-1896). On December 15, 1832 – the first matriculation day – he was summoned to appear before a special faculty meeting to explain the "letter of an improper character" which he had sent to Henry L. Baugher. The case was closed only after Hoshour explained the reasons for his missive and made the required "satisfactory acknowledgments."[111]

Although there are other instances of alleged "disrespectful conduct" toward faculty members, it was much more likely that a student would find himself in difficulty for violation of some other part of his matriculation oath, perhaps the promise to refrain from what was termed, without further definition, "all indecent, disorderly behavior."[112] He would step beyond the limits of acceptable conduct by attending a ball, dancing or cotillion party, dancing school, theatrical performance, circus, or billiard saloon.[113] Any student was courting trouble by leaving "the institution and without permission marching to the mountain under the real or feigned expectation of a riot among the Irish on the railroad" (1837); by going to the Mount St. Mary's commencement after being told not to, because of the questionable behavior of students who had attended in previous years (1838); by stealing, if that be the word for it, some of Mother Aughinbaugh's pies (1841)[114]; by helping to burn down one of the privies (1841, 1844, 1847)[115]; by staying overnight at a camp meeting – attending was acceptable, staying overnight was not (1844); by keeping a pistol in his room (1852); by attending a widely advertised Indian exhibition in town, "contrary to the expressed requirement of the Faculty," which was that he return to campus by 8:30 P.M. (1854); by being out of his room and in the belfry at a late hour on Christmas eve (1855); by leaving his room, after being denied permission to do so (1861); by being accused of stealing a horse (1864); by "firing off torpedoes in the building" (1865); and by playing cards (1867). Those students were also remiss who engaged in the activity which required the faculty to direct John Hopkins "to remove at once the offensive writings that deface the walls of the halls and some of the private rooms of the edifice." (1867)

---

[111]Hoshour was never graduated. He returned to York county, where he became a leading citizen of Glen Rock: merchant, surveyor, teacher, industrialist, banker, and churchman.

[112]For a brief discussion of the trouble experienced by John F. Wilken, the German professor, see p. 281n.

[113]The rule against attending "any political celebration" continued in force.

[114]For more on the pies, see Basil L. Crapster, "Rhetorick and Mince Pies," *Gettysburg College Bulletin* (October 1962), pp. 4-7.

[115]The rules carefully specified that a student would have to pay for any damage to College property which he had caused or which occurred in his room. All other damage caused by unknown persons was charged "to the whole community of Students."

Cases involving the use of alcoholic beverages came up from time to time and were always treated seriously. In 1860 one student found to be "under the influence of liquor" was required to "make an acknowledgement for his offense." Three years later seven students were warned that they would be dismissed if they visited a "drinking saloon" one more time. In the fall of 1866 the secretary entered into the minutes the names of seven students who entered a similar establishment and recorded that the faculty viewed their conduct "with disapprobation." In the mid-1850s the faculty was most angered at tavernkeepers who violated the law by selling alcoholic beverages to students. In 1856 they urged the trustees to institute a suit against such offenders and to seek additional state legislation on the subject. The early rules and regulations did no more than forbid students from unnecessarily visiting taverns. The version published in 1865 was much more explicit: "no student shall be permitted to use intoxicating liquor as a beverage; to frequent or unnecessarily visit any tavern or place of resort, at which intoxicating liquors are sold." The relatively few cases of immoral conduct which came before the faculty were dealt with in stern fashion. Within one week in April 1854 two students so charged were dismissed. One was told that he could not return, and he never did.

Although there were certainly many things students did which were in violation of some existing rule, but which never came to the attention of the faculty, the latter had ways of finding out what was going on, beyond the obvious disappearance of pies and the burning of privies. The College community was a small one and the professors took turns visiting student rooms at times of their own choosing. Equally important, they accepted as an indispensable part of their duty overseeing student conduct. In 1843, after reviewing the regulations governing behavior in the College building, they directed the president to read them to the students in chapel and to "inform them of the determination of the Faculty to enforce them." In 1856 they passed a resolution "that those students who manifest an unwillingness to be governed by the rules be requested to withdraw from the institution."

Sometimes the violator, or violators, of the accepted standards of behavior were so obvious that only the penalty remained to be assessed. More often, either the president or some designated faculty member would need to conduct an investigation, during the course of which the accused could expect to be summoned to appear before the faculty for a hearing. The judges in these cases had a wide range of penalties from which to choose. They could (and did) affectionately admonish; privately admonish; publicly admonish in a paternal manner; publicly admonish without qualification; and require satisfactory acknowledgments. In 1840 they promulgated a

We whose names are hereunto affix-
ed hereby ~~and~~ confess that we did wrong
in attending the Indian exhibition on
the night of the 3 Because we acted contrary to the expressed requirement of the Faculty, by remaining after
8½ o'clock I do ex-
press our sorrow for it.

É. H. Mc Sell   J. P. Robinson
C. D. Eichelberger   M. G. Stick
M. Hay   J. F. Warmpole
C. J. Trearly   H. R. Fleck
C. C. Riley   C. P. Muhlenberg
A. C. Gardner   Abraham L. Guss.
G. Mitchell

"We are heartily sorry for these, our offenses."
The students who in August 1854 did not leave the Indian exhibition in town and return to campus at the agreed-upon time were suspended until they appeared before the faculty and students in order to make the required *"satisfactory acknowledgments."* The handwriting of the text of the statement which they signed is that of President Baugher.

special set of punishments for what they considered lesser offenses. A College student might be required to study with the preparatory students; he might have to study in one of the professor's recitation rooms; he might be forbidden to go into town at any time without special permission; and, if his offense occurred in the dining room, he might have to take the seat to which the faculty directed him. Students in good standing were cautioned to avoid associating with those who were being disciplined.

For more serious offenses, which the faculty minutes sometimes called crimes, a student might be suspended for a week, a month, or the rest of the session. He might be dismissed for an indefinite period of time. Sometimes the order to depart resulted from an accumulation of failings which exhausted faculty patience. Between

1832 and 1868 many a parent or guardian was told simply to come and take a young man away. The minutes record a spectrum of reasons. He is incorrigible (1835). He is "unprofitable to himself and pernicious to others" (1835). He should leave, "as the Faculty has lost confidence in him" (1841). He has lost "the privileges of this institution" (1847). He is "sent home for repeated acts of wickedness" and the fact is to be announced to the students (1848). His offense is contumacy (1849, 1854, 1863). He "will be dismissed for the first violation of the rules," but his mother is told that "it would be better to remove John from the Institution" at once (1864). Two students are "advised to leave on account of their habitual absence from recitation and their rooms during hours of study" and the president is directed to "write at once to their Parents requiring them to remove them." (1865). His parent is "requested to remove him from the Institution on account of his repeated profanity" (1866).

The faculty could be expected to react quickly and vehemently whenever a group of students violated the rules and regulations. In June 1853 nine or more sophomores refused to attend classes. They were told that, if they did not return on the next day, they would be dismissed. At its next meeting, after they had gone back to class, the faculty resolved that they "cannot treat with any student so long as he is in rebellion against the authorities of the Institution" and, furthermore, that they "regard any thing like conspiracy among the students to defeat the discipline of the institution as one of the greatest offenses, that can be committed by them." The footnote came at the end of the term, when the faculty decided that notice should "be taken in the character bills of those Sophomores who participated in the rebellion of the class." When the members of the freshman class tried the same thing four years later, their actions generated the same response, and the faculty decided that, "the best scholars in the Freshman class having participated in the rebellion," there would be no awards to them from the recently established prize fund for their class.[116]

---

[116]There were three College prizes established by 1868. Between 1856 and 1861 a donor identified in the records only as a friend of the institution gave $500, the interest of which was awarded to the student who attained the highest rank in the freshman class. Until 1887 known simply as the Freshman Prize, in that year it was renamed the Muhlenberg Freshman Prize and credited to Professor Frederick A. Muhlenberg who, according to the contemporary records, was the intermediary in passing the gift from the donor to the College. The second prize was made possible by the 1866 gift of $250 by Major Charles W. Hassler, United States Navy. The interest was used to purchase a gold medal to be awarded to the most proficient student of the Latin language in the junior class. The third prize was established by John E. Graeff in 1866 and was named for him. This award went to the senior student who wrote the best essay on an assigned topic.

In September 1861, five months after the Civil War had begun, thirteen of the twenty-two seniors refused to deliver the commencement addresses which were required of them. Not only were they not awarded their diplomas, but they had to wait until the next session began for the first opportunity to make their amends. The faculty devised a statement for each one of them to sign, acknowledging his failings. Some members of the class of 1861 did not receive their diplomas for more than a year after they expected them. One did not comply with the faculty requirement until June 1871. The version of the matriculation oath which was published in 1865 included an additional provision, perhaps prompted by the experience of 1861: the promise to refrain "from all combinations to resist" the authority of the faculty.

The death rate in mid-nineteenth century America was much higher than it was in the twentieth. This may help to explain why the College publications usually referred to the parents or guardians of students. By the time many of them reached College, one or both of their parents had already died. The personal information which students gave when they signed the matriculation oath testifies to this fact. Students themselves were more likely not to survive their college years than those of later generations. Perhaps as many as twenty College and preparatory students died either at home or in Gettysburg between 1832 and 1868. In 1854, when the Evergreen cemetery in Gettysburg was organized, the College and seminary joined to buy a lot on which to bury students whose bodies, for some reason, were not to be sent home. Epidemics did not spare campuses. In January 1847 the students petitioned the faculty to suspend classes because there were numerous cases of typhoid fever in the seminary building and because three College students who were living there had already died. The faculty refused the request, but they did permit any student who wished to return home. The president issued a circular to the constituency, declaring that the College building was "unusually healthy," and that local physicians believed "there is no more healthy location in the United States" than Gettysburg. A similar response greeted what the minutes of the faculty called "the stampede of the students" which followed the discovery of one case of varioloid, a mild form of smallpox, in the College building in 1861.

Gettysburg students who attended two or more worship services every day of the week while they were in College were nevertheless not immune to the periodic religious revivals which swept many parts of the country in the mid-nineteenth century. Whenever the revival fever reached Adams county, members of the faculty believed strongly that it was their duty to encourage students to participate in the "religious" or "protracted" meetings which accompanied it. Sometimes these meetings were separate from the regular worship services, but on other occasions the latter appear to have been the forum in which the heightened religious feeling occurred. From time to time the College church, College chapel, and student rooms were all pressed into the service of the revivals.

There was no faculty meeting on February 1, 1837. The minute book records that "religious meetings" had been held for several days and were expected to continue. "The students especially professors of religion have been deeply impressed. Our prayer is that the Lord may continue to revive his work." In March 1840 "religious meetings" once more superseded the weekly faculty gathering. Years later Joseph B. Bittinger (1844) attributed this particular revival to the sudden death of a student, who "seemed a voice from the grave calling to repentance." Bittinger remembered the years 1842-1844 as "a revival season pretty wide-spread," during the course of which there were no "scenes" or anxious bench and everyone "maintained orderly deportment."[117] When Henry L. Baugher entered the minutes of the faculty meeting of January 24, 1849, he stated that no business had been transacted on that day, but then added: "the secy. avails himself of this occasion to record the fact that God has blessed the institution with a precious revival of religion by which both students and teachers have been greatly refreshed and many souls profess to have experienced a change of heart." The early months of 1854 were another period of "spiritual refreshing."

In 1866 and again in 1868 the faculty indicated their continuing support of revivals by excusing from class any students "under religious impressions" or "exercised in reference to their personal salvation during the religious meetings." Writing in 1882, Milton Valentine believed that these "many special seasons of religious awakening and numerous conversions" were worthy of both notice and praise, "on account of the large number of students who became Christians in connection with them and through their influence."[118] Nevertheless, not every parent was pleased by these "special seasons." In April 1868 an irate father from Reading wrote to Henry L. Baugher about his son, Daniel, who had informed him that during the revival then in progress he had been converted, without explaining "what he means by being converted." The father was adamant: "I peremptorily forbid him to join any church without my consent. I intend that he shall, after he is a few years older, join the Reformed church." If Daniel was taking any steps to join some other church, the father wanted Baugher to "put an immediate and

---

[117]*1882 History*, pp. 440-441.
[118]Ibid., p. 64.

effectual stop to it." The president died before he was able to answer this letter.[119]

Student Organizations

Faculty members of early and mid-nineteenth century American colleges promoted those student organizations which, if they could be sustained over a period of time, might advance the goals of the institution. In some cases, these organizations supplemented some particular curricular interest, such as science. In other cases, they were broader in purpose and scope. For example, many early and mid-nineteenth century colleges had two literary societies, to one or the other of which almost the entire student body belonged and whose interests might actually be wider than those of the curriculum itself. Dickinson had its Belles Lettres and Union Philosophical societies; Jefferson its Philo and Franklin; Washington its Union and Washington; Allegheny its Allegheny Literary and Philo-Franklin; and Marshall its Diagnothian and Goethean societies.

At Gettysburg, two literary societies were formed in the Gymnasium, even before the College came into existence. On February 4, 1831 Michael Jacobs and John H. Marsden called thirty-five students together in the academy building and explained the purposes which they had in mind. Marsden then took half of the students, those whose last names were at the beginning of the alphabet, and organized the Phrenakosmian Society. Jacobs took the other half, those who names were at the end of the alphabet, and organized the Philomathaean Society. Both Phrena and Philo, as they were called, were carried over into the College in 1832.

The first catalogue, issued in 1837, explained that these two societies, "besides the regular duties of the College of a similar character, furnish abundant opportunities to the Students for their improvement in composition and declamation." It is evident that the faculty intended that the programs of Phrena and Philo, carried on both independently and in direct competition with each other, should contribute in a major way to a student's education. Writing in the 1882 history, Luther H. Croll, a member of Philo and vice president of the College, argued that the goal of Jacobs and Marsden in 1831 was "to form literary societies whose generous rivalry would stimulate the members to mutual intellectual and moral im-

---

[119]Diary of Charles A. Hay, Adams County Historical Society. For a fuller treatment of student life, see Anna Jane Moyer, *The Way We Were: A History of Student Life at Gettysburg College, 1832-1982* (Gettysburg, 1982).

provement." At least as far as Philo was concerned, Croll thought, by 1882 more than 1,100 students had "received an important part of their education in this society, a training in the knowledge of men, and power to control them; in reading the thoughts of others, and so presenting the truth as to become the moulders of sentiment."[120]

Faculty members may have organized Phrena and Philo; they may have had high aspirations for both of them; but students ran the literary societies, with only occasional guidance and direction from the faculty and board. Students elected the members, both active and honorary. In 1835 the faculty ruled that preparatory students under twelve years of age could not join; in 1846 the age was increased to fifteen. Over the years the initiation fee grew from 50¢ to $5, which was fifteen percent of the annual tuition fee in the 1850s. Honorary members included College and seminary faculty (only they were eligible for election to both societies), local worthies, and such national figures as John Marshall, Andrew Jackson, Henry Clay, and Daniel Webster.

In 1831 the two societies agreed to maintain a certain balance in strength. When the membership of one was double that of the other, its rolls were closed until half of the difference was eliminated. Four years later, when a case involving Philo and a student was brought before the faculty, that body passed a series of resolutions applying to both societies. One of these required that "all the public performances of the students be submitted to the Faculty before they are presented to the public." Another required Philo and Phrena to exchange membership lists regularly and specified that when the membership of one exceeded that of the other by one-third, its rolls would be closed until full equality was reached. In 1836 the faculty required Philo to drop a new member because this regulation had not been obeyed. The society appealed in vain to the trustees to overrule the decision. In June 1857, giving as its reason the belief that "the ground is already covered by the existing societies," the faculty rejected a request for permission to form a third literary society.

---

[120]*1882 History*, pp. 112, 121. The minute book of the Phrenakosmian Society opens with the following statement: "The cultivation of the mind is not only the duty of every member of the community, but it is the desire also, of every one to improve the mind, that he may be useful in the society in which he may be placed. Guided and induced by a sense of duty, and moved by a desire to improve the mind; the students of the Gettysburg Gymnasium called a meeting on Friday evening – the 4th of February 1831, with a view to form a literary society. After a statement was given of the nature and effects of such societies by Mr. M. Jacobs and Rev. J. Marsden (teachers in the Gymnasium): It was resolved to form a literary society, the object of which is, to improve the mind."

When the College building was occupied in the fall of 1837, Philo and Phrena moved into temporary quarters on the second floor. After the interior was finished, the trustees assigned to Philo the large room at the east end of the fourth floor and to Phrena a similar room at the west end. Eventually frescoed, these were possibly the most elegant quarters in the entire building.

In 1840 the faculty set aside Wednesday afternoons as the time for the literary societies to meet. By means of essays, debates, and similar exercises, each member had ample opportunity to improve his skills in "composition and declamation." Those who did not perform their assigned tasks at these meetings were subject to fines. Several other activities soon became established parts of the program of Philo and Phrena. Each February from 1832 to 1849 they held anniversary celebrations. From 1833 to 1849 there were debate, essay, and other competitions. Both of these exercises ended when the officials of Christ Lutheran church, in which they were held, demanded compensation in advance for the out-of-pocket costs incurred in the use of their facilities. The students took their case to the board, which decided that the church was justified in asking to be paid, and in advance.[121] As early as 1844, each society contributed something to the events of commencement week, beginning in 1857 in alternate years. Many of the seemingly endless succession of speeches delivered on most of these occasions were published in pamphlet form, and both societies issued several printed catalogues, listing their members and giving other information about their activities.

Philo and Phrena had their own library collections. In 1839 the trustees granted each a library room on the north side of the fourth floor adjacent to their meeting halls. Later, as their holdings grew, they were given additional space. In the 1860s, after the steward system was abolished, each society was assigned a reading room on the ground floor of the building. Here its holdings of newspapers and periodicals were available for student use. In 1855 the College catalogue listed for the first time the size of the Philo (2,850 volumes) and Phrena (2,950 volumes) libraries. In that year there were but 3,000 volumes in the College library. In 1868 the figures were 4,850 volumes for Philo, 5,353 for Phrena, and 6,000 for the College library.

---

[121]When the literary societies declined to resume their contests, the faculty in 1850 established what came to be called the junior exhibition, in which all members of the class were required to deliver public orations. The first of these exhibitions was held in April 1851. It is evident by the numbers of petitions from students to be excused from this requirement that they would have preferred to see it abolished, but the junior exhibition lasted for many years beyond 1868.

A SALUTARY INFLUENCE

SEVENTEENTH ANNIVERSARY CELEBRATION

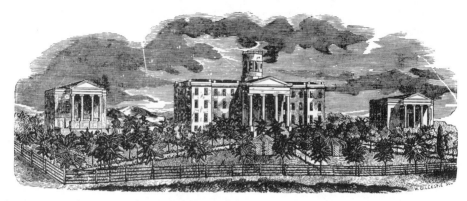

OF THE

PHILOMATHÆAN SOCIETY

OF PENNSYLVANIA COLLEGE.

Gettysburg, Feb. 18, 1848.

" Ἐὰν ᾖς Φιλομαθής, ἔσῃ πολυμαθής."

ORDER OF EXERCISES:

Music—"*Gabriella Waltz,*"—Strauss.

PRAYER ·························by Rev. J. Few Smith.

Music—"*The Bark before the Gale,*"—J. Willis.

ORATION—"Triumphs of Mind," ···························by P. Born, of Muncy, Pa.

Music—"*Yes, Brothers, Yes!*"—(Round,) G. H. Rodwell.

ORATION—"Confidence, the Mother of Great Deeds," ···········W. D. Roedel, of Lebanon, Pa.

Music—"*Desolate is thy Dwelling,*"—Calcott.

ORATION—"Napoleon at Waterloo," ························· A. W. Lilly, of Milton, Pa.

Music—*Miller's Maid,*"—(Quartette,) arranged by G. Hews.

ORATION—"The Despotism of Woman,"····················D. W. Badham, of Edenton, N. C.
Music—"*Ravel Polka,*"—M. Keller.

BENEDICTION ··········· ···········by Dr. Krauth.

Music—"*Lizzy Waltz,*"—Strauss.

☞ *Music by the "Haydn Association."*

[STAR OFFICE.]

Program for Philomathaean Celebration, 1848

162

In 1854 Philo applied to the Adams county court for a charter of incorporation, a move which prompted immediate and vigorous action from both faculty and trustees, who insisted that no student organization should enjoy corporate status. The trustees engaged legal counsel and the petition for a charter was denied. This episode appears not to have soured appreciably the relationship between the societies and the College authorities. In 1858 both faculty and trustees endorsed the plans of Philo and Phrena to erect a campus building to house their meeting rooms and libraries; as already noted, the College proposed that the intended structure be large enough to house its own library. The Civil War intervened and no such building was ever constructed. However, in 1868 the two literary societies were still strong and thriving College organizations, which could count almost all students as members.

A third important early student organization was the Linnaean Association, which was founded on June 8, 1844 by more than thirty students of the College and seminary. John G. Morris was elected president. The constitution which they adopted on that day described their purpose as follows:

> the advancement of Science in Pennsylvania College, by fostering among its members a spirit of investigation, and a love for the works of God. For this purpose, Zoological Specimens shall be collected, Minerals, Dried Plants, Fossils, Coins, Antiquities, and such Curiosities in general, as commonly constitute a Museum, and meetings, held for the delivery of Lectures, the reading of Essays, and the transaction of such business as shall promote the interest of the Association.

Named for the famed Swedish botanist Linnaeus (1707-1778), the society began its existence with a burst of activity in several directions. First, it secured from the faculty a scheduled hour on the calendar for its monthly meetings (Saturday at 10 A.M.), during which there were lectures, essays, and discussions on "Scientific and Philosophical Questions." Second, it used a small contribution from the trustees to purchase cases for its developing "cabinet." Third, it resolved to publish a monthly journal. Fourth, it named a committee to determine the feasibility of building a hall for the association's use. Fifth and finally, it resolved "to take under its special care the improvement of the grounds around the College edifice."

As with Philo and Phrena, there were two categories of membership in the Linnaean Association. College and seminary students were the active members. They paid an initiation fee of fifty cents and dues amounting to twenty-five cents per session. Most students then in College joined in 1844. Honorary members included Louis Agassiz, John James Audubon, George Bancroft, Lewis Cass, Vice

President George M. Dallas, Herman Haupt, Francis Lieber, Benjamin Silliman, and Daniel Webster, in addition to trustees and faculty, including those of the medical department in Philadelphia.

The first decade or so of the Linnaean Association was its period of greatest brilliance. Members assembled a commendable and sizable collection of specimens for their cabinet.[122] Between November 1844 and October 1848, when there were no longer sufficient funds to carry on, they published the monthly *Literary Record and Journal of the Linnaean Association of Pennsylvania College*. This publication included articles on scientific subjects by members of the College and medical school faculties. For example, Michael Jacobs wrote on Indian summer and Washington L. Atlee on the philosophy of storms. It also carried general College news, book reviews, and occasional literary works. In 1847, thanks in large measure to the association's efforts, Linnaean Hall was dedicated and put to use. As already noted, Linnaeans carried through with their resolve to improve the campus. In addition to all of this, between 1848 and 1860 they sponsored annual lectures, most of which were delivered during commencement week. They also developed a small library.

Writing in 1882, Milton Valentine concluded, quite correctly, that the "first years" of the Linnaean Association "were marked by enterprises which have left results of enduring benefit to the Institution." Nevertheless, from a vantage point a third of a century later he had to say that "the association has met with great variations in its success." He noted that "at times great zeal and activity appeared among the membership," but that "at other times no interest was taken."[123] The first revival of the society occurred when Martin L. Stoever became president in 1851, succeeding Morris, whose many other commitments left him little time to devote to the Linnaeans. Soon after Stoever resigned in 1862, the society ceased functioning. Its brief resuscitation in the later 1870s will be discussed in the next chapter.[124]

---

[122]In 1861 the first historians of the society wrote that "in their delving amid rock, digging among roots, poring over antiquities, chasing butterflies, hunting birds, torturing bugs, in short, declaring war against all the inhabitants of air, earth and sea, and confiscating everything within reach, it were indeed strange had nothing been accomplished." *Sketch of the Linnaean Association of Pennsylvania College, . . .* (Gettysburg, 1861), p. 4.

[123]*1882 History*, pp. 125-126.

[124]The feeble condition of the Linnaean Association may have been responsible for the rule included in the 1865 regulations that "if any society of students shall, at any time, be dissolved, the books, apparatus and furniture shall become the property of the College."

Although no student organizations which appeared in Gettysburg before 1868 rivaled Philo, Phrena, and Linnaean in importance or longevity, there were several others which deserve mention. A German society formed in 1836 dissolved five years later, entrusting its small library and treasury to the faculty. When Charles F. Schaeffer became professor of German in 1856, he revived the organization, but it lapsed again with his departure for Philadelphia in 1864. Undaunted by this record, the faculty in 1867 authorized the students to try again.

In the fall of 1837 a few students organized the Athanaeum Society of Pennsylvania College, for the purpose of purchasing periodicals and other publications for student use. Having quickly exhausted their treasury before meeting all of their commitments, they turned in April 1838 to the board of trustees for help. "By granting the donation solicited, you will not only enable us to discharge all our debts, and place the society on a firm basis," they wrote, "but likewise enable us to sustain our association which we think ought to exist in the institution under your direction, as well as every other literary and Scientific institution."[125] The board gave the society $30, but warned that it "cannot continue such appropriations." The society soon disappears from the records.

There are passing references to several early musical organizations, among them the Euterpean Society (1830s) and the Glee Club (1859). Among the other shortlived organizations were an anti-tobacco society (1830s); a temperance society (1840s); a Bible society, in conjunction with seminary students (1850s); and a missionary society (1860s). The College branch of the Young Men's Christian Association, organized in 1867, will be discussed in the next chapter.

Social fraternities began making their appearance in American colleges in large numbers by the 1830s and 1840s. Unlike other student organizations, these were secret societies which neither trustees nor faculties had helped to organize or had in any way sanctioned. Most college authorities could not see that these organizations were serving any useful purposes. Consequently, many of them tried to eliminate fraternities from their institutions. Some required students to sign promises not to join secret societies. Some required faculty members to pledge that they would not participate in any way in their activities.[126] Nevertheless, the fraternities continued to exist, indeed to thrive.

---

[125]Petition of the Athanaeum Society, April 17, 1838, GCA. Between 1824 and 1837 Jefferson College had an Athanaeum or Athenian Society with the same purpose. Its holdings were incorporated into the college library. Coleman, *Banners in the Wilderness*, p. 173.

[126]Rudolph, *American College*, pp. 144-150; Sack, *Higher Education*, pp. 713-715.

By 1868, five fraternity chapters had been instituted at Gettysburg College: Phi Kappa Psi (1855), Phi Gamma Delta (1858), Zeta Psi (1861), Sigma Chi (1863), and Chi Phi (1867). All of the five charter members of Phi Kappa Psi were seniors who were graduated in 1856, when they first made known the existence of their organization. Four of these members were twenty-six years of age or older. One was valedictorian of his class; a second was chosen to deliver the Latin salutatory; and a third, to deliver the Greek oration. Three became pastors and two, lawyers.

The faculty and trustee minutes before 1868 contain few references to the fraternities. In 1862 the faculty denied the request of a member of Phi Kappa Psi to be absent for two or three days, on the grounds that "the regulations of the Institution will not allow absence for the reason assigned, viz., to attend a Convention of a Secret Association." Two years later, when a student went to a similar meeting without first getting leave to do so, he found himself in serious trouble upon returning to the campus. In June 1864 the faculty suspended him indefinitely for absenting "himself without permission in obedience to a secret association, and in violation of the rules of the College." On the next day the faculty relented, but only after the student appeared before the body; "manifested penitence;" agreed "not to commit a similar offense;" and consented, "after a season of probation," to be rematriculated.

Two months later, in their report to the board of trustees, the faculty recommended that the matriculation oath be amended to include a promise by a student that he would not join a secret society while enrolled in the College. They gave as the reason for this request their belief that "these associations lead in various ways to the violations of the rules of the Institution" and cited the recent "case of conflict" involving one of them.[127] With a nice sense of the established polity of the College, the trustees resolved "that the matter of suppressing Secret Societies be left to the discretion of the Faculty." Exercising that discretion, the latter decided, after all, not to deal with the problem by changing the matriculation oath. Instead, they included among the rules and regulations published in 1865 one calling for the immediate dismissal of any student "who shall join or countenance any combination, which has a tendency to create opposition to the discipline of the Institution, either by making promises of secrecy or otherwise."

---

[127]Faculty Report, August 11, 1864, GCA.

Class of 1868
By the time this class was graduated, students had firmly established the
tradition that graduating seniors should have their pictures taken by a local
photographer and that, in some form, they should appear together.

Alumni Association

The Alumni Association of Pennsylvania College was organized on commencement day, September 16, 1835. There were eleven initial members, the graduates of 1834 and 1835. Ezra Keller (1835) was the first president. The constitution which was adopted in 1838 defined the purposes of the association as follows: "the cultivation of friendly and social feelings among its members, the advancement of the cause of education and literature, and the promotion of the best interests of the *Alma Mater*." Since most of the early presidents served one-year terms, it was left to two other officers to provide the continuity so needed if the organization were to survive. Martin L.

Stoever was secretary from 1842 until his death in 1870, during which time he went out of his way to keep in close touch with the growing body of alumni. No one knew as many of them as he did. Henry J. Fahnestock (1844), of Gettysburg, was treasurer from 1850 until 1886. Beginning in 1835, the alumni association met annually during commencement week, in almost every year contributing one more address to the speech-filled climax of the academic year.

The routine business of the annual meetings included receiving into membership the most recent graduates, adopting resolutions memorializing deceased alumni (many of whom died in their twenties or thirties), ordering the publication of the current year's alumni address, and electing next year's speaker (a complicated procedure because the first choice frequently declined and it had to be left to a committee to find a replacement, sometimes at the last minute). As early as 1844, the association began discussing the financial needs of the College. It then adopted a lengthy report calling upon all alumni to join in purchasing a telescope, books for the library, and specimens for the cabinet. It urged them to pledge an amount payable over a period of five years and to encourage many other friends of the College to do the same. Little came of this effort, which was undertaken during the hard times of the 1840s. In 1859, when the College was engaged in an endowment campaign, the association voted to raise $15,000 to establish an alumni professorship. By 1868 it had secured more than $7,000 in pledges. Of this amount, about $3,200 had actually been paid to the College treasurer.

One of the major activities of the Alumni Association was trying to keep track of what was happening to its members. On two occasions, in 1860 and 1870, committees published the comprehensive reports which they had compiled and submitted to the annual meeting. The later of these reports showed that of 455 graduates in the classes of 1834-1870, 390 were still alive. Of the larger number, 231 (about one-half) had entered the ministry, 57 were lawyers, and 33 were physicians. About three-fourths of the total number were or had been residents of Pennsylvania (281) or Maryland (53). About fourteen percent were or had been residents of New York (17), Virginia (16), Illinois (15), or Ohio (15). The rest were scattered among sixteen other states, the District of Columbia, Canada, India, and Ireland.

By 1870, at least seven alumni were or had been college or seminary presidents: David F. Bittle (1835), Roanoke; Ezra Keller (1835), Wittenberg; Theophilus Stork (1835), Newberry; James A. Brown (1842), Lutheran Theological Seminary, Gettysburg; Daniel H. Bittle (1843), North Carolina; Josiah P. Smeltzer (1846), Newberry;

and Milton Valentine (1850), Gettysburg.[128] Samuel Sprecher, who had attended both Gymnasium and College but was not graduated, succeeded Keller as president of Wittenberg College. Both Simeon W. Harkey and Francis Springer, who were students in the Gymnasium but not the College, were presidents of Illinois State University, the predecessor of Carthage College.[129]

Town and Gown

In the mid-nineteenth century there were built-in tensions between the residents of college towns and the students who lived in college buildings, even those described as being located a short distance from the village. Most townspeople had only a minimal formal education; they had to earn their living by using their wits and by hard physical labor. In an era of increasing political equality in the United States and of decreasing deference to one's betters, many townsmen were tempted to look upon college students as a highly privileged, if not aristocratic, group. This was true even for those young men who were preparing to enter the generally respected professions of the ministry, law, and medicine. As the letters written to the Gettysburg editors in 1833 and 1834 eloquently testify, some Adams countians regarded college students with a mixture of envy and resentment. There is reason to believe that much of this sentiment remained a third of a century later.

For their part, some students were exuberant young men only too ready at times to burst out of what they considered to be the stultifying confines of the well-regulated college family and play their pranks. They might reserve for afterwards any careful thinking about the consequences of their actions. Whether or not while they were at home they took seriously the rights of others to enjoy their property and their peace of mind, students sometimes forgot to respect these rights while they were in college.

Probably it would be correct to say that, between 1832 and 1868, the people of the borough of Gettysburg and the members of the College within its limits got along about as well as could be expected, it not better than could be expected, given the tensions

---

[128]North Carolina College was located at Mount Pleasant. Henry Ziegler (1841) was theological professor of the Missionary Institute at Selinsgrove for many years, but did not have the title of president.

[129]The material in the two preceding paragraphs has been taken from *Decennial Report Made to the Alumni Association of Pennsylvania College, . . .* (Gettysburg, 1871). Both 1860 and 1870 reports listed known alumni publications. In 1862 the faculty set aside an alcove in the library for such writings and issued an appeal for the authors to send in copies.

which their respective positions generated. Neither board and faculty minutes nor the three local newspapers yield much evidence of any serious or long-continuing differences between town and gown. After all, Gettysburg had a long tradition of interest in education, going back to the school conducted by Alexander Dobbin and the Gettysburg Academy. In 1826 the community raised what must be regarded as a large sum of money for that time to attract the seminary to locate in its midst. The resident trustees who played so important a role in the government of the College during this period were influential townspeople who were at the same time among the firmest and most consistent of its supporters.

When the board of trustees met in September 1854, its members listened to a generally pessimistic report from the faculty. At a time when national wealth and population were increasing, the professors wanted to know, why was the College making no progress at all, either in increasing its endowment or its enrollment? Perhaps, they thought, "another set of men" could "carry forward the operations of the Institution with more vigor and success." As a closely related matter, they urged the trustees "to discuss and settle" the "recently agitated" question of whether the College should be moved to another place where the prospects for its success might be greater.[130] When the subject of relocation was brought before the trustees for debate and action, John B. McPherson introduced the following resolutions:

> Resolved, That we consider it important that this question be now definitely settled.
> Resolved. That we can see no good reason for the removal, but that it would be a breach of faith and unjust to the people of Adams county, who contributed largely of their means to procure the location of the Theological and Literary Institutions here.
> Resolved, That any want of success is not to be found in the location of the College, but may be found elsewhere.

What the minutes describe as "a protracted discussion" now followed. Aware that the question of moving the College was coming before them, the resident trustees sent to Lancaster for Thaddeus Stevens, who responded by attending his first board meeting in six years and only the second since he had moved to Lancaster in 1842. Using his well-known and often feared talents for invective and sarcasm, Stevens took the lead in closely questioning, indeed in browbeating, those who opposed McPherson's resolutions

---

[130]Faculty Report, September 21, 1854, GCA.

and in denouncing the proposal to move the College from Gettysburg.[131] In the voting that followed, the resident trustees (Samuel Fahnestock, Samuel H. Buehler, Robert G. Harper, Moses McClean, Henry S. Huber, John B. McPherson, and David A. Buehler) contributed seven of the ten affirmative votes which the resolution received. John G. Morris, Benjamin Keller, and Thaddeus Stevens cast the other three. The four negative votes were those of Benjamin Kurtz, Charles P. Krauth, Henry L. Baugher, and Samuel Simon Schmucker.[132]

Townspeople were aware of the benefits of having a "literary and scientific institution" in their midst. There were few years without local students in the preparatory department or the College. It was sometimes possible for local residents to take a course offered by Michael Jacobs or some other instructor. There were always a few students who provided an income for townspeople offering room and board. Faculty members not only lived in town, but also contributed to its life in many ways. William M. Reynolds was elected secretary of the Adams County Antislavery Society when it was organized in 1836. Henry L. Baugher was one of the ardent supporters of the local temperance movement. Several faculty and trustees were directors of Evergreen cemetery when it was founded in 1853-1854. The weather observations of Michael Jacobs were published in the weekly newspaper. Having urged the community to introduce gas for lighting, he was one of the incorporators of the Gettysburg Gas Company and was elected president when it was organized in 1860. Frederick A. Muhlenberg was a fellow-incorporator and also one of the first managers of the company. Faculty members were often called upon to give addresses in town.

Among other places, people from the town and campus met in the drug stores of Samuel Buehler, his son Alexander, or Henry S.

---

[131]In an obituary of Schmucker, George Diehl describes how Stevens questioned Baugher, Schmucker, and Benjamin Kurtz on this occasion. Kurtz said that he had always opposed Gettysburg as the location for the College and would support any proposal to move it which had a chance of success. According to Diehl, Kurtz met the invective and sarcasm of Stevens with some of his own. When Stevens quoted Juvenal, Kurtz quoted Horace. When Stevens quoted the Bible, so did Kurtz. "Whatever weapon Stevens would try," Diehl wrote, "Kurtz would seize the same, and wield it with an arm equally powerful and equally skillful in giving and parrying blows." The "keenest intellectual gladiature ever witnessed in Pennsylvania College" continued for more than an hour. G. Diehl, "Dr. S. S. Schmucker," *Quarterly Review* 4 (1874): 45-47.

[132]In September 1854 the seminary trustees also rejected a proposal to relocate that institution. According to a communication, from an unidentified source, which appeared in the *Lutheran Observer* for September 22, 1854, the "principal ground taken in favor of removal is want of easy access to Gettysburg-fourteen miles of staging must be endured." This writer thought railroads might be necessary for businessmen, but not for students.

Huber, all of whom were trustees of the College. Many were the occasions on which the faculty adjourned classes for part or all of the day to enable both them and the students to join the community in some event: memorial services for the Marquis de Lafayette (1834), cornerstone laying for St. James Lutheran church (1848), memorial services for Henry Clay (1852), formal opening of Evergreen cemetery (1854), the arrival of the first train (1858), dedication of Soldiers' National Cemetery (1863), and dedication of Soldiers' Orphans' home (1866). Most of the churches in town usually joined the College late in February in holding services on the annual day of prayer for colleges. In 1853 the trustees purchased $1,000 worth of stock in the Gettysburg railroad, and four years later, as the track approached the town, dutifully loaned the College level to the engineer in charge of construction.[133]

Despite generally good relations, the faculty were not without their grievances against the community. As early as 1840 they expressed the fear that the townspeople who were using the ball-alley were going to damage it. More seriously, in reporting to the board in 1854 that several students had been dismissed for immoral conduct, they argued that "much of the lewdness . . . has grown out of the visits of persons from Town to the college at unseasonable hours over whom the Faculty have no control and against whom they can bring no legal process." Four years later, they lamented to the trustees that "there seems to be no adequate protection against rude persons of both sexes who enter the campus and take away whatever it pleases them to take." The best way to deal with the problem, they concluded, was to enclose the campus "within a high and strong fence."[134]

One of the faculty's major grievances, already discussed, arose from the practice of some tavernkeepers who sold alcoholic beverages to students, most of whom had not yet reached their majority. Another resulted from the persistent refusal of the borough council to pay much attention to the condition of the walks leading from the campus into town. On at least six occasions between 1852 and 1867 the faculty requested the town fathers to do

---

[133]The interest of the College in the railroad was not entirely the result of public spirit. As noted earlier, lack of rail connections was one reason given for wanting to move both College and seminary in 1854. The 1859 College catalogue, printed only months after rail service was begun, announced that Gettysburg was now in "direct communication with Philadelphia, Baltimore, Pittsburg and other prominent points." Actually, the communication was much more indirect than this statement would lead the uncritical reader to believe. Concerned about the high cost of firewood, the faculty in the early spring of 1858 were hoping that the rail service to Gettysburg would enable the College to convert to a cheaper fuel: coal.

[134]Faculty Reports, April 1854 and September 1858, GCA.

what its members considered to be the borough's duty, but there was little response. In February 1862 an unidentified correspondent told the *Sentinel* that "if the Faculty and Students of Pennsylvania College are found submerged, one of these days, in the mud between" town and campus, "we do not suppose that either the Town Council or the citizens would endeavor to extricate them: for their skulls would make a better pavement than the present one." Both property owners and council members would thus be saved the trouble and expense "of doing their duty, and carrying out the laws." Finally, in 1867, the town fathers took action to have a sidewalk constructed from the railroad to the College grounds.

The College and the Lutheran Church

It is true that the College charter of 1832 made no reference whatsoever to the Lutheran church, and that it contained the statement forbidding discrimination on religious grounds which could be found in almost every similar grant made by the state legislature since 1783. It is true that the board of trustees offered the presidency of the College to a non-Lutheran in 1833. It is also true that, in November of that year, eight trustees, in an address to the citizens of Adams county, declared that while the seminary "belongs to one religious denomination alone," the "College is the property of all denominations." And yet, at the same time, it is equally true that Samuel Simon Schmucker was an accurate prophet in 1831 when he told some of his fellow-townsmen that the College would be "prevailingly under Lutheran influence and control."

The evidence for the latter statement is convincing. Most of the trustees before 1868 were Lutheran. This is not surprising. The large majority of the patrons who chose many of them were members of that church. In fact, most of the resident trustees whom they named after 1832, including Samuel Fahnestock, the Buehlers, David Gilbert, and Henry S. Huber, were or became members of the College church. After the board of trustees became a self-perpetuating body, its members usually filled vacancies with members of their own faith. Both Charles P. Krauth and Henry L. Baugher were Lutheran pastors; the first non-Lutheran chief executive was elected only in 1956. Most faculty members before 1868 were not only Lutheran pastors, but also churchmen who participated actively in the affairs of congregations and synods. For example, Henry L. Baugher was corresponding secretary of the Parent Education Society of the General Synod for more than thirty years (1835-1868). This organization was established to help poor young men prepare for the Lutheran ministry. Michael Jacobs was secretary of the General Synod (1845-1848) as well as treasurer (1846-1849, 1853-1856, 1859-1862) and president (1849-1852) of the West Pennsylvania Synod. Martin L. Stoever, a layman, was secretary of the General Synod (1857-1866), treasurer of the Parent Education Society (1853-1870), and editor of the *Evangelical Review* (1857-1870). More than three-fourths of the students enrolled in the College before 1868 were from Lutheran families. While they were on campus, virtually all students attended Sunday services in a Lutheran church. At the same time, although the instruction in the College had a decidedly religious cast, there is no reason to believe that it was anything other than unsectarian, as Schmucker promised in 1831 it would be.[135]

Although, as was the case with most other American colleges which were in operation during this period, Gettysburg trustees were not chosen by any church body, the Lutheran synods from whose territory most of her students came soon began to consider her in a very real sense their college.[136] The minutes of their annual meetings contain frequent references to "our institutions at Gettysburg," meaning both seminary and college.[137] The successive editors of the *Lutheran Observer* consistently advanced the cause of both of these institutions and urged their readers to support them.[138] Long before 1868, many men who had attended first the College and then the seminary had become pastors of congregations. Most of them looked upon the College as an institution of the Lutheran church and worthy of the consideration which that standing warranted.

---

[135]For a treatment of the church-college relationship as it affected Gettysburg College, see Harold A. Dunkelberger, *Gettysburg College and the Lutheran Connection: An Open-Ended Story of a Proud Relationship* (Gettysburg, 1975).

[136]In the 1850s the College sent catalogues to pastors in the following Lutheran synods (the dates given are those of synodical organization): Pennsylvania (1748), Maryland (1820), West Pennsylvania (1825), Virginia (1829), Allegheny or Alleghany (1842), East Pennsylvania (1842), and Pittsburgh (1845). At the time these synods, which brought together most Lutheran pastors and congregations in three states, were the College's normal Lutheran constituency. By 1868 the founding of Roanoke College at Roanoke (1853), Missionary Institute at Selinsgrove (1858), the Lutheran Theological Seminary at Philadelphia (1864), and Muhlenberg College at Allentown (1867) had narrowed that constituency to central and western Pennsylvania and Maryland. In central Pennsylvania it overlapped that of Missionary Institute.

[137]Although the seminary and College were always recognized as separate and distinct institutions by those who were familiar with them, the relations between the two during this period were very close. They shared some of the same trustees and faculty. College students lived and ate in the seminary building. The schools coordinated their end-of-the-year activity. An increasing number of Lutheran pastors were graduates of both.

[138]Benjamin Kurtz was editor of the *Lutheran Observer* from 1833 to 1858 and again in 1861-1862. Frederick W. Conrad was editor from 1862 to 1898.

Although the catalogue nowhere proclaimed the fact, it is evident that most of the trustees, faculty, and alumni also considered the College a Lutheran institution. At no time was this clearer than during the hard years of the 1840s, when the College desperately needed money. Less than a week after the board meeting in April 1844, David Gilbert wrote a letter which appeared in the *Lutheran Observer* for May 3 of that year. After reviewing the plans to liquidate the College debt and increase the library as well as the "philosophical and chemical apparatus," Gilbert explained that both president and faculty were giving up their vacations in an effort to raise the necessary money. Observing that the College had for more than a decade relied on tuition income and state aid (the latter recently withdrawn), he stated that now, for the first time, it was turning to the church and the general community for assistance. "Will not the Evangelical Lutheran church, especially, come forward," he asked, "and do for her single – only, College" what many other denominations have been doing for their colleges from the time they were founded? Although "much might be said in regard to the immense good which this College has accomplished for the church, as well as what may be expected from it in time to come," Gilbert hoped that the announcement of the need would itself be enough to call forth the desired response.[139]

Five years later, in the spring of 1849, when the financial situation of the College was still precarious, the faculty tried its hand at cultivating one of its key constituencies by means of a letter addressed to many Lutheran ministers. "Pennsylvania College, at Gettysburg, has grown out of the necessities of the Lutheran Church," they argued:

> Thus far it has been sustained chiefly by students from the Lutheran Church. Its Faculty belong to the Lutheran Church, and its Boards of Trustees and Patrons are controlled by the Ministers and Members of the same Church. It may then with truth be said to belong to that Church. It may be added that it will continue to exist only so long as the Ministers and Members of the Church shall defend it from the false aspersions of enemies and support it by sending Students to its halls.

As might have been expected, these two letters in and of themselves yielded few dollars and few students. Nevertheless, they are important in illustrating the arguments which responsible representatives of the College advanced in presenting the claims of

---

[139]The committee which the Alumni Association appointed in August 1844 to propose a plan to aid the College described it as "the first Literary Institution sustained principally by Germans, that has survived an ephemeral existence, having the support of the largest German Church in this country and situated in the heart of Pennsylvania." Minutes of the Alumni Association, September 18, 1844, GCA.

the institution to the Lutheran church. About this time they began sending copies of the catalogue each year to the pastors in the several synods which they considered to be part of the College constituency.

In the 1850s two separate but related developments provided the first legal ties between Gettysburg College and the Lutheran church. The first of these followed from the act of April 19, 1850, which resulted in the organization of Franklin and Marshall College and in the transfer of the Lutheran interest in Franklin College to Gettysburg. The act vested in the Synod of Pennsylvania the power to nominate candidates for the Franklin professorship after the first incumbent had completed his tenure. A few years later, the College entered into an agreement with the same synod, authorizing it to nominate candidates for the German professorship which the synod had endowed. Charles F. Schaeffer, the first German professor, served until 1864. Frederick A. Muhlenberg, the first Franklin professor, resigned from the faculty in 1867. When the time came to choose their successors, changed conditions in the Lutheran church had created problems for the synod and the College which few people would have predicted a decade and a half earlier. These will be discussed in the next chapter.

For several decades after the seminary in Gettysburg was established in 1826, Samuel Simon Schmucker was the most influential Lutheran in the United States. As a theological professor and prolific author, he was able to influence a large number of young men as they prepared themselves to devote the rest of their lives to the Lutheran ministry. A leading pastor in the General Synod and the West Pennsylvania Synod, he was able to convince many of their pastoral and lay members that the numerous causes which he advocated from time to time promoted the best interests of their church and of Christianity in general.

It is clear that Schmucker was convinced that the Lutheran church in this country should participate fully in the movements which were occurring in American Protestantism and not necessarily hold to positions adopted in sixteenth century Europe. Although prepared to subscribe to the Unaltered Augsburg Confession as a "substantially correct" statement of Lutheran belief, Schmucker argued that it contained outmoded and even erroneous provisions which should be repudiated. He was inclined to favor revivals and prayer meetings; advocated strict Sabbath observance and temperance; and opposed slavery. He was committed to the use of the English language and essentially nonliturgical worship services. Schmucker maintained that Lutherans should cooperate with members of other denominations in promoting Sunday schools, distribution of Bibles and religious tracts, and home and foreign missions. In 1846 he

Samuel Simon Schmucker
This picture appeared in the 1882 College history and shows the chief founder of the College near the end of his life.

traveled to London to attend the organizational meeting of the World Evangelical Alliance, whose purpose was to explore the possibility of closer relations among the world's Protestants. In the fall of 1849 he stated his convictions in a series of articles published in the *Lutheran Observer* under the title "American Lutheranism." These were followed two years later by the first edition of *The American Lutheran Church, Historically, Doctrinally, and Practically Delineated, . . .* (Philadelphia, 1851).

Even during his years of greatest influence, Schmucker encountered opposition from other Lutherans who believed that he was straying too far from a proper orthodox position. After about 1850 the dissenters became more numerous and vocal. Some of them, including John G. Morris, Charles P. Krauth, and Michael Jacobs, were men who had worked closely with him in founding and supporting the seminary and College, but who now were beginning to affirm their commitment to the Augsburg Confession as it stood and to champion those things which set the Lutheran church apart from other denominations rather than those which it might have in common with them. These men found allies in the growing number of Lutherans recently arrived in the United States from Germany and Scandinavia.

In 1855, at the urging of several of his supporters, Schmucker published his *Definite [Synodical] Platform, Doctrinal and Disciplinarian, for Evangelical Lutheran District Synods*. Each minister of the General Synod received a copy of this anonymous pamphlet, whose author was soon identified. In this work, Schmucker reaffirmed his commitment to American Lutheranism. Stressing the authority of the Bible rather than that of long and detailed creeds or confessions, he identified errors in several of the Lutherans symbols and proposed a simpler doctrinal statement for synods to adopt. Within a short time, most synods either rejected or sidestepped his proposal and almost all of his ministerial friends deserted him. One of the few who did not was Benjamin Kurtz, who in 1857 led a shortlived secession from the Maryland Synod and in the following year was instrumental in organizing the Missionary Institute of the Evangelical Lutheran Church at Selinsgrove. Kurtz intended this institution, which became Susquehanna University in 1895, as an alternative to the College and seminary at Gettysburg rather than a counter to them. Revivalist that he was, he wanted to found a school in which older men, presumably also revivalists at heart, could be prepared for the ministry, in less time than it took to complete the courses in the College and seminary at Gettysburg.[140]

After thirty-eight years as a seminary professor, Schmucker retired in 1864. His last years at Gettysburg were spent surrounded by associates who had repudiated his position and who were directing the seminary toward a definitely more conservative, confessional Lutheran position. Despite this development, the leaders of the large Synod of Pennsylvania had lost confidence in both of the institutions at Gettysburg to such an extent that in 1864 they organized their own seminary at Philadelphia. In that year Charles F. Schaeffer resigned his position as German professor at Gettysburg to join the faculty of the new seminary as professor and chairman. In August 1865 a committee from the Synod of Pennsylvania met with the Gettysburg trustees and proposed that the

---

[140]For a discussion of Schmucker and American Lutheranism, see Wentz, *Schmucker*, pp. 169-242. Kurtz's determination to have a separate theological seminary to train older men for the ministry recalls one of the arguments advanced for the Gettysburg Classical School. See p. 26.

College be moved to Allentown.[141] After a long discussion the board declared – as it had eleven years earlier – that it "cannot perceive any sufficient reasons for removing the College from Gettysburg." In its report to the synod later, the committee stated that the Gettysburg trustees "acknowledged the necessity of a Lutheran College in the eastern part of Pennsylvania" and "advised the committee to proceed" with plans to establish their own institution in Allentown, extending "their best wishes for success."[142] After serving for seventeen years as Franklin Professor at Gettysburg, Frederick A. Muhlenberg resigned in 1867 to become the first president of Muhlenberg College in Allentown. In his inaugural address, he gave this explanation of why the German Lutherans of eastern Pennsylvania needed a college of their own:

> Our population is large, and rapidly becoming anglicized, and the distance to Gettysburg, the seat of Pennsylvania College, from the centre of our population, as well as its difficulty of access, have been felt by many of us to be serious objections to it as a place of education for our students. We had doubts of its appropriateness from the very beginning, but our necessities urged us to assent to the arrangement, with the hope of its ultimate removal. That these considerations had much to sustain them, we can readily believe, from the present condition of things in Pennsylvania College. Though the institution had a larger number on its catalogue this year than it ever had, there are but twenty-five students receiving instruction there from our territory; and during the previous stages of its history the number has been still less. It is scarcely necessary for me to remind you how inadequate a representation this is for our great Synod of fifty thousand communicants. It allows us but one college student for every two thousand communicants. Such a small attendance of our young men will never develop our church in Eastern Pennsylvania, as the necessities of the case require.[143]

---

[141]Three members of the Pennsylvania Synod asked the Harrisburg endowment convention in October 1864 to consider moving Gettysburg College to eastern Pennsylvania, specifically to Allentown. The convention declined to discuss the matter, deeming it "foreign to its purpose, hence its consideration inexpedient." *Lutheran Observer,* October 28, 1864.

[142]*Minutes of the Pennsylvania Synod* (1867), p. 29.

[143]*Muhlenberg College. A Quarter-Centennial Memorial Volume,* . . . , ed. S. E. Ochsenford (Allentown, 1892), pp. 65-66. Henry Eyster Jacobs claimed that Muhlenberg took with him to Allentown "probably thirty students as a nucleus for the classes at the new College." The actual number was probably much smaller. The total Gettysburg enrollment for both 1866-1867 and 1867-1868 was 195. Some students from eastern Pennsylvania remained in Gettysburg and were graduated there. Jacobs, *Memoirs,* p. 101.

In the World of Higher Education

Although in 1832 there were virtually no educational associations or journals in existence to coordinate the efforts of separate institutions and keep them informed of what was happening in American higher education, the founders of Gettysburg College were aware that theirs was but one in a growing company of colleges of the liberal arts and sciences. They had a lively sense of the need to strive to make theirs one of the very best in that company. Writing in the *Lutheran Observer* on May 1, 1832, less than one month after the charter was granted, John G. Morris predicted that the new college would "afford literary advantages equal to any similar institution in the country." Its faculty and other resources would be superior in quality. "We do not despair of success in our enterprize," he wrote, "but expect in a very short time to see Gettysburg the Cambridge of Pennsylvania, with its academic halls crowded with orderly and diligent students." Beginning in the 1840s, when friends of the College were looking for new sources of financial support, they often used other colleges as models worthy of emulation. "Had not the Alumni of Yale and Princeton at an early period united in their power and influence, in sustaining those institutions," a committee of the Alumni Association argued in 1844, "it is highly probable they would never have risen to their present eminence." The committee was certain that "the sons of Pennsylvania College" would "not be less grateful or less zealous than others in advancing the interests of their *Mother.*"[144] Frederick W. Conrad used the columns of the *Lutheran Observer* for August 25, 1865 to remind the friends of Gettysburg that Eliphalet Nott, Asa Packer, and Ezra Cornell had given at least $500,000 to Union, Lehigh, and Cornell, respectively.

It is clear that the College curriculum of 1832 was a development and expansion of the course of study in the classical school and Gymnasium, rather than the result of consultation with faculty members in older colleges in Pennsylvania or elsewhere. At a time of general curricular stability in American higher education, Michael Jacobs, Henry L. Baugher, and their associates drew upon their own experiences in other colleges when they designed the first Gettysburg courses, as they had when they organized two literary societies in the Gymnasium in 1831. In later years, members of the faculty did sometimes confer with colleagues in other schools when they were contemplating changes in or additions to their program. Charles F. Schaeffer told the Synod of Pennsylvania in 1856 that, before assuming his duties as German professor, he had engaged in

---

[144]Minutes of the Alumni Association, September 18, 1844, GCA.

"extended consultation with various experienced teachers" concerning an appropriate course of instruction.[145] Ten years later, while the preparatory department was being reorganized, the board of trustees instructed Charles J. Ehrehart "to visit several of the best schools of this class, inspect the arrangements, and furnish the [preparatory department] Committee with such information as may thus be acquired."

The faculty supported a number of early efforts to bring together representatives from many colleges for mutual benefit. For example, in 1840 they asked Charles P. Krauth and William M. Reynolds to represent Gettysburg at "a general convention for education" scheduled to meet in Washington during the spring. Nine years later, Martin L. Stoever joined Horace Mann and others in issuing a call for a "national convention of the friends of common schools and of universal education." As a result, the American Association for the Advancement of Education was founded in Philadelphia in December 1849.[146] In succeeding years, the faculty named its delegate to attend the annual conventions of this organization and instructed him to express in writing the College's support of its objectives if he could not attend the sessions in person. On several occasions during the 1860s, the faculty supported similar efforts undertaken on a statewide basis. In 1860 they gave their blessing to participation by Gettysburg students in the publication of a short-lived national student magazine.[147]

The Civil War

When the Civil War began in April 1861, following the Confederate firing upon Fort Sumter and President Abraham Lincoln's call for volunteers to come to the defense of the Union, the winter term of the 1860-1861 academic year at Gettysburg was ending. After a six-weeks vacation, students came back to the campus for the summer term late in May.

The town of Gettysburg to which they returned was located less than ten miles north of the Mason-Dixon line, in a border region where most residents yearned for a peaceful solution to the national

---

[145]*Minutes of the Pennsylvania Synod* (1856), p. 25.

[146]*American Journal of Education and College Review* 1(1856):3-8. Among the early presidents were Horace Mann, Eliphalet Nott, Joseph Henry, and Henry Barnard. For further information, see *A Cyclopedia of Education,* ed. Paul Monroe (Washington, 1911) 1:109. Hereafter cited as Monroe, *Cyclopedia.*

[147]The *University Quarterly: Conducted by an Association of Collegiate and Professional Students, in the United States and Europe* was published in 1860-1861. *Union List of Serials* 5:4335.

crisis. While some Adams countians had spoken out strongly against slavery for many years, few if any championed the use of warfare to overthrow it. The leading industry in the town in 1861 was the manufacture of carriages, most of which were sold in markets to the south of Gettysburg. Nevertheless, once hostilities began, even the Democratic *Compiler,* which had vehemently opposed the election of Abraham Lincoln and the policies of his administration, agreed on April 22, 1861 that its duty "in this terrible emergency" was to "stand by the old flag."

During the excitement which followed the outbreak of hostilities, the members of the College community reacted in much the same way as other citizens did. Members of the faculty participated in public meetings in the courthouse, churches, and elsewhere as volunteers came forward, organized, and left for duty. Students formed a military company in June 1861 and drilled regularly. On June 29, in line with what was happening in hundreds of Northern communities both large and small, the students placed a forty-foot staff on the cupola of the College building and then, with appropriate ceremony, raised what the Adams *Sentinel* for July 10 called "a magnificent streamer, red, white and blue, with the thirty-four stars upon the Union." The significance of this particular flag was that it had a star representing Kansas, which for some five years Southerners had steadfastly prevented from entering the Union as a free state. Only after the Southern members withdrew from Congress did that body have enough votes to admit Kansas on terms acceptable to the North. On July 4, 1861 the College Guards and the literary societies participated in the elaborate parade and celebration staged to demonstrate Gettysburg's support for the Union cause. Frederick A. Muhlenberg delivered the major address of the day.

The initial excitement soon wore off. As the hopes for a quick victory faded, along with the rest of the North the College community had to face the grim realities of a long civil war. During the next four years enrollment suffered. Some students enlisted in the Union army, as did many young men who in quieter days might have become students. Some parents refused to allow their sons to come to Gettysburg because of its proximity to the Mason-Dixon line and the resulting threat of Confederate invasion. In addition, the war reduced the number of students from Lutheran families in slaveholding states.[148] The average enrollment in the four College

[148]Except for Maryland, this number was small to begin with. For example, in the 1859-1860 year, of the 93 students in the four College classes, 14 came from Maryland, 1 from Virginia, and 1 from North Carolina. For a fuller treatment of the College and the Civil War, see Robert Fortenbaugh's chapter in Samuel Gring Hefelbower, *The History of Gettysburg College, 1832-1932* (Gettysburg, 1932), pp. 178-229. Hereafter cited as *1932 History.*

classes for the years 1857-1861 was 90 students. There were 66 in attendance in 1863-1864 and 61 in 1864-1865. Enrollment in both departments dropped from 166 in 1860-1861 to 112 in 1864-1865.

From the start of the war, there were occasional threats of Confederate incursions into Adams county. One such occurred in the late summer of 1862, when the Union Army of the Potomac and the Confederate Army of Northern Virginia clashed at Antietam. A month later General J. E. B. Stuart's cavalry, in the course of a raid on Chambersburg, penetrated into the western townships of Adams county, less than ten miles from Gettysburg. There were rumors that the College would not open for the fall term as scheduled. Robert G. Harper used the columns of the *Sentinel* for September 16, 1862 to insist that they were without foundation.

The actual invasion of the county occurred late in June 1863, after the Army of Northern Virginia had come up the Shenandoah valley, entered Pennsylvania in Franklin county, and then halted to determine what its next move should be. General Robert E. Lee sent some units up the Cumberland valley to probe the defenses of Harrisburg, while others moved through Adams county in the direction of the Susquehanna river. These latter passed through Gettysburg on June 26, occupied York on June 28, and reached Wrightsville, only to find the bridge across the river already burned.

On June 15, 1863 Governor Andrew G. Curtin issued a proclamation calling upon able-bodied citizens of Pennsylvania to come to the defense of the state against the threatened invasion by the Army of Northern Virginia. Among the very first men to respond to this call were members of a company in which there were fifty-four students of the College, more than half the enrollment in the four classes. On June 16, the day following the governor's call, the faculty decided that "we do not disapprove of those who are not minors enlisting in the service of their country in the present emergency, but in the case of minors we cannot give our sanction, unless the permission of their parent or guardian is first secured." With or without such permission, the students went to Harrisburg to be mustered in. Because, unlike some other volunteers, they did not object to entering United States service for the duration of the emergency, they were quickly organized as Company A, 26th Regiment, Pennsylvania Volunteer Militia. A week later this regiment was sent back to Adams county, where the students performed creditably, although they were no match for the seasoned Confederate troops who appeared in the county during the last week in June. In the skirmishing which preceded the battle itself, some students were captured, while others retreated with their regiment to

Harrisburg, serving with it until they were discharged at the end of July.[149]

Upon learning that the Army of the Potomac, now under a new commander, General George B. Meade, was approaching his own army from the south, General Lee recalled his units from near Harrisburg and from York. The immediate purpose of these two great armies was to do battle with each other. The encounter began on July 1, 1863.

The summer term at Gettysburg College began in mid-May 1863 and was scheduled to end with commencement on August 13. When the governor issued his proclamation in mid-June, the faculty decided to continue instruction for those students who remained on the campus. The professors met for their regular weekly meeting on June 30 and transacted several necessary items of business. They decided there would be no classes on July 4, named a tutor for the preparatory department to teach until the regular appointee returned from service in Company A, and decided that the temporary tutor should ring the College bell while the janitor was absent. John Hopkins, a black, had probably decided his own safety required that he leave Gettysburg for a time.

Classes began as usual at 8 A.M. on July 1. Soon the normal routine of instruction was disturbed when Union signal officers came into the building. Michael Jacobs accompanied one of these officers to the cupola, where he called attention to the strategic importance of the high ground south of town. A little later the increasing confusion prompted President Baugher to tell his class: "We will close and see what is going on, for you know nothing about the lesson anyhow."[150] The discipline of the well-regulated family had broken down to such an extent that when one student suggested to his friend that they ought to get the customary permission before leaving the campus to investigate what was happening, the latter replied: "Let the faculty go to grass and you come on."[151]

During the course of the day on July 1 Union fortunes worsened. Its army retreated southward across the campus, through the town, and to the higher ground which it occupied for the remainder of the battle. In the late afternoon or early evening the Confederates took possession of the College building. There was no question but that they would use it for an immediate purpose. With the number of wounded men increasing and soon to run into the thousands, every large building within reach was almost certainly going to be pressed into service as a hospital.

[149]The account of Edmund W. Meisenhelder (1864), a member of Company A, is reprinted in the *1882 History*, pp. 420-426.
[150]*Quoted in the Spectrum* (1902), p. 182.
[151]Ibid., p. 179.

The Confederates removed nearly all of the possessions of students from their rooms and piled them into the president's office, which was then locked and guarded. Student rooms, recitation rooms, the halls of the literary societies, and the libraries were filled with the wounded and dying. Most, but not all, of the patients were Confederates. A building which under normal circumstances housed about one hundred students was now accommodating perhaps as many as seven hundred soldiers. During the course of the battle the building was hit several times, but no serious damage was inflicted.

Most, if not all, of the faculty spent their time during the battle in whatever safety their houses might provide. In his memoir, Henry Eyster Jacobs, son of Michael Jacobs, recounted how his family, augmented by some relatives and friends, retreated to the basement of their home at the corner of Washington and Middle streets. The professor himself made frequent trips to the cupola of the house, where he used the College telescope to observe the progress of the battle. President Henry L. Baugher and his family remained in their residence on the campus, where they took in some eighteen wounded Union soldiers and successfully hid a Union officer. Martin L. Stoever, who lived with his family in the southwest quadrant of the square, also took care of wounded Union soldiers, including several officers concealed in the cellar. Charles F. Schaeffer told the Synod of Pennsylvania that his dwelling on Chambersburg street, which the synod owned, was damaged, "partly by a cannon ball, and partly by violent measures on the part of the Rebels."[152]

After the repulse of Pickett's charge on the afternoon of July 3, General Lee decided not to continue the fight on the field at Gettysburg; he prepared to retreat. On the night of the third or early morning of the fourth of July the Confederate military abandoned the College building. Union troops promptly occupied it, taking charge of the hospital and its patients. Writing years later, Michael Colver (1863), a senior who had waited out the battle with several families in town, gave his recollection of what he learned upon returning to the campus on July 6:

On our arrival we found in and around the building, according to the estimate given us, seven hundred wounded rebels. When I came to my room I saw it afforded ample accommodation for three

[152]Jacobs, Memoirs, pp. 50-60; quoted in the Lutheran Observer, July 31, 1863; dispatch of L. L. Crounse, New York Times, July 9, 1863; Minutes of the Pennsylvania Synod (1864), p. 20.

185

– one on the bed and two on the floor. Upon investigation I ascertained that all my books, trunks and other effects were gone. But the information concerning their whereabouts was soon communicated that all the property of students which could be gained possession of was, according to the instruction of a rebel officer, placed in the president's room and that during the time of the battle a guard had been furnished by the officer to protect such property. President Baugher's room was filled from floor to ceiling with students' books and clothing. The rooms that were locked and into which was no entrance by those who gathered up the effects were subsequently broken into and robbed of their valuables. All rooms, halls and hallways were occupied with the poor deluded sons of the South. The moans, prayers and shrieks of the wounded and dying were heard everywhere. Only a heart dispossessed of all feeling of humanity could refuse sympathy and help in such a time as that. These unfortunates were of our then conquered foe. But had even the tide of battle gone the other way still a sense of a common brotherhood would have impelled us to feed our enemies and our conquerors. While these men of the rebellion were with us they received the courtesies and attention due them. Students and citizens combined to act the part of the good Samaritan. And from all to whom we ministered we received a hearty thanks and from many a "God bless you."[153]

One of the leading good Samaritans in Gettysburg both during and after the battle was Martin L. Stoever, who worked tirelessly with the United States Christian Commission in bringing relief to the wounded.

The faculty passed up its regular weekly meeting on July 7, but the secretary dutifully made the following entry in the minute book: "no meeting, in consequence of the excitement connected with the recent battles fought in Gettysburg, July 1st, 2nd, and 3d." A week later they decided to cancel classes for the remainder of the term and to graduate the senior class without a formal commencement exercise, "in consequence of the College edifice and all the other public buildings being occupied with the wounded and the dying."

When they met during what would have been commencement week, the trustees formally commended the students "who rushed so promptly to the defence of their country during the late Rebel invasion" and expressed their gratitude that faculty members and their families were "saved from injury, both in life and limb," even though they were much affected by both "alarms and losses." The board decided, "notwithstanding the recent interruption in the exercises of the Institution," to pay in full the salaries of the professors,

[153]Quoted in the *Spectrum* (1902), p. 180.

tutor, and janitor. They also named a committee to assess the damages to the College edifice and Linnaean Hall. Shortly thereafter, President Baugher presented to the Office of the Quartermaster General a claim for the use of and damages to the two buildings. In response, the Acting Quartermaster General replied that his office was authorized to compensate only for the use of the College edifice and Linnaean Hall and for returning them to the condition in which they were on July 1. Any claim for damages to or loss of furniture and similar movable items would have to be made to some other office. The amount which he suggested as compensation was $625, which the College accepted.[154]

Another source of funds for restoring College property came from a joint appeal which the seminary and College issued to the "Christian public" in July 1863, even before the wounded were evacuated from their buildings. Published in many newspapers, the text of the appeal described the "sad scene of devastation and ruin" in and around the two campuses. It asked whether every donor would not be proud to have "contributed to the prosperity of institutions of literature and religion, located in the place, hereafter ever memorable in our national history, as the seat of one of the greatest battles and most glorious victories of the federal arms," and where students, "in response to the call of the Governor . . ., formed the first Volunteer Company, that reached the place of rendezvous at Harrisburg." On behalf of the College, the faculty and resident trustees signed the appeal, which yielded about $4,200. The share of the College was $1,864.[155]

When one considers the losses suffered during the battle of Gettysburg, including some 6,000 killed and 50,000 wounded, it is remarkable that the town recovered as rapidly as it did. Charles F. Schaeffer told the Synod of Pennsylvania that "after the lapse of a few weeks," the damage to his dwelling house was satisfactorily repaired."[156] The College building was used for hospital purposes from July 1 to July 29. Then it was cleaned thoroughly and the fall session of a new academic year opened on schedule on September

---

[154]The government moved quickly to compensate the College. The Assistant Quartermaster General in Gettysburg informed President Baugher on September 3 of the government offer of $625. One month later the money was paid to the treasurer. GCA.

[155]*Sentinel*, July 21, 1863. In keeping with their customary stance when approaching the general public, the College authorities stated that their institution, "whilst it is decidedly Christian and Protestant, is as entirely unsectarian as . . . Princeton or Yale." *1932 History*, p. 218.

[156]*Minutes of the Pennsylvania Synod* (1864), p. 20.

24.[157] Two months later, on November 19, classes were suspended to enable the students to participate in the dedication of Soldiers' National Cemetery. President Baugher gave the benediction at the close of the exercises. It was about half as long as the dedicatory address of Abraham Lincoln.

In the fall of 1863 Michael Jacobs, a strong supporter of the Union cause who had carefully observed as much of the battle as he could from his house and who later spoke to many other eyewitnesses, published one of the first of innumerable accounts that have been written about the battle of Gettysburg. Though not free of errors, his *Notes on the Rebel Invasion of Maryland and Pennsylvania and the Battle of Gettysburg . . .* has the advantage of authorship by one who was close to the events which it describes, who had long experience as a disciplined observer, and who had often covered much of the ground on which the battle was fought while conducting field trips for his students. In January 1864 he published a second account, entitled "Later Rambles Over the Field of Gettysburg," in the newly established *United States Service Magazine.* A third account followed in April 1864 in the *Evangelical Review.* Entitled simply "The Battle of Gettysburg," it was intended to give the readers of that Lutheran periodical "a condensed account of those great events which transpired at Gettysburg on the first days of July 1863."

One of the most controversial claims in Jacobs' writings, first made in the *Notes on the Rebel Invasion* and repeated in "Later Rambles," was that on the last day of the battle Robert E. Lee used the College building as an observation post. He stated the case in "Later Rambles" as follows:

> In his eagerness to gain a victory, and to make good the rebel boast, repeated so frequently as to make it almost laughable, that "they could not be beaten," he transcended the rules held sacred amongst belligerents, whilst he ascended the College cupola, for the purpose of gaining a nearer and a more perfect view of our left centre, although that building was at the time used by the enemy as a hos-

---

[157]The faculty included in the catalogue which they published in the summer of 1863 the information that "in consequence of the great and sanguinary battles, fought, on the 1st, 2nd and 3d of July last, in and around the borough of Gettysburg, between the invading Rebel army, under General Lee, and the Union army, under General Meade, the College edifice was used, by Government, for four weeks, as a hospital for the wounded after the defeat and repulse of the enemy." This prevented holding "the ordinary public Exercises of the Commencement," but would not prevent opening the fall session at the regular time. In conclusion, they noted that "it is but due to the patriotism of the students of this Institution to state, as a matter of history," that a company, most of whose members were College students, "were the first to reach Harrisburg, June 17th, and to be mustered into the service for the 'Emergency.' "

pital, and the usual flag designed to give information of that fact was floating in the breeze by his side.[158]

Scholars have argued that using a hospital facility for observation was out of character for Lee; that there would have been more advantage for him to have used the seminary building, which was also controlled by the Confederates, if he found it necessary to violate what may or may not have been a ground rule of war; or that the account cannot be considered credible because it lacks independent corroborating evidence. Writing in the 1882 history of the College, Milton Valentine noted that Lee's use of the cupola "is well known to the citizens of Gettysburg, though attempts have been made to call it in question." He claimed that the general's action was "abundantly established by the positive testimony of a number of witnesses, some of whom are still living."[159] Unfortunately, Michael Jacobs never claimed that he himself saw Robert E. Lee on the cupola and Milton Valentine never presented any of the "positive testimony" which might have removed, once and for all, the lingering doubts.

When rumors that the Confederates were about to embark upon yet another invasion of Pennsylvania reached Adams county in the early summer of 1864, the students appealed to the faculty to suspend classes. Their petition was turned down, but those whose parents or guardians requested that they come home were permitted to leave. Although the fears remained – the Confederates did burn Chambersburg at the end of July – the faculty decided to go through with commencement as scheduled on August 12. Only two seniors appeared, but on this occasion, unlike that of 1861, all twelve candidates whom the board of trustees approved were awarded their diplomas.

In the August 1865 report to the board, the faculty stated that, during the "rebellion, now happily suppressed," twenty-seven undergraduates and an equal number of former students (graduates and nongraduates) had entered military service. These numbers did not include the men of Company A who enlisted in June 1863. The faculty knew of two Gettysburgians who had given their lives in defense of the Union. One, who was killed during the battle of Gettysburg, was buried in the College and seminary lot in Evergreen cemetery. Some "students were severely wounded," the faculty told

[158]The other controversial claim which Jacobs made in "Later Rambles" was that Robert E. Lee used the house of Mary Thompson on Seminary ridge as his headquarters. M. Jacobs, "Later Rambles over the Field of Gettysburg," *United States Service Magazine* 1(1864):74.

[159]*1882 History*, p. 92.

the board, "all acted nobly and some have merited high honors."[160]

Changing the Guard

President Henry L. Baugher died in the president's residence on April 14, 1868. He had become a member of the Gymnasium faculty in 1831 and had served the College from its very beginning. Janitor John Hopkins died in his home on the campus on July 19, 1868. Jack the Janitor began working for the College as its first custodian in 1847. Trustee Thaddeus Stevens died in Washington on August 11, 1868. Elected to the board in 1834 and largely inactive since moving to Lancaster, he had nevertheless retained his interest in the College and attended a trustee meeting as late as 1865.

These three deaths are representative of the departure from the scene about this time of a dozen or more persons who had contributed in a major way to the operation of the College during the early years of its existence. Between 1864 and 1870 four men left the faculty: Charles F. Schaeffer joined the Philadelphia seminary faculty in 1864, Michael Jacobs was retired because of ill health in 1866, Frederick A. Muhlenberg became president of Muhlenberg College in 1867, and Martin L. Stoever died suddenly in 1870. During roughly the same period of time, seven veteran trustees either died or were dropped for nonattendance at meetings: Robert G. Harper (1864), David Gilbert (1865), Benjamin Kurtz (1865), Charles P. Krauth (1867), Moses McClean (1870), Samuel Simon Schmucker (1873), and Charles A. Morris (1873). During the 1870-1871 year, following the death of Professor Stoever, the two senior faculty members were men whose tenure had begun only four years earlier. With the passing of Samuel Simon Schmucker in 1873, the only remaining trustees from 1832 were John G. Morris and Augustus H. Lochman, neither of whose tenure since that date had been unbroken.

A new generation of trustees, faculty, and janitors was thus taking charge of Gettysburg College. In 1868 they found an institution firmly planted and with good prospects for the future. Enrollment in the College had exceeded one hundred students for the first time in the fall of 1867. The long-sought building for the preparatory department was available for use in the fall of 1868. At $110,000, the endowment was triple what it had been only a few years before. In large measure this was due to the efforts of loyal alumni, whose record of performance was a good omen for the future.

---

[160]Faculty Report, August 1865, GCA.

For some years after 1868, the catalogue and other College literature gave the impression that the ideal of the well-regulated family as developed in the 1830s was still central in the philosophy of the institution. Clearly, the board and faculty continued to assume that this was the case. Nevertheless, it was obvious that some things had changed. The president had long since moved out of the College building. Although he now lived on the campus, his family life was not woven into that of the students in the way which must have been envisioned in 1837. The steward was also gone, and the idea of a student body eating together had been abandoned as unworkable. It remained to be seen how long it would be before the rules and regulations adopted in 1837 and still in force, with only minor alterations, would undergo major revision. In writing the faculty report to the board of trustees in August 1866, Henry L. Baugher commented on the great and continuing difficulty experienced in maintaining the level of discipline which he and others still believed was necessary for the proper education of young men. He had to confess that "if our standard of government is that of the family we have thus far failed to reach it."[161]

[161]Ibid., August 1866, GCA.

New Recitation Building
Completed in 1889, this structure provided the College with the wider place for the greater work which President Milton Valentine envisioned. Only in 1912 was it named Glatfelter Hall. This picture appeared in the first *Spectrum,* which was published in 1891.

4.

A WIDER PLACE FOR A GREATER
WORK (1868-1904)

This chapter deals with the history of Gettysburg College between 1868 and 1904, during which years the United States became the world's leading industrial power. Major developments in steel, petroleum, milling, and meat packing were accompanied by changes of similar magnitude in many other basic industries. In steel, for example, the Bessemer and open hearth processes made it possible for the first time in history to produce low-cost steel in large quantities. The demand for this product appeared to be never-ending. Production of raw steel increased from 30,000 tons in 1868 to 15,205,000 tons in 1904. For many years much of this basic metal was used to construct the nation's railway network, which was a major factor in creating our first truly national market. By 1904 many consumer products fashioned in one part of the country were readily available in all other parts. Nationwide fame, as well as fortune, had come to such captains of industry as Andrew Carnegie, John D. Rockefeller, Charles A. Pillsbury, and Philip D. Armour.

Between the censuses of 1870 and 1900 American population almost doubled, increasing from about 39,800,000 to 76,000,000. Part of this growth resulted from a continuing high birth rate, but much of it was contributed by the more than 11,000,000 immigrants who came to this country during those thirty years. Until about 1890, most of the newcomers were from Great Britain, Germany, and Scandinavia, from which most of the earlier immigrants had come. After about 1890, most of the arrivals were from Italy, Austria-Hungary, and Russia (including Poland). Urban population in the United States increased from about 25 percent of the total in 1870 to about 40 percent thirty years later. Some old cities, such as New York and Philadelphia, doubled in population. Newer cities experienced even greater growth. Pittsburgh was three times, and Chicago five times, as large in 1900 as they had been in 1870.

The years from 1868 to 1904 were important ones for American education at all levels. States improved their systems of elementary instruction. For example, by the latter year most had laws requiring compulsory attendance and a considerably longer school term than had been usual before the Civil War. By 1904 public high schools, few of which existed in 1868, were becoming increasingly common, although in the later year a public secondary school education was still the exception, not the rule, for a teenager. Fewer than 7 percent of the seventeen-year olds in 1904 were high school graduates. The number of colleges and universities increased from about 350 in 1868 to 450 in 1904. During the same period their enrollment grew from about 54,000 to 90,000 students. In 1903-1904 about 13,000 persons, nearly 30 percent of whom were women, received the degrees of bachelor of arts or bachelor of science.[1] Increases in the numbers of institutions and students tell only part of the story in higher education. There were important curricular changes, as new courses were introduced which were deemed to be more necessary for an increasingly complex industrial age than the time-honored classics. The latter either had to share the stage with, or yield to, the pure and applied sciences, the new social sciences, and other subjects.

Probably the most significant educational development of all was the appearance of the university as we know it in the twentieth century. While its founders continued to respect the body of knowledge which was already available to them, their idea of an education was not merely to master what was known, but rather to advance beyond it in order to investigate the unknown. As far as they were concerned, the possibilities for new learning were almost, or altogether, limitless. The cooperation of teacher and student in its quest was uppermost. There was little or no place in this scheme of things for the development of character or for administering the university "as nearly as possible after the manner of a well regulated family." In his inaugural address as president of the University of California at Oakland in 1872, Daniel Coit Gilman attempted to define a university. It is "not a high school, nor a college, nor an academy of sciences, nor an industrial school," he declared. Rather, a "university is the most comprehensive term that can be employed to indicate a foundation for the promotion and diffusion of knowledge – a group of agencies organized to advance the arts and sciences of every sort, and train young men as scholars for all the intellectual callings of life."[2]

As existing colleges such as Harvard, Yale, and Columbia transformed themselves into universities, and as new schools such

---

[1]The annual reports of the United States Commissioner of Education, which begin in 1870, contain much valuable information about the development of American higher education in this period.

[2]Quoted in Rudolph, *American College,* p. 333.

as Cornell, The Johns Hopkins, and Chicago were created, these institutions began to exercise an increasingly influential role in American higher education. So impressed was Professor John W. Burgess with the possibilities of the university that he wrote in 1884:

> I confess that I am unable to divine what is to be ultimately the position of Colleges which cannot become Universities and which will not be Gymnasia. I cannot see what reason they will have to exist. It will be largely a waste of capital to maintain them, and largely a waste of time to attend them. It is so now.[3]

In the period between 1868 and 1904, Pennsylvania was one of the leading industrial states. Until 1890, when Chicago surpassed it, Philadelphia was the second largest city in the nation. The name Pittsburgh was synonymous with steel. Pennsylvania produced more bituminous and anthracite coal than any other state. Unlike its neighboring counties of Dauphin and York, Adams did not share directly in these developments. It attracted almost no industry. Its population, which was 30,315 in 1870, was only 34,496 thirty years later. The county seat, Gettysburg, grew from 3,074 inhabitants to 3,495. By 1904, thanks to soil, topography, location, and a small group of enterprising businessmen, the county was contributing to increasing industrialization and urbanization by beginning to develop one of the state's leading commercial cherry, peach, and apple growing and processing industries. Long before 1904, the battlefield at Gettysburg was attracting visitors in large numbers from far and wide. Also long before 1904, the college at Gettysburg, although far removed from the oil refineries of Cleveland or the packing houses of Chicago, had begun to respond in its own way to the far-reaching changes occurring in American life.

Trustees

Under the terms of the original charter of Gettysburg College as amended by the act of April 19, 1850, ultimate responsibility for the institution was vested in a self-perpetuating board of thirty-six trustees. Chosen for life terms, they could be dropped from membership if they were absent from three successive meetings without an acceptable excuse. Between 1868 and 1904 the trustees made two changes in the method of replenishing their numbers, both of which will be discussed at some length later in the chapter. First, in 1886 they agreed that a total of six trustees should be chosen from nominees presented by the Alumni Association. Second, eight years

---

[3] Quoted in ibid., p. 330. For a detailed discussion of its subject, see Laurence R. Veysey, The Emergence of the American University (Chicago, 1965).

later they secured an amendment of the charter requiring that, henceforth, three-fourths of the trustees must be members of the Lutheran church.[4]

During the period covered by this chapter, a few more than one hundred men served as trustees of the College. More than a dozen were dropped for failing to meet the attendance requirement. A few never answered the call of the roll. Several found the obligations which they had assumed either excessively burdensome or distasteful, or both; they soon resigned. A large number died in office, some of them well-advanced in years and unable toward the end to attend meetings.

Many of the one hundred trustees were Lutheran pastors, some of whom had been elected to office long before 1868. Among those deserving mention were Augustus H. Lochman of York, who served from 1832 to 1851 and again from 1853 to 1889; John G. Morris, of Baltimore, who served from 1832 to 1835 and again from 1844 to 1895; George Diehl (1814-1891), of Frederick, who served from 1856 to 1891; Augustus C. Wedekind (1824-1897), pastor in New York City for twenty-five years, who served from 1856 to 1897; William M. Baum (1825-1902), of York and then Philadelphia, who served from 1861 to 1902; Frederick W. Conrad, long-time editor of the *Lutheran Observer,* who served from 1844 to 1850 and again from 1862 to 1898; John G. Butler (1826-1909), pastor in Washington and chaplain of both the United States Senate and the House of Representatives, who served from 1862 to 1909; Reuben A. Fink (1824-1895), of Johnstown, who served from 1868 to 1894; Luther E. Albert (1828-1908), of Germantown, who served from 1870 to 1908; John G. Goettman (1840-1905), of Pittsburgh, who served from 1877 to 1905; Henry Baker (1816-1894), of Altoona, who served from 1877 to 1894; William H. Dunbar (1852-1920), of Lebanon and Baltimore, who served from 1890 to 1920; and John Wagner (1852-1935), of Hazleton, who served from 1893 to 1934. Ten of these thirteen men were alumni. Lochman and Morris were the last surviving of the first twenty-one trustees of 1832. Their tenures – fifty-five and fifty-four years respectively – stand as records. Of the two, Morris was by far the more active and influential trustee. With good cause his colleagues observed in 1895 that "the death, at the advanced age of

---

[4]There were four changes in the charter between 1867 and 1904. First, an act of March 22, 1867 repealed the $6,000 limit on annual gifts in the original charter and clarified the College's borrowing capacity. Second, on February 20, 1880 the Court of Common Pleas of Adams county gave the College complete control of the Franklin and German professorships. Third, on March 5, 1888 the same court, apparently unaware of the act of March 22, 1867, increased the limit on annual gifts from $6,000 to $20,000. Fourth, a court order of May 21, 1894 amended the charter to require that, henceforth, three-fourths of the trustees be Lutherans.

John G. Butler (1826-1909)

William M. Baum (1825-1902)

George Ryneal (1835-1917)

Charles A. Hay (1821-1893)

The combined tenure of these four trustees was 173 years. Butler and Hay pictures courtesy Abdel Ross Wentz Library, Lutheran Theological Seminary, Gettysburg.

92 years, of Dr. Morris, the sole survivor of the founders and patrons who participated in the incorporation in 1832 of Pennsylvania College, is an event well calculated to arrest the attention of every one bearing any relation to this institution."

As was the case during the early years, a considerable burden of responsibility fell upon trustees who lived in Gettysburg. They still manned the committee named to repair and improve College property; they were still the ones for the faculty to consult when something required immediate attention. It was the resident trustees who approved moving the day of commencement in 1869 so that it would not conflict with the dedication of the large monument in Soldiers' National Cemetery, who were charged in 1888 with making the best possible bargain in purchasing land west of the campus which was needed for a new building, who in the same year approved placing a battlefield monument on the campus of the preparatory department, and who were authorized in 1900 to secure on short notice a replacement for an unpopular German professor who had been persuaded to resign.

At the same time, it is evident that some trustees resented the special role which their Gettysburg-based colleagues were called upon to play. The latter were not unaware of this sentiment. In 1873, when there was a vacancy in the Graeff professorship, Milton Valentine informed John E. Graeff that his candidate for the position had met with the faculty and the resident trustees, but that the latter were reluctant to commit themselves to him or any other person in advance of a full board meeting. "In view,...of the frequent complaint made by non-resident members against the resident members of the Board," Valentine wrote,

> for presuming to forestall, as they have said, the free action of the Board itself, the brethren did not seem to be willing to do as you intimated would be desirable, i.e., "practically settle the matter." They thought it not advisable for the so-called "Gettysburg Ring" to give any formal expression on the subject.[5]

Among the most influential resident trustees were David A. Buehler, attorney and editor, who served from 1852 to 1887; Alexander D. Buehler, book and drug store proprietor, who served from 1856 to 1889; Edward McPherson (1830-1895), attorney, editor, author, and clerk of the United States House of Representatives, who served from 1861 to 1895; Edward G. Fahnestock (1829-1907), merchant, who served from 1872 to 1885; David Wills (1831-1894), attorney, judge, and banker, who served from 1877 to 1894; John M. Krauth (1846-1890), attorney and postmaster, who served from 1879 to 1890; John A. Swope (1827-1910), physician and banker, who served

---

[5]Milton Valentine to John E. Graeff, May 5, 1873, GCA.

198

from 1882 to 1907; Charles H. Buehler (1825-1896), coal dealer, who served from 1888 to 1896; Samuel McCurdy Swope (1850-1931), attorney and judge, who served from 1890 to 1931; John B. McPherson (1863-1934), attorney and editor, who served from 1896 to 1932; and Harry (or Henry) C. Picking (1859-1925), banker, who served from 1898 to 1925.[6] In addition, during these years there were always several resident trustees who were also members of the seminary faculty, including Charles A. Hay (1821-1893), who served from 1852 to 1893; James A. Brown (1821-1882), who served from 1856 to 1882; Milton Valentine (1825-1906), who served from 1868 to 1906; and Thomas C. Billheimer (1842-1923), who served from 1892 to 1923. All of these men, with the exception of Alexander D. Buehler, were alumni of the College. The Buehler brothers; the McPhersons, father and son; Fahnestock; and Krauth were all second- and third-generation members of families influential in the governing of the institution since the 1830s. Except for the McPhersons, Wills, and Samuel McCurdy Swope, all were Lutherans.

In no small way, the success of the institution in a period of increasingly rapid social change would depend upon its ability to attract and keep the support of trustees willing to assume major leadership in providing the financial resources necessary to carry out whatever educational program the board and faculty determined was most appropriate for Gettysburg College. While Lutheran parish pastors and resident trustees (including the president of the College) could be counted upon to participate in this crucial task, a large part of the burden would almost certainly have to rest upon the nonresident business and professional men who were members of the board. Among them were Martin Buehler (1806-1880), a Philadelphia hardware merchant, who served from 1856 to 1880; Daniel Eppley (1817-1887), a Harrisburg merchant and banker, who served from 1862 to 1887; John E. Graeff, a Philadelphia coal merchant, who served from 1864 to 1898; George P. Ockershausen, a New York sugar refiner, who served from 1865 to 1897; Edward G. Smyser (1820-1887), a York iron merchant, who served from 1869 to 1880; John Loats (1814-1879), a Frederick industrialist, who served from 1862 to 1876; John W. Rice, a Baltimore hardware dealer, who served from 1871 to 1893; George Ryneal (1835-1917), a Washington paint dealer, who served from 1873 to 1917; Samuel D. Schmucker (1844-1911), a Baltimore attorney and judge, who served from 1875 to 1911; Jeremiah Carl (1829-1909), a York banker and businessman, who served from 1879 to 1899; Benjamin S. Kunkle, a Philadelphia businessman, who served from 1880 to 1905; Charles A. Schieren

---

[6]John A. Swope and John B. McPherson both moved from Gettysburg during their tenure.

Edward McPherson (1830-1895)

Philip H. Glatfelter (1837-1907)

John E. Graeff (1820-1898)

David A. Buehler (1821-1887)

The combined tenure of these four trustees was 122 years. Buehler, Graeff, and Glatfelter in turn presided over the board between 1870 and 1903. McPherson picture courtesy Adams County Historical Society.

(1841-1915), a Brooklyn leather manufacturer, who served from 1885 to 1891; John F. Gwinner (1833-1916), an Easton banker, who served from 1882 to 1905; Philip H. Glatfelter (1837-1907), a Spring Grove paper manufacturer, who served from 1888 to 1907; and James McMillan (1822-1896), a Johnstown iron manufacturer and banker, who served from 1889 to 1896. Given the tradition and continuing commitment of the College, it is not surprising that most of these trustees were Lutheran laymen. In addition to being active in their own congregations, several served on synodical and national church agencies and as delegates to regional or national conventions. A number were elected to the board only after they had begun giving money to the College.

Between 1862 and 1895 the board of trustees held one regular meeting each year, convening for one or two days in Gettysburg during commencement week. Then, for a period of four years (1896-1899), they met twice annually: in January and June. In 1900 the members decided to return to their former practice of holding one regular meeting each year, in June. From time to time it became necessary to call special meetings, but the surprising thing is that so few of these were deemed necessary.

Three men served as president of the board between 1870, when Moses McClean died, and 1904. They were David A. Buehler (1870-1887), John E. Graeff (1887-1898), and Philip H. Glatfelter (1900-1904).[7] When the board selected John E. Graeff in 1887, it had its first nonresident president in almost half a century. In part because of this, it then created the position of vice president and chose John A. Swope as the first incumbent. Alexander D. Buehler, who became treasurer in 1856, remained in that office until he died in 1893. His successor, Harry C. Picking, continued the practice of treasurers with long tenure, dying in office in 1925.

In 1872 the board created a new standing committee. Consisting of five elected members, the president of the board, and the president of the College, the executive committee was instructed to consider all proposals made by the faculty or by any board members and then make a recommendation upon which action could be taken. In 1874 this committee was authorized "to originate any new business they may deem proper." The executive committee was used for its intended purpose and quickly became one of the more influential agencies in the College. The board was disposed to re-elect its members; several served terms of twenty years or more.

---

[7]In 1871 the trustees decided that their president and secretary should be chosen for three year terms, but they eventually forgot to enforce this rule. Glatfelter resigned as president, effective at once, in September 1903, but his resignation was not accepted until June 1904.

During the period under consideration, the members of the board of trustees continued to interest themselves in all phases of College life, although there is less evidence of concern for some of the small details than characterized the early years. Trustees still played the major role in the recruitment of faculty and sometimes suggested new courses and programs. In an effort to limit expenditures during a time of financial stringency, in 1880 and again in 1881, the board rearranged teaching assignments, redefining the duties of several endowed professorships and switching work in specific subjects from one faculty member to another. Writing years later, Henry Eyster Jacobs said of the changes affecting him which were made in 1880:

> I was not consulted concerning the arrangement either before or when it was made. Some days elapsed after the adjournment of the Board before I learned of the action. I had to learn of it first from Rev. Mr. Demarest, the Presbyterian pastor.[8]

On two occasions during the 1870s, the faculty challenged long-standing board practices in a way which might have seriously jeopardized the generally good relations which had long prevailed between them. The first of these challenges dealt with honorary degrees. Ever since the beginning of the College, both faculty and board members had suggested candidates for these degrees, but the latter made the actual selection. In 1873, in response to a question which someone raised, the trustees entered into their minutes a statement of their belief that the role which the charter assigned to the faculty in awarding degrees was discharged by its chairman, the president of the College, "in publicly conferring the degrees ordered by the Board." The response of the faculty, in its annual report to the board a year later, was to ask that no more honorary degrees be awarded without the vote of both bodies, "unless an interpretation of the language of the Charter by competent disinterested legal authorities shall be adverse to that mode which the Faculty is decidedly of opinion that the Charter clearly defines." Obviously, in the opinion of the faculty, the president of the College could not act on its behalf in this matter unless it had so instructed him.[9]

After the board reaffirmed the action which it had taken in the previous year, the faculty in January 1875 sent letters to at least nine attorneys, all of them alumni, asking for their opinions of the meaning of the charter provisions concerning honorary degrees. The responses, most of which supported the faculty position, were submitted in June 1875 to the trustees, who referred the documents to a committee consisting of three of their own members who were

---

[8]Jacobs, *Memoirs*, p. 213.
[9]Faculty Report, June 23, 1874, GCA.

also attorneys. One year later, the committee presented its report, which regretted that, "notwithstanding the decided expression of opinion of the Board on this subject, the Faculty has deemed it proper to place itself in antagonism to the Board, by seeking to revise the long settled policy of the institution on this subject." While the faculty-solicited opinions were "from respectable members of the bar," they were all based "on abstract questions as to the interpretation of certain verbiage in the charter, and ignoring very important factors in the case." Simply put, the "very important factors" were these:

> For more than forty years the policy and practice of this Institution in the matter of conferring degrees has been uniform, unchallenged, and acquiesced in both by the Board and the Faculty, under every successive administration. The founders of the Institution, those who had largely to do with the framing of the charter and its practical interpretation, both in the Board and Faculty, may be reasonably supposed to have understood what was intended to be the scope of the powers of the Board over this subject. And, if there be any ambiguity or uncertainty in the phraseology of Sect. 9 of the Charter on this subject, the committee submit that it is too late to undertake to reverse the interpretation thus acquiesced in through a long series of years; nor are they able to conjecture why the Faculty should seek to reverse it, if practicable.

The board had not retreated one inch from the position which it had taken in 1873. At this point, the faculty decided not to continue the contest.[10]

The second faculty challenge to the board of trustees, which occurred simultaneously with the first, dealt with the length of time required before a faculty resignation could become effective. The departure of several professors on short notice and the difficulty encountered in replacing them led the board in 1867 to demand six months' notice of an intended termination of services and to specify that a copy of its resolution be given to each person subsequently hired. Persistence of the problem, at least as far as the trustees perceived it, led them in 1875 to direct the officers to secure an amendment which would incorporate their wishes into the charter of the College. A petition was filed with the Adams county court in Feb-

[10]On its own initiative the board awarded an honorary doctorate of laws to one of its members, John G. Morris, in 1875. When a notation of this degree did not appear after Morris' name in the 1876 catalogue, the board formally censured the catalogue committee for having committed "an improper act towards the eminent friend of the College referred to" and directed that Morris' degree, "and any others resting on the same authority, shall be inserted." When it met in the fall, the faculty, without attempting to explain why the Morris degree had been omitted, unanimously endorsed it and then asked that, in the future, the secretary of the board provide the copy for the trustee page in the catalogue.

ruary 1876, requesting the following addition to the charter:

> That any Professor or Instructor may resign his position in the College or Preparatory Department, on giving, in writing, six months' notice of such intention to the Board of Trustees, or to either of its officers; and the Board of Trustees may remove any Professor or Instructor in the College or Preparatory Department, at discretion, to take effect in six months from the date of such action by the Board.

When the text of this proposed amendment was advertised in the local newspapers, as was required by law, the faculty asked the officers of the board to withdraw it from further consideration until they had the opportunity to present certain objections to the published text. David A. Buehler reminded them that he was not empowered to withdraw the application, but promised to secure postponement of any final action until after the next board meeting. This gave the faculty time to formulate and state their case. They suggested a period of three months, exclusive of vacations, instead of six months in the case of resignation or removal. Rather than permitting the latter to occur simply "at discretion" of the board, the faculty proposed that in all such cases formal charges should first be preferred against a professor and voted upon, that he should have a copy of the charges, and that the board should grant him a hearing if he desired one.[11]

At their meeting in June 1876, the trustees found the faculty suggestions "inadmissable, as placing upon the necessary power of removal, existing in the Board, a limitation exceptional and undesirable." However, since they were "at present unwilling, for prudence's sake, to have an unseemly wrangle over this question, either in courts or elsewhere," they instructed their officers to seek a discontinuance of the efforts to amend the charter. Clearly, the trustees were not disinclined to do this, because they were convinced that it was "in the power of the Board to accomplish the object they chiefly desire in ordinary forms of procedure, at their discretion." The court allowed the application to be withdrawn in August 1876. In subsequent years, the trustees made acceptance of the principles embodied in the proposed amendment one of the conditions of

---

[11]Fearful that the proposed charter change would work to the detriment of the German professorship, in 1876 the officers of the Synod of Pennsylvania prepared to engage counsel to argue against it before the Adams county court. The College's application for a charter change, with the record of action on it, is on file in the office of the Adams County Prothonotary.

faculty employment. In 1884 they incorporated these principles into a standing rule.[12]

These two brief confrontations did not impair the generally good relations which had long existed between the trustees and the faculty. Even while the differences were occurring, the two sides continued to deal with each other in civil fashion. The annual faculty reports were still the starting point of much of the business which the trustees transacted. Sometimes the faculty declined to accept recommendations which the board made. On at least two occasions they informed the trustees that the teaching arrangements in the preparatory department which the board had prescribed were impractical and hence had not been put into effect. In 1887 they spurned the trustee suggestion that the class day begin at 9 A.M. instead of 8 A.M. during the winter months. As before, the board was consistent in its support of faculty disciplinary actions.

About 1890 the trustees proved that the determination which they had exhibited in the 1870s was still very much with them, when they successfully resisted considerable pressure to change the legal name of the College. As early as March 1878, the editor of the *Pennsylvania College Monthly* observed that there were at least five educational institutions with Pennsylvania in their names: Pennsylvania College of Gettysburg, University of Pennsylvania, Western University of Pennsylvania, Pennsylvania Female College, and Pennsylvania State College.[13] Confusion resulted. Sometimes mail was delivered to the wrong place. The Gettysburg College exhibits at the 1876 centennial exhibition in Philadelphia were credited in error to Pennsylvania State College.

In February 1887 the editor of the *College Monthly* returned to the subject of the name of the institution. "To avoid this confusion," he asked, "would it not be well to change our name?" If legal reasons made a change unwise, then more people should do what many had been doing for years: simply call the school Gettysburg College. Those who referred to the College of New Jersey as Princeton, he noted, were setting a good example.

Alumni who read the *College Monthly* were quick to respond to the editor's suggestion. "It would certainly be wise to adopt some nomenclature," wrote J. Howard Wert (1861), "that will prevent the

---

[12]The standing rule also affirmed the right of the trustees "in their discretion and to meet emergencies, to modify the duties of . . . President or Professor, or his compensation."

[13]The *Pennsylvania College Monthly* was published from February 1877 to December 1893. Its editor was Professor Philip M. Bikle. For further information about it, see pp. 343-345. Hereafter identified, with few exceptions, as *College Monthly*, with the month and year of issue given.

mortifying confusion that sometimes arises by which graduates of our *Alma Mater* are supposed to represent the alleged institution of learning in Centre county." William Gerhardt (1841) confessed that he almost always answered the question of which college he attended by saying: Gettysburg. Entirely apart from the confusion, he thought that the name should be changed because of the battle. "The signal Union victory achieved, and the significance of that victory in giving course and color to the future of our country," he argued, "have not only made the name of Gettysburg familiar to every household of our nation, but given it a worldwide notoriety. The name has passed prominently into history, and carries with it a prestige that cannot fail to give prominence to our institutions located there." Rev. Philip C. Croll (1876) wrote that he was "interested in the re-baptism of *Alma Mater*." He offered his services to the president of the College and the editor of the *College Monthly,* urging them to serve as godparents and to invite faculty, trustees, and alumni to witness his performing the ceremony: "Gettysburg College, I baptize thee in the name of propriety, custom, and reason."[14]

After 1887 the editor of the *College Monthly* continued the pressure by including more comment and by identifying a sixth, and then a seventh, school with Pennsylvania in its name. However, neither he, the alumni, nor the president of the College could bring about the desired change. That was the prerogative of the trustees, and of the courts. Not until 1889 did the board name a committee "to consider the propriety and expediency" of changing the name of the College and its preparatory department to "Gettysburg College and Grammar School." A year later, the committee recommended that the change be made. Its report was deferred until the next annual meeting, in 1891. After what was described as an "earnest and interesting discussion," the board voted to postpone the matter indefinitely. President John E. Graeff performed his own rebaptism: "Let it continue to be Pennsylvania College both now and forever."

The trustees had not spoken the final word on this subject. In 1892 the students organized the Gettysburg College Press Association for the purpose of providing "full and accurate reports of the daily events" in the institution. They resolved always to call it Gettysburg College. The editor of the *College Monthly,* who came to regret not calling the publication the *Gettysburgian* when it was begun in 1877, accepted a student suggestion and changed its name to the *Gettysburg College Monthly* in January 1893. More and more people abandoned the old name, the impracticality of which became

---

[14]These letters were in the March and May 1887 issues of ibid.

increasingly evident in the 1890s, with each passing year of Gettysburg's participation in an intercollegiate athletic program. The trustees were not convinced to accept the inevitable until 1921.

Finances

As noted in the preceding chapter, between 1832 and 1868 the annual income and expenditures of the College averaged slightly less than $6,000. The trend in both was upward.[15] By 1868-1869, thanks in part to wartime inflation and in part to the yield of the College's first endowment fund, income had doubled. Unfortunately, expenditures had more than matched this increase. The deficit for that year of $2,200 may seem tiny and scarcely bothersome by contemporary standards, but it amounted to about 20 percent of total income. In the following year, 1869-1870, the shortfall exceeded $5,000. The construction of Stevens Hall and of a double house for professors had been undertaken and completed in 1867 and 1868 before all of the money needed to pay for them could be collected. As a result, the College had an unwelcome debt of about $20,000.

The deficits which began in 1867-1868 continued unrelieved during most of the 1870s, a decade which ranks with the 1840s as a period of financial troubles for the College.[16] Time and again it became evident that there was no room in the budget to absorb even moderate unexpected expenditures, such as payment of President Baugher's salary for several months after his death or of paving ordered by the borough council along the streets bordering the campus. On more than one occasion the repair committee noted that maintenance of College buildings was needed, but complained that there was no money for it. In 1870 the trustees asked the faculty to propose a commercial course for the College, but by the time the latter responded, the board decided that financially it was "inexpedient at this time to introduce such a course." Faculty and trustees often reminded each other that both must work to "adjust expenditures to

---

[15]The report of the United States Commissioner of Education for 1889-1890 contains the following statement: "As is well known higher education is not and can not be self-supporting and needs considerable aid from outside sources, either in the form of endowment funds or annual gifts or appropriations for current expenses." If this section needs a text, here it is. *Report of the Commissioner of Education for the Year 1889-90* (Washington, 1893), 2:755. Hereafter cited as *Report of the Commissioner* with the year of issue. The College endowment fund in 1868 was valued at $110,046.27, of which $17,169.61 was designated for support of the Franklin professorship.

[16]College financial records for 1868-1904 are less complete than those for 1832-1868. It appears that the deficit continued through the 1877-1878 year.

income." If the College could be said to have had a motto in the 1870s, this was it.

In an effort to keep things going, the trustees took from the endowment principal and borrowed from other sources. During their 1873 meeting six of them pledged $100 each "to meet the current deficiency in the income of the institution, so as not to require the curtailment of its work and hamper its efficiency." One source of their difficulty was the bankruptcy of John R. Turner, the contractor for Stevens Hall and the professors' houses. On the advice of counsel, the College paid about $6,000 in liens filed against Turner, an amount over and above the contract price for the buildings. During the 1870s it attempted to recover this amount, first by instituting action against Turner and then against his sureties. The effort dragged on until 1879; the College recovered only part of the $6,000.

Since more than half of what the College spent each year was used to pay faculty salaries, the trustees were sorely tempted to revise them downward in trying to adjust expenditures to income. The first person to be threatened by the financial exigencies of the moment was Michael Jacobs, to whom on the occasion of his retirement in 1866 the trustees had solemnly promised "an appropriation of $1000 per annum during the term of his natural life." Three years later, "in view of the large deficiency in the College treasury and our consequent inability to carry on its operations without extreme embarrassment," the trustees considered a resolution to reduce the pension to $500, "until our finances shall be improved." When it was learned how meager Jacobs' other sources of income were, the resolution was withdrawn. Two years later, in 1871, since things were worse, the trustees returned to this expenditure and, this time, decided reluctantly to eliminate it altogether, without making any promise of restoration at some future time. Michael Jacobs died on July 22, 1871, without ever learning that his pension had been withdrawn.[17]

During the 1870s the trustees not only respected several faculty pleas not to reduce the size of the teaching force, but also in 1874 they created a new professorship in the sciences. While this step was sound academically, it made the immediate financial situation that much worse. In that very year the faculty informed the board that "the Professors' salaries, small in themselves, are no longer promptly paid," resulting in "serious inconvenience." They

---

[17]"Mÿ father never learned of this action," wrote Henry Eyster Jacobs. "My mother and I dreaded the effect which its communication would have upon him. He asked several times what the Board had done; but I managed to evade the answer." Jacobs, *Memoirs,* p. 145.

expressed "their sense of constant obligation to the Treasurer for doing his best to relieve this condition of things."[18] In response, the trustees decreed that the treasurer should give faculty salaries top priority in making payments, but obviously he could not disburse money which he did not have. In 1878 the trustees voted that, unless current expenditures matched current income, faculty salaries would be reduced by $100, or about 8 percent. They directed the secretary to write a "courteous note" to the faculty, explaining that

During the 1887-1888 year, the treasurer made about 160 payments on behalf of the College, most of which went for salaries. Faculty were paid once a year; janitors, once a month.

---

[18]Faculty Report, June 23, 1874, GCA.

their "action was taken with reluctance and because of pressing financial difficulties."

As early as 1870, the trustees began seeking new sources of income for the College. In that year they appointed a financial agent and appealed to the supporting synods to help raise at least $50,000. Two years later, they asked the faculty to relieve the president of his teaching duties for at least one month in each of the three terms, so that he could visit congregations in search of students and monetary contributions. The faculty cooperated, but a year later the president reported to the board that he had secured less than $1,250, only $400 of which was in cash. In explaining the disappointing results, he identified three obstacles to success. One was a faculty vacancy, which required his presence on the campus most of the year. A second was "the peculiar dulness [sic] of business and financial stringency throughout the country, almost discouraging the expectation of any success," which prevented some persons who expected to give "liberally and largely" from doing so. A third obstacle was the fact that in some quarters "the needs of the College are not appreciated, nor the importance to all the interests of the Church of at once relieving its wants and strengthening its power."[19]

Undaunted by the pessimism of this report, the trustees decided in 1873 to undertake an ambitious effort to add $125,000 to its endowment fund and to rely upon its Lutheran constituency to contribute most of that amount. They proposed to three synods (Maryland, West Pennsylvania, and East Pennsylvania) that each cooperate in raising $25,000 for an endowed professorship and to four other synods (Allegheny, Pittsburgh, Central Pennsylvania, and Susquehanna) that they join together in attempting to raise a like sum for a fourth professorship. The trustees encouraged the College Alumni Association to provide the remaining $25,000 by concluding their efforts, begun more than a decade earlier but long stalled, also to endow a professorship.[20]

The board named a three-man endowment committee to work with the president of the College in carrying out this ambitious campaign. They were instructed to conduct an endowment convention similar to the one held in Harrisburg in 1864 and to present the College's requests to the synods during their annual fall meetings. The endowment convention met in St. Paul's Lutheran church in York on September 16, 1873. John G. Morris was its chairman. Several representatives of the College presented their statements of its needs and why Lutherans should take the leading role in meeting

---

[19]Milton Valentine to the board of trustees, June 25, 1873, GCA.

[20]For further information about these efforts among the synods and alumni, see pp. 374, 387-388.

them. Since the purpose of this gathering was to provide information, no attempt was made to secure public pledges, as was done in 1864. Most of the synods responded favorably to the request that they participate in the endowment campaign. The response of the West Pennsylvania Synod, only three days after the York convention, was typical. In a series of five resolutions, its members (1) approved the action of the College board, (2) urged that the College make "vigorous efforts" to raise $25,000 in its congregations, (3) invited the president of the College and the endowment committee into the congregations to make these efforts, (4) asked each pastor to present the "claims of Pennsylvania College" to his members, urging them to support it by sending both monetary contributions and students, and (5) urged the College to carry the campaign "to a speedy and successful consummation," so that it would not interfere with the synod's regular benevolent program.[21]

In the three-day interval between the endowment convention and the West Pennsylvania Synod meeting, newspapers announced the collapse of the well-known Philadelphia banking firm of Jay Cooke and Company. This event marked the beginning of a severe nationwide depression which lasted until about 1878. Under these circumstances, the high hopes of the board of trustees had little or no chance of being realized. In reporting on progress to date, the endowment committee in 1876 presented this explanation, "respectfully, but with much regret," to the board:

The business and monetary depression throughout the country has been in the way of successful effort among those from whom the money for this purpose must be, for the most part expected – those who succeed in making money. To fail among this class defeats a successful movement. They have been almost entirely inaccessible during the past year. It seemed inadvisable to press the matter.[22]

The results obtained thus far, while welcome enough, were nevertheless discouraging. From Harrisburg, Shippensburg, Easton, York, Frederick, Hagerstown, and other places, the endowment committee had secured slightly less than $13,400 in cash and notes. At this point, it fades from the scene. In 1877 and again in 1878, at the request of the board, two members of the faculty in succession canvassed for funds. While they were thus engaged, colleagues taught their courses, without extra compensation.

By the end of the 1870s it was evident that the depression had run its course and that recovery was beginning. At the end of the 1878-1879 year, there was a small surplus, $450 of which the trustees decided to divide among the seven professors. Within a few years

---

[21]*Minutes of the West Pennsylvania Synod* (1873), pp. 17-18.
[22]Endowment committee to the board of trustees, June 1876, GCA.

the salary cuts were revoked, some year-end surplus funds were transferred to the endowment, and the College was at last out of debt. Elimination of the latter burden was due in large part to the $20,000 bequest of Charles A. Morris, veteran trustee, who died in 1874.

Although the financial experieces of Gettysburg College in the 1870s were very much like those of most other institutions of higher education, there were a few colleges and universities which were in a much stronger fiscal position at the end of the decade. In November 1881 the *College Monthly* identified the five which, according to its information, had endowments in excess of $1,000,000.[23] One month later it observed that "in this country the growth and extent of the custom of making gifts to educational institutions is really surprising, and scarcely a day passes that there are not new donations to chronicle." For the benefit of his readers, the editor listed large contributions made by Johns Hopkins to The Johns Hopkins University, by John C. Green to Princeton College, by Ezra Cornell and Henry W. Sage to Cornell University, by Ario Pardee to Lafayette College, by Samuel Williston to Amherst College, by William Bucknell to what was then the University at Lewisburg, and by many others.[24]

The main purpose of the *College Monthly* was to keep the alumni informed of what was happening on the campus, among their own numbers, and in the world of American higher education. Beginning in 1878, most issues contained at least one notice whose purpose was either to inform the readers of specific pressing needs of Gettysburg College or of the success of sister institutions in attracting gifts, both large and small. Clearly, those who were managing the periodical hoped that among the readers so informed there would be several motivated to respond. "Where are the generous men of wealth who will come to the relief of the college treasury?" they asked in December 1883. "Few things are more evident than the necessity of an adequate endowment for an educational institution," they claimed three months later. "Location is next to nothing compared with it.... Endowment is second in importance only to well qualified instructors." When the board of trustees was engaged in electing a new president in June 1884, the *College Monthly* insisted that "notwithstanding the good work Pennsylvania College has been

---

[23]In the parlance of the time, what we call endowments were usually referred to as productive funds. The five institutions named were Columbia, Harvard, The Johns Hopkins, Lehigh, and Cornell.

[24]Most of these gifts represented pre-Civil War money gained from dealings in lumber, coal, canals, early railroads, shipping, the telegraph, domestic and foreign trade, real estate, and investments.

doing in all its years and its present fair condition of prosperity, there must be a step forward, and a long one too, if it is to hold its present relative rank among the better colleges of the land." Those colleges which were progressing "have made their advance by improving their treasury, and we must do the same."

These sentiments were echoed in the June 1884 faculty report to the board, which presented "the great importance and necessity of at once inaugurating and carrying through some plan for the better endowment of the institution and enlarging its work." The faculty insisted that, "as the efforts for the increase of the endowment, for the last eight years, have failed to bring in any considerable amount," the immediate needs of the College "will not allow any further delay." They took "the liberty of pressing the matter upon the best and most earnest attention of the Board."[25]

In June 1879 the *College Monthly* reported that the recently deceased Asa Packer had bequeathed an additional $2,000,000 to Lehigh University and $30,000 to Muhlenberg College. "It has not yet been announced how much he left to Pennsylvania College," the editor stated. "We are waiting for it." In November 1881 he informed his readers that Edwin B. Morgan, the first president of Wells Fargo and later associated with the American Express Company, had promised $200,000 to Wells College, Aurora, New York. "Would that we could make a similar announcement as to Pennsylvania College!" he exclaimed, "but the day may come." All of which raises the serious question: how could Gettysburg College have generated $200,000 in the 1880s, or indeed at any other time during the third of a century dealt with in this chapter? What old methods might have been tried again? What new methods gave any realistic expectation of success? One thing was certain. Past experience with efforts to raise large sums through the supporting Lutheran synods suggested that these were not promising sources.

As an alternative, the Lutheran pastors who were members of the board of trustees could solicit contributions from wealthy parishioners and other acquaintances, both Lutheran and non-Lutheran. The trustees could maintain a contingent of New York, Philadelphia, Baltimore, and western Pennsylvania business and professional men within their ranks. The staff of the *College Monthly* could portray Gettysburg as a well-established, strong institution which now needed large infusions of new money simply to maintain its already enviable position. It was hoped that alumni readers would contribute to the best of their ability, but even more

[25]Faculty Report, June 1884, GCA. The board replied by calling upon the faculty to present an endowment plan. See pp. 229-230.

important that they would call the College to the attention of wealthy friends and associates.

Not only could the foregoing steps be taken, but they were taken. Regrettably, none of them yielded $200,000, either from one or many donors. The several gifts that came from wealthy merchants, coal operators, iron manufacturers, and investors did not equal those which many sister institutions received. Sometimes Lutheran pastors found it easier to obtain contributions for the seminary than for the College, a fact which irked the staff of the *College Monthly*. Especially in the troubled 1870s, several trustees who might have made substantial contributions appear to have lost interest in the College. Some gave their money for other charitable and educational purposes. For example, John Loats, the Frederick industrialist who served on the board from 1862 to 1876, bequeathed a large sum of money to endow an orphans' school for girls. Charles A. Schieren, the New York leather merchant who served from 1885 to 1891, made his major gift about twenty years later, to the seminary in Philadelphia. Perhaps if the trustees had deliberately recruited more business and professional members with non-Lutheran backgrounds, they would have been more successful in attracting funds for endowment and other purposes. However, it is difficult to believe that, at the time, they ever considered this an option which they should have used. After all, was it not a Lutheran college with a Lutheran constituency?

In November 1888 the *College Monthly* reported that, several years before, a stranger visited the Bowdoin College campus and asked to be shown the facilities. One of the professors gave him an extended tour, at the end of which the visitor left his card. Within a short time the college received a check for $40,000 and subsequently the promise of a bequest of an additional $20,000. Undoubtedly, there were at this time numerous contributions to colleges and universities, the initiative for which came almost, or altogether, entirely from the donor. Although a few of these were made to Gettysburg College, none approached $60,000.

Among the sources of endowment income which the College had used before the Civil War and which were still available after 1868 were transient or permanent scholarships, bequests, and endowed professorships. The faculty had not changed its mind about the undesirability of the first of these sources. In reporting to the board in August 1867, the professors compared the yield of the capital derived from this source with that represented by the loss of tuition income brought about by the thirty-four scholarship users during the previous year. "It seems to be the manifest interest of the College," they wrote, "to sell no more scholarships." In fact, they went beyond that position to advise the board to encourage holders of

214

existing ones to donate them to the College.[26] The board took no action on this suggestion, and as late as 1871 the catalogue still announced that "a permanent Scholarship in the Institution may be obtained by the payment of five hundred dollars, which secures to the holder perpetually the right of gratuitous instruction for one student." Two years later, when it appeared that the College might be a major beneficiary of a bequest made to the East Pennsylvania Synod, the board offered to grant one perpetual scholarship for each thousand dollars the College received. In 1880 a committee of the faculty made a detailed study of these scholarships. It found that only one of the forty-three issued during the previous thirty years had been sold since 1868. Only five had never been used. About thirty were being presented annually in payment of tuition, several of which belonged to persons who rented them out as sources of income. As they had thirteen years before, the faculty in 1880 suggested that the board encourage people to turn in their certificates, either immediately or by means of a bequest. As before, the board did not act, and College records demonstrate that these scholarships continued to be used to the end of the period under study. The 1904 catalogue made known that "a number of permanent scholarships, securing free tuition, have been endowed, and are under the control of synods, congregations, or individuals."

For many American colleges and universities in the generation after the Civil War, bequests were a major, perhaps the major, source of long-term financial strength. The alumni editor of the *College Monthly*, writing in October 1890, urged potential donors to Gettysburg College to give while they were living. "Be your own executor in this matter " he advised, and see that your wishes and plans are literally and fully carried out." Colleges need aid immediately, he stressed, for endowed professorships, new departments, or other worthy purposes. However, for a variety of reasons, many persons chose to retain control of their assets as long as they were able to do so, just in case, and to use their wills to provide for the ultimate disposition, according to their instructions, of whatever might be left. Testamentary gifts to the College in this period, following the precedent set by Isaac Baugher, usually came from Lutheran laymen who also made bequests to other Lutheran institutions and agencies.

Henry Stroup, who died in Montour county in 1873, left his wealth to be divided by the East Pennsylvania Synod, at its discretion, among a number of church agencies. Between 1874 and the final liquidation of assets in 1887, the patient and painstaking trustees whom the synod appointed distributed money as it came into

---

[26]Ibid., August 1867, GCA.

their hands to ten agencies, including the seminary and what later became Susquehanna University. Gettysburg College's share was $3,712.92. Miss Theodosia E. Weiser (1803-1889), member of a prominent and wealthy York family engaged in the dry goods business and in banking, left $5,000 each to the Home Missionary Society, the Church Extension Society, the seminary, and the College. The two last-named recipients were directed to use the interest from their bequest to aid worthy candidates for the ministry. In his will, dated January 10, 1889, Matthew Eichelberger (1807-1893), a local resident who was associated for many years with the Gettysburg Gas Company, left money to the seminary, College, and several Lutheran church agencies. Later, when the board of directors of the seminary were seriously considering moving the institution to a city, such as Baltimore or Washington, he added a codicil leaving the seminary $20,000, on condition that it remain "in Gettysburg, where it is now located." Otherwise, it would forfeit the entire bequest to the College. Partly in response to this will, the seminary decided to remain in Gettysburg. The College received $2,000 from the Eichelberger estate. Trustee Charles A. Morris, the York druggist, did not fit into the characteristic pattern of testator. His will, dated August 15, 1872, left $20,000 to the College, with the expressed belief that "the interest of the Lutheran church would be better promoted, by the endowment of its colleges, than by contributions to its theological Seminary, or other benevolent institutions." In addition to these four, there were other bequests, all of them gratefully received and quickly put to use, but none of them approaching in size that of Charles A. Morris.[27]

In 1868 the College had four endowed professorships: the Franklin (1853), German (1856), Graeff (1865), and Ockershausen (1865). The principal for the first, which amounted to $17,169.61, was invested in a separate account until it was placed in the general fund in 1880. The principal for the second was held by the Pennsylvania Synod until 1879-1880, when it was transferred to the College. John E. Graeff gave a $20,000 note, which he subsequently paid, in carrying out the pledge he made at the Harrisburg endowment convention in 1864.

The Ockershausen brothers set aside four hundred shares of Staten Island Railroad stock as collateral for their pledge. For a number of years the College included the estimated value of the securities – $20,000 – as part of its endowment and the Ock-

---

[27] East Pennsylvania Synod minutes from 1874 to 1887 record the disposition of the Stroup legacy. The Morris and Weiser wills are recorded in York County Will Books Z, p. 69, and FF, p. 304. The Eichelberger will is recorded in Adams County Will Book J, p. 570.

ershausens annually paid the College $1,200. By 1878, thanks to the depression, these securities were worthless. The finance committee hoped that they would quickly be replaced by assets of equal value, but the future worth of this endowment was sharply called into question by the death of August Ockershausen. In May 1878 his brother George informed the College that business reverses had forced him to ask that he be excused from any further responsibility for payment of interest or principal on his half of the 1864 pledge. Also, as executor of his brother's estate, he reported that counsel had advised him that under New York law the $10,000 claim which the College had filed against the estate was invalid. If it wished to attempt to recover anything, the College would have to submit its case to a referee and be represented by counsel. When it met in June, the board of trustees decided to attempt to recover what it could. One year later, after the referee had awarded the College $10,000 from the estate, the board released George P. Ockershausen from his pledge to pay an equal amount.[28]

The board of trustees created a fifth endowed professorship in August 1868, only a few days after it was informed officially that the recently probated will of Davis Pearson (1811-1868) left the College four hundred shares of Honey Brook Coal Company stock, with a par value of $20,000, to be used to found a professorship bearing his name. Pearson was an early developer of the anthracite coal trade in eastern Pennsylvania, an active member of St. Matthew's Lutheran church in Philadelphia, and a supporter of several charitable institutions in the city. Since the Honey Brook stock yielded little or nothing in dividends, the finance committee sold it for $12,000 in 1872 and invested the proceeds in railroad bonds. In 1887 Pearson's widow agreed to give the College $8,000, the difference between what her husband intended to bequeath and what his gift actually was worth. The last payment on her pledge was made in 1894.

Twenty years passed between the Pearson bequest of 1868 and the creation of the sixth endowed professorship. The will of William Bittinger (1820-1888) of Abbottstown, which was probated on March 9, 1888, left the College a two hundred acre farm and mill

---

[28]According to a treasurer's record dated November 6, 1878, the College received $10,738.89 from the Ockershausen estate. David Wills charged $500 for representing the College in these proceedings. The faculty was incensed. By a unanimous vote of all members, they resolved that, "inasmuch as the regular salaries of the Professors have been made contingent, this year, on the sufficiency of the income of the College to meet its expenses, and in view of the fact that they are asked to do a large amount of gratuitous labor in its straitened financial condition," they would ask the board to "inquire into the propriety, equity, and legality of the charge of $500." Wills then contributed half of the fee to the alumni professorship fund.

property near Thurmont, Maryland, and also made it the residuary legatee of his estate, if it would in return establish a William Bittinger professorship. The College was expected to keep the farm in good repair and use part of the proceeds to maintain the donor's widow during her lifetime. In June 1888 the board of trustees accepted the bequest and established the professorship. Bittinger had been a successful merchant and farmer. He was a member of one of the earliest German Lutheran families in Adams county.[29] "This is the largest contribution, by subscription or bequest," thought the *College Monthly* in April 1888, "that the College has ever received." For several years the value of the gift was placed conservatively at $42,000. As the initial enthusiasm passed, and as the bills for keeping the farm in repair continued coming in, the estimates of its worth began dropping. In 1899 the executor paid the College as residuary legatee $14,800.23. Five years later, after the death of Eliza Bittinger, the College sold the farm for $8,000.

The seventh endowed professorship resulted from a visit which the president of the College made in 1889 to Peter Graff (1808-1890), Worthington, Armstrong county, a merchant whose financial interests included iron and woolens, and who was an active Lutheran. He was the father of three graduates of the College. One of these, Charles H. Graff (1854-1889), was a successful physician in Duluth, Minnesota, before his early death in the fall of 1889. His father agreed to give $25,000 from the estate of his son, who was a bachelor, to support the chair of physical culture and hygiene which the board of trustees had established in January of that year. The 1890 catalogue identified it as the Dr. Charles H. Graff Professorship of Physical Culture and Hygiene. The death of Peter Graff in April 1890, before his gift could be completed, complicated matters. However, his will did call for the sale of his interest in fifty-seven acres of land in Chicago and for the proceeds to be given to the College. In June 1902 the trustees acknowledged that they had received "a full and satisfactory settlement and satisfaction"from the Graff executors.

The eighth and last endowed professorship before 1904 was established by the board of trustees in April 1892. James Strong (1842-1908), a Philadelphia lumber merchant and banker, agreed to give the sum of $25,000 to found a chair in memory of his first wife, Amanda Rupert Strong, through whose influence he had become a Lutheran. The donor was a member of Messiah Lutheran church in Philadelphia; at his urging, its pastor became the first incumbent of

---

[29]In the 1870 census Bittinger is called a retired merchant and in 1880 a capitalist. According to an article in the May 1890 *College Monthly*, President Harvey W. McKnight tried to persuade Bittinger to contribute during his lifetime, but he preferred a bequest.

the new chair. As had happened so often in the past, here was a donor who gave the College a note for the amount of his pledge. Until a year or two before his death, Strong regularly paid interest on this obligation at the rate of 6 percent. Financial reverses and a debilitating illness made it impossible for him to pay the principal.[30]

Although in a number of ways the constituency had been made well aware of the need for an adequate endowment to maintain the standing of the College, the results of the efforts to build that endowment must have been disappointing to many of her most ardent supporters, especially when compared with the greater successes of many other institutions. Their unhappiness may have been tempered by the generous support given during the major building program which began in 1888 and was completed a decade later (and which will be discussed in a succeeding section), but it could not have been dissipated entirely.[31] The facts are these: the endowment of Gettysburg College in 1868 was $110,046.27. In 1904 it was about $200,000. Among nine Pennsylvania colleges founded before 1865, Gettysburg's endowment ranked a poor ninth in 1904. Dickinson had "productive funds" amounting to $390,000; Washington and Jefferson (combined since 1865), $325,000; Allegheny, $430,000; Western University (not yet the University of Pittsburgh), $498,000; Lafayette, $464,000; Haverford, $1,000,000; Bucknell, $490,000; and Franklin and Marshall, $235,000. Among newer Pennsylvania institutions, Lehigh had $1,250,000; Swarthmore, $557,000; and Ursinus, $185,000. Gettysburg had the largest endowment of the four Lutheran colleges in Pennsylvania. Muhlenberg had $170,000; Thiel, $62,500; and Susquehanna, $40,000.[32]

---

[30]In her will, dated August 31, 1877, Adeline Sager left the College a sum of money to endow a professorship. Since this money was not received until 1922, her bequest will be discussed in the following chapter. For a discussion of the Alumni Professorship of Mathematics and Astronomy, see pp. 374-376.

[31]In remarks made during the semicentennial and quoted in the *College Monthly* for July 1882, Milton Valentine observed that "the story of *Alma Mater's* struggles in doing its work with inadequate money, and her unwearied efforts through all the weary years to get more, forms a pathetic chapter in her unwritten history." He could have said much the same thing in 1904.

[32]Information on endowments was taken from the *Report of the Commissioner* (1904), 2:1508-1525. It was derived from data submitted by the colleges and universities. The commissioner stated that Thiel College was reported to have closed. The figure given above for Thiel is for 1901-1902, the last previous year for which a report was made. Among the most heavily endowed American colleges in 1904 were those in New England. Dartmouth had about $2,350,000; Amherst, $1,700,000; Wesleyan and Williams, each about $1,400,000; and Bowdoin, $925,000. In New York, Hamilton had $550,000; Hobart, $510,000; and Union, $550,000. Elsewhere in the country Colorado College had $350,000; Wabash, $480,000; and Cornell College in Iowa, $710,000.

A review of the current operating budget of Gettysburg College during the entire period under study demonstrates clearly that it was still an era of small things. In the mid-1870s the treasurer paid about 110 vouchers each year, and a decade later about 160. Total expenditures for 1867-1868 amounted to $13,220.02 and for 1906-1907 (the year closest to 1903-1904 for which a detailed financial statement is available) to $31,992.47.[33] Faculty salaries consumed the largest single portion of these amounts: in the earlier year about 84 percent. The salary level of $1,300 for professors, which was set in 1865, continued unchanged until 1891, when it was increased to $1,400, a figure which continued in effect beyond 1903-1904.[34] The salary of the president was increased from $1,400 in 1868 to $1,700 in 1873 and $2,000 in 1891. In addition, he continued to enjoy, rent free, use of a house on the campus. In 1867-1868 all noninstructional expenses, including the salary of the janitor, an appropriation for the library, coal, and repairs, amounted to about $2,000.

By 1906-1907 salaries were consuming slightly less than 72 percent of annual expenditures. As the number of buildings on campus increased, so did the cost of maintaining the physical plant. The two largest items of College expense after faculty salaries were other employees' salaries (long gone were the days of one janitor) and coal. All other expenditures, which included advertising, canvassing for students, commencement expenses, and printing the catalogue, amounted to $4,454.49. In 1906-1907 $972.81 was spent for the chemistry laboratory, $381.91 for the biology department, and $264.21 for the library.

Total College receipts in 1867-1868 were $12,796.37, slightly less than half of which came from endowment income. In 1906-1907 receipts were $33,401.58, about 70 percent of which represented tuition and room rent and 30 percent endowment income. Tuition, which was $39 per year in 1867-1868, was increased to $50 in 1871-

---

[33]The treasurer's report for 1906-1907 is in *The President's Report for the Academic Year 1907-8* (1908), pp. 15-16.

[34]Because of the continuing deficits, in 1878 the trustees reduced annual salaries by $100. This cut was not rescinded until 1882, but the trustees did begin dividing among the faculty the small surpluses which began appearing in 1879. These amounted to between $75 and $100 a year for each professor. There were no deductions from these salaries for federal, state, or local income taxes; for social security; or for a number of items in a later day called fringe benefits. However, in 1875 the board began remitting tuition for sons of professors. In 1889 this benefit was extended to the son of a preparatory janitor and in 1891 to daughters of professors. "The salaries paid to professors at American universities and colleges are very small when compared to the general wealth of the country and the cost of living," according to the February 1889 *College Monthly*. "The highest are those in Columbia, a few of which exceed $5,000 a year. In Harvard, Yale, Johns Hopkins and Cornell they generally fall below $4,000."

1872 and remained at that level in 1903-1904.[35] Annual room rent was $9 until the College edifice was remodeled and turned into a dormitory in 1890, at which time a schedule of charges was adopted. In 1903-1904 the least desirable rooms cost $12.50 per year, while the most desirable ones rented for $62.50, assuming double occupancy in both cases. The 1868-1869 catalogue estimated the costs of a year at Gettysburg College at $211.50, which did not include books, clothing, furniture, and travel. The 1903-1904 catalogue estimates for the same charges ranged from $150 to $241.50, depending upon the room chosen. At no time between 1868 and 1904 did the College operate a dining hall for College students. The catalogue estimate for charges in boarding houses or clubs ranged from about $2 to $3.50 per week.

It is evident that, if the professors had been setting tuition charges, they would undoubtedly have been higher than they actually were. The increase which the trustees did vote in 1871 resulted from strong faculty urging. Their report of that year observed that only two Pennsylvania colleges had lower tuition than Gettysburg, and that such other schools as Harvard, Amherst, and Princeton had recently approved increases ranging from 10 to 50 percent. From time to time in later years the *College Monthly* ran brief articles which demonstrated that annual expenses at Gettysburg were still considerably less than at Williams, Union, Hamilton, Amherst, Lafayette, and other colleges. In 1904 the tuition at many of the Pennsylvania colleges with programs similar to Gettysburg's was between $75 and $200. An occasional article in the *College Monthly* argued that, whatever the student paid in tuition, either at Gettysburg or elsewhere, it did not cover the actual cost of his education. He could not in truth say that he had paid his way and thereby discharge any obligation he might have to his alma mater. Tuition income at Harvard in a recent year, wrote the editor in October 1890, amounted to only one-fifth of university expenditures. At Columbia, it amounted to about one-third.[36]

[35]Beginning in 1896, $30 of this figure was described as tuition and $20 as "general expense."

[36]Faculty Report, June 28, 1871, GCA. The *Report of the Superintendent of Public Instruction of the Commonwealth of Pennsylvania, for the Year Ending June 4, 1906* (Harrisburg, 1906), p. 581, listed estimated expenses at fifteen Pennsylvania colleges to at least twenty of whose graduates teaching certificates had been issued under the act of 1893. Gettysburg was the least expensive of the fifteen to attend. Hereafter cited as *Report of the Superintendent* with the year of issue. Between 1868 and 1904, some Gettysburg students placed themselves even more in debt to the benevolence of others by using a permanent scholarship or, if they were preministerial students, by accepting substantial grants from synodical committees.

Presidents and Faculty

When Henry Eyster Jacobs joined the faculty of the College on September 1, 1870, he found that none of the professors under whom he had studied as a member of the class of 1862 was there to welcome him back as a colleague. Charles F. Schaeffer had left in 1864 to join the faculty of the new theological seminary in Philadelphia. Ill health had forced his own father to retire in 1866. Frederick A. Muhlenberg became first president of Muhlenberg College in 1867. Henry L. Baugher died in 1868. Martin L. Stoever died suddenly in Philadelphia in 1870. Years later, Jacobs wrote that he thought it was best for a college if a new faculty is "constantly growing up within the old, the older members maintaining the historic continuity and representing the reasons for established rules and precedents, and the younger members infusing their warm blood and aggressive spirit into the work."[37] Whatever might have been the advantages of such a mixing, the College was deprived of them in the late 1860s.

The most immediate task of the board of trustees when it convened in special session on May 15, 1868 was to select a new president. Henry Eyster Jacobs believed that Martin L. Stoever, who was then forty-eight years old, was the "natural" candidate for the position, a man qualified by ability and experience. Although he thought Stoever really wanted the presidency, the latter presented the trustees with a letter in which he declined to be a candidate. Charles A. Hay, then forty-seven, a trustee and a seminary professor, wrote in his diary that some of his fellow-trustees had tried to prevail upon him to allow his name to be considered. "Disciplinary ability, such as is needed there, I greatly lack," Hay wrote. "General culture I am deficient in. I know my own weaknesses better than others can know them." In short, he professed to have "an unconquerable aversion to the duties chiefly required of the President of a College."[38]

When the discussion ended and the ballots were counted, Milton Valentine (1825-1906) had eighteen votes. One ballot was left blank. The newly elected president asked for some time to determine upon his answer, but agreed to carry out the duties of the position if the trustees decided, as they did unanimously, that his serving as president was "essential to the interests and prosperity of the Institution." At the regular annual board meeting in August, Valentine stated that he

[37]Jacobs, Memoirs, p. 139. "Where are the fathers and prophets?" asked an 1858 graduate after a visit to the campus in 1874. "Do they still live? Ah! not one of them is left." Quoted in the Star and Sentinel, January 1, 1875.

[38]Jacobs, Memoirs, p. 140; Charles A. Hay diary, Adams County Historical Society.

preferred not to continue in office, but that if "the present exigencies of the Institution" required it, and if the board would so declare by re-electing him, he would accept. On this occasion he received the affirmative vote of every member present.

The very reluctant new chief executive was born near Uniontown, Maryland. A member of the graduating class of 1850, he was the first alumnus to become president of the College. After completing his work at the seminary, he served parishes in Winchester, Virginia; Pittsburgh; Greensburg; and Reading. In 1866 he returned to the seminary as Professor of Biblical and Ecclesiastical History. Charles A. Hay gave his assessment of the relative importance of the seminary and College positions when he wrote that "some other post should have been robbed that can be more easily supplied than that occupied by Brother Valentine."[39]

Milton Valentine (1825-1906)
Valentine was president of the College from 1868 to 1884.

---

[39]Hay and Valentine had been elected to the newly created third and fourth positions on the seminary faculty in August 1865. Hay took up his duties in the following month. Valentine began one year later.

The inauguration of the third president occurred in Christ Lutheran church on December 21, 1868. Taking as his theme the "Present Necessities in Collegiate Education," Milton Valentine reminded his audience that he had not sought the office upon which he had recently entered; that he had, in fact, resisted it; and that it was only a pronounced sense of duty which had finally persuaded him to accept. Turning to the subject at hand, he distinguished between the tasks of the college and those of the university. "The field of the College is general science [knowledge]," he argued, "as distinct from and preparatory to professional training. Its work is mental discipline and the awakening of the broad scientific spirit." American colleges must reject "the gross utilitarianism that loses sight of the man, in an excluding gaze upon professions and business, and looks, in education, only towards capacity for making money, winning honors, or reaching conditions of worldly ease and comfort." After all, "immediate use must be accounted less than the worth and excellence of intellectual culture and power."

Valentine called particular attention to two present necessities in education. The first related to methods. Collegiate experience must stimulate "the student to make his own achievements. The plan must be, not to do the mental work for him, but to move and aid him to do it himself." Instead of being "a passive recipient," the student must become "a vigorous and active inquirer, urged along by the quickening of an inner impulse." Since, in his opinion, "the practical tendencies of American life dispose men to hasten over a large field, and compass a large aggregate of results," scholarship was often "crude, unsystematic and loose." His solution to this problem was to raise entrance and graduation requirements, so that the entire college course could be "thrown forward to an advanced grade of scholarship."

A second necessity related to proper fields of study, a subject which he believed was even more important than methods. Rejecting the idea of abandoning Greek, Latin, philosophy, mathematics, and German, he declared that "we are not ready to bury the Classics." Instead, he urged that necessary new subjects be accommodated within the existing time schedule. It was obvious to him that what he called the natural sciences must be given a larger place in the curriculum. "Investigation in the Natural Sciences has been achieving grand conquests," he noted, "and opening such results as deeply to engage the attention and interest of the age." He was pleased to note that many institutions, including his own, had recently established professorships in English. Not only was this language "the great instrument of advancing culture and science," but also "the millions that constitute the ruling race of mankind, and march at the head of the grand column of enterprise and progress, speak it as their native and only tongue." Finally, he urged that greater attention be given to the study of psychology.

It should not be surprising that a Lutheran pastor, upon assuming the presidency of a Lutheran-related college in 1868, would express his conviction that the world needs an education that is "deeply and vitally Christian." True education, he was convinced, "must have Christ at its heart, and work to the high moral ends and aims of redemption." The student of science should encounter "the presence of the Omnipotent, the token of the Almighty," as well as hear "the ceaseless voices that speak of Him in the tones of Nature's thrilling eloquence." The psychology which the College offers should be "true, comprehensive, spiritual, and theistic Psychology." Since "if there is anything that ought to be regarded as ultimate in education, it is soundness and purity of character," the College should promote "the development of mental life in the excellence and power of right moral life." In closing, Valentine insisted that "Pennsylvania College must stand in its lot, among the other Colleges of our land, in zealous promotion of the high interests of true learning and religion."[40]

Although Milton Valentine was undoubtedly more comfortable as a teacher than as an administrator, in part at least because of a gentle personality and strong scholarly interests, it is clear from his reports and letters that he was not hesitant in taking positions which one would expect the chief executive officer of a college to assume. The annual reports to the board which he wrote on behalf of the faculty are forceful documents. In May 1873 he advised a synodical officer to withdraw financial aid from a ministerial candidate who had recently left College and to give him no further encouragement. "This will be the easiest way out of the matter," he argued. "It will save the Synod of what I am sure will end in an unpleasant experience." The letters which he wrote to parents explaining why their sons were being disciplined were models of charity but firmness. He usually maintained his aplomb in responding to irate fathers who refused to admit that their offspring could do any wrong, but in July 1877, in effect, he suspended both generations from the institution. "You could not do a worse thing for your son, in matters of this sort," he admonished the father, "than to make out his offenses to be of little or no account." Furthermore, he insisted, "if it is your habit to do so, instead of sustaining just and necessary discipline for his right training, it explains the reason of a good deal of the trouble he has been causing all along by his disregard of the

---

[40]*Inauguration of Milton Valentine, D.D., as President of Pennsylvania College,...* (Gettysburg, 1869). Hereafter cited as *Valentine Inaugural.*

rules of the College." In conclusion, Valentine hoped the second letter would "disabuse your mind of the wrong views you have taken in these things, and [that] you will see them in their right light."[41]

In the midst of the financial troubles which began in the late 1860s, the board of trustees turned to the president to lead the effort to attract more money and students to the College. As already noted, in 1872 they asked the faculty to release Valentine from his teaching and other campus duties for at least one month each term. In the following year, when they undertook their ambitious program to raise $125,000, it was understood that the president would be asked to become the busiest member of the endowment committee. At this point, in June 1873, Valentine announced his intention of resigning, effective in six months. The reasons he gave were the extra burdens placed upon him and a call from the seminary. At a special meeting two months later, the board refused to accept the resignation and increased his salary. Once again, as five years earlier, Valentine agreed to stay, with the understanding that the board would make "earnest efforts" to improve the financial position of the College and take steps to relieve him "from some of the confinement and drudgery hitherto attached to his office." In March 1884, after he accepted a call to return to the seminary as successor of a recently deceased faculty member, Valentine again presented his resignation as president of the College and as a trustee. The first was accepted, effective with the end of the academic year, but the second was refused. Valentine continued as an active member of the board until his death in 1906, regularly attending its meetings and serving as a leading member of the executive committee from 1884 to 1906.[42]

After voting to accept the resignation of Milton Valentine in June 1884, the trustees unanimously elected Charles S. Albert (1847-1912) to succeed him. Salutatorian of the class of 1867 and a graduate of the seminary in Philadelphia, Albert had served parishes in Lancaster and Carlisle before going to St. Mark's Lutheran church in Baltimore in 1882. Undoubtedly, the trustees left Gettysburg in June believing that they had successfully performed one of their most important duties. Three weeks later, however, they were summoned back to a special meeting, during which the secretary read a letter in which Albert explained why he was declin-

[41]Milton Valentine to P. Anstadt, May 15, 1873, and to Lewis Shindel, July 14, 1877, GCA. In the form in which these two letters are preserved, they are signs of the times. They are in the letter copying press which the College bought in 1872. A cyclostyle followed in 1889 and a typewriter in 1893. In 1901 the College for the first time hired a secretary for the president.

[42]There is a perceptive sketch of Valentine's career in Abdel Ross Wentz, *Gettysburg Lutheran Theological Seminary*, 1:400-403. It discusses his theological and literary contributions to the Lutheran church.

ing the appointment. Agreeing to accept his reasons and not to urge him to reconsider, the trustees then unanimously elected Harvey W. McKnight (1843-1914) to the presidency.

Born in what later became known as McKnightstown, Adams county, where his father kept a tavern, McKnight entered the College in the fall of 1861. His undergraduate career was interrupted by three separate enlistments in the Union cause, one of which was in the student company in June 1863. Upon graduation in 1865, he entered the seminary and, after two years of study there, the Lutheran ministry. His parishes were in Newville; Easton; Cincinnati, Ohio; and Hagerstown, Maryland. During this time he maintained close ties with the College, returning on several occasions to give talks during commencement week and, as a member of the East Pennsylvania Synod, serving as a trustee of the Stroup legacy. Elected a trustee of the College in 1878, he may have come to the special meeting in July 1884 without any thought that he was about to be elected to the presidency. Possibly because it had apparently become part of the ritual of presidential selection, and possibly because he had been serving his Hagerstown congregation for less than six months, McKnight at first declined the election. Before the meeting adjourned, however, he changed his mind.

The new president assumed his duties at the end of September 1884, a few weeks after the fall term began. Formal inauguration was delayed until September 3, 1885. McKnight's address on this occasion covered much the same ground as that of his predecessor seventeen years before. Colleges and universities, he proclaimed, perform the special and distinct functions which they happen to have. Education must be thorough and strive to prepare men to be "strong, independent, alert, exact." College education "should be soundly Christian, yielding nothing to those secularizing tendencies which have never been stronger than now"; it must stress both scholarship and character.

McKnight demonstrated a keen awareness of the seriousness of the days through which the College was passing. "The very time in which we live thrusts upon educators responsibilities unknown before," he declared. "In education, as in all else, our age is one of rapid and often radical change. The old and the new are facing each other in an antagonism, out of which has grown controversies, earnest and often bitter, touching the essentials of educational work." The central theme which he chose to develop in his address was "what in the collegiate education of the present should be held in sympathy with conservatism, and...what should be conceded to the demands of progress."

Convinced that contemporary education was being "moulded and modified too much by the spirit of this age of steam and railroads and enterprise, in which everything is done in a hurry, and there is a manifest impatience with plodding and prolonged effort," McKnight would retain the core of the old curriculum. Greek, Latin, and mathematics were studies "which are mainly disciplinary, and have proved to be most conducive to robust and rounded mental development." New studies should be added, but only as they demonstrate their usefulness. McKnight was even willing to consider the introduction of electives into the curriculum, but only in the upper classes, whose members were presumably experienced enough to make intelligent choices.

The new president was convinced that "the college of the present, to be worthy of the present and meet its demands, must recognize the new relations into which it is brought and, by wise and necessary advances, adapt itself to the new requirements of the age." He would have Gettysburg College proceed "in the spirit of praiseworthy conservatism," resisting the temptation facing all colleges to move from one extreme to another. He would have what is valuable

Harvey W. McKnight (1843-1914)
McKnight was president of the College from 1884 to 1904

in the old "preserved and carried up into the new by a safe and healthful evolution."[43]

Harvey W. McKnight may not have understood it fully in 1884, but he had assumed a college presidency which was undergoing a notable evolution of its own. Although each of his three predecessors had some responsibilities for fund raising, each considered teaching and administering the discipline of the institution as the tasks which would consume virtually all of his available time and energy. The financial difficulties of the 1870s and an increasing awareness of developments in higher education convinced both faculty and trustees that the College had to begin putting much more effort, indeed the most effective effort, into the task of raising funds. In June 1884 the *College Monthly* expressed the case as follows:

> Notwithstanding the good work Pennsylvania College has been doing in all its years and its present fair condition of prosperity, there must be a step forward, and a long one too, if it is to hold its present relative rank among the better colleges of the land. Others are advancing, and we must not fall in the rear by standing still. The others have made their advance by improving their treasury, and we must do the same.... The man to collect this money should be the President. He goes before the people supported by an official relation to the institution which no other man has. A mere Financial Secretary will not do. Good as some of them have been, it is clear that we can look for large results only through the efforts of the President.

Before adjourning, following the election and acceptance of McKnight, the board of trustees adopted a resolution presented by his predecessor, Milton Valentine. This resolution restated the tasks of the presidency of the College for the first time since the duties of Charles P. Krauth were defined in 1834. The board affirmed that the president was still "the head of the Faculty of Education," whose duties were "mainly those of scholarly instruction and the immediate administration of the educational work of the institution." However, these words were merely the preamble for what the trustees really wanted to say. "In the present emergency calling for the enlargement and better endowment of the College," they asked the faculty to relieve the president

> of both teaching and administrative duty [so] as to enable him to devote as much time to seek endowment and the general interests of the College abroad as he may find necessary or best, in accordance with the action already taken or which may yet be taken by the Board.

Further, even apart from the "present emergency," the board asked the faculty to reassign duties in order to lighten the president's work

---

[43]The address was reprinted in the *College Monthly* for October 1885.

load, which it considered "very heavy and exhausting."

Since the members of the faculty had on more than one occasion urged the trustees to embark upon a financial campaign, they could scarcely do anything but honor the board's request. Immediately, in the fall of 1884, they granted the relief which enabled McKnight to enter upon a campaign to raise large sums of money. Probably few people realized fully the needs of the College at this juncture or how much it would take to meet them. Time and again during his tenure, relief from campus duties was renewed for McKnight, either by engaging a seminary faculty member to carry the teaching load or by distributing his courses among his colleagues. The extent and success of McKnight's fund raising efforts will be discussed in the next section.

On February 23, 1903 Harvey W. McKnight sent to the president of the board of trustees a letter of resignation, effective on September 1 of that year.[44] Explaining that he had served the College for many years and was no longer in good health, he insisted that the time had come for a younger man to assume his duties. The trustees accepted the resignation and began looking for a new president. This proved to be a much more formidable task than at any previous time in the history of the College. Since McKnight had agreed to serve until his successor was elected and ready to begin his duties, he continued to function as president until September 1904.

Upon resigning the presidency, McKnight also attempted to resign from the board of trustees. His request was refused and he continued to serve until 1910, at which time he was elected president emeritus of the College, becoming the first person to hold that title. After an illness of about a year, McKnight died in Gettysburg in May 1914. Active beyond the circles of Lutheran higher education, he had been a founder of the Pennsylvania Chautauqua, a director of the Gettysburg Battlefield Memorial Association until the federal government took over the battlefield, and a director of the Western Maryland Railroad. Proud of his other-than-German paternal heritage, he belonged to the Scotch-Irish Society of Pennsylvania and St. Andrew's Society of Philadelphia. He was a member of the Loyal Legion of the Grand Army of the Republic.

In August 1868 the board of trustees established the office of vice president of the College.[45] The sole stated requirement for the position was that the incumbent live on the campus. The sole stated duty was that he "relieve the President in case of necessary absence or

---

[44]As will become evident in a later section, this was not McKnight's first letter of resignation.

[45]In 1848 and again in 1859 the faculty called the attention of the board to the need for a vice president. Their candidate in the latter year was Michael Jacobs.

temporary disability." The first vice president was Edsall Ferrier of the English department, who served from 1868 until 1872. His successor, Luther S. Croll of the mathematics department, held the office from 1873 until his death in 1889. In June of that year the board changed the title of the position to Dean of the Faculty, decreed that the duties were unchanged, and elected Philip M. Bikle of the Latin department as Croll's successor. He served until 1925.

Ferrier, Croll, and Bikle were chosen from the faculty and continued to carry full teaching loads. They lived in one of the two houses for professors built on campus in 1868 and were paid $100 annually for their administrative work. In the period under study, the offices of vice president and later of dean were not, in and of themselves, very influential ones. The incumbents might share responsibility with the president for morning chapel or assign dormitory rooms, but they did not have the responsibilties which later deans were given. Neither in 1884 nor in 1903-1904 did the board of trustees consider them as candidates for the presidency.

At the beginning of the 1868-1869 year there were eight faculty professorships. Between then and 1903-1904 there were some additions to, and subtractions from, the number, which stood at nine in the latter year. In addition, there were several lectureships and assistantships, which were filled by persons who did not have professorial rank and whose duties, in most cases, did not occupy all of their working time.

The first professorship, that of Intellectual and Moral Science, was the one traditionally reserved in American colleges and universities for the president, whose special task was to offer courses for the seniors. Between 1868 and 1904 Milton Valentine and Harvey W. McKnight occupied this professorship, which beginning in 1888 carried the name of William Bittinger.

The second professorship, that of Greek Language and Literature, became vacant upon the resignation of Frederick A. Muhlenberg in 1867. With the exception of three years, Henry Louis Baugher (1840-1899) taught the Greek courses between 1869 and 1896. Son of the second president, he was a graduate of the College and seminary. Following further study at Andover, he became a pastor and was called to the faculty from a parish in Indianapolis, Indiana. Between the time Baugher resigned in 1880 and then returned in 1883, Henry Eyster Jacobs taught the Greek courses.[46] Baugher's successor was

---

[46]Baugher usually referred to himself as H. Louis and will be so identified in later references. He was elected to the faculty in August 1868 and assumed his duties in January 1869. See pp. 392-403 for a discussion of the events which led to his departure from the faculty in 1896.

Oscar G. Klinger (1860-1934). A graduate of the College and seminary, and a student at Cincinnati and Cornell universities, he had served as parish pastor and principal of the preparatory department. His tenure ended in 1912.

In 1867 the trustees changed the Franklin professorship, which Frederick A. Muhlenberg held, from Ancient Languages to Greek. One year later they made it a chair of history. The professorship which H. Louis Baugher occupied from 1869 until 1880 was the newly established Pearson chair. During his second period of service, as a result of board action in 1880 and 1881, he was Franklin Professor of Greek, which title Klinger also held.

The third professorship, that of Latin Language and Literature, was held by Martin L. Stoever, the last surviving member of the old faculty, until his death in 1870. He was succeeded by Henry Eyster Jacobs (1844-1932), who held the position until the board realignment of faculty responsibilities in 1881. After being graduated by the College and seminary, and before joining the faculty, Henry Eyster, the son of Michael Jacobs, was a home missionary and principal of the school which later became Thiel College. He was the Greek professor between 1881 and 1883, when he accepted a call to the seminary in Philadelphia, which he served as faculty member, dean, and president before his retirement in 1927. Jacobs' successor was Philip M. Bikle (1844-1934). After being graduated by the College in 1866, he taught mathematics and Latin at the York County Academy, was Professor of Latin and Greek at North Carolina College, and was Professor of Latin at Lutherville Female Seminary before becoming Professor of Physics at Gettysburg in 1874. Seven years later he exchanged that responsibility for the Latin chair, which he occupied until 1925.[47] By board action, the Latin chair was the Franklin professorship between 1870 and 1881 and the Pearson thereafter.

The fourth professorship in 1868-1869, that of mathematics and astronomy, represented the field of study which Michael Jacobs chose to retain when his work was divided in 1865. Upon his retirement a year later, the trustees elected Luther H. Croll (1834-1889) to succeed him. A member of the graduating class of 1855, Croll returned to the College after eleven years of experience as a teacher and administrator in academies and colleges in Pennsylvania, Illinois, and Indiana. In addition to his teaching duties, he was vice president of the College from 1873 until his death in 1889. Ill health forced him from the classroom in November 1888, at which time the

---

[47]His last name is sometimes written with an accent: Biklé. As already noted, he was the first dean of the faculty, serving from 1889 until 1925.

faculty engaged Henry B. Nixon (1857-1916) to conduct his classes. In 1889 the board formally elected him to the professorship, in which he served until he died in 1916. Nixon was a native of North Carolina and an 1878 graduate of the university there. At The Johns Hopkins University, which awarded him a Ph.D. degree in 1886, he was a member of the faculty while he engaged in graduate work.

The fifth professorship, that of German Language and Literature, was supported with an endowment held by the Pennsylvania Synod, which by agreement with the College had the right to nominate candidates for the board of trustees to consider and, if it chose, to elect. The resignation of the first German professor, Charles F. Schaeffer, in 1864 created a vacancy which lasted for two years, during which time other members of the faculty, including a tutor in the preparatory department, conducted the German courses. In 1866 the board of trustees elected a nominee presented by the synod: John F. Wilkin (1810-1876), who was then pastor of a congregation in Tennessee. Although in his first report to the synod he felt "called upon gratefully to recognize" in his unsought election "the hand of Providence," by the summer of 1868 enough students had demonstrated their dislike of him and his subject to persuade him to resign at the end of the academic year.[48] As a one-year replacement, for 1868-1869, the board elected Frederick William Augustus Notz (1841-1921). Born in Germany and an ordained Lutheran pastor, he received his Ph.D. degree from the University of Tuebingen in 1863 and came to the United States three years later. After leaving Gettysburg, he was a member of the faculties of Muhlenberg College and Northwestern College at Watertown, Wisconsin.[49]

Notz was succeeded in 1869 by Adam Martin (1835-1921), a native of Germany and an 1858 graduate of Hamilton College. Ordained in 1861, he had a parish in New York and was later (1865-1869) principal, or president, of Northwestern College.[50] His tenure as German professor continued after the Pennsylvania Synod turned over its endowment to the College and yielded its right to nominate candidates for the professorship. Martin resigned in 1898 and moved to New Haven, Connecticut, where he spent the rest of his life in study and research. His three immediate successors each had two year tenures: Charles F. Brede, Charles F. Woods (1868-1912), and Samuel G. Hefelbower (1871-1950).

The sixth faculty position was the Graeff Professorship of English

---

[48]Quoted in *Minutes of the Pennsylvania Synod* (1867), p. 42.

[49]John Philipp Koehler, *The History of the Wisconsin Synod*, ed. Leigh D. Jordahl (St. Cloud, Minn., 1970), pp. 135-138.

[50]Ibid., pp. 121-123.

Language and Literature which the board of trustees established in April 1865. At that meeting they elected Joseph B. Bittinger (1823-1885) as the first incumbent and the 1865 catalogue identified him as professor-elect. After he declined to accept and refused to reconsider, the board in April 1866 chose Charles A. Stork (1838-1883), who also declined. The trustees had more success with their third election, in August 1866, when Edsall Ferrier (1831-1903) accepted their offer. An 1854 graduate of Lafayette College, Ferrier served as pastor of several Presbyterian congregations before he became Professor of English Language and Literature at Washington and Jefferson College in 1865. He took up his duties as the first Graeff professor in January 1867 and was elected to the newly created post of vice president of the College in August 1868. Apparently tiring of academic responsibilities, he resigned his administrative post in July 1872, gave up his teaching duties several months later, and returned to the parish. For the ten years prior to his death, he was a member of the Lafayette College faculty, where he taught Hebrew.

Fearing that the board of trustees would respond to the hard times by not replacing Ferrier, the faculty warned that even a temporary reduction in their numbers would be "fraught with great damage to the work and reputation of the Institution." At their urging, the trustees named John A. Himes (1848-1923) Acting Graeff Professor in June 1873 and made the appointment permanent one year later. An 1870 graduate of the College and recipient of the Graeff prize, Himes studied briefly at Yale University. He held the title of Instructor in Physics at Gettysburg in 1871-1872 and was a tutor in the preparatory department in 1871-1873. Before his retirement in 1914, he had become one of the country's better known authorities on John Milton.

The seventh professorship of 1868-1869 resulted from the Ockershausen endowment and the division of the work which Michael Jacobs had performed for many years. When he chose to retain the courses in mathematics and astronomy, the board of trustees in 1865 established the Ockershausen Professorship of Natural Science. At the same meeting, John G. Morris nominated Alfred M. Mayer (1836-1897) for the position and he was unanimously elected.[51] A native of Baltimore, Mayer was not a college graduate, but had served on the faculties of the University of Maryland and Westminster College, Fulton, Missouri. When he was elected at Gettysburg, he was completing two years of study in physics,

---

[51] According to the *Lutheran Observer* for April 28, 1865, Joseph Henry, director of the Smithsonian Institution, recommended Mayer to the College.

Edward S. Breidenbaugh (1849-1926)

Philip M. Bikle (1844-1934)

George D. Stahley (1850-1939)

John A. Himes (1848-1923)

These four faculty members, whose combined years of service exceeded 175, were well-established long before 1904 and provided continuity as the College moved into a new century. These pictures appeared in the 1904 Spectrum.

mathematics, and physiology at the University of Paris. Joining the faculty in September 1865, he moved energetically and quickly to improve the quality of instruction. Two years later he left for the faculty of the recently organized Lehigh University, where correctly he saw considerably greater opportunities to pursue his research interests. After four years there, he transferred to Stevens Institute of Technology, also newly organized, and where he remained until his death. Mayer, whose major interest was in physics, published more than fifty papers based on his research into sound, heat, light, gravity, and electricity.[52]

In August 1867 the board of trustees elected Victor L. Conrad (1824-1900) to succeed Mayer. A graduate of the College and seminary, Conrad did not enter the parish ministry. Instead, he became a secondary school administrator and later a New York businessman. Not only were his credentials far different from those of his predecessor, but also his success as a teacher. In the spring of 1870, after three students had been suspended for their conduct in his classroom, eighteen juniors petitioned the faculty, acknowledging that it had acted properly in taking the action which it did, but asking to be excused from attending any more of Conrad's classes, lest the incident be repeated. By that time Conrad had presented his resignation to the president of the board of trustees, effective at the end of the term. He then joined his brother on the staff of the *Lutheran Observer,* from which he retired in 1899.[53]

In August 1870 the board of trustees elected Samuel P. Sadtler (1847-1923) to succeed Conrad. The new Ockershausen professor was the son of Benjamin Sadtler, who was a member of the board, and a grandson of Samuel Simon Schmucker. After being graduated by the College in 1867, he studied at Lehigh and Harvard Universities. He was not prepared to assume his new duties at Gettysburg immediately, since he wished to complete his studies at the University of Goettingen, from which he received his Ph.D. degree in 1871. Sadtler's stay at Gettysburg was brief. After three years, in 1874, he became Professor of Chemistry at the University of Pennsylvania and later joined the faculty of the Philadelphia College of Pharmacy. While in Philadelphia, he was widely known as a consulting chemist, especially in cases of patent litigation. In addition, he was author or coauthor of several chemistry textbooks.[54]

Despite the poor financial condition of the College when Sadtler

---

[52]*Dictionary of American Biography,* 12 (1933): 448.

[53]In accepting Conrad's resignation, the trustees commended him for "the enthusiasm with which he sought to develop the responsible department under his care" and noted "his eminent capacity as a Teacher of Physical Science."

[54]*Dictionary of American Biography,* 16 (1935):285-286.

left in 1874, the board of trustees decided to divide the work for which he had been responsible between two professors. A major reason for this step was the promise of Frederick W. Conrad to contribute $700 in each of three years toward the salary of one of them. Accordingly, the board elected Philip M. Bikle Ockershausen Professor of Physics and Astronomy and Edward S. Breidenbaugh Conrad Professor of Chemistry and Mineralogy. The career of Bikle has been discussed. Breidenbaugh (1849-1926) was an 1868 graduate of the College who studied for a short time at the seminary before transferring to Yale University, where he was briefly an instructor in chemistry and from which he received a master's degree in 1873. Following one year as Professor of Physics and Natural Science at Carthage College, he returned to Gettysburg in the fall of 1874. Seven years later, as the financial troubles of the 1870s were ending and after Frederick Conrad's pledge had been met in full, the trustees in their wisdom abolished the Conrad professorship and made Breidenbaugh Ockershausen Professor of Chemistry and the Natural Sciences, a position which he held until his retirement in 1924.

The eighth faculty position listed in the catalogue of 1903-1904 was the Dr. Charles H. Graff Professorship of Physical Culture and Hygiene, which the board of trustees had established in January 1889. The first incumbent was George D. Stahley (1850-1939), an 1871 graduate of the College to whom the University of Pennsylvania awarded an M.D. degree in 1875. Between then and 1887 he was assistant physician in the State Hospital for the Insane in Harrisburg. In the latter year he returned to his native Easton, where he engaged in private medical practice. In 1882 Stahley was elected alumni editor of the *College Monthly* and began contributing many brief stories and articles stressing the importance of physical exercise for promoting the good health and best performance of people of all ages. His tenure in the Graff professorship terminated with his retirement in 1920.[55]

The ninth faculty position in the 1903-1904 catalogue was the Amanda Rupert Strong Professorship of English Bible, which the board of trustees established in April 1892. The enabling legislation

---

[55]The eighth professorship in the 1868-1869 catalogue was the Franklin Professorship of History, Ancient, Medieval, and Modern. The board of trustees assigned these subjects to the Franklin chair in August 1868, but when it elected Henry Eyster Jacobs to the faculty in June 1870, he was called Franklin Professor of the Latin Language, and of History. The last three words in his title survived until 1880, when the board transformed the Franklin chair into one of ancient languages, which is what it had been earlier. Beginning in 1882, the principal of the preparatory department also held the rank of professor.

Henry Eyster Jacobs (1844-1932)

Luther H. Croll (1834-1889)

Adam Martin (1835-1921)

Henry B. Nixon (1857-1916)

Except for Professor Nixon, these four faculty members had completed their service to the College before 1904.

prescribed that the incumbent would also be chaplain of the College. As such, he would share with the president "supervision of the moral and spiritual interests and welfare of the students" and have charge of "all the religious instruction of the Institution." After passing this legislation, the board proceeded to elect Eli Huber (1834-1911) to the newly created position. The first Amanda Rupert Strong Professor was an 1855 graduate of the College. After attending the seminary he became a Lutheran pastor. His fifth parish was Messiah Lutheran in Philadelphia, from which he came to Gettysburg in the fall of 1892. He retired at the close of the 1903-1904 academic year.[56]

In addition to the eight or nine professors, the College always had several instructors of lesser rank, some of whom were full-time employees while others gave only a few lectures each year. Although his name appeared in the catalogue as Lecturer on Natural History only in 1868-1870 and 1871-1874, John G. Morris continued functioning in that capacity at least to the end of the decade. As late as March 1879, a writer in the College Monthly wondered when the ever-popular old gentleman was going to deliver the series of eight lectures which he had promised the students. Three alumni who were physicians – John M. Radebaugh (1851-1920), J. Bion Scott (1859-1904), and George D. Stahley – lectured on anatomy, physiology, or hygiene during most of the decade before the chair of physical culture and hygiene was established in 1889.[57] After that occurred, a succession of upperclass students with the title of Physical Instructor assisted Stahley in his work, most of them serving for one year or two. Three alumni held the rank of Assistant in Chemistry. They were George S. Eyster (1848-1937), from 1874 to 1877; Franklin Menges (1859-1956), from 1886 to 1896; and Clyde B. Stoever (1873-1948), from 1896 to 1910. Between 1886 and 1903 three attorneys –William McClean (1833-1915), John Stewart, and Donald P. McPherson (1870-1937) – lectured on constitutional law or jurisprudence.

In 1903-1904, as the period under study was drawing to a close, the College was not about to repeat what had happened a third of a century before, when within a period of six years there was a complete turnover of faculty. Three remarkable professors in 1903-1904, who joined the faculty thirty years earlier and whose combined service was to exceed 140 years, were men with teaching

---

[56]For a discussion of the result of the establishment of this professorship upon the relations between the synods and the College, see pp. 392-403.

[57]In the May 1888 College Monthly, Stahley reported on the twelve lectures which he had recently given. His salary for the first year was zero, he wrote, but it was to be doubled annually in the future.

careers of ten or more years still ahead of them. They were John A. Himes, Philip M. Bikle, and Edward S. Breidenbaugh. At the same time, in Henry B. Nixon, George D. Stahley, and Oscar G. Klinger the faculty had three somewhat younger men with less experience, but they had already established themselves as professors and would continue well into the new century.

By 1904 the contemporary pattern of preparation for college and university teaching, which had scarcely existed in 1868, was already well-established in the United States. After earning their undergraduate degrees, candidates for the profession could enroll in a university to engage in a program of study and research which, it was hoped, would culminate in the awarding of a Ph.D. degree. In 1903-1904 thirty-six American universities conferred a total of 301 such degrees, two-thirds of which were granted by Harvard, Yale, The Johns Hopkins, Chicago, Columbia, and Pennsylvania.[58]

As indeed was the case at many other undergraduate colleges throughout the country, the older methods of faculty selection long continued to prevail at Gettysburg College. Of the twenty-two men who held the nine professorships just discussed, fourteen were alumni of the College and twelve were ordained Lutheran pastors. One of the three or four non-Lutherans was an ordained Presbyterian minister. In 1874 Milton Valentine urged that the temporary appointment of John A. Himes be made permanent because he was "an alumnus, a Lutheran, actually and successfully in the work."[59] Sixteen years later, in March 1890, the alumni editor of the College Monthly, Charles R. Trowbridge (1859-1937), himself a Lutheran pastor, argued that

> fitness and adaptability for demands in the teaching of any branch of study ought to far outweigh any minor points of denominational or other condition or connection. What is needed is competent instructors, first of all, and the choice between two or more candidates for the same position ought to be made principally on that ground.

Give the students the best, he insisted, "even if you do have to go outside of the ranks of the graduates of the College to get it."

It is obvious that the board of trustees tried to choose candidates who had demonstrated outstanding academic promise as undergraduates. Oscar G. Klinger was valedictorian of his class. Luther H. Croll, Philip M. Bikle, and John A. Himes were salutatorians. In fact, only five of the fourteen alumni faculty had not received some senior class honor. Among the nonalumni faculty, Edsall Ferrier was salutatorian of his class. Edward S. Breidenbaugh and John A.

---

[58]Report of the Commissioner (1904), 2:1425.
[59]Milton Valentine to Frederick W. Conrad, March 12, 1874, GCA.

Himes had some university experience, but it was brief and did not result in their receiving an earned Ph.D. degree. Those members of the faculty who were concerned about keeping abreast of their fields in order to offer a strong instructional program had to engage in their own routine of study, without whatever benefit formal training beyond their undergraduate days might confer upon them.

Four of the twenty-two faculty members between 1868 and 1904 had an earned Ph.D. degree when they came to Gettysburg. The first of these, William Notz, the German professor during 1868-1869, brought his from the University of Tuebingen. The second was Samuel P. Sadtler, one of the five alumni faculty members who did not receive a senior class honor. After study at Lehigh and Harvard, he earned his Ph.D. from the University of Goettingen. Both Henry B. Nixon and Charles F. Woods received their degrees from The Johns Hopkins University. Only one of these four men – Nixon – remained at Gettysburg for any length of time.

In five cases the College recognized its own faculty members by awarding them honorary degrees. In 1866 it conferred a Ph.D. degree on Alfred M. Mayer. In 1880, after he resigned his professorship, the trustees gave H. Louis Baugher a D.D. degree. Seven years later, they granted Sc.D. degrees to Luther H. Croll and Edward S. Breidenbaugh, and a D.D. degree to Adam Martin. In 1884 Roanoke College conferred an honorary Ph.D. degree upon Philip M. Bikle. Thirteen years later the Dickinson College chapter of Phi Beta Kappa elected him to honorary membership.[60]

After 1868 the Gettysburg College faculty continued its earlier practice of meeting at least once each week during the academic year. The president presided or, in his absence, the vice president or dean. Minutes were kept by a secretary who was expected to stay in office for a long time: H. Louis Baugher (1870-1877); Philip M. Bikle (1877-1889); Huber G. Buehler, principal of the preparatory department (1889-1891); and George D. Stahley (1891-1911). In the meetings, there was considerably more discussion of curricular matters than was true before 1868. Here faculty agreed upon the frequent readjustments of teaching schedules made necessary by the president's absences, a vacancy, or an illness. Here they arranged for admitting students into the College and for examining those already there. Nevertheless, the striking thing about the minutes is the evidence they give of continuing preoccupation with the many rules and regulations of the College, determining who had violated them, disciplining the offenders, granting permission for students to leave town, and excusing absences from courses or other obligations.

[60]The Hamilton College chapter of Phi Beta Kappa elected Adam Martin to alumni membership in 1890. In the same year, the Lafayette College chapter similarly honored Edsall Ferrier, long after he resigned his Gettysburg position.

The Campus

In 1868, the College campus consisted of about twenty-one acres of land. The older part, on which the College edifice, Linnaean Hall, and the president's house stood, extended west from North Washington street about 520 feet, with its northern limit about fifty feet south of West Lincoln avenue and its southern limit stopping short of the Tiber. In preparation for building Stevens Hall, the College purchased four small tracts of land within the square bounded by Carlisle, Lincoln, North Washington, and Stevens streets. In 1868 it owned all of this square but the southwestern corner, on which Christ Chapel now stands.[61]

Not surprisingly, the College acquired no more land during the financially troubled 1870s. Only when in the mid-1880s they were about to undertake serious planning for a large new building did the trustees begin expanding the campus again by purchasing three lots to the west and one to the south (1885-1888). In 1892 they bought the property on which Christ Chapel was later built. About this time a local insurance agent, Martin Winter (1854-1918), began acquiring and developing land north of the campus. The first four houses which he built, located at 59-71 West Lincoln avenue, were constructed in 1892. Two years later Winter opened a new street to the north, which he called College avenue but was soon renamed Broadway.[62]

The response of the College to this development was to purchase (1892-1894) all of the lots which it did not already own on the south side of West Lincoln avenue, on one of which a house had recently been built. In 1894 Winter and the College exchanged a number of small parcels of land, so that the former's holdings would henceforth be north and the latter's south of West Lincoln avenue. In the same year the two parties joined in asking the Gettysburg borough council to abandon that section of the old Gettysburg-Black's tavern turnpike which ran in a northwesterly direction through the campus and also to extend Washington street north to West Lincoln avenue.[63]

---

[61]For further information on the campus, see Gregory J. Landrey, "A History of the Gettysburg Campus," (Gettysburg College paper, 1977), pp. 25-34.

[62]The borough council ordained the present Lincoln avenue in 1869. It was first called Stevens street.

[63]One can try to follow the course of the old turnpike by attempting to walk north on the present Mummasburg street and then continue in a straight line through the campus, across the properties fronting on West Lincoln avenue and West Broadway, and onto the Mummasburg road. In 1897 the borough council passed an ordinance vacating the old turnpike road through the present campus.

The transactions just described brought to an end the expansion of the College campus until after 1904. By expending about $7,800, the trustees had doubled its 1868 size from about twenty-one to forty-three acres. In 1904 the campus extended west from North Washington street to near the present Constitution avenue, with its northern limit the south side of West Lincoln avenue and its southern limit, except for one small property on Washington street, along Constitution avenue. The campus now also included the entire square enclosed by Carlisle, West Lincoln, North Washington, and Stevens streets. In June 1900, when someone sought to buy from the College a building lot on Carlisle street, north of Stevens Hall, the trustees wisely declared that they deemed "it inexpedient to alienate any of the Corporation's property."

In 1868 there were six buildings on the campus, all of which remained in use in 1904. They were the College edifice, Linnaean Hall, the president's house, the janitor's house, Stevens Hall, and the double frame house occupied by two professors and their families.

The College edifice continued to dominate the campus until the construction of what is now Glatfelter Hall in 1888-1889. Milton Valentine was correct when he declared in 1882 that, "in view of forty-three years' use, by so many renters and renters of all classes,

The campus as it appeared between 1868 and the building program of the late 1880s.

tormented by day and by night by the laborious investigations of enterprising young men into the possibilities of things," the building was indeed "in a good state of preservation."[64] But he was correct only because the College tried as best it could to meet the almost constant need for repairs. In 1870-1871, for example, a tin roof replaced the original shingle roof. New steps were built to the main entrance, and the cupola was painted. Every so often a coat of whitewash was applied to the building.

In an address to the Philadelphia alumni in 1884, Valentine expressed his concern for the safety of a building "with fifty-four fires going day and night, and an almost equal number of lamps." It was "a hazard too great to be thought of with quiet nerves."[65] Students were no longer permitted to use wood for their fires; the coal bins were located inside the building in two basement rooms. In March 1882 the *College Monthly* warned students not to use kerosene, or coal oil, in kindling their fires and called attention to the almost daily accounts of serious accidents in other places, resulting from this practice. Several fires were started in the old building, but they were all quickly extinguished. Although gas was available for lighting, many students continued to use kerosene for that purpose.

In 1861, when the Civil War began, a flagpole was placed on the building and a flag ceremoniously raised. There is insufficient evidence to establish whether the flag was flown regularly either during or after the war, but the pole remained until in October 1878 a heavy storm brought it down. The students were pleased when it was replaced, but were disappointed that it was not regularly used for its intended purpose. After Secretary of War Robert Lincoln presented the seminary students with a flag, which they began to display, the *College Monthly* for March 1883 asked: "Cannot we be as patriotic and procure a flag for our cupola?" They did, and after it had worn out, students and faculty in 1894 contributed enough money to buy two new ones. However, no one assumed the thankless responsibility of raising and lowering the flag each day, which prompted the following lament in the *College Mercury* for June 1895:

> We cannot understand why the flag is not allowed to float every day, especially in a town of such military interest as Gettysburg. The only reason we can think of is the trouble which would necessarily be involved. But this should have been thought of before the students were asked to buy the flags.

---

[64]Quoted in the *College Monthly* (July 1882), p. 176.
[65]Quoted in ibid. (March 1884), p. 42.

> When the idea was first mentioned, all were in favor of it, and now since we have the flags we think they should be used as they were first intended.

In spite of this appeal, flying the flag over the building every day, let alone day and night, had not become the custom by 1904.

Into the 1880s one called the structure erected in 1836-1837 either the College edifice, the building, or the main building. In the College Monthly for December 1886, the editor argued that it

> should be called Pennsylvania Hall. It certainly should have some specific name, and we know of no other more appropriate than the one we suggest. The College bears the name of our State, and as most of the money for erecting the main building was contributed by the State, there is special propriety in having it bear the name of the State. We have a Linnaean Hall, Stevens Hall, McCreary Hall or Gymnasium; let there be also a Pennsylvania Hall, and let the building erected chiefly with the State's money bear that name.

Especially after the present Glatfelter Hall was built and the old structure was used as a dormitory, many agreed that some more fitting designation was in order. Until 1898, the catalogue referred to it as Dormitory Hall; then for the first time it was called Pennsylvania Hall. Faculty minutes in the same year (McKnight Hall was now in use as a dormitory) refer to it for the first time as the old dormitory. The next step was to call it simply Old Dorm.[66]

During the first twenty years of its existence, Linnaean Hall housed the collections of the Linnaean Association on the main floor and the classrooms of the preparatory department in the basement. With the construction of Stevens Hall in 1867-1868, the vacated space was used briefly as a gymnasium and then for instruction in the sciences, especially chemistry. Although the Linnaean Association was revived in the 1870s, it did not thrive. However, the collections which it had inaugurated grew considerably during the period under study and were housed in the building until 1890.

Between 1868 and 1904 one janitor and three professors (one of them the president) lived on the campus. The houses of all four families were less than ten years old in 1868 and needed no major repairs for some time after that date. In asking the board to build residential facilities on campus, the faculty argued that such a step would improve discipline by enabling more of the professors to assemble on short notice when immediate action was required.[67]

---

[66]Subsequent references call this building Pennsylvania Hall. To most students before extensive changes were made in 1969-1970, it was Old Dorm.

[67]Faculty Report, August 8, 1867, GCA.

[68]For a discussion of Stevens Hall, see pp. 113-115. The first major renovation of the president's house occurred in 1898. Friends of the College contributed $1,800, which paid the bills.

Whether this alleged benefit ever resulted is hard to say, but it is apparent that for many years two faculty families enjoyed living on the edge of the campus. Among the tenants were Edsall Ferrier and Luther H. Croll, while they were vice presidents of the College; Samuel P. Sadtler; Philip M. Bikle, whose occupancy began many years before he became dean; and Henry B. Nixon. The Bikle and Nixon families were the tenants in 1904.[68]

During the twenty years between 1868 and 1888, only a few, relatively inexpensive, facilities were added to the campus: a skating pond in 1869-1870, a gymnasium in 1872, an observatory in 1874, and tennis grounds in 1885.[69] The first of these improvements was initiated when in October 1869 the faculty named a committee to bring in a plan to furnish "the students with increased facilities for skating." The resulting pond was located in the northwest quadrant of the square bounded by Carlisle, West Lincoln, North Washington, and Stevens streets. Students helped to build, maintain, and repair it. As late as 1881, the *College Monthly* reported that the pond was still being heavily used.

Interest in a gymnasium for Gettysburg College reflected a nationwide revival of interest in physical exercise and education which began about the time of the Civil War. By 1880 few Pennsylvania colleges and universities lacked such a facility or some sort of program to encourage students to remain physically fit.[70] In August 1865 the board of trustees commissioned the faculty to prepare "a detailed and specific plan of buildings etc. for gymnastic exercises" and to submit it at their next meeting. The report presented one year later consisted primarily of letters from two of the country's leading authorities on physical education and fitness. Dio (or Dioclesian) Lewis (1823-1886) was the author of the well-known book, *New Gymnastics* (1862), and founder of the Boston Normal Institute of Physical Education. Edward Hitchcock (1828-1911), Professor of Hygiene and Physical Education at Amherst College since 1861, held the first such position in an American college. The faculty believed that the statements by these two men contained "all that is needed on the subject," the importance of which, they argued, "cannot well be overstated."[71] Nevertheless, since the trustees were then busily engaged in planning for a new preparatory building, they did not take final action on the report. Two years later, in 1868, after the students had petitioned the faculty for a gymnasium and begun to raise funds for its construction and after the faculty added its bless-

[69]A diagram of the campus prepared in 1876 identified a ball ground located north of Pennsylvania Hall and south of the present Lincoln avenue.
[70]Rudolph, *American College,* pp. 151-153; Sack, *Higher Education,* 2:634-638.
[71]Faculty Report, August 1866, GCA.

ing to the effort, the trustees named a committee of their own members to propose a workable plan. In June 1869 this committee reported that no suitable structure could be built for less than $650 (this must rank as one of the major understatements of the year), whereupon the trustees named another committee to procure the necessary funds.

Obviously, the financial condition of both College and country at this time afforded little promise of early success. No definitive action was taken until the trustees appointed still another committee in 1871. On November 9 of that year its members met with the faculty and students. The latter agreed to try to collect the money required and in a few vacation months they succeeded in raising about $500. This prompted the committee to enter into a contract with a local carpenter, George Cashman, directing him to begin construction and proceed until the available funds were exhausted. Work began in the spring of 1872. In June, just before the trustees met, John B. McCreary of Philadelphia, president of the Honey Brook Coal Company, sent the president of the board a letter, enclosing $1,000 and promising $500 more at the end of the year, if the completed structure were named for him. At their next meeting the board members promptly thanked McCreary, accepted his condition, and directed the committee to complete the task.

McCreary Gymnasium
Completed in 1872, this building was converted into a chemistry laboratory in 1890 and was used for that purpose until it was removed in 1927.

247

The John B. McCreary Gymnasium was dedicated on October 17, 1872. Located between Pennsylvania Hall and Washington street and just north of the former, it was a frame building of about ninety feet by fifty feet. It had an earthen floor with a ten-pin alley "of the latest pattern" on either side. Eventually, the equipment included swings, climbing ropes, and suspended circles. The cost was about $2,200.[72] Although the prime mover of the gymnasium was trustee Charles A. Hay, who introduced the first motion in 1865 and served on each of the many committees subsequently appointed to bring about its construction, the honors on the day of dedication went to two elderly gentlemen of great experience, but not in gymnastics, who were called upon to break in the new facility. A writer in the *Lutheran Observer* for October 25 recounted its initiation as follows:

> The winding up of the affair was the funniest of all. It was determined that two reverend divinities should roll the first balls. To the professor emeritus [Samuel Simon Schmucker] was accorded the honor of opening the game, but it was evident that he could lecture on dogmatics better than play nine-pins, for in four rolls he did not bring down a pin. His competitor [John G. Morris], who stripped for the occasion, did not do much better, but it was no wonder, for the "boys" crowded round the alley so densely and kept up such an unearthly yelling at the failure of the combatants, that the latter was rendered nervous, and somehow the balls would not run straight.[73]

In the generation before the Civil War, there was considerable improvement in the means available for careful astronomical observation, and many observatories were built, especially in the North and West. Not all of these were connected with educational institutions. During the 1865-1866 academic year, John E. Graeff purchased a German-made telescope for Gettysburg College, which paid for it from unused Graeff professorship funds that year. The instrument had been used for some time in an observatory near Philadelphia. The 1866 catalogue claimed that it "has already done good work in astronomical science, and has been pronounced, by the first astronomers in the country, to be a perfect instrument." It predicted that the telescope would "soon be mounted and ready for

---

[72]On October 17, 1872 the gymnasium committee reported to the trustees that the cost of the facility was about $2,180, a figure which did not include several small unfinished items.

[73]"Could one have prophesied that the venerable Dr. S. S. Schmucker, a puritan of puritans in his theories, would ever have raised his hand to roll a ball?" asked Henry Eyster Jacobs. When he told Schmucker's son what had happened, the latter was incredulous. "Who would have thought that my father could ever have been persuaded to handle a ten-pin ball?" Jacobs confirms that the score in the Schmucker-Morris game was 0-0. Jacobs, *Memoirs,* pp. 155-156.

the use of the students in Astronomy." Eight years were to elapse before this prediction came true.

The College's first task was to bring the telescope to Gettysburg. As late as January 1868 it was still in Philadelphia, where Martin L. Stoever inspected it. Upon his return he told his colleagues that the instrument was not properly protected and needed immediate attention. Moreover, the person in whose custody it was placed wanted to be relieved of his responsibility as soon as possible. One year later, Graeff loaned the instrument to naval authorities to be used in observing the solar eclipse of August 7, 1869.[74] For that purpose it was taken to Iowa. Not until 1872 did the federal government finally agree to pay for the damage incurred during the trip out and back. Although the College was at this time short of funds needed to meet already existing obligations, at the request of the trustees Milton Valentine had begun raising money specifically for an observatory building. In June 1872 he told them that he had raised about $3,000 and hoped to secure the remainder soon. The College then engaged a

Observatory
Completed in 1874, after a period of little or no use this building was removed in 1925.

[74]For an account of this eclipse, the first total eclipse of the sun visible in the United States since 1834, and of the part to be played by the College telescope in observing it, see the *Star and Sentinel* for August 6 and 13, 1869.

Baltimore architect, William F. Weber, who visited several existing observatories and what were described as "some of the most eminent astronomers of the country." He then prepared a set of plans for Gettysburg College. In July 1874 a contract was entered into with Elias Roth of New Oxford, and by the end of the year, or shortly thereafter, he had completed his work.[75]

Located directly east of Washington street, on ground now occupied by the southern part of Hanson Hall, the Observatory consisted of a central section sixteen feet square, with a western and an eastern wing, each twelve by sixteen feet. The dome on the central section rested upon iron balls, which revolved in an iron groove and made rotation possible either by hand or by a wheel, so that "the whole visible hemisphere of the sky may be laid under contribution at any time." The telescope and several other pieces of equipment were mounted on masonry piers resting on solid rock. The frame of the building itself was covered by corrugated and galvanized iron. The reported cost was $3,406.[76]

The distinctive appearance of the Observatory gave rise to expressions of College humor. Said a prep student on seeing the building for the first time: "Chum, what fur house is that over there with a balloon on it?" Some visitors to the campus apparently had trouble deciding the purpose of the building and concluded that, because it had a ball on top, it must be a gymnasium.[77]

In May 1885 the faculty granted permission to an alumnus, John B. McPherson (1883), and several other local persons to use the area to the rear of the Observatory for playing tennis. In the next issue of the *College Monthly,* one writer noted that the grounds were being laid out for this purpose, but concluded that they would be equally suitable for star gazing and for moon-struck lovers.

Even before the College recovered fully from the hard times of the 1870s, members of the faculty began urging the trustees to prepare for the construction of a new College building. Although some of them seemed to believe otherwise, increasing enrollment could scarcely have been much of a factor in their thinking. The number of students in the early 1880s was only then returning to the levels reached, and accommodated, in the late 1860s. Not until 1887 did enrollment in the College proper exceed the number of students in

---

[75]The Franklin and Marshall College observatory was dedicated in 1886.

[76]*Star and Sentinel,* July 28, 1874. The 1875 catalogue, noting the completion of the observatory, stated that "in a few months" it would be "furnished with a full equipment of Astro and Meteoro instruments. The Equatorial Telescope has been mounted, the Transit Instrument has been purchased, and efforts are now being made to add an Astronomical Clock and Chronograph."

[77]Quoted in the *College Monthly* for March 1879, p. 64, and February 1880, p. 31.

1871. The faculty were still actively looking for students to maintain existing enrollment. The major reason for advocating a new building was the conviction that the times required more adequate facilities than the existing campus buildings could provide for larger classrooms, better-equipped libraries, and a more appropriately appointed chapel. Morever, these facilities should be more fire proof than Pennsylvania Hall could ever be, at least as long as those fifty-four fires were kept burning. The old building would still be highly useful, but as a dormitory for students. We can trace the campaign for a new building in a number of sources. Evidence appears in the columns of the *College Monthly* as early as 1880. In October 1881 it described the proposed new structure as "an imperative necessity."

Some persons hoped that the trustees would use the occasion of the College semicentennial in 1882 to begin raising money. No one was quite sure how much was needed, but the early estimate was an unrealistically low $20,000. The semicentennial came and went. As we shall see, it was a gala affair in which many participated and enjoyed themselves, but it did not produce a major financial campaign. Trustees remembered the minimal success of past efforts to raise money, especially those which followed the construction of Stevens Hall. They were reluctant to embark upon yet another attempt until there was a good prospect of its success.

The faculty were determined not to allow the matter of a new building to be forgotten. In December 1883 the editor of the *College Monthly* declared: "we again press our appeal." In February 1884 Milton Valentine told the Philadelphia alumni that "the wonderful enlargement of the universities and colleges in the last few years, should be a stirring and effective appeal to us." In response to the demands resulting from "the progress of science and the practical industries," many of them had already added new departments, increased their "apparatus and appliances," and built "themselves up in grand proportions and into great strength." He told the Philadelphians that "college work is advancing all along the line, and *Alma Mater* must advance." The most pressing immediate needs of Gettysburg were two new professorships, a large increase in endowment, and "at once . . . a new hall – as a fire-proof library, with recitation rooms.[78] The faculty report to the board several months later restated these needs in even stronger language than the president's and referred them to "the best and most earnest attention of the Board."

While Milton Valentine fully shared in the faculty sentiment, he was undoubtedly relieved when presented with the opportunity to

---

[78]Quoted in ibid. (March 1884), pp. 39-41.

return to the more agreeable task of seminary teaching and entrust the responsibility of College leadership at this particular time to someone else. As already noted, it was widely believed that while trustees, faculty, and financial agents were necessary for successful fund raising, the main burden would have to be borne by the president of the College. That understanding was clearly in the minds of the trustees when they elected Harvey W. McKnight in July 1884. At that time, however, they were obviously not ready to commit themselves definitively to a building program. In 1885 they did begin buying for future use land west of the campus. But during their annual meetings in that year and again in 1886, they did nothing more than commend McKnight for his fund-raising efforts and promise their cooperation in advancing them. Meanwhile, national developments demonstrated once again how vulnerable the College was to economic conditions. Another in the long line of recessions which began in the early 1880s dropped enrollment of degree candidates from 110 in 1881-1882 to 94 in 1885-1886.

Soon after taking office, Harvey W. McKnight began visiting and soliciting potential donors to the College. It is evident that he confined his attention largely to Lutheran circles and that this was what was expected of him. He came to doors which were closed, some of them because of the recession. He found others open, but not to his immediate purposes. William Bittinger, for example, was ready to give money to the College, but only after his death and for an endowed professorship. The first real breakthrough came when he called on Philip H. Glatfelter, the Spring Grove paper manufacturer and not yet a trustee of the College. He promised to give $10,000 toward the construction of a building, but attached certain unspecified conditions to his gift.[79] Nevertheless, at last McKnight had a promise which he might use to challenge other donors. The faculty continued to press. Their 1887 report referred once more to "the imperative need of a new building and better facilities."

When the board of trustees met on June 29, 1887, its members were finally ready to act. They established a committee to select a site and erect a new building, proceeding with construction, however, only so long as funds were available. The newly elected board president, John E. Graeff, named the following trustees to the committee: Harvey W. McKnight, Edward McPherson, Frederick W. Conrad, Milton Valentine, and the board officers. By the end of the meeting, members of the board had increased the total pledged to about $25,000. Most of the amount beyond Glatfelter's gift came

---

[79]Philip M. Bikle, "Recent College Improvements," ibid. (May 1890), p. 17. Philip H. Glatfelter later removed the conditions.

from five trustees: John E. Graeff, John A. Swope, Charles A. Schieren, Benjamin S. Kunkle, and George Ryneal. The building committee was authorized to call special meetings of the board whenever it deemed appropriate. One such meeting occurred in 1887 and three in 1889.

The building committee promptly engaged the services of John A. Dempwolf (1848-1926) to present plans for the new building. Born in Germany, Dempwolf came to York in 1867 and learned the carpentry trade. Becoming interested in the work of an architect, he took a course at the Cooper Union Institute in New York, from which he was graduated in 1873. After working in Boston and Philadelphia, he opened his York office and began a fifty-year practice in 1876. Dempwolf was an active member of Christ Lutheran church, whose retired pastor, Augustus H. Lochman, was still a trustee of the College.[80] The plans which he prepared were presented to a special meeting of the board in September 1887. They were approved, with the understanding that changes would be made as the work progressed. The president was now relieved of all of his campus duties so that he could devote his entire time to raising money.

The plans which the board sanctioned called for the construction of a building 162 feet long and 69 feet in depth, except for a 52-foot central extension to the west, which was to be used for a chapel. The tower above the main entrance would be 143 feet high. The new structure was to be located on a site between the president's house and Linnaean Hall, apparently chosen as early as 1885, when the land on which it stands was purchased. It was to be constructed with an estimated 1,200,000 bricks, with Hummelstown brownstone trim. An article in the *Star and Sentinel* for October 4, 1887 described the style of architecture as "the classic Romanesque, a style greatly admired and adapting itself readily to a modern structure of this character – its forms suggesting dignity and strength." Five contractors submitted bids ranging from $77,457 to $91,318, all of them far cries from the estimates being made only a few years before. These bids did not include the chapel, already being regarded as too much of an added expense. The building committee selected the lowest bid and in December 1887 awarded the contract to William A. Slagle, who had completed buildings in Hanover (where he lived), Frederick, and Baltimore. At the groundbreaking ceremonies on March 1, 1888, Philip M. Bikle threw the first shovel of ground and

---

[80]*Christ Lutheran Messenger,* January 1927, pp. 5-6, has a summary of Dempwolf's career. He designed several hundred structures in York and numerous other places, including more than a dozen in Gettysburg (1883-1900). For the data of buildings erected by Dempwolf, see File 11022, Historical Society of York County, York.

the construction began. It had not proceeded far before the College's plans were dramatically changed.[81]

On April 10, 1888 Lieutenant Colonel John P. Brua (1813-1888), a retired army paymaster and brother-in-law of Simon Cameron, happened to meet William M. Baum in Philadelphia. He told this veteran College trustee of his desire to erect a monument to his parents somewhere in Gettysburg, and preferably on the College campus. Baum immediately referred the colonel to another veteran trustee, Charles A. Hay, who had once been pastor of Zion Lutheran church in Harrisburg, of which Peter (1771-1842) and Catharine (1777-1833) Brua had been long and faithful members. Hay responded immediately to this initiative, suggesting that Brua might best memorialize his parents by providing the funds for a combination chapel and auditorium. "This would be a most conspicuous object, right on the theatre of the first day's battle," he wrote, "and would forever associate your name, and that of your deceased parents, with the great event that turned the tide of war and secured the perpetuity of the Union." On May 1 the colonel replied, pledging $15,000 for Brua Memorial Chapel, asking only that "a slab of Italian marble" be erected with a simple inscription, the text of which he furnished. On May 26, quite unexpectedly, Brua died, but not before giving the College his note for $15,000.[82]

The cornerstone of the New Recitation Building (it did not become Glatfelter Hall until 1912) was laid, on schedule, during commencement week, on June 27, 1888. John G. Morris, one of the two surviving original trustees of the College, was the main speaker. Former President Valentine made brief remarks and formally laid the cornerstone. He referred to the original building of the College which since 1837 had "furnished place and convenience for its prosperous and enlarging work of Christian education." Now, half a century later, the College was responding to the Lord's "summons to arise and build again, because the old place is too narrow for the greater work now given to the institution."[83] Once the ceremonies were concluded, the workmen returned to their tasks. By fall they had reached the top of the third story windows and by December the roof was in place. The work on the interior remained to be done.

[81]For further information about this building, see Norman O. Forness, "Glatfelter Hall: Gilded Age Building Reflects a Past Era in Academic History," Gettysburg Bulletin (October 1972), pp. 3-7.

[82]There are several accounts of this sequence of events. The one used here, believed to be the most credible, comes from Charles A. Hay's statement on September 7, 1890, when Brua Memorial Chapel was dedicated. Quoted in College Monthly (October 1890), pp. 222-225.

[83]Quoted in ibid. (June 1888), pp. 186-187. Philip H. Glatfelter was elected to the board of trustees at its annual meeting in June 1888.

Laying the cornerstone for the New Recitation Building, June 27, 1888

By the end of the year 1888 the building committee had committed all of its available funds and needed about $25,000 to complete the structure. Its clear mandate was to halt at this point and return to the trustees for further instructions. What these would be was uncertain. Many believed that President McKnight and others had already approached almost every likely prospect for pledges. While it would undoubtedly be unsettling to halt construction, going into debt promised to be even more disturbing. "The experience with the Preparatory Hall," commented the *College Monthly* for December 1888, "is warning enough for a century." Its editor advised that a second approach be made to those who had already given.

The board of trustees, with fifteen members present, convened on January 22, 1889 to hear McKnight's progress report. Their deliberations and actions concerned not only the hall under construction, but also four other campus buildings whose uses would be affected in some way by its completion. After considering the alternatives before them, the trustees directed the building committee to (1) complete the hall "at once," (2) borrow the funds required, and (3) make those alterations in the old College building which were necessary to fit it for use as a dormitory. Further, they authorized the committee to (1) change Linnaean Hall into a gymnasium, (2) change McCreary Gymnasium into a chemistry building, and (3) construct a heating plant to serve all campus buildings. The trustees gratefully acknowledged the gift of $5,000 made a few days before their meeting by James McMillan and directed McKnight to canvass the constituency once more in the search for additional money. Well might the *College Monthly* for February 1889 conclude that "never was there a more important meeting of our College Board, or one characterized by a better spirit." At its annual meeting in June, the board confirmed all of the decisions made five months earlier. By then, work on the interior of the new hall was nearing completion.[84]

The New Recitation Building was dedicated, on schedule, on September 11, 1889. The ceremonies had to compete with those marking the dedication of about eighty Pennsylvania monuments recently erected on the battlefield, but the College authorities minimized the competition by securing the services of Governor James A. Beaver, who was in town for the other events, as master of ceremonies. A heavy rain forced the exercises into one of the large rooms on the third floor of the new building. To John E. Graeff fell the difficult task of trying to raise $20,000 on the spot. This was the sum needed to pay what was still due on the building and to purchase needed furnishings. When he asked who would contribute the first $5,000, Philip H. Glatfelter stated that he would, if the entire sum could be raised. When no one responded to Graeff's call for a second $5,000 quickly enough to suit him, he announced that he himself would give it. Within less than half an hour, more than twenty pledges, ranging from $2,500 to $50, had raised the entire amount asked for. The main address of the day, which lasted almost one hour, was given by Attorney General William S. Kirkpatrick of Pennsylvania. Milton Valentine then formally dedicated the building and turned over the keys to Harvey W. McKnight. "Who will be the man to name the new building?" asked the *College Monthly* in December 1889. "Where is he? Let him show his face that we may all see him." The new hall might have been named for Graeff, an old and frequent benefactor of the College. Glatfelter urged that it be named for McKnight. But everyone would have to wait until 1912 for the answer to the *College Monthly's* question.

The New Recitation Building had three floors and a basement. At first, the latter was used for instruction in physics, but later, mostly for storage. There were nine classrooms, four on the first, four on the second, and one on the third floor. As early as 1889, the large room at the north end of the second floor, which was set aside for examinations, was named the "sweat box." On the first floor, there was an office for the president to the left of the main entrance and a

---

[84]James McMillan and Luther R. Keefer, the latter the nephew and executor of John P. Brua, were elected to the board at this time.

reception room to the right. Space for the library was also on this floor. The museum collections which had been in Linnaean Hall for many years were placed in the center section of the third floor, where there was also space which could be used for an infirmary, if needed. The literary societies had their meeting rooms on this floor; Philo had the north and Phrena the south wings. Neither the library nor the literary society rooms were ready for use until the spring of 1890, but the formal opening exercises for the 1889-1890 year were held in the sweat box, which also served as the chapel for that year.[85]

The decision made in 1887 to construct a new College hall virtually determined that substantial alterations would have to be made in the old College building if its space were to be used effectively. In January 1889 the board of trustees directed the building committee to proceed with the changes. John A. Dempwolf drew up a set of plans, but the committee was so staggered by the estimates received that it decided not to enter into a contract with anyone. Instead, the employees of William A. Slagle did the work under the general direction of the architect. In an effort to give Slagle's workmen the maximum amount of time to do what needed to be done, the faculty held commencement three weeks earlier than usual in June 1889 and scheduled the opening date of the fall term two weeks later than usual in September. Although the remodeling began as soon as the students left the building, when they returned three months later it was not ready to receive them. Fortunately, temporary accommodations were found in town for what was a record enrollment. "Too much cannot be said in praise of the students," noted the *College Monthly* in October 1889, "for the philosophical way in which they took in the situation and adapted themselves to present circumstances." The first to occupy the building did not move in until mid-October; it was not fully in use until November. The workmen did not complete all of their tasks until May 1890. The building committee hoped to keep costs to $10,000 or less, but it was not successful.

The thoroughly renovated Pennsylvania Hall contained eighty-six rooms for student occupancy, some of which were arranged so that two students could use one of them for study and one for sleeping. The building committee quickly abandoned the plan to add a large extension to the north center of the building, but it did install new

[85]In 1892, at a cost of $1,200, the College purchased a clock and bell for the tower. The old bell which had been moved from Pennsylvania Hall but was soon found to be unsatisfactory in its new location was then retired from service. The cost of these improvements was met by contributions from Mrs. John Wiseman and William L. Glatfelter.

windows, doors, floors, concrete hallways, and iron and brick stairways. It placed an extension to the east and west ends of the building, each of which became a stairwell. Cast iron steps with brick cheek walls topped by cast stone replaced the old wooden steps of the portico.

Prompted by an act which the state legislature passed on June 3, 1885, one to which the trustees had for several years avoided responding, the building committee installed fire escapes. Pennsylvania Hall was now divided into three distinct divisions or parts, which the catalogue described prosaically as east, middle, and west. With a more highly developed sense of style, the *College Monthly* in November 1889 suggested naming them Gentlemen's Retreat, Devil's Den, and Fools' Gallery. Some young men returning in the fall of 1889 may have thought for a moment that the devil was indeed making a fool of them. Gone were the days of the $9 annual room rent. In its place there was a scale ranging from $21.75 for the least desirable and usually avoided basement rooms to $48 for the best quarters. Two students using a room could divide the cost between them. Except for the old chapel, which was now turned over to the Young Men's Christian Association for its use, and for the reading rooms of the literary societies, the entire building was devoted to dormitory purposes.

The groundbreaking ceremonies for Brua Memorial Chapel occurred on June 27, 1888, a few minutes after the conclusion of those during which the cornerstone of the New Recitation Building was laid. Trustee William M. Baum spoke about the generosity of John P. Brua. The daughters of Presidents Valentine and McKnight broke the first ground. However, construction did not begin immediately. Not until December did the trustees actually enter into a contract with William A. Slagle, who agreed, for the sum of $15,400, to erect and complete the structure. Work began in the early spring of 1889 and was far enough advanced to permit formal laying of the cornerstone on May 16 of that year. The speaker on this occasion was Charles Emory Smith, editor of the *Philadelphia Press*. Unexpected and extended delays in securing the special roofing tiles rendered impossible the expected completion date of September 1889 and forced the faculty to conduct chapel service during the 1889-1890 year in the sweat box. Commencement exercises were held in the new structure in June 1890 and it was used for opening College exercises and for daily chapel services for the first time in the following September. It was dedicated on September 7, 1890. Charles A. Hay preached the sermon and Harvey W. McKnight dedicated the building "for uses, religious and literary, in the cause of Christian education."

Brua Chapel
Completed in 1890. This picture appeared in the first Spectrum, *published in 1891.*

According to an account in the *College Monthly* for December 1888, the site of Brua Chapel (as it will now be called) was selected because it was "close to the principal entrance to the college grounds, within full view of the Gettysburg and Harrisburg Railroad." It was placed so that "the northern entrance, which will be most ordinarily used, will be in a direct line from the main entrance to the dormitory building." The article described the architectural style as "the later Romanesque," similar to that of the New Recitation Building. "Local common brick" and Hummelstown brownstone were used to achieve the desired effect. A seventy-foot tower stood at the southeast corner. The estimated seating capacity was 750, of which one-third would be accommodated in what was described as the morning chapel. Located at the north end of the building, the morning chapel could easily be separated from the rest of the auditorium by movable partitions. In addition, there were three vestibules, a small sacristy, and a gallery along the east wall.

While the faculty and trustees were considering the best use of the space which would be available once the New Recitation Building was completed, Edward S. Breidenbaugh proposed that the functions of Linnaean Hall and McCreary Gymnasium be reversed, at least in part. Move the chemistry laboratory into the existing gymnasium building and the latter into Linnaean, he advised, and move the mineralogical collection into the new building.[86] In January 1889 the board of trustees accepted his plan. In spite of the fact that expenditures for building and renovations were running far ahead of projections, the trustees, during a special meeting in December, directed the building committee to proceed at once. Consequently, in January 1890 the College entered into a contract with Calvin Gilbert and Joseph J. Smith, members of a local firm, to execute the plans which John A. Dempwolf had prepared. The value of the contract, which was $7,359.70, included alterations to the existing gymnasium and preparation of a room in the new building to receive the mineralogial collection. Supervised by Breidenbaugh, the work was completed in the spring of 1890 and the new facility was ready for full use in the fall.

Abandoning an early proposal to move the old gymnasium to some other part of the campus and renovate it there, the building committee, in the words of Breidenbaugh, raised "the frame shell . . . about two feet from the ground and entirely remodeled [it], only the old frame work remaining."[87] When completed, it included several laboratories, with space for more than ninety students; a large class room; balance room; assay room; and several supply rooms. Writing in the College Monthly for March 1890, Breidenbaugh stated that "the building is very convenient and comfortable in arrangement – and is a very great improvement over the contracted space and inconveniences of the present quarters."

On February 1, 1890 the College entered into a contract with Gilbert and Smith to carry out the plans which Dempwolf had prepared for remodeling Linnaean Hall. The amount of the contract was $7,140. Except for a few items, the work, supervised by George D. Stahley, was completed by the end of December 1890. During the fall term students used one of the large rooms in the new building for their calisthenics. Writing in the College Monthly for February 1891, Stahley described Linnaean Hall as "enlarged and entirely reconstructed." A twenty-four foot extension was added to the north end and the portico on the south side was considerably altered. On the first floor, there were some 270 lockers, a wash room, dressing room, two bowling alleys, and toilet facilities.[88] The second floor

[86]As early as December 1887, President McKnight asked John A. Dempwolf to determine whether McCreary had the "capacity for the apparatus of a first class gymnasium." A few months later he announced that he had found someone who would contribute part of the $3,600 needed for its renovation. College Monthly for December 1887 and March 1888.

[87]Quoted in the Spectrum (1893), p. 45.

[88]The College Monthly described the toilets as "a water closet 24 feet by 18 feet constructed according to the 'Smead dry closet system.' "

contained the main gymnasium, office space, a gallery with a felt and canvas track, and an observation gallery. "The alumni and friends of the College can rest assured," Stahley wrote, "that this is a strictly first-class gymnasium in all its appointments and appliances."

Advocates of enlarged College facilities had urged the trustees to reduce the danger of fire on campus by constructing one facility which would heat all of the buildings. In January 1889 the board committed itself to this end. "The heating of all the buildings on the campus, from one central point, is the one thing in all our improvements that promises to pay its own way and possibly more," argued the College Monthly in April. "To fail in this, or postpone it, will be a disappointment to all and detract largely from the important changes now going on." There was to be no retreat from the decision to proceed. In September the trustees accepted the bid of $2,839 made by Gilbert and Smith to construct the boiler house and that of $16,000 made by Kelly, Jones, and Company of Pittsburgh to install the steam-heat system. Work began promptly enough, but it took more time than anticipated to complete the necessary digging, lay the pipes, make the connections, and get the system working properly. Students complained that the radiators at first did not radiate anything. They seemed to function best, it was reported, when used for cracking nuts. Early in December the faculty decided that "in view of the uncomfortable condition of many of the college rooms and recitation rooms, due to the delay in completing the steam-heating apparatus," classes would end a week before scheduled, "unless the weather prove too unfavorable, in which case we will close earlier." The heat was not turned on for the first time until mid-December. In March 1890 the College Monthly reported that steam heat had now been introduced into all of the buildings but the still uncompleted gymnasium and that, except for a few rooms on the fourth floor of Pennsylvania Hall, where larger radiators were necessary, it was working reasonably well. "The convenience and comfort of the heating," wrote Edward S. Breidenbaugh in 1892, "is only understood by those who had experience with the old system of stoves."[89]

In conjunction with the heating plant, the building committee drilled a deep well near the boiler house and used some of its water for campus use. In Pennsylvania Hall, water was available on the first floor only. The 1891 catalogue described the "water works" of the College as a well two hundred feet deep, "from which the water is pumped by a wind mill and hot air engine, as occasion requires,

---

[89]Spectrum (1893), p. 46.

into a large tank in the tower of the Recitation Hall, whence it is distributed to the various buildings on the campus."[90]

To recapitulate, between June 1887 and December 1890 the building committee had supervised the planning and construction of three new buildings (New Recitation Building, Brua Chapel, and the heating plant) and the extensive renovation of three others (Pennsylvania Hall, McCreary Gymnasium, and Linnaean Hall). Compared to all of the previous efforts of the College to provide facilities for carrying out its educational program, this was by far the most imposing. The costs incurred were even more imposing. According to the report which the building committee submitted to the board of trustees at the conclusion of its work, the total attributed to each of the buildings was as follows: New Recitation Building, $92,850.11; Brua Memorial Chapel, $19,025.34; Pennsylvania Hall, $17,631.07; heating plant, $20,558.19; chemistry building, $9,761.25; and Linnaean Hall, $10,676.75. The sum total of these six items was $170,502.75.

When one recalls the reluctance of the board of trustees to embark upon this building and renovation program in the first place, it is remarkable that, once having committed themselves, they were so determined to carry it through to completion. Time and again, noted the *College Monthly* for December 1889, "our Trustees have shown their purpose to take no backward step nor even halt in carrying out the liberal things they devised about a year ago." The editor attributed this to the fact that "there are men in the Board who will not rest till we have what every first-class college ought to have." He was pleased that "they are men, too, who not only help to pass resolutions but help also most liberally in furnishing the wherewithal to carry them out." What he did not note was that a number of these trustees were newcomers to the board.

The College could accurately say that it was able to dedicate the New Recitation Building free of debt. The amounts which President McKnight collected for that purpose and which were subscribed on the day of its dedication did cover its costs. In addition, the contribution of John P. Brua paid for about 80 percent of the cost of the chapel. In order to meet the remaining financial obligations, the board of trustees borrowed $25,000 from local banks and $30,000 (on June 27, 1889) from the Spring Garden Insurance Company of Philadelphia.[91]

---

[90]The College installed its own water system because no satisfactory arrangements could be made at this time with the Gettysburg Water Company, which feared that the College might use more water than it could supply.

[91]This latter obligation, payable in five years, was secured by a mortgage on the real estate of the College. The interest rate was 4½ percent. Adams County Mortgage Book J, pp. 254-258.

In the absence of any large gifts to erase this indebtedness, the trustees asked President McKnight to resume his travels. Although he diligently covered many miles and secured some contributions, the results were disappointing. There were at least three reasons for his scanty success. First, the depression which began in 1893, while not as long as the one twenty years earlier, was nevertheless severe. Second, there appears to have been an unwritten understanding, once the seminary decided to remain in Gettysburg and begin a building program, that it would have priority in approaching congregations in supporting synods for contributions.[92] Third, a dispute between the trustees and Professor H. Louis Baugher, which lasted from 1892 to 1896, alienated some congregations and potential donors. In June 1898 the board named a committee to appeal to the state legislature for financial help, but nothing came of this effort. When McKnight left office in 1904, the notes had been paid, but the $30,000 mortgage remained. It was not satisfied until March 28, 1913.[93]

After no discernible upward trend in student enrollment during the first eighteen years of the period under study (1868-1886), a rather dramatic change began in 1887. Enrollment in each of the two preceding years was about average for the period: 94 students. In 1887 it was 166; in 1889, 136; and in 1892, 175. Assuming that this trend was going to continue, President McKnight told the Philadelphia alumni in January 1892 that the College needed an additional dormitory. Soon the *College Monthly* began echoing his call. In May it claimed that "the students want to room in the college buildings, their parents prefer to have them do so, and it is the desire of the College authorities to have them together instead of scattered through the town." The depression which began in the following year not only made it more difficult to raise money for building purposes, but it also reduced enrollment from 175 in 1893 to 134 in 1896. With the return of prosperity in the following year, the board of trustees named a committee to call the attention of the church to the continuing need for additional dormitory facilities. A story to that effect appeared in the *Lutheran Observer* for January 29, 1897.

In June 1897 the board of trustees named President McKnight,

---

[92]In 1902 McKnight informed the Superintendent of Public Instruction that "our Theological Seminary has had the field for the last eight years in a canvass for funds to pay for its new buildings, and, according to an unwritten law, we have kept out as much as possible." *Report of the Superintendent* (1902), p. 921.

[93]The mortgage was assumed on February 10, 1897 by William W. Hafer of Abbottstown, whose estate transferred it to Farmers and Merchants Trust Company of Chambersburg on April 20, 1910. Adams County Deed Book XX, pp. 592, and Adams County Miscellaneous Books B, pp. 524-525, and C, p. 386.

James Strong, Philip H. Glatfelter, Charles M. Stock, and J. Emory Bair members of a building committee and charged them with constructing two or more dormitories. Using the plans which John A. Dempwolf prepared, they advertised for bids. In July 1897 they entered into a contract, amounting to $14,782, with a local builder, Merville E. Stallsmith, to construct the first of what was intended to be a series of three new dormitories. By September the walls were going up. The students first occupied South College, as it was called (it was not named KcKnight Hall until 1916), when they returned to the campus early in January 1898. The total cost of the building was $19,242.

Constructed of brick, with Indiana brownstone trim, South College was eighty-five by thirty-four feet. Rooms located on its three floors could accommodate about fifty students, some in single and others in double rooms. There was hot and cold water on each floor and lavatories in what were described as convenient places.[94] "The erection of this dormitory has proved very advantageous to the College," wrote a proud President McKnight in his report to the board of trustees in January 1898. "It has already secured for us four

South College
First occupied as a dormitory in January 1898, this building was renamed McKnight Hall in 1916.

---

[94]When McKnight Hall was connected to the heating system, Stevens Hall was disconnected and given its own system.

students, who otherwise would probably have gone to Yale or Harvard."

The days when the College could get along with one janitor ended about the time John Hopkins died in 1868, the same year in which Stevens Hall was first occupied by students. The trustees now found it necessary to employ two janitors, one for the College proper and a second for the preparatory department. In the mid-1880s it hired a night watchman. In the fall of 1889 John B. Hamilton (1849-1933) began a career of forty-four years with the College, most of them as superintendent of buildings and grounds, with special responsibility for maintaining the heating plant.

Between 1868 and 1904 a number of janitors and watchmen came and went. Except for surviving treasurer's vouchers, most of them are not remembered. The man who was the true successor of John Hopkins in the life of the College was Adam Foutz or Pfoutz (1841-1911), whose tenure began in 1876 and ended with his retirement, on a pension of $5 per month, thirty years later. In a sense, his position was demoted from the rank enjoyed by his predecessor. While Hopkins was known as the Vice President, Pfoutz had to be content with the title of Governor, or Guv, or even plain Jan. Adam was a good-natured and long-suffering man. If we are to believe the writer of his obituary in the Gettysburg *Compiler*, "when he pretended to be cross at some pranks of the boys it was always with a twinkle in his eye and a smile on his lips." Patiently, we are led to believe, he would clean out the keyholes of some class or dormitory rooms which students had plugged tightly with something which hardened like cement.[95] Without complaining, he brought students down from the cupola which was off limits to them because the faculty believed they could be up to no good when they were on top of it. Guv was also confident of his own ability to handle general College affairs. In June 1891 the *College Monthly* gave his reported response to a townsman who asked him how things were going at a time when most of the faculty were out of town: "All right – better than when they are all here."

While it was the assigned duty of the janitor to trim the trees, repair the fences, and keep the paths covered with tanbark and ashes, long after 1868 students continued helping to take care of the campus. Each spring, in April or May, classes were dismissed on one day for the freshmen, on another for the sophomores, and on still another for the juniors. Those who chose not to work were

---

[95]Benjamin V. D. Fisher, of the class of 1881, recalled one such incident. Irate students prevented Jan and a particularly obnoxious group of visitors from leaving the cupola by filling the keyhole of the locked door with melted lead. It took two hours to release them. *Spectrum* (1902), p. 188.

Adam Foutz (1841-1911)
Janitor from 1876 to 1906. While his predecessor was called vice president, Adam had to be content with the title of governor.

expected to attend classes as usual. One wonders whether any ever appeared to recite. During these campus days, as they were called, students worked under the direction of the janitor to clear away the debris left by the winter and prepare the grounds for another growing season. It is evident that for many young men that day was a spring holiday, but, nevertheless, enough work was accomplished to justify the faculty's continuing the practice into the 1880s.

George P. Ockershausen bought the College its first lawnmower in 1871, but the machine soon fell into disuse and was forgotten. It was the custom to allow the grass to grow until the janitor decided that the time had come to cut it, with a scythe. The resulting hay crop was his to use for his own benefit. It was also the custom for the students to spend most of one night making a crop of their own before leaving the campus. They fed theirs to no horse or cow, but packed it tightly into some classroom or the chapel. One item in the *College Monthly* for July 1883 was news of the breaking of this custom. "Jan harvested his hay this year without its going through the usual process of chapel packing."

According to the *College Monthly* for June 1885, Jan was complaining that little boys were beginning to pay attention to the "no trespassing on these grounds" signs at the College entrances, but cows were not. They wandered in from the farm to the north and from the outlots to the west.[96] There is little evidence of fences along these entrances to the campus, but there was a four-foot fence along Washington street. In 1887 it was replaced by an elaborate iron fence extending about nine hundred feet from the old gymnasium to the southeast corner of the campus.

In 1886 trustees David Wills and John G. Butler secured for the College the services of William Saunders (1822-1900), the famous horticulturist and landscape gardener for the United States Department of Agriculture, who in 1863 designed Soldiers' National Cemetery in Gettysburg. Saunders concluded that the campus was much too cluttered with trees. He recommended removal of the arbors which had graced it for years, as well as of many ailantus and silver poplar trees. Over the objections of those who opposed any such changes as destructive of the beauty which they saw in the old campus appearance, the College took his advice. Citizens of Gettysburg contributed about $500 to help pay for the new arrangement. "Workmen have been busy from day to day pulling down trees, cutting them into cord wood and logs, clearing away rubbish, filling up and leveling off the grounds, and making new drives," reported the *College Monthly* for December 1886. All of the ailantus and silver poplars were going, "leaving the center of the campus quite bare and giving a much better view of . . . Pennsylvania Hall, . . . There is no question but that the shade was too dense both for health and the growth of grass." The editor advised his readers "to wait till the drives and walks are finished and the grass has had time to grow before saying whether you like the changes or not." He judged it necessary to repeat this advice in the spring of 1887, when the grass was sown and when Norway spruce trees and hedges were planted. As an integral part of these changes, the College now purchased one large and one small lawnmower, retiring the janitor's scythe.[97]

Eleven years later, in 1897, the board of trustees authorized the president "to employ a landscape gardener to make a plan of the grounds, indicating drives, walks, clusters of trees, building sites,

[96]In 1874 the faculty instructed the janitors to pen up all stray cattle found on campus and threatened to prosecute their owners for trespassing.

[97]In 1897-1898, with the approval of faculty and trustees, students raised an estimated $1,200 in an unsuccessful effort to erect a life-size bronze statue of Samuel Simon Schmucker midway between Pennsylvania Hall and Brua Chapel. In 1902-1903, trustees listened sympathetically to the plans of the Young Men's Christian Association to build its own building on campus. Although they gave the proposal their blessing, almost twenty years elapsed before the building became a reality.

etc." In 1901 Edward H. Bissell of Philadelphia proposed turning the northern and western parts of the campus into a park area. In carrying out his plan, the College constructed new driveways and planted more than four hundred new trees and shrubs.

As was the case during the period discussed in the previous chapter, so between 1868 and 1904 Christ Lutheran church, at 30 Chambersburg street, should be regarded as a functioning part of the College campus. Through the 1888-1889 academic year, baccalaureate and commencement exercises were held in the sanctuary. Well into the 1889-1890 year, many other College functions occurred in the church. For long after 1904 students were required to worship there each Sunday, unless they had written permission from their parents to worship elsewhere. Some students became members of the congregation. In 1904, all nine professors were also members.

Nevertheless, the relationship between the congregation and the College was not always a smooth one. For one thing, the faculty had long wanted a more satisfactory place in which to hold commencement exercises. The two alternatives which they considered briefly in the early 1870s were Agricultural Hall on the fair grounds in Gettysburg and McCreary Gymnasium which was completed in 1872. Lack of funds made it impossible to construct the latter so that it could serve both purposes. The faculty did not achieve their goal of an auditorium on campus until Brua Chapel was ready for its first use in the late spring of 1890.

Another faculty dissatisfaction with Christ church stemmed from the fact that it had no full-time pastor. Clerical members of the seminary and College faculties were still expected to provide it with

Panoramic view of t

preaching and other pastoral services. Albeit with some occasional grumbling, members of the College faculty fulfilled these duties during the early years, for some sixteen of which Henry L. Baugher functioned as stated pastor of the congregation. If nothing else, he was first among equals in this capacity.

Baugher resigned his position in 1866, and the congregation chose Charles A. Hay of the seminary faculty to succeed him. Within two years all of the old clerical professors were gone from the College faculty, and their successors were much younger men who were less tolerant of the existing arrangement. Years later, Henry Eyster Jacobs wrote that what had once been voluntary "had grown into a rule which was executed as though by written statute. The freedom and joy of preaching were in measure lost."[98] In 1876, during the course of a dispute with the church council, most of the clerical members of the faculty announced their intention of withdrawing from the pulpit. This caused immediate consternation in the board of trustees, whose members believed that the College had a responsibility to provide preaching for worship services which the students were required to attend. in June 1876 the executive committee appealed to "the uniform custom for the last forty years, which thereby became the unwritten law of the institution," in asking the faculty pastors to reverse their decision. After what was described as a "protracted discussion" of the case, the full board declared that, "in view of the paramount importance of properly caring for the spiritual interests of the students committed to their care," it was requesting all of the clerical members of the faculty "to take their

---

[98]Jacobs, Memoirs, p. 144.

campus taken in 1897.

turn in preaching in the College church, trusting that, by mutual efforts, under the blessing of the Prince of peace, the harmony between them may be restored." At the same time, the board made it clear that it was not expressing any opinion regarding the merits of the differences between the faculty and the church council.[99]

In response to this appeal, the concerned members of the faculty agreed to fulfill their preaching assignments during the academic year and to discuss with their seminary counterparts filling the pulpit during the summer months. A year later they reported to the board that, "without recognizing any right of the institution inherent in their position as Professors to require them to preach in Christ's Church, Gettysburg," nevertheless since the history of the College demonstrated that such preaching "was a voluntary and gratuitous service," which they rendered "feeling a responsibility, under their general call as Christians and ministers," they had "unanimously and cheerfully" agreed to the request of the board, and they had worked out mutually satisfactory preaching arrangements for the entire year.

The final resolution of this matter had been delayed, not effected. In June 1888, as Hay prepared to resign his position in the congregation, the *College Monthly* declared that "the present state of affairs is abnormal, and the sooner it is changed the better," In the months that followed, the journal urged the congregation to call a full-time pastor. In October the members voted to do just that, but then reelected Hay when the pledges made toward a pastoral salary fell far short of what was required. A renewed effort in 1891 was more successful, and Hay resigned again in the following year. Because students were still being required to attend worship services, the board of trustees now agreed to contribute $300 annually toward a pastor's salary. In the spring of 1893 Luther S. Black, a member of the class of 1888, became the first full-time pastor of Christ Lutheran church. In 1895 he married a daughter of President and Mrs. McKnight.

Preparatory Department

In 1868 few people doubted the necessity of the preparatory department – what the faculty on one occasion called their training

---

[99]In his diary, Charles A. Hay touches upon some of the reasons which led to the dispute between the faculty and the church council. Hay was able to see both sides in the dispute. He recorded the observation of a seminary colleague who took a dim view of the "rich men who can give parties that cost them over $100 and set up Christmas trees that cost over $50," but who want their preaching "for almost nothing." For Henry Eyster Jacobs' explanation of the reasons for the dispute, see Jacobs, *Memoirs*, pp. 181-183.

school – in assuring the continued success of the College. At a time when public high schools were still the exception rather than the rule, at least two-thirds of the students entering Gettysburg College had first spent two or three years in its prep. Well might the editors of *Our Olio,* the junior class publication of 1874, feature the preparatory department with a statement whose inspiration was taken from a well-known Civil War song: "We are coming Father Valentine, Some sixty strong or more."

The trustees had demonstrated their concern for prep by resolving in 1865 to seek its "immediate resuscitation and improvement." To that end they asked the faculty to revise the course of study, revived the office of principal and named Charles J. Ehrehart to the position, and built Stevens Hall. Under Ehrehart's vigorous leadership, enrollment more than doubled, increasing from a low of 40 in 1862 and 1863 to 94 in 1868, when Stevens Hall, although still uncompleted, was first occupied. But the high hopes that these measures would introduce a new and sustained era of prosperity for the preparatory department were not to be realized.

In April 1870 Ehrehart resigned his position, effective at the end of the academic year. In a long letter to the board of trustees, he recited the troubles which he had encountered ever since the new building was first used and which had now become unbearable. He placed much of the blame on the fact that the hall was not large enough to accommodate all of the students and, particularly, on the fact that there were no facilities to accommodate himself and his family. "A preparatory school for boys can never be a success," he wrote, "unless the Principal and his family occupy the same building, or one immediately adjoining." In addition, Stevens Hall had too much large dormitory space; students , he argued, should have their own separate rooms for study and sleeping. By the terms of his agreement with the College, Ehrehart had furnished the rooms in Stevens Hall at a cost of more than $2,100 to himself and was responsible for providing the students with such essential services as board and fuel. Now he found that collecting the money from them on his own account "weakens his influence, and interferes with the discipline of the Institution." In concluding, he expressed the hope that the department could be strengthened, "for upon its success depends in a great measure the success of Pennsylvania College."[100]

Ehrehart's successor was Solomon Sentman (1807-1871), a veteran trustee who gave up his parish to become superintendent of

---

[100]C. J. Ehrehart to the board of trustees, April 19, 1870, GCA. Ehrehart's wife died in 1867, leaving him with several small children. In ill health himself for some years, he died in November 1870, a few months after leaving office.

the preparatory department. Presumably he was given that title because he was not expected to teach. The trustees quickly recognized the validity of one of Ehrehart's complaints by building partitions in the large dormitory space in Stevens Hall to create separate rooms for study and sleeping. The boarding arrangements which Ehrehart had inaugurated proved to be no more successful than the earlier College efforts had been. Responding to student complaints, the faculty in 1871 made boarding voluntary. A few years later, it abandoned the service entirely.[101] Sentman moved his family into Stevens Hall, where their residence was terminated by his unexpected death in December 1871.

The faculty then named a recent graduate and tutor in the department, Hart Gilbert (1845-1898), as acting principal. Between 1873 and 1877 Philip L. Harrison (1829-1897) served as superintendent and lived in the building. He resigned to become a fund raiser for the College. His tenure coincided with the worst times of the 1870s. Prep enrollment dropped, as did that in the College proper. When he resigned in 1877, the board of trustees revived the title of principal and named Philip M. Bikle to the position. In the interests of economy, it asked that most of the faculty do some teaching in the department and that Bikle continue to perform his previous duties. Although the members of the faculty accepted their added responsibilities, they did not hesitate either to tell the trustees that some of their proposals were unwise or unworkable or, in a few cases, to decline to carry them out. "The lower the grade of the pupil," they advised the board in April 1879, "the more needful it is that the teaching and discipline be concentrated in the hands of the smallest number."

As better times eventually returned, the trustees elected John B. Focht (1851-1924) principal and made him a member of the faculty with the rank of professor. He served from 1882 to 1887. His successor, Huber G. Buehler (1864-1924), the son of David A. Buehler, was principal from 1887 until he resigned in the summer of 1892 to join the faculty of the new Hotchkiss School, Lakeville, Connecticut, of which he eventually became headmaster. Oscar G. Klinger was principal from 1892 until he was chosen Franklin Professor of Greek four years later. The board then elected Charles H. Huber (1871-1951), son of Eli Huber, who remained in charge of the preparatory department (later the Gettysburg Academy) until it closed in 1935.

Between 1868 and 1904 annual catalogue statements of the purposes of the preparatory department changed, but three basic

---

[101] Apparently meals were never served in Stevens Hall itself, but in a house located to the north of it which the College had purchased before the hall was built.

themes were present in all of them. First, prep continued to provide instruction in what were called "all the branches of a thorough English education." These included reading, grammar, composition, penmanship, arithmetic, history, and geography. Second, it prepared young men (and later women) for entrance into college, especially into the college of which it was a part. As the 1887 catalogue explained it, "the primary design of the course of study is to prepare students of either sex for the Freshman Class of Pennsylvania College." This explains the presence in the curriculum of such subjects as mathematics, philosophy, Latin, and Greek. Third, the department claimed to prepare students for entry into careers as accountants, engineers, and teachers. One looks in vain for more than a few courses apparently designed to serve this third purpose. There was one in bookkeeping and the catalogues did state that prep students could choose certain College courses for which they might be qualified. In later years, the catalogue asserted

Charles H. Huber (1871-1951)
His professional career with the College began when he became principal
of the preparatory department in 1896. It ended when he retired as director
of the women's division in 1941.

273

that the quality of work expected of all students in the department was enhanced because it was supervised by a college faculty in a college atmosphere and also because preparatory students had access to a college library. As before, the full course of study was expected to take most students three years.

On more than one occasion after the legislature provided for a system of normal schools to train public school teachers, the College considered establishing such an agency as part of the preparatory department. For example, in January 1872 the county superintendent of schools proposed that the College do this. Two months later, without rejecting the idea, the faculty decided that it was "inexpedient at this time to organize such a Department." Probably the recent death of the principal and the current hard times were the major reasons for the decision. Some twenty years later, in 1893, the board of trustees approved a special course of study for prospective teachers to be organized within the preparatory department. In 1898 it authorized the faculty to give it full recognition, and the catalogue which appeared later that year announced that the College was now offering a teachers' course during the spring term. According to the statement. the course recognized both "the existence of a science and an art of education which imposes the duty of preparation on those who would teach" and "the paramount importance of the thorough knowledge of the subject-matter to be taught." That being the case, the prospective teacher was offered instruction in both the theory and practice of teaching and in "all the 'common school' branches." Experienced teachers supplemented the work of the regular prep faculty. In 1903-1904 about twelve students were enrolled in the teacher's course, at the conclusion of which they hoped to be able to pass the teacher's examination which the county superintendent administered.

Except for the brief period in the 1870s when the College faculty did most of the teaching, the instructional staff of the preparatory department usually consisted of the principal and from one to three tutors, depending on enrollment. Most of the tutors were recent College graduates who remained for one or two years before actively pursuing their intended careers. By the 1890s, this long-established pattern was beginning to change. Abraham B. Bunn Van Ormer (1869-1941), a nongraduate hired as tutor in 1894, remained until 1901 and conducted courses in the program for teachers. For the last two years of his tenure he was styled Instructor in Pedagogy.[102]

---

[102]Van Ormer, who held a Pd.D. degree awarded by New York University, earned college and seminary degrees at Gettysburg and entered the parish ministry in 1901. Later he was a member of the faculties of Ursinus, Irving, and Juniata Colleges.

In the early days enrollment in the preparatory department often exceeded that in the four College classes. The last year in which this occurred was 1865-1866. Between 1868 and 1888 the average preparatory enrollment was 52, while that in the College was 98. Between 1888 and 1904 the respective figures were 73 and 170. Many of the prep students continued to come from Gettysburg and the rest of Adams county. In June 1883, acting with the permission of the board of trustees, the faculty decided that it was "expedient" to admit women to the department. Nine enrolled for the fall term.[103] The catalogue made very clear that women were day students who were not eligible for dormitory accommodations. However, out-of-town parents were assured that lodging and board were easily found with reputable Gettysburg families. The 1897 catalogue stated that there was now a separate study hall for women students, who were "not obliged to mingle with the general classes except at regular recitation periods." In addition, while on campus they were "under the care of a lady superintendent." This was Emily B. Horner (1870-1942), who upon her graduation by the College in 1901 was chosen Instructor in History for the preparatory department. She was the first woman to be listed among the College's instructional staff. After Principal Charles H. Huber reported in 1902 that more than a quarter of the students in prep were now women and that there needed to be some formal recognition of their place in the school, the board of trustees authorized the listing of a preceptress in the faculty section of the catalogue. The name of Rosa E. Plank (1879-1980), a 1903 graduate, appeared in the 1903-1904 issue.

In 1898 the faculty informed the board of trustees that major work needed to be done on the exterior and interior of Stevens Hall. They asked the board to consider as one of its options abolishing the preparatory department. In their January meeting, the trustees rejected this option and directed the building committee which had just completed South College to bring in recommendations for Stevens Hall. In June the committee presented figures for constructing a new preparatory building on a different site, for extensive remodeling of the old building, and for moderately repairing it. Not having yet found all of the money to pay for South College, the trustees authorized the expenditure of up to $3,500 to repair and refurnish Stevens Hall.

---

[103]For a discussion of women in the College, see pp. 302-304. The first nine women were Maggie M. Blackwelder, Henrietta L. Forney, Anna R. Miller, Rosa B. Pitzer, Laura M. Spangler, Beulah M. Tipton, Esther A. Valentine, Mary R. Wolf, and Bertha L. Ziegler. Blackwelder was from Arendtsville and Miller from Keysville, Maryland. The other seven were from Gettysburg. Miss Tipton's father was W. H. Tipton, well-known Gettysburg photographer. Miss Valentine's father was president of the College.

The committee was directed to borrow temporarily from the endowment in order to pay the bills.

The Curriculum

The 1868 catalogue of Gettysburg College used less than three pages to describe the curriculum which the faculty offered. As already noted, of 122 topics or combinations of topics listed under "the studies of the several classes," 43 dealt with Greek and Latin language, literature, and culture, while 13 dealt with mathematics. A glance at these and other subjects, including philosophy, chemistry, and surveying, shows that there had been little curricular development since 1832. Most of that which had occurred was in German and in English language and literature. Most of the "studies" listed were required of all candidates for the bachelor's degree. Although there was optional work which a student could take, there were no elective studies, at least not in the sense in which that term was later used.

The inaugural address which Milton Valentine gave in December 1868 shows clearly that he was well aware of major changes which were then occurring in American life, and especially in higher education, which those persons responsible for a college curriculum could not ignore. In some way they would have to respond to these far-reaching developments, either by re-endorsing all of their old positions, by rejecting the traditional and adopting the new, or by attempting to select from the old and the new what they believed was best for their students. Virtually every major pronouncement which Valentine and his successors made during the next thirty-six years gave evidence that those persons charged with administering Gettysburg College were fashioning responses which they thought were most appropriate for the institution which they wanted the College to become.

Every alert college needed to determine to what extent it should adopt the approach of the developing university to higher learning. The belief that neither traditional Christianity nor classical learning was the sufficient source of truth and the conviction that higher education should stress the acquisition of new knowledge convinced some that, whatever might have been true in the past, study in a liberal arts college was now largely a waste of time. The supporters of Gettysburg rejected this view. In his inaugural, Milton Valentine proclaimed that both colleges and universities had their place in American higher education. In a letter which appeared in the *College Monthly* in April 1879, John G. Morris expressed a similar view. He asked this question: Do undergraduates get a better education at The Johns Hopkins University than at Gettysburg? "I answer decidedly, No!" was his response. "Any studious young man will come out from Gettysburg as good or a better educated man than from the Hopkins, and I could give good reasons for it too!" The university was the place for those desiring to continue their studies, because it had "the men, the apparatus, the libraries, and all other instrumentalities." From time to time the *College Monthly* noted the precipitous decline in the percentage of university graduates preparing for the ministry. Gettysburg never discriminated against students intent upon other professions or occupations, but neither did she apologize for the fact that until after 1904 it was not unusual for at least half of her graduating class to enter the seminary. A good college course such as the faculty believed it was offering appeared to be the best preparation for the Lutheran ministry as well as for other careers. "Pennsylvania College, . . . is not a University," declared the 1892 catalogue, "and is content to do good collegiate work, preparing men for the learned professions and for whatever post-graduate studies or activities they may wish to engage in."[104]

Every alert college also needed to determine how it would respond to the action of Harvard University in eliminating course requirements and introducing the elective system. Between 1872 and 1897 the university, prodded by President Charles W. Eliot, abolished all required work for seniors, juniors, and sophomores in the undergraduate college; freshmen were left with a required course in rhetoric.[105] In June 1873, when Eliot's changes were just beginning, the Gettysburg faculty proposed to the board of trustees that the study of Latin and Greek terminate at the end of the junior year and that "an Elective System" be introduced, in which seniors would devote the time thus released to physiology, political science, and history.[106] The board took no action on this request, and as Harvard

---

[104]This catalogue statement did not deter the alumni editor of the *Mercury* from asserting in the October 1893 issue that the Lutheran church ought to have "at least one powerful university." Gettysburg was the logical place for it. In the November 1896 issue he congratulated Princeton on its becoming a university as it celebrated its sesquicentennial and expressed the hope that "long before Pennsylvania College has reached her sesqui-centennial Princeton will have the pleasure of returning congratulation to Gettysburg University."

[105]Rudolph, *American College*, p. 294. The *College Monthly* for April 1885, pp. 84-86, included a history of the elective system at Harvard up to that time. Eliot argued that giving the student the right to choose his subjects was necessary to obtain his interest, initiative, and best work. Ultimately, only complete freedom of choice would yield the opportunity to achieve the depth required for a thorough undergraduate education. The elective system, he believed, was much better than one which produced a jack-of-all-trades and master of none.

[106]Faculty Report, June 25, 1873, GCA.

continued with its changes, voices at Gettysburg were raised against a wide-ranging elective system.

"There is no doubt that electives may be introduced with profit," wrote the editor of the *College Monthly* in March 1885, "but if done too early or too extensively the whole course may become so emasculated as to utterly defeat the true ends of a collegiate education." Enough Harvard freshmen had abandoned Latin, Greek, and mathematics for what were called the "easy studies," he believed, to prove the contention that "youth still in their teens, as most Freshmen are, are not qualified to select the studies best adapted for their education – not even Harvard Freshmen." A month later, the same publication reported a famous debate on the elective system which took place before the Nineteenth Century Club in New York in February 1885, between Charles W. Eliot and James McCosh, president of Princeton. The latter defended required courses. The editor was pleased that a number of university presidents who were interviewed after the debate disagreed "with the extreme views of President Eliot" and that "the general drift is against electives before the Junior Year."

An elective system came to Gettysburg, with little preliminary fanfare, in 1891. One year earlier, the board had named a joint trustee-faculty committee to recommend whether or not to arrange "our College Curriculum as to provide for elective courses of study." In May 1891, just before the committee reported, the editor of the *College Monthly* observed that "we are prepared for some electives now, but prudence calls for caution in making changes under present conditions." Obviously, he was aware of one of the major requirements of a successful elective system. "The more the matter is considered," he wrote, "the more evident becomes the necessity for an increase of the number of professors and an enlargement of facilities in all directions."[107]

While lacking the funds to support expansion in these two crucial areas, in June 1891 the board of trustees adopted the plan of the joint committee and it went into effect in September. During a total of sixteen periods of work each week, sophomores could take one elective, juniors three, and seniors six. The two rules announced in the 1892 catalogue, and repeated in the one for 1904, were simply stated. No student could choose as an elective a study for which the instructor did not believe him qualified. Electives had to be picked

---

[107]The *Report of the Commissioner* (1889-1890), 2:756-757, made the same point and praised those schools which were "strong by the zeal and capacity of their teachers, and while not attempting to teach everything, teach the subjects which they do undertake with increasing thoroughness."

at the beginning of the year and then pursued until completed. For many years after these changes were introduced, College periodicals routinely listed all the electives which individual students had chosen.[108] There is little evidence that the students who enrolled at Gettysburg in the 1890s and early 1900s were dissatisfied with this limited elective system.

Every alert college also had to decide how it would react to Eliot's proposal in 1890 to shorten the undergraduate course of study to three years. In justifying this further departure from long-accepted ways, Eliot explained that the liberal arts college was being threatened by the longer time now required for graduate and professional studies. Making it possible for students to complete their course in three years by coming to college better prepared and by taking more than the standard course load while enrolled would increase the college's chances for survival. In the long run, it would also force an improvement in the quality of secondary education, which was another of Eliot's objectives. The alumni editor of the *College Monthly* was quick to react to what he described as "this radical intention." Writing in the October 1890 issue, he maintained that a three-year course would offer "an opening for superficial work" and put "a premium on the undue haste and foolish scramble that are becoming so much, and too much a part of our American life." If time is to be saved, it should be accomplished somewhere else. "This thing of searching for more liberty, wider range of freedom in thought and action," he insisted, "approaches perilously near something like misrule." Returning to the same topic in the April 1891 issue, he insisted that "there is a great deal of silent but powerful influence exercised by such colleges as our own, that wisely adhere to the time honored and always useful curriculum which is largely classical in character, to the maintenance of a natural and sensible average of age in its student constituency, – an influence of good, always." It soon became evident that Eliot's proposal was not about to alter the traditional four-year college course, either at Gettysburg or elsewhere.

One of the major goals of the university was to make learning an active exercise for students. Few, if any, of the Gettysburg faculty ever took issue with this goal. Both Milton Valentine and Harvey W. McKnight embraced it in their inaugurals. College publications subscribed to it. An editorial in the April 1893 issue of the *College Monthly* declared that "the great need of the college student of to-day is that

---

[108]The 1893 catalogue listed all of the available elective courses. It could be argued that the bachelor of science program which the College introduced earlier provided an elective for students.

he be trained along a line which will lead up to original investigation." Students "must reason out the problem for themselves and not allow other brains to do their thinking" for them. They must "not be mere reflectors but radiators." In its issue of January 17, 1900, the student weekly, the *Gettysburgian,* urged students to engage in "original work", by which it meant "investigation as opposed to mere receptivity, . . . construction as opposed to reproduction." One may ask to what degree Gettysburg College students in 1904 were personally committed to investigation and construction. Given the size and availability of the library and the extent of the laboratories, how far could those who were so committed proceed?

During the semicentennial exercises of the College in June 1882, Harvey W. McKnight was assigned the task of describing and evaluating the incumbent Valentine administration. In carrying out this duty. he identified what he believed was the Gettysburg style of responding to the educational needs of the post-Civil War era. The changes which had been made since 1868, he explained, were not "in any sense antagonistic to the old order of things but rather the results of a healthful development . . . . New branches have been engrafted on the parent tree, but the old ones have not been lopped off or pruned even to make room for them." The old and the new "have grown side by side"; they exist together. McKnight was proud that "Pennsylvania College has not, in obedience to the modern demand for a so-called practical education, committed the unpardonable mistake of neglecting her classical course or entrusting it to Tutors or Adjuncts." There have indeed been changes in the curriculum, he concluded, "but they have been improvements, made by enlargement, not by revolution." Two years later, McKnight succeeded to the presidency, and in his inaugural announced that this approach would be continued: "the old shall not be removed by revolution, but preserved and carried up into the new by a safe and healthful evolution."[109] It remained to be seen whether the result of that evolution would be a proper curriculum for students in an increasingly rapidly changing America or a bloated mixture of the old and new which lacked the strengths of either.

The 1872 catalogue was the first to list departments of instruction. Seven of these were enumerated: Intellectual and Moral Science, Physical and Natural Sciences, Mathematics and Astronomy, Latin Language, Greek Language, English Language and Literature, and

---

[109]Quoted in the *College Monthly* for July 1882, pp. 206-207, and October 1885, p. 229. In the July 1877 issue of this journal, a writer who signed himself H. E. I. (was he Henry Eyster Jacobs?) decried the current emphasis on change for change's sake and argued against "heedless tampering" with an existing curriculum which had proved itself in preparing men for "a broad culture or . . . one of the learned professions."

German Language. One or more paragraphs described the purposes and procedures of each.[110] There were frequent changes in statements about the curriculum in succeeding catalogues. By 1904 the list included twelve departments: Philosophy; Mathematics and Astronomy; Greek; Latin; English; French and German; History, Political Science, and Law; Chemistry; Geology and Mineralogy; Biology; Physical Culture and Hygiene; and Biblical. It is evident that these divisions had more reality on paper than they did in fact. They existed for the purpose of explaining the curriculum to the interested public by means of the annual catalogue. They bore little or no resemblance to the organized departments of instruction of later days. Course descriptions appeared for the first time in the 1895 catalogue. They included the name of the course; a description; whether it was required and, if so, in what year; the number of times per week it met; and the name of the instructor. The 1904 catalogue listed eighty-two courses, forty-seven of which were required for the bachelor of arts degree.

Through and beyond 1903-1904 candidates for the arts degree were required to take both Latin and Greek language and literature: four years of each until the elective system was introduced and three years thereafter. Students accepted these stipulations as two of the givens at Gettysburg. There is virtually no evidence from faculty minutes or College publications of individual or group opposition to either of them. The same cannot be said of the requirement of four (later reduced to three) years of German study. Time and again the faculty disciplined one or more students for their conduct in the German classroom, occasionally involving use of what the minutes call explosives or torpedoes. Often the punishment was an apology and then return to the scene of the discontent. There was somewhat less of this during the later years of Adam Martin's tenure, possibly because more students exercised their option of securing a parental letter asking that they be excused altogether from the requirement.[111] There was a penalty attached to this option in 1870;

---

[110]The Department of Physical Science was the only one listed in the 1866-1871 catalogues, undoubtedly because of the improvements made in science instruction at that time.

[111]Between 1868 and 1904 not a year went by without at least one of these requests, which were routinely granted. Student dissatisfaction, which in each case had some justification, led to the departure of two German professors: John F. Wilken and Charles F. Brede. In May 1900 the faculty disciplined a student for throwing an "explosive" in Brede's classroom, then for refusing to leave when asked, and finally for throwing a second explosive at Brede when the latter forced him out. A few days later, some twenty-five students were disciplined for burning an effigy of Brede near his house. When the board of trustees met a year later, it named a committee of three to visit the professor "and as delicately as possible secure his with-drawal."

COURSES OF INSTRUCTION.

The whole course of instruction occupies four years. The classes attend three recitations or lectures a day, except on Wednesday and Saturday, when they have but two.

The following schedule presents a general view of the studies of the various classes. Equivalents for the books mentioned are used by the various Professors at their discretion.

CLASSICAL COURSE.

FRESHMAN YEAR.

FIRST TERM.

Mathematics: Algebra (Wentworth); Geometry (Wentworth).

Greek: Historians—Selections (Boise and Freeman); Syntax (Boise).

Latin: Livy; Prose Composition (Arnold).

History: English (Montgomery).

French: Keetels' Oral Method.

Science: Lectures on Practical Hygiene.

SECOND TERM.

Mathematics: Algebra (Wentworth); Geometry of Planes (Wentworth).

Greek: Historians—Selections (Boise and Freeman); Syntax (Boise).

Latin: Odes of Horace; Prose Composition (Arnold).

English: History of English Literature (Shaw).

French: Grammar (Keetels); Reader (Keetels).

THIRD TERM.

Mathematics: Algebra (Wentworth); Geometry of Solids (Wentworth).

Greek: Historians—Selections (Boise and Freeman); Syntax (Boise).

Latin: Cicero de Amicitia, *or* de Senectute; Prose Composition (Arnold).

English: History of English Literature (Shaw); Bacon's Essays.

German: Grammar (Sawyer; Colloquial Exercises and Reader (Deutsch).

English Composition and Declamation throughout the year.

SOPHOMORE YEAR.

FIRST TERM.

Mathematics: Plane Trigonometry and Mensuration (Wentworth).

Greek: Lysias.

Latin: Satires and Ars Poetica of Horace; Prose Composition (Arnold).

English: Anglo-Saxon (Sweet).

German: Grammar (Sawyer); Reader (Deutsch).

SECOND TERM.

Mathematics: Surveying and Navigation (Wentworth); Analytical Geometry (Loomis).

Greek: Homer; History of Greece (Smith).

Latin: Cicero's Tusculan Disputations; Prose Composition (Arnold).

English: Rhetoric (A.S. Hill).

German: Grammar (Brandt); Schiller's Maid of Orleans.

THIRD TERM.

Mathematics: Analytical Geometry (Loomis); Spherical Trigonometry (Wentworth).

Greek: Plato; History of Greece (Smith).

Latin: Plautus.

English: Chaucer's Canterbury Tales.

German: Schiller's Ballads.

Science: Physiology (Martin); Botany (Gray's School and Field).

English Composition and Declamation throughout the year.

> The curriculum as described in the 1887 catalogue.

JUNIOR YEAR.

FIRST TERM.

Mathematics: Differential Calculus (Loomis).

Greek: AEschylus.

Latin: Quintilian; Composition.

English: Dramatic Art—Shakespeare.

German: Goethe's Iphigenia of Taurus; Composition.

Science: Lectures on Inorganic Chemistry.

Philosophy: Intellectual Science (Porter).

SECOND TERM.

Mathematics: Integral Calculus (Loomis).

Greek: Sophocles.

Latin: Tacitus; Composition.

English: Logic (Jevons).

German: Goethe's Faust; Composition.

Science: Lectures on Inorganic Chemistry; Physics (Daniell).

Physiology: Intellectual Science (Porter).

THIRD TERM.

Mathematics: Integral Calculus (Loomis).

Greek: Euripides.

Latin: Juvenal; Composition.

English: Epic Art—Milton.

German: Goethe's Hermann and Dorothea; Composition.

Science: Physics (Daniell); Crystallography; Lectures and Practical Exercises.

Philosophy: Intellectual Science (Porter).

English Composition and Written Debates throughout the year.

SENIOR YEAR.

FIRST TERM.

Latin: Terence; Composition.

German: Lessing's Minna Von Barnhelm; Original Composition.

Science: Astronomy (Newcomb and Holden); Mineralogy: Descriptive (Dana's Text Book) and Determinative (Laboratory Work); Lectures on Lithology with practical work; Lectures on Organic Chemistry.

Philosophy: Natural Theology (Valentine); Evidences of Christianity (Paley).

History: History of Civilization (Guizot).

Political Science: Political Economy (F.A. Walker).

SECOND TERM.

Greek: Demosthenes on the Crown.

Latin: Tertullian.

German: Lessing's Nathan der Weise. Original Composition.

Science: Astronomy (Newcomb and Holden); Lectures on Applied Chemistry: Geology (Le Conte).

Philosophy: Moral Science (Haven).

Political Science: International Law (Woolsey); Constitution of the United States and of Pennsylvania.

THIRD TERM.

Greek: Demosthenes on the Crown.

Latin: Tertullian.

German: Lessing's Nathan der Weise.

Science: Astronomy (Newcomb and Holden); Geology (Le Conte).

Philosophy: Moral Science (Haven).

Political Science: International Law (Woolsey).

English Original Orations throughout the year.

students not completing the German requirement lost their eligibility for honors. In 1868 the faculty permitted a student, again with parental permission, to substitute French for German, but here too there was a penalty: payment of an extra fee for the instruction. The German professor taught the French course, which was considered to be over and above his regular teaching load. Few students availed themselves of this opportunity. Then, in 1880, French also became a required course of study for bachelor of arts candidates, and Instructor in French was added to the title of the German professor. In 1904 the French requirement was one year of work.

All students took some studies in English during each of their four years in College. In 1904 this included writing essays, elocution, rhetoric, as well as English and American literature. Since the Graeff professor taught most of these courses himself, and also several in other fields, he had little time in which to offer elective courses.

For many years it was the responsibility of college presidents to offer courses for seniors, or for juniors and seniors, in what was usually called moral and intellectural science or philosophy. Presumably the ranking officer in the institution was in a better position than any of his colleagues to lead students through the last stages of the institutions's efforts to form their character along desirable lines.[112] In 1904, as in 1868, the Gettysburg faculty assigned a very high priority to the careful discharge of this responsibility. The task fell almost entirely to Milton Valentine and Harvey W. McKnight, both of whom bore the titles of President and Professor of Intellectual and Moral Science. The topics which the former announced as the themes of his department were Mental Philosophy, Moral Science, and Evidences of Christianity, to which he soon added Natural Theology. It is probable that the instruction which he began in 1868 was very similar to that he had received as an undergraduate twenty years earlier. Shortly after McKnight became president, he entered in the catalogue (first in 1887) the statement that the studies of his department were "deemed of great importance, not only because of their educational value for the mind, but for their direct and practical bearing on the character and life of the student." He claimed that recent discussion had indicated great interest in these subjects and "rendered imperative such a discriminating examination of the various theories and systems as will lead to the discovery and rejection of those which are false and dangerous," enabling the student to "settle for himself the great questions of being and duty by the application of the principles of a sound philosophy."

---

[112]Rudolph, *American College*, pp. 140-141.

McKnight's increasing personal involvement in fund raising, which did not end in 1890, required the trustees to release him at times from some or all of his teaching duties and to entrust them to others. For some, this must have raised questions about how long the old teaching arrangement could survive. The establishment of the Strong professorship in 1892 also forced the trustees and faculty to consider how teaching assignments in the fields of philosophy and religion should be divided. The question was not settled by 1904, but it should be noted that, when the faculty first listed course descriptions in 1895, they abandoned the traditional heading of Intellectual and Moral Science in favor of Philosophy. Of the five courses listed under that rubric, McKnight taught but two (Psychology and Ethics, required of juniors); John A. Himes taught one (Logic, also required of juniors), H. Louis Baugher taught one (Rational Theism, required of seniors), and Eli Huber taught one (Christian Evidence, also required of seniors.) By 1904, only one change had been made in these assignments; Oscar Klinger now taught Rational Theism.[113]

When the trustees accepted James Strong's endowment of a chair of English Bible and the chaplaincy of the College in April 1892, they chose to define the teaching and other duties of the incumbent in more detail than was used in establishing any other professorship, before or since. The resolution which President McKnight introduced and which was adopted specified that "English Bible" become a required course of study, that the original languages in which the Bible was written become electives, and that the "teaching in the department shall be positively Christian, according to the accepted standards of Evangelical Christendom, but in no sense denominational."[114] At their next meeting, the trustees transferred the Christian Evidence course from the president to the Strong professor. In the first listing of course descriptions in 1895, three of the five courses listed in the Biblical Department, including one in Hebrew, were electives. The two required courses were in Old Testament History, one in the freshman and the other in the sophomore year.

---

[113]It is instructive to read the description of the Christian Evidence course which first appeared in the 1898 catalogue: "While opposing theories are duly considered, the argument for Christianity from Miracles is accepted and defended. This argument is supported by others derived from various sources such as the fulfillment of Prophecy, the adaptedness of Christianity to the needs of human nature, the superiority of Christian Doctrine, and the benevolent fruits of the religion of Christ." This course, it should be recalled, was required for all seniors.

[114]For a discussion of the reaction of the several synods to this resolution, see pp. 394-395.

For reasons best known to themselves, the trustees in 1868 transferred the then-vacant Franklin professorship from the ancient languages to history. The new chair remained vacant until 1870, when Henry Eyster Jacobs was elected. The board then assigned Jacobs the title of Franklin Professor of the Latin Language, and of History, but it could not grant him enough time to do justice to both subjects. In fact, believing that Latin had the priority, he taught no history. In desperation, he asked the trustees in 1872 either to reduce his teaching responsibilities in Latin or to change his title. They responded by directing the faculty to arrange Jacobs' schedule so that he could offer work in history to the members of the senior class. This he did, during two of their three terms.

In 1880, when the trustees undertook a major rearrangement of the professorships, they transferred history from Jacobs to John A. Himes, the English professor. History was not listed in the catalogue among the departments of instruction after 1875, although some work in the subject was offered in the Greek, Latin, German, and English departments. In presenting the various needs of the College in the 1880s, spokesmen called for two new professorships, one of which was in history. "A thorough, accurate and ready acquaintance with History," declared Milton Valentine in 1884, was never "more necessary than in the present reconstructions of social ideas and political systems."[115] Necessary or not, no professorship was forthcoming at this time. In 1895, when course descriptions first appeared in the catalogue, the faculty created a paper department of history, political science, and law. Of the seven courses listed under it, two were in history. Modern European History, required of freshmen, was taught by the German professor. American Political History, required of sophomores, was taught by the English professor. These assignments, first made some years before 1895, were still in effect in 1904.

Defenders of the traditional liberal arts in the post-Civil War era considered mathematics on a par with the classics as a fundamental study in the curriculum. In 1885 Harvey W. McKnight said it was one of those subjects "which are mainly disciplinary, and have proved to be most conducive to robust and rounded mental development."[116] As it had been ever since 1832, mathematics at Gettysburg was a required subject in 1904. Students took algebra, geometry, trigonometry, and surveying in their freshman and sophomore years, as well as astronomy in their senior years. For the latter subject, they used the College Observatory. Henry B. Nixon, who taught all of the courses in mathematics and astronomy, was the

---

[115]Quoted in *College Monthly* (March 1884), p. 41.
[116]Quoted in ibid. (October 1885), p. 235.

only one of the nine professors in 1904 who had an earned Ph.D. degree.

There were science courses at Gettysburg College from the time it opened for instruction in 1832. Michael Jacobs distinguished himself as a teacher of chemistry and related subjects, while John G. Morris upheld the tradition of natural history by coming from Baltimore to deliver his occasional lectures. In 1868 all degree candidates were required to take as many as fifteen "studies" in science during their junior and senior years. These included physics, chemistry, anatomy, physiology, zoology, botany, and geology.

In the period after the Civil War, no fields of study were mentioned more frequently than the sciences by those who were describing the changes that were then taking place in American education. The emphasis which the developing universities placed on research and on the possible vast new learning applied especially to the sciences. Presidents Valentine and McKnight both used the occasion of their inaugurals to contend that increased attention to these subjects should not be limited to the universities alone. "The importance of giving them a larger space in the Collegiate course," declared Valentine in 1868, "is, every year, more and more felt and acknowledged."[117] It is evident that the trustees were in agreement. In 1865 they assigned the Ockershausen endowment to the sciences. Then, in 1874, when they were experiencing one deficit year after another, they established a second science professorship, which they continued for seven years. In the 1880s, when College spokesmen were outlining their pressing needs, they included a second science professorship among them.

Without a doubt, chemistry was the strongest of the sciences at Gettysburg College during the period under study. There were a number of reasons why this was true. The tradition of Michael Jacobs was still a force to be reckoned with. Soon after the Ockershausen professorship was established, the trustees appropriated what was for them the large sum of several thousand dollars to replace most, if not all, of Jacobs' old equipment. During his brief tenure as professor, Samuel P. Sadtler reorganized the instruction in chemistry, his major scientific interest. Finally, Edward S. Breidenbaugh was forceful enough over a long period of time to secure from the trustees what must have been close to the maximum available financial support for the chemistry program. From 1874 to 1877 and after 1886 he had the services of a full-time assistant; he was the

---

[117]It should be noted that Valentine was interested in promoting what he called true science, not the false science which leads to atheistic materialism. True sciences "provide useful knowledge, but they also lead us to a fuller understanding of God and His works." Quoted in *Valentine Inaugural*, pp. 39-42.

only professor who did. In 1904 these men were offering courses in inorganic and organic chemistry as well as in qualitative and quantitative analysis. For many years the catalogue proclaimed that the College's chemistry instruction "gives the student a general acquaintance with the science as established by recent investigation, and shows the value of its applications and conclusions to the arts and economy of life."

Instruction in physics was much less developed than that in chemistry. Certainly this would not have been the case if Alfred M. Mayer, who was a physicist, had remained as Ockershausen professor. During his brief tenure at Gettysburg, and at his urging, much new equipment was purchased, some of it with his own funds. After his departure, physics eventually became the responsibility of Edward S. Breidenbaugh, who in 1904 offered one course in the subject. When the catalogue began listing needs of the College in 1891, the first one named was a department of physics. Seven years later the New York alumni club resolved to raise money for this purpose, but by 1904 it had not succeeded in gathering enough to make it a reality.

In 1868 there were required courses in the Gettysburg curriculum which, in a later day, one might find in a department of biology. These included botany, zoology, anatomy, and physiology. Usually, they were taught by the science professor, but in 1878 the College lightened his load slightly by reviving the part-time position of Lecturer in Anatomy and Hygiene which had been allowed to lapse more than a decade before. In 1886 George D. Stahley was appointed to this position, and it may have been at his urging that the board of trustees three years later created the Professorship of Physical Culture and Hygiene, at the same time naming him its first incumbent.

Writing in the *College Monthly* for February 1890, Stahley presented a statement of the purpose and scope of his new position. "This feature of educational work has only of recent years been made an integral part of collegiate training," he explained, "and has not yet become familiar by general adoption." Assuming that "sound bodies conduce to sound minds," Stahley argued that a department of health should be operated "on a broad scientific and thoroughly educational basis" and "with the same diligence and regularity as the other branches in the college course." It should draw for its development upon the experience of already established departments, such as those at Amherst, Cornell, Harvard, The Johns Hopkins, and Yale. For Gettysburg students Stahley proposed several thorough physical examinations, prescription of appropriate required exercise during the entire College course (at least two hours a week, he hoped), and required course work in physiology and personal hygiene. He assured his readers that the trustees "desire that the department shall have primarily in view the physiological good health of the students, rather than that it should become a training school for professional athletes." That is why they had entrusted it "to the medical control of a physician."[118]

The transformation of Linnaean Hall into a gymnasium gave Stahley the facility which he needed to carry out his program. In 1890 Anatomy, Physiology, and Personal Hygiene became a required freshman course. At the same time, physical culture or gymnastic exercises became a requirement extending over the entire four years. To help carry the considerable teaching load which this program entailed, the College provided Stahley with an assistant, who was usually an upperclass student and whose title was Physical Instructor.

A proposal made by several Philadelphia medical schools in the spring of 1895 resulted in a significant change in Stahley's course offerings. These schools had recently increased the length of their program to four years. Now they announced that they would admit college graduates who had completed acceptable courses in anatomy, physiology, chemistry, and physics into their second-year curriculum without further examination. As a physician who had for many years spoken and written in favor of more and better training for doctors, George D. Stahley moved promptly to secure the approval of the board of trustees for adding the courses necessary to qualify Gettysburg graduates for the three-year program.[119] Having secured it in June 1896, by fall he was ready to offer what he called a two-year junior and senior course in biology, designed "to comply with the requirements of certain of our high-grade medical schools." It included zoology, mammalian anatomy, general biology, human anatomy, physiology, histology, and embryology. "The course aims to be modern in its methods and rigidly practical," he wrote for the 1897 catalogue. "A biological laboratory has been fitted up, the equipment of which is being greatly added to by interested alumni

---

[118]The February 1890 issue of the *College Monthly* also carried an extract from a paper which Professor Edward Hitchcock of Amherst had read at the famous Boston Conference, held in November 1889. It dealt with essential principles to be followed in directing departments of physical education and hygiene.

[119]In an article entitled "College Degrees and Medical Doctors" which appeared in the April 1884 number of the *College Monthly*, Stahley called medical education reform "a crying necessity" which could be achieved only by requiring a bachelor's degree or its equivalent for medical study. He used Charles W. Eliot, the American Medical Association, and the American Academy of Medicine to bolster his argument. The latter, two of whose founders (Robert L. Sibbet and Edward H. M. Sell) were alumni of the College, was organized in 1876 to improve the quality of medical education.

and friends of the college." By 1904 the seven topics mentioned above had evolved into six separate courses (human anatomy and physiology were combined), each with its own description. Perhaps more important, Stahley now announced them as courses aimed "to teach fundamental principles" and "calculated to interest and profit any student of nature, whatever his future calling is expected to be."

To recapitulate, in 1904 Edward S. Breidenbaugh and George D. Stahley and their two assistants were responsible for eighteen science courses. Four of these were required of all candidates for the bachelor of arts degree: Botany of sophomores, Elementary Inorganic Chemistry of juniors, Physics of juniors, and Geology of seniors. The required course in anatomy, physiology, and personal hygiene was dropped in 1899. The four-year requirement in physical culture remained.

In 1868 the fields of study which are now often called the social sciences were only beginning to emerge as separate and distinct disciplines in the college curriculum. Economics, political science, psychology, sociology, and anthropology had been in existence for a long time, but it took the impact of Darwinism and the example of the sciences just described to move them much beyond the stage of development which they had reached in the eighteenth century, and to give them clear identities of their own.

The Gettysburg curriculum of 1868 included only two studies which fall into the category of political science: the Science of Government and the Constitution of the United States. The Latin professor, Martin L. Stoever, taught both. After his death they were assigned to the English professor, in whose custody the field remained in 1904. The description of the English department in the 1874 catalogue included the statement that "the Senior year is devoted to the subjects of Political and Social Science." Eight years later, the statement was more informative: "In response to the popular demand for instruction of College students in matters of public interest and duties of citizenship, two hours a week during the whole of the Senior year are given to the study of Political Economy [the old name for Economics] and the Science of Government." In 1887 Himes's title was changed to Graeff Professor of English Literature and Political Science, and the trustees began to supplement his work by engaging a lecturer to offer a course in the fields of law and government., All three of the men who served in this capacity by 1904 were attorneys, two from Gettysburg and one from Chambersburg.

The titles of the courses which Himes offered were changed slightly from time to time. Those which he listed in 1904 under the heading History, Political Science, and Law were Political

Economy, Lectures on Money and Banking, International Law, and Science of Government. The first three listed were required of seniors. There were no courses in sociology or anthropology, at least none bearing those names. The only one in psychology was the junior required course which was listed under Philosophy in the catalogue and which President McKnight taught.[120]

Three new programs were added to the curriculum between 1868 and 1904. The first, which instituted what was called the scientific course, was begun quite informally in 1874, when Samuel P. Sadtler asked the faculty to approve the degree of bachelor of science in course for Edgar Fahs Smith, a senior, and George S. Eyster, a member of the class of 1868. Upon the recommendation of the faculty, the board awarded this degree to both men. The 1875 and subsequent catalogues contained the announcement that "the degree . . . of Bachelor of Science is conferred upon students who, with adequate previous attainments, pursue a special scientific course and sustain an examination for the degree." However, there was as yet no established course of study for this degree. Beginning in 1877, the faculty recommended such a course to the board, but the latter routinely postponed action on the subject until the next year, possibly because the recommendation included a warning that additional staff would be required.

Finally, in 1884 the board authorized preparation of a diploma for the degree of bachelor of science. One year later, the announcement of the scientific course appeared for the first time in the catalogue. Soon this course was being described as one "arranged to provide for those who wish to give less time to the classics" and as one "particularly adapted to those who intend entering the profession of Medicine or Pharmacy or engaging in industrial or manufacturing pursuits." While the work was "principally of a practical nature," the student in the course was "required to understand the principles of the Sciences studied and the methods of their application." Thus the design was, according to the catalogue, "not only the obtaining of information, but also substantial mental discipline." The reader was informed that "no fact that can possibly be treated is allowed to pass unchallenged. Thus the student is taught to think and judge for himself."[121] Entrance requirements for the scientific course differed from those for the classical course in only one respect: no Greek was

---

[120]There were no courses in music or art in the 1904 curriculum. Noting the absence of the former, in the section dealing with the preparatory department the catalogue stated that arrangements for music instruction could be made in town.

[121]The early catalogues describing the course stated that "in order to promote scientific reading and study" a number of periodicals were available to students in the chemistry quarters. Included were the *American Journal of Chemistry, Chemical News, Scientific American,* and *Popular Science Monthly.*

required. Course requirements were the same in both programs, except that science candidates took no Greek and only two years of Latin. Eleven of the twelve studies required in place of the classical languages were in chemistry. The twelfth was in physics.

Between 1874 and 1904 the College awarded eighty-three degrees of bachelor of science. There were two in 1874, then none until 1882, one in 1884, one in 1885, and three in 1886. Between 1900 and 1904 the average number of all graduates was forty and of bachelor of science recipients, six. All but three of the eighty-three science degrees were granted to undergraduates.[122]

The second new program, for special students, was announced in the 1887 catalogue. It was designed for persons, especially those in chemistry, "whose time is limited, to prepare for the study of Medicine or Pharmacy, or for manufacturing pursuits." These special students were not candidates for a degree. They had to qualify for the courses in which they wished to enroll and were required to take about three-fourths of the normal course load. Their numbers remained small.

A third new program, one offering graduate study, began informally in the spring of 1876, when Abram R. Horne, a graduate of the class of 1858 who was then principal of the normal school at Kutztown, asked to be admitted to candidacy in a course of study leading to the degree of doctor of philosophy. While granting his request, the faculty decided that, since the step was "something beyond the custom of this College," they would ask the trustees about the "propriety of providing a scheme by which degrees may be obtained on examination by persons not on the roll of students on the ground." The board members quickly referred the matter back to the faculty, asking them to return in a year with "some general plan, in harmony with the usages of our American colleges, whereby postgraduate degrees can be conferred upon applicants having the attainments requisite for such degrees." In June 1877 the professors reported that they could "find no definite or prescribed courses which show any uniformity of plan or custom prevailing among the Colleges of our land."[123] That being the case, they then exercised their own judgment in proposing that postgraduate study be established in twelve specified fields. To be considered, candidates for an advanced degree would have to present an acceptable thesis and pass an examination to the satisfaction of the faculty. The board

---

[122]The exceptions were George S. Eyster (1868) in 1874; Sterling G. Valentine (1880) in 1882, and Murray G. Motter (1886) in 1887. Valentine's degree was granted upon completion of two years of work beyond the arts degree and an examination.

[123]Faculty Report, June 26, 1877, GCA.

of trustees gave its approval to this new venture.

Beginning in 1878, the catalogue announced that "provision is made for post-graduate degrees upon completing a prescribed course of study, according to the degree for which the student is a candidate." In 1884 an examination fee of $25 was introduced. Five years later this was changed to include a registration fee of $25, plus a $50 examination fee at the end of the course. From time to time, the fields of study in which one might pursue graduate work were redefined. In 1900 these were the twelve major fields open (a candidate also needed two minor fields): Moral Science, Greek, Latin, German, French, English Literature, History, Political and Social Science, Mathematics, Chemistry, Geology, and Physics and Astronomy. The 1900 catalogue listed these degree requirements: possession of a bachelors's degree "equivalent to those given in this College"; three years of work under faculty direction, two of which must be in residence in the case of nongraduates and one in the case of graduates; such examinations as the faculty might prescribe; and "a satisfactory thesis showing evidence of original investigation." Students not in residence who failed to report progress for two years would be dropped from the list of approved candidates which began appearing in the catalogue in 1892.

Between 1876 and 1904 about forty persons were admitted to candidacy for the degree of doctor of philosophy. The usual procedure for establishing candidacy was to apply to the faculty, choosing major and minor fields. If accepted, the candidate was assigned one or more faculty advisers. Nine persons entered during the first ten years; all of the remainder, after 1888. The 1893, 1894, and 1895 catalogues listed sixteen current graduate students. Until 1890 almost all of the candidates were alumni. After that, at least eight qualified from southern Lutheran colleges: six from Roanoke, one from Newberry, and one from North Carolina. Two were women, both recent Roanoke graduates. Many were Lutheran pastors; at least three were missionaries or teachers in Japan or India. The first few graduate students chose science as their major field. After 1888, almost all of the rest elected others topics, psychology and moral science being the favorites.

Between 1882 and 1900 the College actually awarded fifteen Ph.D. degrees in course. The recipients were George S. Eyster (1882), Sterling G. Valentine (1886), Daniel Fleisher (1888), Franklin Menges (1888), Gottlieb C. H. Hasskarl (1890), Junius B. Fox (1890), Martin L. Young (1892), William H. Klose (1893), Michael M. Kinard (1894), Rufus B. Peery (1895), Henderson N. Miller (1896), Milton H. Stine (1896), James A. B. Scherer (1897), Julia Painter (1897), and William P. Swartz (1900). Eight of these persons were alumni. The average length of time between establishment of candidacy and awarding of the degree was slightly less than three years. Eyster and Valentine had distinguished careers as chemists. Menges was a well-known science teacher, author, and member of the United States House of Representatives. Peery, Miller, and Scherer were college presidents. Fox and Klose were college professors.[124]

This graduate program was begun and continued at a time when the financial situation of the College was given as the reason why the board of trustees could not hire enough faculty to staff adequately the undergraduate courses of instruction. As graduate training in the universities increased and improved, the Gettysburg faculty began to question whether, given their extremely limited resources, they were not engaged in an activity which they could scarcely expect to perform to their own satisfaction. In 1897 they ceased registering candidates for the advanced degree while they proposed to the board of trustees that postgraduate study be abolished or, if that were not the wish of the board, that at least it be made more rigorous. The trustees responded by taking the second course of action; it was at this time that they introduced minimum time and residence requirements. However, in spite of trustee optimism, the graduate program was on its way out. The last doctorate was awarded in 1900. The last announcement of graduate work appeared in the 1904-1905 catalogue.[125]

There were at least three other programs which the trustees and faculty considered between 1868 and 1904, but did not adopt. The first was what the former called a commercial course, initially proposed in 1870 but never approved. The second would have added a military instructor to the faculty. In June 1880 Congressman Frank E. Beltzhoover, an 1862 graduate of the College, informed President Valentine that a recent revision of federal law allotted three military instructors to Pennsylvania colleges, of whom only two were already assigned. He believed that Gettysburg should apply for the third. With the approval of the faculty and board, Valentine did make a formal request of the War Department, and for a brief period it was believed that an officer was coming. Then it was announced that there were no vacancies in Pennsylvania after all, and the matter

---

[124]"Ph. D., Gettysburg," *Gettysburg College Bulletin* (May 1962), pp. 14-15.

[125]See Sellers, *Dickinson College*, p. 290, for an account of the Dickinson graduate program, which was apparently urged by President George E. Reed. According to the *Report of the Commissioner* (1890-1891), 2:1408, there were eight universities and colleges in Pennsylvania with graduates departments in 1890. The number for 1903-1904 was fifteen, and included Allegheny, Dickinson, Haverford, Lafayette, Lehigh, and Swarthmore. The average number of graduate students enrolled in each institution, excluding the University of Pennsylvania, was six. *Report of the Commissioner* (1904), 2:1485.

was dropped.[126] In 1889, when the possibility of a military instructor redeveloped, the board of trustees named a committee to apply again on behalf of the College, with no better results than the first time. Three years later, the editor of the *College Monthly* called attention to a bill before Congress providing for one hundred more military instructors. If the bill passes, he thought, the College should try again. "Much can be said in favor of military drill and discipline among college students," he wrote, "and we hope the day is near at hand when we can announce that an army officer has been detailed for our institution." It was not.[127]

A third proposal made from time to time, and one which also produced no results, would have added a formal teachers' training program to the College curriculum. Neither trustees nor faculty could forget the responsibilties which the College assumed in the 1830s for the training of teachers. Some of this responsibility might have been removed when the state set up a system of normal schools, but it was not eliminated. Before 1868 the College briefly entertained the idea of establishing a normal school in the district of which Adams county was a part, but it was Shippensburg which occupied that ground in 1871. For the most part, Gettysburg was then content to use the pages of its catalogue from time to time to remind school boards that it was in a position to recommend qualified teaching candidates. The introduction of a teachers' course into the preparatory department in the 1890s has already been discussed. A report in 1906 showed that during the preceding thirteen years 41 Gettysburg graduates had received permanent teaching certificates. The number for Bucknell was 88; for Franklin and Marshall, 83; for Allegheny, 76; for Dickinson, 43; and for Washington and Jefferson, 38.[128]

It is evident that there was considerable curricular development at Gettysburg College during the years between 1868 and 1904. The

---

[126]In approving the application, the trustees asserted their right to terminate any arrangements made with the government, decreed that a professor of military science and tactics would not be considered "a full member of the Faculty in the general working of the Institution," specified that any military instruction should be in addition to existing work, insisted that there should be no "considerable expense" to the College, and decreed that any such program would have to be voluntary. For Dickinson's experience with a military instructor in 1879-1881, see Sellers, *Dickinson College,* p. 273. Franklin and Marshall had a department of military science and tactics from 1894 to 1901.

[127]The numbers of professors of military science and tactics in American colleges, universities, and other schools had increased from 28 in 1882 to 79 in 1893. Pennsylvania Military Academy and Allegheny College had one in both years. Pennsylvania State College and Girard College had one in 1893. *Reports of the Secretary of War* (1882), 1:183-184 and (1893), 1:161-165.

[128]*Report of the Superintendent* (1906), p. 581.

faculty were aware, from several sources, of what was happening in other institutions and used that information in developing their own programs. The descriptions which they wrote for the annual catalogue made the claim that they were committed to recent scholarship and methods of research. For many years, as already noted, the chemistry professor asserted that his purpose was "to give the students a practical acquaintance with the science as established by the most recent investigations." In the 1890s John A. Himes was announcing that in his economics class textbook theories were put "to the test of the student's personal observation" and that "problems for investigation are assigned to the members of the class, with directions to inquire into actual industrial and social conditions and operations."

It is also evident that, long before 1904, the Gettysburg faculty realized that, however much they may have altered their curriculum to suit the style to which they were accustomed and which they wished to preserve, it still had serious shortcomings. During the building program of 1888-1890, the editor of the *College Monthly* expressed the hope that, once the physical plant had been enlarged and improved, the board of trustees would launch a campaign to increase the endowment, enlarge the faculty, and meet other equally pressing instructional needs. "The college that no longer has any needs," he wrote in June 1890, "is ready to close its doors." In 1891 the faculty introduced a new section into the catalogue. Called "Needs of the College," it listed five so-called departments in which additional "teaching force and apparatus" were required: Physics, Biology, Applied Mathematics, Philosophy and History, and Rhetoric and Elocution. In addition, it called for an increase in the library fund and the general endowment. It is a stark commentary on the fate of the College during the next thirteen years to observe that the very same notice, with only a word changed here or there, appeared in the 1904 catalogue.

It is difficult to determine how well the Gettysburg faculty carried out the curriculum which they offered to their students between 1868 and 1904. Given the wide range of topics which most of them were called upon to teach, the brevity of their own formal study beyond the undergraduate level, the financial restraints under which everyone in the College worked, and indeed the capacities and interests of the students who were attracted to Gettysburg, one may wonder about the quality of the academic work expected and offered. In attempting to reach some answer to the question, one must take into consideration the evidence that most of the faculty were able and conscientious men who were confident of their ability to perform their duties well and who attempted to keep up-to-date in ways similar to some of those which faculty before and since have employed.[129]

From Admission to Commencement

Beginning in 1861 the academic year consisted of three terms or sessions. In 1868 the board of trustees determined that these terms should be fifteen, twelve, and twelve weeks in length, with vacations of nine, three, and one weeks between them. Under this arrangement, classes began in late August or early September and commencement occurred on the last Thursday in June. With minor adjustments, this was the calendar in effect in 1904. One of those adjustments was made in 1902, after the faculty told the trustees that "the great majority of institutions of our class" have academic years of thirty-six weeks and that, in any event, "the first week in September is rather early to begin work on account of the continuance of the summer heat." The first term of the 1903-1904 year began on Thursday, September 10. Commencement exercises took place on Wednesday, June 15.

The academic year was punctuated by days on which no classes were held. One such was Thanksgiving day. Christmas and New Year no longer presented the problem which they did during the early period, since the vacation between the first and second terms included both of these days. Once it was switched to a Sunday, the annual day of prayer for colleges ceased being a holiday. There was an abortive attempt to make Lincoln's birthday a day without classes. Washington's birthday fared much better; it was as dependable a day off in 1904 as it had been in 1868.[130] When Easter did not

---

[129]Two burlesques, one of which appeared in 1892 (*The Bloody Lutheran*) and the other in 1897 (*The Gettysburg Kindergarten*), were unsparing in their characterization of almost every faculty member, but one cannot accept their criticisms as credible without subjecting them in turn to criticism.

[130]Through 1886 February 22 was a day for the literary societies to take turns in holding public exercises. In 1879, if not earlier, a new feature was introduced for this day. According to the *Compiler* for February 27, 1879, "the 22d – Saturday –brought out the flag, the drums corps, and an unannounced fantastical parade of more than ordinary point and wit." This custom lapsed in the mid-1890s, was revived in 1896 by a student mass meeting, and was still alive in 1904. The *College Monthly* for March 1884 described the parade in that year as follows: "As customary on the 22nd of Feb. the students, about 65 or 70 in number, clad in fantastic garb, formed a procession and marched through town. The procession headed by a drum corps, which performed its part admirably under the efficient leadership of the drum major, left College about 10 o'clock A. M., and proceeded directly to the 'diamond,' where the entire party was photographed by W. H. Tipton. From here they marched back and forth through the principal streets of town, creating everywhere much amusement for the crowds of spectators that could be seen everywhere. The characters and impersonations were very creditable indeed, and many of them worthy of special notice, if space would permit. But suffice it to say, the whole affair was a grand success, and was highly appreciated by the citizens as well as the entire body of students."

occur during the vacation between the second and third terms, Good Friday offered students a relief from classes. They complained when they did not have at least half a day off on Ascension day. Memorial day became an American holiday after 1868. It would have been most unusual had a battlefield town such as Gettysburg failed to make special efforts to observe it properly. With few exceptions, the faculty cancelled classes on May 30 for at least half a day. Since the academic year now closed in June rather than August, there was no need to decide to call off classes on July 4.

In addition to these holidays, which occurred every year, there were others which the faculty decreed from time to time for what it took to be good reasons. Hundreds of battlefield monuments were dedicated with imposing ceremonies, many of them about twenty-five years after the July days of 1863. The faculty could be expected to suspend classes on Ohio day (1887), when the monuments of that state were dedicated, as well as on the day when the high water mark monument (1892) and the Hancock and Meade equestrian statues (1896) were formally set aside. For very different reasons there were other days without classes: the funeral of President James A. Garfield (1881), the four hundredth anniversary of the birth of Martin Luther (1883), the centennial of the inauguration of George Washington (1889), the four hundredth anniversary of the landing of Christopher Columbus (1892), the parade in Gettysburg by the Order of United American Mechanics (1896), and the birthday of Abraham Lincoln, decreed specifically for this year only (1904).

Between 1868 and 1904 there was considerable change in the long-established patterns of admission to American colleges. As the numbers of academies and high schools increased, it became more difficult for colleges to influence the preparation of their entering freshmen than it was at a time when most beginning students were veterans of preparatory departments under their complete control. Although the number of college-bound students was increasing more rapidly than the number of institutions offering undergraduate instruction, some of the newer schools had large endowments and offered superior programs which were attractive to able and ambitious students.

During this period Gettysburg College experienced the same sort of competition faced by any other pre-1868 institution. Three new Lutheran colleges appeared on territory on which it was once unchallenged. Muhlenberg awarded its first baccalaureate degree in 1868, Thiel in 1874, and Susquehanna in 1896. Some of the students who might not have considered another college in years past might now weigh the advantages of attending Lehigh or The Johns Hopkins University. In responding to the changed conditions, Gettysburg increased its advertising in Lutheran and other newspapers, journals, and reports. It urged pastors and other friends of the College to influence prospective students to come to Gettysburg. In a number of ways, it encouraged its own students to sell their alma mater to their younger friends, especially during hard times. "A word from a student in favor of the institution he is attending has more influence, perhaps," according to the *College Monthly* for July 1884, 'than that of anyone else in leading a young man to decide upon what college he will enter, and we ask the students to bear this in mind." On occasion, the College engaged recruiters (sometimes faculty) to bring in the students needed to pay the bills.

In 1904, as in 1868, the catalogue announced that entrance examinations were held on several days before commencement and at the beginning of the fall term. There could be examinations at other times, but obviously the faculty expected prospective students to present themselves on these preferred occasions. There was, nevertheless, a major difference between the two catalogue statements. The later one reported that those graduates of the College's preparatory department who were recommended by the principal were now admitted without examination. In addition, students recommended by "approved Academies and High Schools" were admitted without examination, "on an extended trial."

One can trace the history of these admissions changes at least to 1876, when the faculty proposed to the board of trustees the appointment of a joint committee. Its purpose was to determine whether it was feasible for the College to establish a "closer cooperative relation" with existing academies "in the matter of preparing students for its classes" and also whether additional academies might be established which would "stand in some recognized and efficient relation to this institution as preparing schools." The board could scarcely reject this proposal out of hand. It dutifully named three influential trustees to the joint committee, which did not make its report until 1880. Then it referred the matter back to the faculty, with the suggestion that the professors consider modifying or omitting entrance examinations for students from certain cooperating preparatory schools. In 1884, after several years of study, the faculty adopted a statement of policy on the subject. The College would admit students without examination on the certificate of principals of academies which would "adjust their course and grade of studies to our entrance requirements." This privilege was extended first to its own preparatory department and in later years to the Missionary Institute at Selinsgrove (before it became Susquehanna University), Baltimore City College, Mercersburg Academy, McEwensville Academy, Lock Haven High School, as well as to other similar institutions. The arrangement did not always work smoothly, but it was continued.[131]

The admissions requirements of 1868 included a stated level of mastery of Latin (grammar, Caesar, and Virgil), Greek (grammar and the reader), mathematics (arithmetic, elementary algebra, and one book of geometry), English grammar, and geography (ancient and modern). Aware of the increasing expectations of what it called "the better-class colleges," the faculty and board in 1884, 1897, and 1898 raised the entrance requirements. The statement in the 1904 catalogue as it applied to the bachelor of arts candidates read as follows: Latin (grammar, three books of Caesar, three books of Virgil, and three orations of Cicero), Greek (grammar, prose composition, and three books of Xenophon), mathematics (arithmetic, elementary algebra, three books of George A. Wentworth's widely used geometry text), English (grammar, rhetoric, and mastery of specified books by Addison, Goldsmith, Coleridge, Tennyson, Lowell, Eliot, and Milton, as recommended by the Assocation of Colleges and Preparatory Schools of the Middle States and Maryland), geography, and history (Greek, Roman, and American).[132] One of the pressing questions facing the faculty after 1904 was whether the entrance requirements needed to be raised again.

As had been the case from 1832, so through and beyond 1904 all students were required to sign their names in the matriculation book and give certain personal information. The oath which most signed during the period under study differed slightly from the earlier version. It read as follows:

I solemnly promise, on my truth and honor, to observe and obey all the laws, rules and regulations of Pennsylvania College, and especially that I will abstain from the profanation of the Lord's day, from the use of profane language, from all kinds of gambling, from disorderly behavior, from disrespectful conduct towards my instructors, and from all combinations to resist their authority.

Between 1868 and 1904 enrollment in the College doubled. The average for the first decade of this period was 91; for the second, 104; for the third, 162; and for the years 1898-1904, 182.[133] There is not enough evidence to state with confidence how selective the

[131]In 1887-1888, for example, there was a vigorous disagreement between Jonathan R. Dimm of Missionary Institute and the Gettysburg faculty over whether graduates of Selinsgrove were prepared for admission to the upper classes at Gettysburg.

[132]Bachelor of science candidates, not needing Greek, could choose to be examined in physical geography, botany, physics, or English or French history.

[133]In the late 1880s, the *College Monthly* noted on at least three occasions and with some pride that the size of the Gettysburg freshman class exceeded those of Dickinson, Franklin and Marshall, Bucknell, Allegheny, and Muhlenberg.

MATRICULATION BOOK OF PENNSYLVANIA COLLEGE.

I solemnly promise, on my truth and honor, to observe and obey all the laws, rules and regulations of Pennsylvania College, and especially that I will abstain from the profanation of the Lord's day, from the use of profane language, from all kinds of gambling, from disorderly behavior, from disrespectful conduct towards my instructors, and from all combinations to resist their authority

FULL NAME.	PARENT OR GUARDIAN.	P. O. ADDRESS.	DATE OF BIRTH.	DENOMINATION.	WHERE PREPARED FOR COLLEGE.	CLASS.	DATE OF ENTRANCE.

Page from the matriculation book, 1883-1884.

faculty was in admitting students, but in October 1878 the editor of the *College Monthly* thought that the faculty was evidencing high standards when it accepted only thirty-seven of the forty to fifty young men who applied for the freshman class.[134] The large majority of students continued to come from Pennsylvania: 28 of the 34 freshmen entering in 1868; 26 of the 35 in 1886; and 43 of the 49 in 1904.[135] In those three years the number of Marylanders was 2, 6, and 4 respectively. Eighty-one percent of the students who signed the matriculation book between 1875 and 1904 identified themselves as being Lutheran. Most of the rest were Presbyterian, Reformed, and Methodist, in that order. It would appear that the Lutherans possessed the greater staying power, since 22 of the 26 juniors in 1891 confessed to being Lutherans, as did 40 of the 42 seniors in

[134] The faculty minutes continued to record refusals to admit transfer students who could not present a statement of honorable dismissal from a previously attended school. Whether they made any unrecorded exceptions is unknown.

[135] Twenty-seven of the forty-nine freshmen of 1904, an unusually large proportion, gave their place of residence as Gettysburg. In April 1890 the *College Monthly* noted that there were seven students enrolled from Pine Grove, Schuylkill county. For forty-five years Elias S. Henry (1849) occupied the Lutheran pulpit in that town and continued an existing tradition of sending young men to Gettysburg College.

1904. The first Roman Catholic student was probably Robert Nicholas Heltzel, who entered in 1901 and was awarded a degree in 1905. Both he and the three other Catholic students who were enrolled before 1904 were from the Gettysburg area.[136]

Women students first entered Gettysburg College in the 1880s. A decade earlier, in 1873, the trustees briefly considered a resolution to open the preparatory department to both sexes. There was no request for such action in the faculty report for that year, and the name of the trustee who introduced the resolution is not given in the minutes. Perhaps at a time when enrollment was down, someone saw admitting women as a way to bring it up. In any event, the trustees referred the resolution to the executive committee for advice, which was not offered until 1875. Instructed by the board to consider the desirability of having women students in either prep or the College proper, the committee reported against them. The trustees accepted this advice.

Writing in the *College Monthly* for May 1877, John G. Morris brought the subject to the attention of the College constituency for the first time. He favored what he called coeducation and suggested that the place to begin was with the preparatory department. J. Clinton Hill, an 1864 graduate and a Williamsport attorney, told an alumni group early in 1880 (as reported in the *College Monthly* for February) that women deserved to have better educational opportunities than were available to them. An article in the *Lutheran Observer* for February 18, 1881 lamented that there were no Pennsylvania colleges open to Lutheran daughters. Women are doing much more in society, according to the author, they will be doing even more in the future, and they deserve to have access to a college education. The writer proposed adding substantially to the endowment of the three Lutheran colleges in the state (he did not say how this could or would be done) and opening their doors to women.

In June 1883 veteran trustee William M. Baum introduced a resolution opening the preparatory department to women students "until otherwise ordered." After discussing the proposal, the trustees referred the matter to the faculty with power to act. The faculty chose to admit women and, as already noted, the first ones entered in the fall of 1883. When the board met in June 1884, Charles A. Hay

---

[136]The matriculation book which was used before 1875 is not in the College Archives. If it were available, one could state definitely whether there were Catholic students earlier. In 1902 the faculty excused the three Catholic students from the English Bible course, in spite of the fact that it was supposed to be taught as an undenominational exercise. A year later, it excused the fourth student from a required history course and advised her to make the substitution which her priest recommended.

proposed that qualified women be admitted to College classes; his colleagues defeated the motion. In the same month, the *College Monthly* observed that "co-education seems to be meeting with more and more favor." More than one hundred colleges had already adopted it and it was the progressive thing to do. A year later, the faculty advised the board of trustees that there were women in the preparatory department who were qualified to become College students. What should be done if any applied? Hay presented his motion again; John W. Rice offered the time-honored substitute motion to delay by appointing a committee to seek more information "from all accessible sources"; and then a majority of trustees decided that the time had come to act. Hay's motion prevailed.

The first woman student in the College proper, Beulah M. Tipton, was not enrolled until the fall of 1888. She was not the first to complete the course. That honor was shared by Cora E. Hartman and Margaret R. Himes, both of whom were graduated in June 1894. By June 1904 some sixty-seven women had been enrolled and seventeen of these had received bachelor's degrees. More than half of the women students who entered before 1900 dropped out after one or

Most of the seventeen women students enrolled for the 1902-1903 year posed for this picture.

two years. Of the 179 students listed in the 1904 catalogue, 27 were women and 15 of these were freshman.[137]

"It looks as though all will adopt co-education sooner or later," declared the *College Monthly* in July 1885, "and we might as well take the step now as to wait a few years longer." But had Gettysburg adopted coeducation or a variant thereof? It was true that in 1894 Miss Hartman won the Graeff prize and Miss Himes first honor; that in 1895 Edna Loomis was an associate editor of the *Mercury*; and that in 1904 Bess M. Drais, Carrie E. Inglebert, and Mary C. Adams were all second honor graduates; yet it was equally true that the catalogue clearly stated women were "day scholars" and that references to the students of the College consistently called them young men, not young men and women. The hope which the *College Monthly* expressed in June 1883 that women would have their own department and dormitory was not realized for more than half a century. An excellent indication of their status, or lack of it, came in April 1904, when the women asked the faculty for a tennis court. "We cannot accede to the request," the minutes explained, "as the ladies are only 'day students,' and there is no proper place on the campus to assign them for the purpose asked."

The student's class schedule consisted of sixteen exercises each week, three on Monday through Friday and one on Saturday. The catalogue described these exercises as recitations or lectures – lasting sixty minutes – or laboratory periods – lasting 150 minutes. Until 1891, classes met at 8 A.M., 11 A.M., and 3 P.M., except on Saturday, when they met at 8 A.M. and 9 A.M. Beginning in 1891, there were classes on the hour, except at noon, from 8 A.M. through 3 P.M., except on Saturday, when the old schedule still prevailed. Until 1899 there was no such thing as an absence system. Students were expected to attend every class. If they planned to be absent, at any time, their proper course of action was first to secure permission to leave the community and then make up the work in advance, if at all possible. Failing that, the disciplinary procedures would begin operating and the case would come before the faculty, an inordinate amount of whose time was consumed, both in and out of session, administering this cumbersome system. As early as March 1893, a committee was appointed "to ascertain the method of other colleges in reference to allowing a certain percentage of absences from recitations and other college duties." Not until January 1899 did the trustees revise the rules and regulations to permit from one to

---

[137]Of the twenty-seven Pennsylvania colleges listed in the 1889-1890 report of the Commissioner of Education, twelve reported women students in their college classes. These latter included Allegheny, Bucknell, Dickinson, and Swarthmore, as well as Gettysburg. *Report of the Commissioner* (1889-1890), 2:1595.

three absences in each course in each term. Subsequently students were warned that "unexcused absences from recitations are counted as zeros upon the grades."

Toward the close of the period under study, the catalogue announced that "a careful record of the attendance, scholarship and conduct of each student is kept" and that "a general statement of which record is transmitted to parents or guardians at the close of each term." Truly, such an announcement could have been included in the very first College publications, since it was in total accord with the policies determined in 1832. One way for the faculty to compile the careful record was to enter a grade for performance during every class session and to give what were called topical examinations. Another was to schedule more extensive and formal evaluations at the close of each term. Sometimes these examinations were oral and sometimes, written.[138] If the former, and the students were seniors, the examiners included both faculty and trustees. As if to add insult to injury, these sessions were thrown open to the general public, which was exhorted to attend by newspaper notices. Final examinations for juniors, sophomores, and freshmen, as classes, were conducted by one or more designated faculty members, mercifully in private. Finally, when all of the reckoning, based on attendance, scholarship, and conduct, was completed, the faculty entered its notations, or grades, on the appropriate form and sent them off to waiting parents or guardians. The grades were given in numbers.

Between 1868 and 1904 much of this procedure changed. First, the public examination of seniors and involvement of the trustees ended; the last mention of trustee participation was in 1885. Second, upon recommendation of the faculty, the board in 1890 adopted a new system of "notations." Henceforth, grades would be reported in letters rather than numbers: A (excellent); B (very good); C (good); D (passed); and E (deficient).[139] Third, in 1891 the professors decided to discontinue what they called "regular faculty examinations" and to authorize each of them to determine the examination he wished to give in his courses.[140]

---

[138]The first reference to the College's supplying paper for use in these examinations was in 1884.

[139]This legislation established numerical equivalents for letter grades: A, 97-100; B, 92-97; C, 80-92; D, 65-80; and E, everything below 65. Unfortunately, it did not state whether 80 was a C or a D, or whether 97 was an A. In 1896, the B range was set at 90 through 96. Grades continued to be recorded by instructors in numbers, even though reported in letters.

[140]In May 1892 the *College Monthly* reported that during the preceding six years some 389 Prussian university students had committed suicide, most of them because of failure in examinations. "American students," the reader was informed, "take such misfortunes more philosophically."

PENNSYLVANIA COLLEGE.

Gettysburg, Pa., *Nrci 26 1885*

DEAR SIR:
                    Annexed is the Official Report of

Franklin Menges

of the *Junior* Class for the Session ending *Ned 26 1885*

The numbers in this Report are on a scale in which the maximum is 100, and
50 is the lowest grade that will enable the Student to remain in the Class. Unexcused absences from recitation are counted as zero upon the grades.

The attention of Parents and Guardians is specially called to the fact that
absences from recitation, whether at the opening of Term or at other times, are
not excused except for sickness or imperative necessity.

Students are graded in Deportment; the highest grade being 100, from which
reductions are made for violations of the Regulations, misdemeanors, and unexcused absences from College duties.

The next session will begin *April 7th* 1885

H. W. McKnight President.

Grade of Scholarship.

IN MATHEMATICS,	
LATIN,	
GREEK,	
FRENCH,	
GERMAN,	
HISTORY,	
ENGLISH,	
ANGLO-SAXON,	
RHETORIC,	
COMPOSITION,	
DECLAMATION,	
LOGIC,	
POLITICAL SCIENCE,	98
NATURAL PHILOSOPHY,	97
CHEMISTRY, *An. chemistry*	100
ASTRONOMY,	100
MINERALOGY,	
GEOLOGY,	
ZOOLOGY,	
BOTANY,	
MENTAL SCIENCE,	
MORAL SCIENCE,	
NATURAL THEOLOGY,	
CHRISTIAN EVIDENCES,	
BIBLICAL RECITATION,	
DEPORTMENT,	100

	Excused.	Unexcused.
ABSENT FROM PRAYERS,		11
" CHURCH,		
" RECITATION,		3
" BUILDING,		

GENERAL REMARKS:

Student Grade Report, 1885.

Commencement week in Gettysburg continued to be a gala affair, with College and seminary often, but not always, coordinating their end-of-the-year activities.[141] From 1834 through 1861 these festivities had occurred in September; from 1862 through 1868 they were in August. Beginning in 1869 they took place in June. In 1869 commencement was on June 30 and in 1904 on June 15. The board of trustees insisted that every senior must participate in the graduation exercises unless excused for a good reason by the faculty. They also believed that all other students should remain in Gettysburg to be present on these occasions. In 1898 they instructed the faculty to refuse requests for permission to leave before commencement and to "provide for keeping the students occupied until that time." In spite of the directive to take "extreme action" against those absent without excuse, about twenty-five students disobeyed this explicit order. The faculty carefully explained to the board how difficult it was to carry out their wishes. At their next meeting, the trustees gave up the effort.

---

[141]Although the seminary had such activities for many years, it held its first formal baccalaureate service only in 1891 and conferred its first bachelor of divinity degrees only in 1899.

306

Commencement week began on Sunday morning with the baccalaureate service, at which the president usually, but not always, preached the sermon. That evening, there was a lecture sponsored by the Young Men's Christian Association. Two commencement events of long standing disappeared during these years. The lectures sponsored in turn by Philo and Phrena were last given in 1886, and the junior exhibition was abandoned two years later.[142]

As early as the 1870s the seniors sometimes had class day exercises. After having been neglected for some years, these activities were revived in 1891.[143] Two years later, the seniors first planted ivy on campus as part of their class day program.[144]

The Alumni Association held its annual meeting during commencement week, until 1896 preceded by an address delivered by one of its members who was cajoled into returning to campus for that purpose. Sometimes the association held a social gathering, at which food might be served. During the 1870s the board of trustees also sponsored "social reunions," some of which were held in the fashionable Springs Hotel, just west of town. For many years the College president gave a reception for people attending commencement. This was in addition to the always well-attended dinner which he gave for the members of the senior class. Sometimes the social fraternities and alumni classes also held reunions. To provide an alternative to or relief from the many speeches and receptions, tennis tournaments and field days were held, beginning in the 1890s.

---

[142]Beginning in 1851, all juniors were required to give orations during the junior exhibition. This task was distasteful to many of them. Some of their requests that it be abandoned resulted in an occasional one-year cessation, usually followed by a trustee request that the custom be fully reinstated. Finally, in 1888, by which time the commencement week schedule obviously needed some relief, the junior exhibition was moved into the second term. In 1891 it was changed into a junior oratorical contest sponsored by the literary societies and not requiring participation by every member of the class. By 1893 the junior oratorical contest was being squeezed into the commencement week program.

[143]They were held on Tuesday evening in front of Pennsylvania Hall. There were lanterns, lamps, streamers, and music. The program included the inevitable oration, class history, class poem, class prophecy, and the final call of the roll. *Spectrum* (1893), pp. 275-276. In 1897, when it was learned that a "faculty roast" was being planned as part of the forthcoming program, the professors registered a vigorous protest and warned the students that their plans were directly counter to specific board action against such performances.

[144]The ivy reportedly came from the Abbotsford home of Sir Walter Scott and was planted along the northern wall of the chapel. *College Monthly* (June 1893), p. 195, and *Mercury* (June 1893), p. 90. A prophetic student in the *Gettysburgian* for October 19, 1898 argued that ivy was not a good class memorial. Years later, he wrote, alumni would return to campus and find nothing to remind them of their gift.

307

Through 1889 commencement exercises were held in Christ Lutheran church; beginning in 1890 they were in Brua Chapel.[145] Although the trustees and faculty had for some years considered following the practice of an increasing number of other institutions by requiring the use of caps and gowns at the exercises, it was the senior class of 1895 which set the precedent by deciding to wear them for the first time. According to the *Mercury* for July 1895, "it was a novel feature of commencement to see the class clad in

Program for the 1886 commencement, when every graduate still delivered an oration.

---

[145]In 1878 the faculty declared that the forthcoming commencement was the forty-sixth, "reckoning from the year in which the College was chartered rather than, as heretofore, from the number of graduating classes." The 1878 commencement program explained that "the former method of reckoning commencements according to the number of classes graduated has been abandoned, and the custom elsewhere prevalent of reckoning according to the number of years the College has been in operation, has been adopted."

uniform costume, which certainly added dignity to the occasion."[146]

It was the long-established custom to have every graduating senior give an oration, on a topic assigned by the faculty but subject to later negotiation. In 1872 the faculty decreed that any senior who did not follow the approved text of his oration but introduced new material jeopardized his graduation. By 1888 the senior class had become sufficiently large (four times in the decade it exceeded twenty) that, even with abbreviated orations, trustees and faculty agreed something had to be done to prevent the program from running to unbearable lengths. The first solution, to schedule half of the orations on one day, with the other half and the actual awarding of degrees on the next, was tried in 1889, 1890, and 1891. Few, if any, liked this awkward arrangement, and beginning in 1892, with trustee approval, and after receiving a petition from the seniors, the faculty chose ten of the highest ranking students in the class to give orations. The debate was not over. Both sides now argued the question of whether Gettysburg should adopt the procedure of an increasing number of institutions, which retired the student orators altogether in favor of an outside commencement speaker. This issue had not been resolved by 1904.

Music was always an important feature of the graduating exercises. Bands or orchestras from York or Baltimore were sometimes engaged to play, at considerable cost. In 1874, when it was having great difficulty in paying its faculty members an annual salary of $1,300, the board authorized the expenditure of $200 for commencement music, simply because the faculty assured it that a suitable musical group could not be secured for much less than that amount. In an effort to promote what it believed to be good order during commencement, the faculty resolved that, beginning in 1887, family and friends could no longer interrupt the exercises by placing flowers or other expressions of approval upon the stage during or after a senior's oration.

Between 1868 and 1904 most honors and prizes for students were awarded during commencement. The honors of valedictorian and

---

[146]The *Mercury* for January 1894 stated that seniors at Amherst, Dartmouth, Harvard, Lafayette, Princeton, Williams, and Yale had recently agreed to wear academic costume. In 1889 the Gettysburg board of trustees considered a motion to purchase enough caps and gowns to supply both juniors and seniors, for a rental fee. No action was taken on this motion, but later in the same year most of the students participating in the junior exhibition wore academic costume, after the faculty told them they could wear whatever they pleased, "provided it be proper for the occasion." The class of 1894 elected not to wear this garb. Once the decision to conform to developing custom was made, seniors began wearing their caps and gowns as soon as they were available. For example, in 1896 the seniors wore theirs for the first time in February, to church. The faculty were still not wearing academic costume in 1904.

STUDENTS IN COLLEGE AND DEGREES GRANTED,
1868-1904

	Degree Candidates	Special Students	Preparatory Students	Total Students	Graduates
1868-69	103		75	178	16
1869-70	101		60	161	18
1870-71	114		63	177	23
1871-72	86	6	37	129	25
1872-73	75	4	50	129	15
1873-74	81	9	54	144	23
1874-75	81	2	69	152	15
1875-76	85	3	44	132	16
1876-77	75	4	46	125	24
1877-78	70	3	47	120	14
1878-79	79	2	51	132	12
1879-80	94	2	44	140	17
1880-81	104	2	46	152	16
1881-82	110	1	60	171	24
1882-83	106		47	153	25
1883-84	100		52	152	18
1884-85	93	1	45	139	24
1885-86	94		50	144	24
1886-87	106	10	48	164	20
1887-88	119	12	62	193	17
1888-89	126	10	62	198	27
1889-90	155	11	60	226	30
1890-91	159	11	59	229	29
1891-92	163	12	62	237	26
1892-93	163	12	64	239	49
1893-94	151	16	58	225	28
1894-95	134	16	67	217	33
1895-96	134	16	77	227	16
1896-97	159	14	97	270	26
1897-98	182	3	78	263	31
1898-99	185	3	66	254	33
1899-1900	182	3	64	249	37
1900-01	192		82	274	50
1901-02	178	1	85	264	38
1902-03	178	1	102	281	32
1903-04	179	3	83	265	43
					914

Sources: College catalogues and *Alumni Directory of Pennsylvania College of Gettysburg, 1832-1918* (Gettysburg, 1918). The number of degrees granted includes only the bachelors' degrees in the arts and in science, but not three awarded to students who completed their work before 1868 whose degrees were withheld for disciplinary reasons. In a few instances graduates of 1869-1904 are listed with their original classes, even though for one reason or another their degrees were actually awarded a year or more later. There were about 609 students who were enrolled in the College between the fall of 1868 and 1904 but who were not graduated.

salutatorian could be traced to 1834. Until 1903, the latter delivered his oration in Latin. Occasional Greek and German orations and an English salutatory were also treated as honors. Beginning in 1862, the faculty chose from among the seniors of highest rank one or more persons to be designated first, second, third, or fourth honor men. In 1870, for example, four qualified; in 1883, eight; and in 1891, seven. Beginning in 1892, the number of honors available was reduced to two.

In 1868 there were three College prizes: the Freshman Prize (it became the Muhlenberg Freshman Prize in 1887), the Hassler Latin Prize; and the Graeff English Prize. Candidates for the latter wrote a senior essay on an assigned topic. A committee of outside persons evaluated the work submitted and selected the winner who, through 1880, read his essay at a public meeting. Thereafter, the essays were published in the *College Monthly* and, later, in the *Mercury*. Three additional prizes were added by 1904. First, in 1892 Charles J. Reddig established a Reddig Oratorical Prize for the junior who placed first in public competition. Second, in 1893 Charles Baum, an 1874 graduate and a Philadelphia physician, contributed money for an award to the sophomore showing the greatest proficiency in mathematics. Third, in 1898 William J. Gies, an 1893 graduate and an instructor at Yale, established three prizes to encourage superior work in English composition.[147]

Most of the degrees awarded at commencement were bachelors of arts or of science. Until 1896 all members of the faculty signed the diplomas. After that the signatures of the president of the College and the secretary of the board made them official. In 1871 the rules for awarding master's degrees in course to graduates of three years' standing were changed significantly. No longer were they granted routinely to most of those who met the time requirement. Henceforth, those eligible and desiring the degree had to apply for it and furnish evidence of their qualifications by virtue of their "professional or literary pursuits." Many responded to these new regulations and the practice continued.[148] Except in rare instances, recipients of these master's degrees did not appear at commencement. An attempt made in the 1870s to have one of their number deliver an oration at the exercises soon ended in failure. Diplomas were first made available to these recipients in 1876 and then were

---

[147]The 1903-1904 catalogue listed a Pen and Sword Society Prize, which disappeared after being listed in the 1904-1905 edition. See the *Spectrum* (1899), pp. 130-133, for a history of each of the first six prizes.

[148]In an effort to counter misunderstandings which had arisen because of these new procedures, the *College Monthly* for June 1878 explained the reason for them and noted that some colleges required an examination of candidates for the master's degree.

given only to those who asked for them and paid a $5 fee.

Between 1868 and 1904 the College awarded 176 honorary degrees: 75 doctors of divinity, 58 masters of arts (separate from those granted in course), 2 bachelors of arts, 18 doctors of laws, 11 doctors of philosophy, 9 doctors of science, 2 doctors of literature, and 1 master of science. Most of the D.D. recipients were Lutheran pastors and alumni. Many of those awarded the M.A. were educators, some were pastors, and a few were physicians. Among those awarded the doctorate of laws were Jeremiah S. Black, Attorney General during the Buchanan administration; Alfred Stillé, professor of medicine at the University of Pennsylvania; John G. Morris; Samuel P. Sadtler; and John S. Stahr, president of Franklin and Marshall College. Recipients were not present to receive these degrees; the president simply announced that they had been conferred. Only in 1902 did the trustees direct the dean to secure diplomas to be given to those who had accepted their honorary degree.[149]

In 1866, only a few years after Yale University awarded the first Ph. D. degree in the United States, Gettysburg College began to use this form of recognition by conferring it as an honorary degree upon one of its own faculty members, Alfred M. Mayer. Between 1869 and 1880 it awarded the degree to eleven other people. Six of these were alumni. Hezekiah R. Geiger (1846), Samuel Aughey (1856), S. Carson Wells (1849), and William Carroll (1850) were college professors. Victor L. Conrad (1848), who succeeded Mayer as Ockershausen professor, was later associate editor of the *Lutheran Observer*. James Macfarlane (1837) was an attorney, author, and businessman in Towanda. Among the nonalumni recipients of the degree were Theodore G. Wormley, professor of chemistry and toxicology in the medical department of the University of Pennsylvania; Thomas J. Turner, medical inspector, United States Navy; and George W. Ruby, long-time principal of the York County Academy.

As the doctorate in philosophy was becoming the highest and most respected earned degree and as an increasing number of colleges and universities were awarding it *honoris causa*, the American Association for the Advancement of Science and the American Philological Association in 1881 both passed resolutions strongly urging that, henceforth, the degree be awarded only to

---

[149]The rules of the board, which were suspended from time to time, called for names of candidates to be submitted at one meeting and then voted upon at a subsequent meeting. Voting was by ballot and, beginning in 1901, a two-thirds vote was required. In 1898 a nominating committee was established to make a preliminary judgment on candidates.

those who had earned it in course. To give some effect to this action, these associations, which were then the two leading learned societies in the country, named a joint committee which sent a letter to 430 colleges and universities, asking them to honor their wishes in this matter. The letter reached Gettysburg in time for the faculty to present it at the board meeting in June 1882. The trustees discussed the recommendation at some length, decided to postpone action for a year, and in June 1883 passed a simple motion "that the conferring of the degree of Ph.D. *honoris causa* be abolished." Three years later, when members of the senior class petitioned the board to award the degree to Edward S. Breidenbaugh, the trustees politely reminded them that the existing rules made granting their request impossible. However, they did institute the degree of doctor of science in 1887 and award it to three persons, one of whom was Breidenbaugh.[150]

Library

In 1868 the College library was located on the north side, center section, third floor of Pennsylvania Hall. A separate reading room held newspapers and periodicals. The College book collection consisted of about 6,000 volumes; the literary societies and other organizations had about 10,500 more. The annual funds for library growth amounted to about $175, which was the interest on an endowment fund established in the 1850s. The yield enabled the faculty to purchase about 150 new volumes each year. Gifts from the federal government, several state governments, and individuals contributed significantly to the annual growth. The hours of service, under the direction of Librarian Luther H. Croll, were limited to one each day.

Despite slow growth of the collection and its limited use by students, the faculty believed that the library needed more adequate and safer quarters. "A separate, fire-proof building should be provided, " they advised the trustees in June 1874, "but as there is no immediate prospect for the erection of such a building," they asked for an appropriation to enlarge the existing quarters. The trustees granted this request and also increased the insurance on the library.[151] A decade later, when Milton Valentine was explaining the

---

[150]Between 1873 and 1889 about twenty-nine honorary Ph.D. degrees were awarded each year by about twenty colleges. In 1904 the Commissioner of Education observed with obvious pleasure that during the preceding academic year the number of these degrees had dropped to five and the number of institutions awarding them to three. *Report of the Commissioner* (1889-1890), 2:759 and (1904), 2:1425.

[151]Faculty Report, June 23, 1874, GCA.

needs of the College to various groups, he told the Philadelphia alumni that it should have a new building, arguing that

> a continuation of the libraries, now numbering together some 20,000 volumes, the accumulation of over fifty-one years, many of the works of much value and difficult of replacement, in the main building, with fifty-four fires going day and night, and an almost equal number of lamps, involves a hazard too great to be thought of with quiet nerves.[152]

Not until the fall of 1889, when the library was moved to the first floor of the New Recitation Building, were Valentine's desires realized.

This picture in the 1898 Spectrum is labeled "General View of College Libraries."

John A. Himes succeeded Croll as librarian in 1888, about a year before the move into the new building occurred. In 1890 Sarah P., or Sallie, Krauth (1850-1924) began a career as assistant librarian which extended to 1922. The daughter of the first president of the College, Sallie replaced the proctors who for about a decade had assisted the librarian in addition to trying to keep order in the old building. Her starting annual salary was $200. By now the library was open to the students for twenty-two hours each week: from 9 A.M. to 11 A.M. and 1 P.M. to 3 P.M. Monday through Friday,

---

[152]Quoted in College Monthly (March 1884), p. 42.

and from 10 A.M. to noon on Saturday.

The 1904 catalogue stated that the library now contained 14,105 volumes, which means that it had more than doubled in the preceding thirty-six years. The growth in the societies' libraries was much smaller. Philo's now had 6,473 and Phrena's had 5,624 volumes. The three collections totaled 26,202 volumes, not including several thousand unbound pamphlets. Among Pennsylvania colleges in 1904, Gettysburg's library holdings ranked with those of Lafayette (23,600), Bucknell (25,000), Swarthmore (22,375), and Pennsylvania State College (21,300). They were behind those of Dickinson (36,000), Franklin and Marshall (39,400), and Haverford (43,000).[153]

In the 1890s, writers for College publications and others demonstrated repeatedly that they were satisfied with neither the library nor student use of it. "Now of course Gettysburg is not a university," said the *Gettysburgian* on February 8, 1899, "but it should make claims, to be nothing less than a first-class college." To validate those claims, it needed a library of 40,000 to 50,000 volumes, which would require a much larger annual expenditure than the accustomed one. Several months earlier, on October 19, 1898, in the same publication, a writer wondered whether a larger and better library collection would indeed be used. "A somewhat continued observation," he wrote, "has led us to estimate that not more than twenty-five per cent of the men are making anything like a proper use of the advantages the libraries afford. This condition is so far from being right that it is entirely wrong." In a day of "broad reading and close research," with the library at hand, and with the time available, "failure to make proper use of the books becomes almost a crime." If the upperclassmen refuse to set a good example for the freshmen, the writer argued, then the latter should set it for everyone else.

Equipment

The first part of the instructional program to be given separate mention in the catalogue was what was ambitiously called the Department of Physical Science. Announcement was made in 1867 that "during the past scholastic year the efficiency of this department of the College has been greatly increased, by the addition of a complete collection of Philosophical Apparatus" and also that "a superior Telescope has recently come into possession of the College, and will soon be mounted and ready for the use of the students in

---

[153]*Report of the Commissioner* (1904), 2:1520-1522. In 1900 the College library was receiving about fifty newspapers and periodicals.

Astronomy." Strongly urged by Alfred M. Mayer, the trustees had appropriated $2,500 for new equipment. Years later, Henry Eyster Jacobs wrote that, when he returned to Gettysburg to join the faculty in 1870, "the apparatus had been completely renewed, and facilities afforded, we as students never enjoyed."[154]

Improvements continued to be made. The basement floor of Linnaean Hall was turned over to the sciences in 1869. Trustee Samuel Appold provided $1,000 for an analytical chemistry laboratory in 1871. The observatory was completed in 1874. Appold contributed money for meteorological instruments in 1877. Nine years later Edward S. Breidenbaugh persuaded the trustees to allow him, under their general supervision, to use the laboratory fees which students

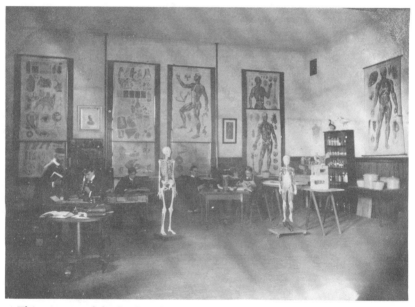

This picture of the biology laboratory in the 1898 Spectrum accompanied Professor Stahley's description of the recently established course in biology.

---

[154]Jacobs, Memoirs, p. 143. In a strongly worded letter, dated April 10, 1866, after the trustees had appropriated $1,000 for the sciences, Mayer complained that although he had given the College $300 worth of equipment and was using $2,000 worth of his own, his usefulness was "very much diminished by the paltry means at my command to carry on my work." He still needed $2,000 to do his job properly. If the trustees would appropriate $1,500, he would raise the remainder from the proceeds of his own lecturing. This act, he argued, "will thus do mere justice to the students and I will not feel that they are wasting their time by studying in an Institution which affords them, in my department, advantages hardly equal to those of a first class preparatory school." Alfred M. Mayer to the board of trustees, April 10, 1866, GCA. The trustees voted the money requested.

paid to purchase chemical supplies and compensate an assistant. This assured him a dependable source of necessary funds without having to make annual appeals to the board. The changes made during the building program of 1888-1890 resulted in much improved facilities for the instructional activities of both Breidenbaugh and George D. Stahley. In 1890 the latter secured from England a set of eleven anatomical diagrams, seven feet by four feet in dimension. Seven of these were life-size representations, while four were drawings of organs and tissues. After Stahley reported this acquisition in the May 1890 issue of the *College Monthly* and asked for someone to make a contribution which would pay for these diagrams, a donor who chose to remain anonymous rose to the occasion. In 1895 Stahley added to his equipment by purchasing from the famous Ward's Natural Science Establishment in Rochester, New York, a mannequin, human skeleton, and human skull.

In 1868 the college had a well-developed museum which included minerals, natural history specimens (such as fossils, shells, birds, reptiles, and other animals), as well as curiosities and relics. In the late 1860s and early 1870s much time and effort were spent in a major reorganization of this collection. Most of it was relabeled, catalogued, and placed in new cases. The collection itself continued to grow. Among the donors were Elizabeth C. Morris of Germantown, who gave her botanical specimens, and John G. Morris, who willed the College his large and varied collection of shells, herbs, and insects. The faculty actively encouraged such gifts in a number of ways. They used the pages of the catalogue and the *College Monthly* both to solicit and to acknowledge contributions: quartz from North Carolina, gold ore from Maryland, silver ore from Colorado, iron ore from Adams county, petrified wood from Arizona, a stuffed mountain lion, Indian implements, an ancient Asian Indian vase, an African canoe, Confederate money, and a piece of wood claimed to be from Abraham Lincoln's birthplace. About 1890 a chemical museum was begun. Its purpose as described in the catalogue of that year was "to contain specimens of raw and manufactured articles in chemical industries." From time to time the College claimed that its museum was one of the largest and most representative to be found in any college. Beginning in 1891, soon after the museum was moved to the third floor of the New Recitation Building, the catalogue stated that there were more than 6,000 items in the mineral, 6,000 in the botanical, and 3,000 in the rock collection.

The faculty consistently maintained that the museum was not intended to be a campus curiosity, but rather a valuable instructional aid. Professor Breidenbaugh, who acquired the title of Curator of Linnaean Hall in 1874 and kept it and its successor, Curator of Museum, through 1904, explained in the catalogue that

This picture of the museum after it was moved to Glatfelter Hall appeared in the 1904 Spectrum.

the senior mineralogy course was taught "by having the students make a personal examination of the specimens" in the collection. Until the novelty wore off and it ceased being the thing to do, the seniors also went on what were described as mineralogical excursions: to Lancaster county nickel mines in 1878; to Lehigh and Northampton county steel mills and zinc mines in 1880; to Luray Caverns in 1882; and to Watkins Glen, Niagara Falls, and the Pennsylvania oil region in 1883. Presumably the students learned something from the trips. It is evident from the accounts which they left that they thoroughly enjoyed themselves on these excursions.

Students

The ideal of operating a college after the manner of a well-regulated family, in which instruction and discipline were seen as equally important and necessary functions, was one shared by virtually every American college before the Civil War. Long after 1865, many of these institutions continued to cling to this ideal, insisting that the development of character in young college men was as important as any other purpose which they undertook to serve. Yet no alert college faculty after the Civil War could fail somehow to reckon with the increasingly evident policy of the developing universities to concentrate their attention, including that of their undergraduate colleges, on scholarship and research. While university leaders might regard the development of good character as indispensable to the well-being of society, they did not believe that its cultivation was their business, at least not to any considerable extent.

It is evident that the postwar trustees and faculty of Gettysburg College were alert to what was happening in American higher education. Not surprisingly, they refused to accept many of the current trends. In 1904, as in 1868, they remained firmly convinced that character development was a responsibility which they could not and would not shirk. The long-used catalogue statement on this subject was changed only when that document underwent a general revision in 1887, but the new pronouncement certainly meant no weakening of the old purpose: "Parents and friends can feel assured that all judicious efforts will be made to secure the highest mental culture and to develop true Christian character among the young men enrolled as students in this institution."[155] Trustees and faculty continued to take a keen interest in the published rules and regulations of the College, which were revised and reissued every few years.[156] The fact that secretaries of the board of trustees sometimes copied the entire text of revised versions longhand into the minute book is one indication of the seriousness which was attached to good conduct, as College officers related it to good character. Another indication is the regularity and detail with which the faculty discussed discipline in each annual report which they made to the board of trustees.

One could also find student voices accepting the change that was in the air and yet reaffirming certain of the old verities. "The idea is slowly dying a natural death that four years of Latin, Greek, and Mathematics will fit a man to deal with all the problems of life," wrote one student in the Mercury for June 1893. "The world calls for more than that, it calls for men . . . . Character is a prime necessity for a man, and here is the place to develop it, for the college is a little world with duties as real as those of the throbbing world about us."

While the Gettysburg trustees and faculty may have clung

---

[155]The comparable statement in the 1904 catalogue made its appearance in 1895: "The College aims to secure the cooperation of each individual student in the preservation of good order and the attainment of a high standard of scholarship and manly conduct." This section of the chapter deals with faculty efforts to keep order and promote good conduct, which to the professors were only part of their attempt to develop character.

[156]There were editions in 1872, 1876, 1883, 1885, 1889, 1893, 1899, and perhaps at other times as well.

tenaciously to the ideals of 1868, they were nevertheless prepared to seek to realize them with a spirit increasingly different from that of, say, Henry L. Baugher. "College government should be secured, as far as possible, through the students' own manly self-government," declared Milton Valentine in his inaugural address in 1868. "Whilst young men are sent to College not to govern, but to be taught, they are, nevertheless, to be trained up in the sentiments and practices of ruling themselves, with the principles and laws of virtue and order written on their hearts."[157] To demonstrate that these were not idle words, Valentine discontinued the regular evening visitation of student rooms. This threw "the students on their honor for the observance of the rules and a frank reporting of any deviation by themselves," he told the trustees in 1869, "and according to them a generous confidence in their fidelity to their pledged word."[158] Baugher may have moved slightly in his grave if he learned what Valentine told the Philadelphia alumni in 1884: "Over against reports of troublesome irregularities in other institutions, I must be allowed to say for the students of Pennsylvania College, that a better-ordered and manlier set of young men could hardly be found anywhere."[159]

In September 1884 Luther H. Croll delivered the traditional faculty lecture at the opening of the College year. Taking as his topic "In Loco Parentis," the vice president of the College insisted that Gettysburg does "advocate the idea of the possibility and the advantage of the adoption of a disciplinary force or influence called parental." He was severely critical of those who assumed that "parental modes are puerile and babyish" and that "college officials are offensively prying into trunks and wardrobes, and constantly chiding and inflicting petty punishments." In the course of his address, Croll answered a series of objections to "parental government" by contending that campus problems often attributed to it resulted instead from youthful exuberance, the failures of biological parents, or the shortcomings of society at large. These problems, he believed, were more pronounced on those campuses where "all interest and influence over the student is abandoned out of the class-room." It was especially unfortunate that so many young men come to college

---

[157]*Valentine Inaugural*, p. 36. "If there is anything that ought to be regarded as *ultimate* in education, it is soundness and purity of character," Valentine maintained. "It is the development of mental life in the excellence and power of right moral life. Good principles are greater than intellectual ability."

[158]Faculty Report, June 1869, GCA.

[159]Quoted in *College Monthly* (March 1884), p. 40. Henry Eyster Jacobs thought that under Valentine "the excessive severity of Dr. Baugher gave place to the reliance upon the honor of the students to an extent that allowed many gross irregularities." Jacobs, *Memoirs*, p. 141.

"anticipating a system of vigilant espionage and rigorous discipline, and fully prepared from the first to regard the faculty as their enemies." Actually, Croll insisted, the only college officers who should be employed and retained are those who "ever find their own happiness in rendering their pupils intelligent, virtuous and happy." He urged his listeners, the student body of 1884-1885, "to uphold and fortify, by every means in your power, the dignity and authority of those to whom are entrusted your dearest interests, rather than reap the bitter fruits of your own imprudence and folly in resisting an influence because some have caviled at its name."[160]

In keeping with the main theme of his inaugural address in 1885, Harvey W. McKnight criticized both the "rigid and exacting discipline" of former years and the current practice, which he traced in part to European universities, which "treats the student as a man, amenable only to himself." Gettysburg should avoid both extremes, blending the "care of the earlier method" with "the liberty of the later." The student who enters as a boy and leaves as a man needs "at first a guardianship which should relax more and more into freedom as his age advances, his principles gain strength, his sense of responsiblity is developed." External restraint should yield to an internal self-control which "recognizes the inherent excellence of right action, puts a curb on passion, and gives fitness for the duties and responsibilities of independent life."[161]

It is both necessary and instructive to turn from the pronouncements of presidents and faculty on formal occasions to the actual rules and regulations governing conduct which were in force between 1868 and 1904 and which, obviously, students were expected to obey. The oath which all matriculants had to both "pronounce and sign" was revised in 1899 to read as follows:

> I, of my own free will, promise to observe and obey all the laws, rules and regulations of Pennsylvania College, and, while a member of this Institution, faithfully to fulfill my duties as a student and conduct myself as a gentleman. If notified by the Faculty that in their judgment I have failed in either respect, and should therefore cease to be a student in the Institution, I will submit to the

---

[160]Quoted in *College Monthly* (October 1884), pp. 214-224. An address by a faculty member inaugurating an academic year was the practice from 1849 through 1886. An editorial in the *Mercury* for February 1896 denied that a student's college years are his most formative ones and argued instead that "the habits which shape his college life have been formed long before." The greater responsibility rests upon parents and the home.

[161]Quoted in ibid. (October 1885), pp. 235-236.

discipline of the Institution or at once withdraw, if permitted by the
Faculty to do so.[162]

In 1904, all students were still required to live in a dormitory,
either Pennsylvania Hall or South College, unless they had permission to reside elsewhere or unless their parents lived in town. A student permitted to live elsewhere whose parents were not
townspeople nevertheless had to pay room rent to the College,
unless the dormitories were filled. The president, dean, and faculty
could visit a room at any time, but regular nightly visitation, once
abandoned, was not reintroduced. The faculty reserved the right to
approve places where students boarded and to withdraw their sanction at any time. It was next to impossible to secure permission to
board at a hotel where alcoholic beverages were served.[163]

In 1904 the College still prescribed hours for recreation (6:45 to
7:45 A.M., noon to 1 P.M., and 5 to 8 P.M. – 8:30 P.M. in the third
term), during which time students were free to leave campus, but
they were expected to be in their rooms or in classes at all other
times. At 10 P.M. the janitor locked the doors and turned loose the
watchdog. Under any and all circumstances, permission of the
faculty was required before leaving town.[164] The class attendance
regulations adopted in 1899 and incorporated into the rules and
regulations have already been discussed. They permitted absences
without special faculty permission for the first time in the history of
the College.[165]

In 1904 all students, except those living at home, were required to
attend daily chapel; all students, except those with written permission from their parents or guardians, were required to attend weekly
Sunday morning worship services at Christ Lutheran church; and all
students were required to attend a Biblical exercise every Sunday
morning. It was extremely difficult to secure an exemption from
these requirements.

In 1904 the rules and regulations contained a list of five categories
of what were called misdemeanors: (1) profaning the Sabbath, using
profane language, gambling, disorderly conduct, disrespect for pro-

[162]The editions of the rules and regulations used in this discussion are those of
1865, 1885, and 1899. By 1885 the rules and regulations no longer contained the statement that the College "shall be administered as nearly as possible after the manner of
a well regulated family."

[163]The *Olio*, published in 1874, listed seven boardinghouses accommodating
ninety-four students. The rest, we are told, ate with their mothers. The *Spectrum* for
1904 listed fourteen boardinghouses.

[164]In the 1885 version of the rules, students leaving the building without permission
except during recreation hours lost eligibility for honor standing for a term.

[165]It is clear from the 1896 faculty minutes that students were expected to wait five
minutes for a professor absent at the beginning of a class before leaving.

fessors, and forming "combinations" to resist faculty authority; (2) unnecessary noise in and near College buildings; (3) smoking, except in one's room; (4) using intoxicating liquor as a beverage or unnecessarily visiting a place were it was sold; and (5) playing ball inside College buildings or throwing anything which could damage College property.[166]

The rules and regulations had long contained the statement that

> an accurate account of the delinquencies, conduct, and attendance of every student, and of the degree of his attainment in scholarship, shall be kept in a book prepared for the purpose; in it shall be entered his merit and demerit, so as to present his standing. A copy of this account shall be transmitted to every parent or guardian.

In 1872 the faculty further systematized this phase of its work by assigning each student a conduct grade of one hundred at the beginning of a term and then deducting points assessed for "disorderly conduct and misdemeanors." Demerits, as they were called, ranged from one for a "single misdemeanor or case of disorderly behavior or violation of the rules" to ten for an unexcused absence from church. The faculty were empowered to levy appropriate penalties for all those offenses not specified in the rules.[167] Incorporating a number of changes made during the intervening thirty years, this system remained in effect in 1904. Students with twenty-five demerits were warned and parents were notified. Those with fifty were subject to suspension.

In all good faith, Luther H. Croll might tell the students of 1884 that the faculty had no higher wish than to make them happy. He might counsel them "against the wicked spirit which would free itself from all wholesome control." But he was speaking more realistically when he admitted that teachers are "commonly regarded as petty tyrants, as the abridgers of youthful pleasures, as unfeeling, little-minded, arbitrary pedants, who delight in imposing unreasonable burdens, and in inflicting undeserved punishment."[168]

---

[166]A glance at the 1865 regulations shows that a number of earlier prohibitions had now disappeared, including riding on a horse or in a vehicle on Sunday, attending a political celebration, and going to a ball or theatrical exhibition. Most versions of the regulations gave the faculty authority to deal with matters of conduct not otherwise provided for.

[167]The proposed faculty rule in June 1872 called for the automatic suspension of any student whose conduct grade fell below fifty. Possibly in part because of the hard times and the low enrollment, the trustees decided that such a course of action "would not be prudent," and it was abandoned.

[168]*College Monthly* (October 1884), pp. 223-224. The *Spectrum* (1901), p. 212, identified the officers of the Gettysburg Secret Service Department: Old Sleuth McKnight was chief, Hawkeye Phil Bikle was trailer, and Sure Shot Traub, the proctor, was informer. The rest of the faculty were dubbed assistants.

As each College term wore on, it became clear anew that boys will be boys. The crescendo of their youthful activity was often reached at term's end, especially in the spring. The last burst of energy had to be released before they parted and went their separate ways for the summer. The faculty after 1868 proved as determined as were their predecessors to respond to the boys by enforcing the rules, as best they could.

The number of discipline cases which the faculty considered between 1868 and 1904 ran into the hundreds. Among the violations arising from residence in the dormitories were these: rolling stones or bowling balls through the halls (1870 and later); blowing horns, especially at night (1872 and later); stealing coal (1875 and later); "misusing the lower story of the building" (1876); stealing the key to the belfry (1880); dropping a heavy block from a fourth story window (1888); throwing water on passersby (1890 and later); fighting (1891); destroying a water closet (we have now progressed beyond the privy) (1896); and not having the required slop pail (1897).[169]

A fairly continuous procession of students sought permission to leave town, and they offered a wide variety of reasons to support their request. It was easy to get approval to go home to vote, to attend the 1876 centennial exhibition, to attend a presidential inauguration, to participate in a Young Men's Christian Association meeting, or to join a Sunday school convention. It was much more difficult to go to a fair or circus with the proper blessing. Sometimes the faculty approved going hunting, but at other times they did not. For years the professors flatly refused their leave to anyone suspected of wanting to participate in an off-campus fraternity gathering. They found it difficult to countenance anyone's attending an intercollegiate athletic contest other than the team members themselves. Some students left town either without having sought the required permission or after their request had been denied. A few seemed to delight in getting approval to go to one place, then actually going to another, and finally, upon their return, lying about where they had been. The trustees demonstrated how important they thought the permission rule was by specifically instructing the faculty as late as January 1896 to enforce it "by such punishment as will prevent its violation."[170]

---

[169]One of the passersby was a telegraph boy (1890). The student who threw the water on him was fined and the boy got the money.

[170]By the 1890s a few students were securing blanket permission to go home every weekend, for reasons acceptable to the faculty. One cannot help having some sympathy for the four young men charged in November 1894 with going hunting without permission, shooting only a chicken, and then getting drunk.

Among offenses involving students' academic obligations which came to the attention of the faculty were these: including unapproved material in a public address (1873 and later); cheating, including plagiarism (1880 and later); setting off what were called explosives or torpedoes in the classroom (1880 and later); breaking into the president's office when everyone should have been in church (1880); not charging library books (1880 and later); plugging classroom keyholes (1882 and later); surreptitiously tampering with College records (1885); breaking into the library (1886); hissing in class (1890); and humming in class (1898)[171]

Although most students professed to be Lutheran, this did not mean that they welcomed the religious obligations imposed upon them or that they intended to fulfill them conscientiously or without complaint. Readers of the *College Monthly* learned that by the mid-1880s Harvard no longer placed any such obligations on its students and that in certain other institutions there was agitation for similar concessions. From time to time the publication chided Gettysburg students for their inattention and occasional disruptive actions in church. In January 1896 the *Mercury* complained about the conduct of some students in Brua Chapel. If they had no respect for the chaplain, it argued, at least they should for the message that he was giving. The writer had two suggestions to be considered: require the faculty to attend chapel or make student attendance voluntary.[172] Neither suggestion was adopted, and the old arrangements con-

---

[171]As already noted, during this entire period, from Wilken to Brede, there were more disturbances in the German classroom than in any others. However, the explosion of 1880 occurred in John A. Himes' classroom. Years ago, an uncle of this writer, a 1904 graduate, commented on the behavior of his fellow-students in a number of their classes. Few if any Gettysburg instructors in the 1980s would tolerate such conduct. Some students used ponies, which they also called bicycles. Most of a Graeff essay of 1882 was found to have been plagiarized. In May 1890 the *College Monthly* reported that "an enterprising New York City concern is sending circulars to college seniors all over the country offering to furnish, for a consideration, orations, essays or theses on any subject required and at short notice."

[172]In February 1882, for example, it complained of inattention, whispering, reading of books, and snapping of watch lids by those seated in the rear pews. Students attending Christ Lutheran church on Sunday sat in pews along the west side of the building. Under the honor system, they were expected to report their presence or absence to College authorities on Monday. The *Centennial Olio* (1876) accused some students of sticking their heads inside the church door at 11:30 Sunday morning, so that they could report the next day that they had been in attendance. In 1885 the faculty assigned each class certain rows of seats and proctors determined who was present. During this entire period a few students had permission to attend other churches in town. Most of them went to St. James Lutheran, where they taught a Sunday school class or were choir members. Until Brua was available for use, the roll was called in daily chapel. After 1890 each student was assigned his own seat and proctors took attendance, marking as absent all who came late.

tinued in effect. Especially after 1890, some students accrued so many demerits for absences from chapel and church that, according to the rules, their continuance in College was in jeopardy. In an effort to close loopholes, the faculty announced that neither the call of nature nor carrying breakfast to a sick friend would any longer be accepted as valid reasons for missing chapel. The faculty considered it a violation of the rules to hiss in chapel (1892), attempt to place a cow in the Brua vestibule (1892), steal one's nameplate from his chapel seat (1900), and throw hymnals (1904).

Especially high on the list of violations which the faculty took most seriously was the use of alcoholic beverages. They continued to advocate legal action against local hotels which sold such drinks to students who were minors, and they protested when there was the prospect of a new hotel on Washington street, near the College. They were much annoyed by the fact that many students who left town, both with and without permission, returned to the campus inebriated. After 1868, the use of alcoholic beverages brought considerably more students, both singly and in groups, before the faculty than was the case in the earlier period; however, this did not result in the professors' deciding finally to accept what apparently they could not change. In 1900, when dealing with six students found guilty of drinking, the faculty declared that their desire was not to punish anyone, but rather "to crush out the evil of using intoxicants."[173] There were also a number of cases of immoral conduct during this period. One which came to the attention of the faculty in 1901 was a precedent in that it involved a male and a female College student.

Another type of violation of the rules which the faculty took very seriously was one which involved, or appeared to involve, a group of students challenging the dignity of the institution or its authority to manage its affairs according to the best judgment of its faculty. In 1867, 1868, and 1869, for example, members of the sophomore class published what was known as a burlesque and distributed it during commencement week. Called the *Revelator* in 1867 and the *Banner of Honor* in 1869, these publications mercilessly ridiculed the faculty in general and most of its members in particular. "Every college in the country has its peculiar characters," insisted the

---

[173]By the 1890s it was becoming the custom for classes to have banquets. The faculty usually granted the necessary permission, but always with the stern admonition that no alcohol was to be served. How well the student heard this admonition and obeyed it is another matter. There is an undated statement in the College Archives signed by about fifty students who promised not to use intoxicating beverages and to report any student "certainly known to us as using them." The document dates from about 1902.

Salutatory

In presenting The Latest Out to the public, we are actuated by the desire to vindicate the cause of truth. That gross misrepresentations of this Institution and those connected with it have wide circulation, we are aware; and we desire to correct at least a few of those falsehoods. The world knows how conceit, love of money and lack of brains largely prevail here; hence it needs no further mention. Lately an effort has been made to place this would-be College on a footing with the first institutions of the country, but, oh, ye gods, how signal has been the failure attending those efforts. We caution the world against believing the contents of the Catalogue. It is an advertising concern and does not adhere closely to the truth. The facts herein mentioned fall under our daily notice and are the truth.

Fearing too much light might be thrown on some of the dark points, every possible effort on the part of Tyrants has been made to suppress this document. Threats and intimidations have been freely used, and even our secret conclave disturbed by certain members of the Faculty, and by him to whom all students must pay "due homage and bow in reverence." But "Truth crushed to earth will rise again," and, in spite of all opposition, the work lies before you, embracing some of the facts which come under our notice....

PROFESSOR HENRY JACOBS. Henry has cultivated his voice until he has attained the most sanctified tone and manner imaginable. Any Methodist minister in the land would give half his salary – which is generally meagre enough – for such a blessed tone. Professor, if you knew what a bore it is to hear you "drawl out" a well-written sermon, – as you do – with no more animation than a "scare-crow in a corn field," you would stop preaching until you had improved your delivery....

DR. MORRIS. One of the fancy touches which the Trustees of Pennsylvania College have added to their list of instructors, is a lecturer on Natural History. This position is held by one, Dr. Morris, who comes here once or twice a year, and with insufferable pomposity, tells a few musty jokes, which would be often more appropriate in a barroom than in a lecture-hall. He then proceeds to enlighten his hearers on the nature of "bugs," (a few decayed specimens of which he usually brings along with him). From his close affinity to, and connection with, bugs, we take great pleasure in conferring upon him the honorary degree of H.B. – (Humbug.)....

PROFESSOR HENRY BAUGHER. Henry is sorely afflicted with the same malady that has taken possession of a majority of his pupils, namely, self-conceit. He has a severe attack....Notwithstanding all, Henry is not as big a fool as you would judge by his appearance.

These excerpts from The Latest Out, dated June 27, 1872, furnish an example of one of the milder student burlesques. Spelling and punctuation in the original have been preserved.

Revelator, "but we readily assert that ours will bear off the palm in every comparison . . . . in all respects our faculty is like his satanic majesty among the fallen angels, the worst, and yet the greatest." In language which might lead the reader to ask what purpose libel laws were intended to serve and when they should be invoked, the Banner of Honor called Milton Valentine "half devil and half man," Martin L. Stoever a "dreadful ogre," William Notz an "arrant swindler, petty thief," Victor L. Conrad one in whom "are blended in perfect harmony and unison all the characteristics of the ass," and Charles J. Ehrehart "the Pine-town Hog."[174]

---

[174]No copies of the 1868 burlesque survive in the College archives, nor do any of one published in 1877. The Bloody Lutheran (1892) and the Gettysburg Kindergarten (1897) were also burlesques. Charles J. Ehrehart gave the harmful effects of the early burlesques on the College constituency as one reason for his resignation in 1870.

The faculty continued to have a wide range of penalties to impose upon students found guilty of violating College rules and regulations. Including unauthorized material in a public address, breaking into the library, or rolling stones through the hallways could bring twenty demerits. Fighting or loud hornblowing could bring twenty-five. The mysterious misuse of the lower story of Pennsylvania Hall in 1876 yielded fifty. Unspecified misconduct on the part of two students cost them seventy-five demerits and the added penalty of being in the building at 7 P.M. every evening for the remainder of the term. Among the offenses which could result in suspension, for varying lengths of time, were "combined and aggravated offenses committed against the law and order of the College" in 1870, "persistent contumacy" in 1878, setting off explosives, cheating, immoral conduct, and use of alcoholic beverages. In 1869 the faculty quickly identified four students responsible for publishing the *Banner of Honor*. The professors suspended them and announced their intention to recommend expulsion to the board of trustees, but before that could happen the guilty parties persuaded the faculty that they were truly penitent and should be received back into the fold. Between 1868 and 1904 the trustees did expel at least six students: two for larceny (1879), one for persistent neglect of academic and financial obligations (1896), one for unauthorized night painting of Philip M. Bikle's house (1899), and two for stealing books from the College library (1901).[175]

In June 1886, after a year or more of discussion and following the example set by Amherst College, the faculty proposed to the student body the adoption of what was then called cooperative college government. If constituted at Gettysburg, it would have been administered by a board of three seniors, two juniors, one sophomore, and one freshman, elected by their respective classes. With the president of the College as its presiding officer, the board would have met at least once a month. Either the president or a student could refer cases of "college order and discipline" to the board, whose decisions, if approved by the faculty, would be final. Although the alumni editor of the *College Monthly,* in June 1886, urged his readers that since "we cannot be the first" to adopt the sys-

---

[175]In 1871 the board of trustees adopted a sense motion that the faculty's recognized power to suspend students should not extend beyond the end of the academic year or the next business meeting of the board. At the same time, they delegated to the faculty their own power to expel students from the institution in cases of offenses "sufficiently grave to merit [immediate] final dismissal or expulsion," requiring a full report from the president in the event the faculty concluded that it was necessary to take such action. In practice, the faculty limited their penalties to suspension, and recommended expulsion to the board where they believed it was warranted.

tem, "let's not be the last," the junior class turned it down several months later. Opponents charged that it would turn seven students into proctors and, in the end, be no improvement over the existing system, as far as students were concerned. Two years later, in November 1888, a writer in the *College Monthly* noted that cooperative government did not seem to be working at either Amherst or Princeton. "Perhaps it is just as well," he concluded, "that the effort to introduce it here was a failure."

Seven years later, in a lead editorial in December 1895, the *Mercury* brought up the matter again and urged the students to use its columns to discuss the question of self-government. "We are not willing to believe that compulsion is necessary in order to have students observe" the requirements, the editor wrote. "Those who are naturally well-disposed grow restless at being compelled to do what they would most gladly do of their own free will," he thought, "while those who have no inherent regard for right or propriety will generally do as they please despite the rules and prohibitions." In terms reminiscent of the arguments of Luther H. Croll more than a decade earlier, the editor claimed that the existing system pitted faculty and students against each other, to the detriment of learning. Although he believed that unfriendliness was declining in the College, he was convinced that "if the students were given a part in their own government, it would disappear entirely." Moreover, he believed, student participation would improve College discipline. No person was then "willing to incur the unpopularity attached to one who gives evidence against his fellow student." Under the proposed arrangement, students "would take a greater interest in preserving the reputation of the college, and cases which would come before them would be almost sure to be decided justly and impartially." The small response to this challenge demonstrated that the students of Gettysburg College were not then willing to exchange a system whose workings they had mastered to their own satisfaction for one with so many unknowns.

In 1884 Vice President Croll was prepared to accept that "the college man is a mirth-loving creature, of an age enjoying the privileges, without being burdened by the responsibilities of manhood, absent from home, associated with many scores like himself, and eager to find avenues for the release of a surplus vital energy."[176] He and his faculty colleagues were prepared to accept, albeit reluctantly at times, students growing moustaches; wearing their distinctive hats, whatever happened to be in fashion at the time; guying passersby; scribbling graffiti; riding bicycles (as early

---

[176]*College Monthly* (October 1884), p. 218.

as 1882 the fever had reached Gettysburg); wearing college pins; putting Limburger cheese on chapel and classroom radiators; and showing up in the dormitory with grapes that were obviously neither purchased nor sent from home. They were prepared to listen as students sang "Grandfather's Clock" in the late 1870s and "Just Tell Them That You Saw Me"in the 1890s. Usually, but not always, they gave permission for students to celebrate their release from a long, hard term by publicly and ceremonially cremating one of their textbooks (perhaps Livy, Olney's algebra, or Wentworth's geometry). They accepted that every year the students would fill the old chapel with hay. They made no attempt to halt the lively class rivalry, unless it took the form of hazing. They expressed themselves clearly enough on that subject when in 1883 they voiced "unqualified disapproval of any attempt on the part of students to subject to personal discomfort any fellow-student."[177]

In welcoming the freshman class in October 1893, a writer in the *Mercury* advised its members that "you may be offended at times by

The editors of the 1904 *Spectrum* described the above as "a typical college room."

---

[177]The *College Monthly* included many notices of hazing on other campuses, always condemned the practice, and believed it was declining. See the issues for December 1881, November 1887, and June 1891.

the strictness of your instructors, by the rigidness of your discipline, and think the Mater has received the wrong appellation." Counseling patience and understanding, he predicted that "what seems strictness now" will in future years "appear the truest kindness, while words of rebuke will be treasured up as incentives to better endeavors." In some cases, his prediction was an accurate one. At least some alumni who in later years wrote about their College experiences recalled the discipline of the institution as something of a game in which the players on both sides, faculty and students alike, acted out the roles which under the circumstances they were expected to perform. In retrospect, they would not have wanted it otherwise.[178]

Student Organizations

Almost all student organizations before 1868 were ones which the faculty had actively promoted in the belief that they would contribute in a positive way to the program of instruction and discipline. Even though the literary societies gained considerable independence from faculty control, they were still an integral part of the establishment. Each successive edition of the rules and regulations specified the time of their weekly meetings and prescribed alternate exercises for those who were not members. One explanation offered for the increasing popularity of social fraternities on many campuses is that these were organizations which students could form and govern by themselves. If secrecy was the price for independence from faculty control, they were prepared to pay it.

Between 1868 and 1904 the number of student organizations on the Gettysburg campus increased. As the old ideal of the well-regulated family disappeared from the published statements and faded in actual practice, these organizations took on more of a life of their own. And yet, the old ways were far from gone. The 1899 edition of the rules and regulations still prescribed the weekly meeting date for the literary societies and special exercises for nonmembers. In fact, the rules in that year placed fences around all student organizations: the faculty could determine their time and place of meeting; they could attend all meetings; they reserved the right to pass upon all speakers the students invited to address them; they could restrict, even dissolve, any organization which interfered

---

[178]See, for example, the recollections of George E. M. Herbst in the *Spectrum* (1902), p. 183. For a fuller treatment of student life in this period, see Anna Jane Moyer, *The Way We Were: A History of Student Life at Gettysburg College, 1832-1982* (Gettysburg, 1982).

"with the good order of the College, by shielding its members from discipline or furnishing facilities for the violation of law"; and they would take the assets of any dissolved organization.

The Phrenakosmian and Philomathaean literary societies continued to flourish after 1868, claiming the membership of almost every student. The 1899 *Spectrum* stated that of 1,068 graduates, 562 had belonged to Philo, 479 to Phrena, and only 27 to neither. Every graduating member of the class of 1904 was affiliated with one or the other of these societies. Philo voted to admit women in 1892; it elected its first female members in the following year. When they gave up their elegant, if small, quarters in Pennsylvania Hall, the societies moved in 1890 into truly ornate rooms on the third floor of the New Recitation Building. The lot had determined that Philo should have the north room and Phrena the south. While society libraries grew less rapidly than did the College collection, together they had more than 12,000 volumes in 1904.[179]

The 1904 catalogue described Philo and Phrena in terms which must have been familiar to the oldest living alumni. They "exert a favorable influence in the intellectual and social culture of their members," readers were told. "The exercises consist of music, essays, orations, and debates. The practical acquaintance with parliamentary law here formed makes these societies the best schools for free citizenship." If these claims conveyed the impression that nothing had happened to the standing of the societies since the early years of the College, they were false, indeed. Time and time again the *College Monthly, Mercury,* and *Gettysburgian* felt it necessary to run articles written by faculty, alumni, and others, explaining why interest in both societies seemed to be flagging.[180] "Must we believe that our literary societies, that have such a creditable history and have been so beneficial," asked the *College Monthly* in March 1885, "are in their death struggle?" Some attributed what appeared to be happening to the general drift of the times, to an increasing fascination with athletics, or to the competition offered by social fraternities. Two signs of the times, whose meanings might nevertheless be susceptible of different interpretations, were the abandonment in the 1880s of the February anniversary exercises which the societies had conducted since the 1830s and also of their sponsorship of an event during commencement week. College publications consistently supported Philo and Phrena, urging new

---

[179]The libraries were moved to the New Recitation Building in 1889, but their separate reading rooms remained in Pennsylvania Hall. In 1899 these rooms were combined and placed under College control.

[180]These and other articles made it evident that declining interest in literary societies troubled people on other campuses as well.

Philo Hall

Phrena Hall

students to be prompt in joining one or the other. All graduates "need the parliamentary training, the celerity and clearness of thought, the grace of speech and the aptness at debate, which you can only acquire within the walls of the properly conducted literary society," advised George D. Stahley in the *College Monthly* for November 1885. "The class-room will not furnish you these accomplishments; the place is too constrained, – the freedom, the inspiration, the mutual incentives of social contact in the society hall, are wanting."

In November 1876, after a decade of growth in the sciences at Gettysburg, the faculty decided it was "expedient" for them to reorganize the Linnaean Society, which had lapsed in 1862. They called a meeting of the students for December 9, at which time the revival was accomplished. Edward S. Breidenbaugh was elected president and a Monday afternoon hour was set aside in the class schedule for its biweekly meetings. Dutifully and at length the *College Monthly* reported on each of these sessions. It is obvious that Breidenbaugh and others were trying to make them both attractive and substantive, but it is equally clear that student interest was minimal. Because of lack of attendance, the faculty soon took away the hour reserved in the daily schedule. Later, in the hope of rekindling interest, it was restored, but in November 1881 the *College Monthly* pronounced the Linnaean Association dead.[181]

In 1867 a new student organization, one which was to exercise a major influence on campus life for many years, made its first appearance on the College scene. On March 16 of that year, the Young Men's Christian Association of Pennsylvania College was founded. According to Henry Eyster Jacobs, who was then a tutor in the preparatory department, President Baugher named him chairman of a student committee to draw up a constitution for an organization through which students could learn about and support missions. Jacobs selected the name for the new society, which happened to be that of an organization founded in England in 1844 and introduced into the United States in 1851.[182] The Gettysburg Y.M.C.A. quickly took root. By 1868 it had forty members and had already gained a place in the commencement week exercises by sponsoring the first in a long series of Sunday evening addresses.

---

[181] In November 1888 Edward S. Breidenbaugh and Franklin Menges organized the Priestly Society and became president and vice president respectively. Designed to "foster a deeper interest in and love for the study of the Physical Sciences," it promptly expired.

[182] Jacobs, *Memoirs*, p. 90. Jacobs may have recalled the Young Men's Christian Association which was formed in Gettysburg in November 1857 and which disbanded in March 1860 because of lack of interest. Minute Book, Adams County Historical Society.

Before long most of the students became members at some point during their undergraduate careers. There were eighty-nine so affiliated in 1904.

While questions were being asked about the vitality of the literary societies and while the Linnaeans were approaching their second and final demise, the College Y.M.C.A. thrived. Meeting at first monthly, it soon moved to weekly sessions. To a large degree, this organization contained and channeled the impulses which in an earlier day had produced that long series of intense campus revivals. Its program included prayer meetings, Bible study, lectures, and musical entertainment.[183] Members conducted services at the poorhouse, as it was called in those days, and gave financial support to several foreign missionaries, one of whom was John Aberly (1888). Toward the end of the 1880s they offered to administer the gymnasium on behalf of the College, but the appointment of George D. Stahley to the chair of physical culture and hygiene resulted in other arrangements being made for the use of that facility. In 1895 they issued the first in a continuing series of annual College handbooks intended for the orientation of new students. An enthusiastic writer in the College Monthly for October 1893 stated that "the Y.M.C.A. of Gettysburg College is, in all probability, the most active and useful organization which adorns the institution."

The Gettysburg Y.M.C.A. was one of the earliest to be established on an American college campus. It may have been the first in a Pennsylvania college. The years from 1868 to 1904 were ones of tremendous growth for the Y.M.C.A. among American students. By 1900 there were almost five hundred associations on college and university campuses. The State Young Men's Christian Association of Pennsylvania was organized in 1869; a few years later the College group established an affiliation with it. In 1877 the national convention of the Y.M.C.A. voted to name a secretary to coordinate and promote student work in colleges and universities. In the years that followed, the Gettysburg association placed itself within the purview of his efforts. Its members attended many of the famous summer Bible study conferences held at Northfield, Massachusetts, beginning in 1886, under the leadership of Dwight L. Moody. They also participated in the even more famous Student Volunteer Movement for Foreign Missions, an ambitious undertaking begun in 1888 whose goal was "the evangelization of the world in this generation." Robert Weidensall (1836-1922), of the class of 1860, provided a close link between the Gettysburg and national Y.M.C.A.'s. His appoint-

---

[183]The Y.M.C.A. sponsored some of the first recitals by off-campus artists. See the Gettysburgian, March 2, 1904.

ment in 1868 as the first national field secretary marked the beginning of a half-century career with the national organization.[184]

In 1889, about the time many other Y.M.C.A.'s were beginning to build structures of their own to accommodate their many activities, the Gettysburg association acquired use of the former College chapel in Pennsylvania Hall. That these quarters were not long considered either adequate or appropriate is evident from the following statement in the *College Monthly* for June 1891:

> Last year the two literary societies were handsomely furnished, this year two [fraternity] chapter houses have been erected, and no doubt in the coming year two more will follow. The Y.M.C.A. seems to have been left to the last, and yet it is by far the most important institution at College . . . . It is an acknowledged fact that the greater part and most effectual spiritual work among the students must be done by the Christian young men in college. The Faculty and Alumni must support the work, but the non-Christian students can, for the most part, only be reached by their fellow-students. Now, the Y.M.C.A. must have a building to keep in touch with the other advancing societies that make up College.

A building fund was inaugurated and in April 1893 the *College Monthly* expressed the hope that some wealthy friend would make a large enough contribution to the fund to create the momentum necessary for its ultimate success. Although the friend declined to step forward, the board of trustees in June 1902 authorized the Y.M.C.A. to begin a fund raising campaign and promised a site on the campus when it was prepared to build. The 1904 and 1905 *Spectrums* published the proposed floor plans for the two-story building. Although about $4,000 had been pledged by 1904, it was not until after World War I that a Y.M.C.A. building became a reality.

In 1868 there were five social fraternities to which Gettysburg students could belong: Phi Kappa Psi (1855), Phi Gamma Delta (1858), Zeta Psi (1861), Sigma Chi (1863), and Chi Phi (1867). According to the *Ragout,* a student publication which appeared in March of that year, these five "secret societies" enrolled a total of thirty-seven members, a few more than one-third of the student body. Because they were secret organizations which did not seek faculty sanction or support, and because they were suspected of being subversive of good order in the College, the professors opposed them. As already noted, when the trustees declined to accept their recommendation that the matriculation oath be amended to include a promise that a

---

[184]C. Howard Hopkins, *History of the Y.M.C.A. in North America* (New York, 1951), pp. 271-308 and 120-122. Three other College graduates spent all or parts of their careers in Y.M.C.A. work: James McConaughy (1857-1934), David McConaughy (1860-1946), and Samuel G. McConaughy (1863-   ). John E. Graeff was an active Y.M.C.A. supporter and, together with John Wanamaker, attended the international Y.M.C.A. jubilee in London in 1894.

student would not join a secret society while enrolled in the College, the faculty revised the rules and regulations in 1865 to include as grounds for dismissal joining or countenancing any combination "which has a tendency to create opposition to the discipline of the Institution."

In the years after 1868, faculty opposition to the fraternities softened. The fact that Professors Baugher, Bikle, Breidenbaugh, Jacobs, McKnight, Sadtler, and Stahley were all fraternity men helps explain why this occurred. Whatever may have been the danger which fraternities presented to the order and authority of the institution in the 1850s and 1860s, College officials, perhaps drawing upon their own undergraduate experience, came to believe that they now saw little or none. They were prepared to grant that students had the right to form such organizations, even secret ones, and to maintain them so long as they did not violate the existing rules and regulations.[185]

In 1877, the first year of its publication, the editor of the *College Monthly* opened its columns for several months between July and December to an extended discussion of fraternities. This gave both friends and foes the opportunity to deal with the major issues being argued at the time: their secrecy, alleged insubordination, reported domination of campus politics, and claimed social and other benefits for both undergraduates and alumni. Clearly, the fraternity case was the one more strongly presented. Ten years later, in October 1887, the same journal ran excerpts from a recent *Forum* article by former President Andrew D. White of Cornell University. Using arguments which probably reflected the sentiments of most of the Gettysburg faculty, White answered many of the charges directed against the fraternities. For example, he thought "their secrecy is rather nominal than real" and that few concerned college officials lacked "a fair knowledge" of their "interior organization." White refused to lay more than a modest share of the blame for the decline of literary societies on the social fraternities. Even that could be removed if "half the lung power expended by college officers in declaiming against the fraternities" were directed to supporting the literary societies. Fraternity involvement in college politics, he argued, is "simply one form of an evil which, in some form, is, as things go at present, inevitable." Wipe out the fraternities and some

---

[185]In June 1885 the faculty lectured the members of Phi Kappa Psi and Phi Gamma Delta, following an incident in which the grades of certain seniors were lowered by other students who gained access to the records. It is not clear who the guilty parties were, but the faculty reminded the two fraternities that, "in all institutions of civilized government,. . . administration of justice rests upon the power to obtain in every case the best and fullest testimony." It called upon all students to cooperate in the investigation.

other "cliques, clubs, parties, and intrigues" will take their place; "it seems a result of our American atmosphere." It was White's contention that fraternities "reduce certain inevitable evils in college life to a minimum, that they produce good in many ways, and that, when college authorities deal with them in a large-minded spirit, they can be made to do still more good."

If most of the Gettysburg faculty were in substantial agreement with White, they were nevertheless reluctant to accord the fraternities that same degree of recognition and acceptance which Philo, Phrena, and the Y.M.C.A. enjoyed. For example, they long refused permission to students who wanted to attend regional or national fraternity conventions. Only in 1889 did they amend their explicit rule on this subject, passed eleven years earlier, to permit a fraternity to send one or two students each year. Even in 1904 the faculty

The editors of the 1899 Spectrum used this theme to introduce the section on fraternities.

were still not listing fraternities in the catalogue, something which an alumnus had suggested be done as early as 1882. That publication contained only a passing reference in the section on buildings to the chapter houses which the "Greek Letter Societies" had erected on campus.[186]

There were six fraternities at Gettysburg College in 1904. Three had been organized before 1868: Phi Kappa Psi, Phi Gamma Delta, and Sigma Chi. Phi Delta Theta dated from 1875. Alpha Tau Omega was chartered in 1882. Sigma Alpha Epsilon was organized in 1883, lapsed in 1885, was reorganized in 1893, lapsed again, and was reorganized again in 1899.[187] Active membership in these six fraternities ranged from eight in the case of Phi Kappa Psi to sixteen for Phi Gamma Delta. Total membership was 67 in a student body of 179. The 1899 *Spectrum* estimated that 417 of the 1,068 men graduated up to that time had been fraternity members.

In the early days, fraternities held their meetings in different student rooms at the College or seminary; the exact location at any one time was one of their secrets. Later, they rented quarters somewhere in town, sometimes a room on the floor above a business place. In June 1881 the board of trustees granted permission to Phi Kappa Psi to erect a lodge, or chapter house, on a campus site to be approved by the executive committee and under such control as would prevent violations of the rules and regulations of the College. The cornerstone for this lodge was laid during the semicentennial exercises in June 1882. William E. Parson, valedictorian of the class of 1867 and then a Lutheran pastor in Washington, gave the principal address, praising the board of trustees for their broadmindedness in permitting the construction to take place. "Certainly we are not seeking to build anything within the bounds of the college domain," he told his listeners, "that would be subversive of good order, or detrimental to the best interests of our *Alma Mater*." Fraternities belong to the days of a person's youth, he said. Since St. Paul did not think or act like a man until he became one, Parson was certain that

---

[186]The pages of the *Spectrum,* the student yearbook, first published in 1891, always gave generous coverage to the fraternities in both pictures and text.

[187]Zeta Psi and Chi Phi had disappeared by the early 1870s, as had a shortlived chapter of Upsilon Beta. In November 1897 the faculty learned of an attempt by about twenty students to organize a chapter of Theta Nu Epsilon, a fraternity with a national reputation for disreputable conduct. The faculty warned that any students joining such an organization would be expelled. In January 1898 the trustees granted the faculty request for authority to deal with any similar situation by authorizing the president to spend whatever was "needed to crush out the said society." Baird's *Manual of American College Fraternities,* 19th ed., edited by John Robson (Menasha, Wis., 1977), pp. 801-802. See *1932 History,* pp. 365-386, for more information about the six fraternities of 1904. A sorority, Iota Lambda Delta, was formed in November 1903.

Miller Hall
Phi Kappa Psi chapter house dedicated on the campus in 1884.

if "he had been a college boy in these days, he would have been a member of one of our Greek Letter Societies." Believing that this address was "the first public defense of college fraternities in our midst," the editor of the *College Monthly* published it in full in the July 1882 issue. Miller Hall, named after its major donor, Daniel R. Miller (1856), was dedicated on June 24, 1884.

Three other fraternity chapter houses were built on the campus before the end of the century. On June 16, 1891 Phi Gamma Delta dedicated Delta Hall on the site of its present house. On the same day Sigma Chi dedicated William L. Glatfelter Hall. Phi Delta Theta dedicated its house, which was located south of the Phi Gamma Delta hall, on June 14, 1899. Each of these four chapter houses consisted of two or three rooms, which were used for meetings and other related purposes. None contained rooming or boarding facilities. On June 3, 1903 Alpha Tau Omega laid the cornerstone for its chapter house on North Washington street, off campus.

In addition to the ones already mentioned, there were many other student organizations which existed in the College at one time or another between 1868 and 1904. Some of them, for example, the College and seminary Bible society, had a fairly continuous existence. The lives of others, such as the Priestly Society (1888), must be measured in terms of months. Several organizations, including the Temperance Constitutional Amendment Club (1888) and the Prohibition Club (1893), were campus manifestations of ongoing national crusades. A few, such as the Pennypacker and Pattison Clubs (1902), reflected student interest in state and national politics. Others, including the Epicurean Club (1860s) and the Lazy Club (1870s), catered to impulses which may well have existed during the first period of the College's life, but which would then scarcely have found expression in an organization. The third attempt to maintain a German literary society, made under faculty auspices in 1867, proved

William L. Glatfelter Hall
Sigma Chi chapter house dedicated on the campus in 1891.

no more successful than the first two had been. However, in the early 1870s students of German and Swiss origin formed an organization of their own, one whose purpose appears to have been to encourage the spoken Pennsylvania German or Dutch dialect, and to promote a good time. Known as the Rauch-Gesellschaft, Deutsche Gesellschaft, or Deitch Gesellschaft, this club had an intermittent existence which carried it beyond 1904, in which year it had thirteen members.

The musical organizations of the years between 1868 and 1904 illustrate one of the signal characteristics of student activity outside the classroom at this time. There was a glee club in 1868 and one in

1904, but the pages of College publications show clearly that the continuity from one year to the next in this organization was minimal. It was almost literally necessary to reorganize the club every fall. Some years there was no one to take this step and to conduct the rehearsals necessary for creditable performances. Occasionally there was enough student interest to sustain more than one glee club. In 1893 the College was able to secure the services of an experienced director for the group. From time to time there was a band, an orchestra, and a chapel choir. There were banjo, mandolin, and guitar clubs, sometimes working together and sometimes separately. These organizations gave concerts on the campus and in town. As early as 1891 their members were granted a stated number of excused class absences, which enabled them to go on tour to nearby towns and cities. Before long their performances were looked upon as good public relations for the College. Occasionally, some of these organizations performed jointly with musicians from other colleges.

In the 1890s Philo and Phrena each organized clubs which sponsored intersociety debates. Later, there were also interclass debates. Similar opportunities to engage in debating and oratory were available by participating in the activities of the Pennsylvania Intercollegiate Oratorical Union, which was organized in the 1890s by six or seven central and eastern Pennsylvania colleges, including

College Musical Clubs
The glee club and the mandolin and guitar club posed together for this picture during the 1902-1903 season.

Gettysburg. The first reference to a dramatic association dates from 1895, when the Philo Dramatic Club was formed. Renamed the Roister Doister Club in 1898, it welcomed members of both literary societies.[188] Its successor, the Mask and Wig Society, presented its first play in June 1904.[189]

From the beginning of its existence, the College had recognized superior academic achievement by its system of commencement honors. Over the years a number of donors established prizes which made it possible to regard classroom achievement in additional ways. On September 4, 1897 a group of students under the leadership of William J. Gies (1893) organized a society whose purpose was to honor broader-based attainments. Five of the thirteen charter members of the Pen and Sword Society were graduates. Writing in the 1899 *Spectrum*, Oscar G. Klinger described the new organization as

> a body which is unique in our Lutheran college world and is designed to exert a masterful influence in the future. It exists for the sole purpose of promoting the interests of the college in any and every possible way. It is an attempt to bridge the chasm which has too long separated the undergraduate body from the Faculty on the one hand and the alumni on the other. To its membership any man is eligible whose loyalty to the institution is expressed in some practical work for her.

The student body elected members to the Pen and Sword Society, subject to confirmation by its undergraduate members. By 1904 about one hundred persons had been so honored.

College Publications

Since 1877 the College has had a regular monthly or weekly publication to keep its several constituencies informed of campus happenings and of the issues before the institution for debate and resolution. The first of these publications was the *Pennsylvania College Monthly*. Aware that other colleges were already issuing journals, in October 1876 the faculty appointed a committee to draw up a plan for such a publication at Gettysburg. A month later they adopted the committee report and committed themselves, if at least 250 subscribers could be secured, to a publication "in which articles of value on general subjects may be published and preserved,

---

[188]In February 1898 the faculty passed a sense motion declaring that "it is proper to give dramatic entertainment in Brua Chapel."

[189]The organization for dramatics is a good example of a student activity with little continuity. The Roister Doister Club disappeared in 1900; later in the year a Minstrel and Dramatic Troupe was formed; in 1903 the literary societies were staging plays; and in January 1904 the Gettysburg Dramatic Club appears.

college interests discussed, matters of college history chronicled." The faculty would retain general management of the journal and elect the editor. Each of the literary societies and the Alumni Association were entitled to choose an associate editor. The required number of subscriptions having been secured, the faculty in January named Philip M. Bikle editor and the first number of the *College Monthly* appeared in February 1877.[190] Within a few months circulation reached 450 copies, equal to the number of the *Cornell Review* and half that of the *Yale Courant.*

The format which the new publication soon took and which it retained was as follows: news about what was happening or should be happening in the College (literary societies, Y.M.C.A., fraternities, and athletics); articles, essays, and poems of general interest; information about individual alumni; reviews of books dealing with higher education; news about colleges and universities elsewhere in the country, gleaned largely from the exchange copies which other institutions sent; notes about events occurring in the town of Gettysburg, taken mostly from local newspapers; and brief notices of campus happenings, many of them humorous and lighthearted, some of them apochryphal.

In the first issue, the editor wrote that "the Professors, Students and Alumni will have in the *Monthly* something of common interest, and this may prove a bond of more intimate union among them." To what extent the bond was ever formed is debatable, but certainly there was much information in every issue which was of interest to all three constituencies. From the alumni columns the faculty learned what their former students were doing. Because of the manner in which they were presented, the notices of campus happenings, in which present students might be most interested, gave them more chuckles than solid campus news. Of the three groups, the alumni stood to gain the most from a careful reading of the *College Monthly.* Along with the generous number of pages devoted to alumni personals, the editors presented what they believed were the strengths of the College; its needs if it were to retain its position in a changing educational world; and much information about what was happening in other colleges and universities, especially about the gifts which generous donors were bestowing upon them. The Alumni Association chose a succession of interested and able associate editors who regularly contributed articles which may have had more influence among alumni than anything a faculty or board member might have written. "Next to the letters, I always open the

---

[190]The title of the journal was *Pennsylvania College Monthly* until 1893, when it became the *Gettysburg College Monthly.* In this text, with a few exceptions, it is called the *College Monthly.*

College Monthly first," wrote John Aberly (1888) from India in 1892. "It comes to me as a letter from *Alma Mater* and is so appreciated."

Although the *College Monthly* had two student associate editors, the guiding force in directing it was always Philip M. Bikle. In the winter of 1892-1893 six or seven students asked him to yield control of the journal to the literary societies. They explained that students were now responsible for similar publications in an increasing number of other colleges (and they were accurate in saying this). Giving them control of the *College Monthly,* they maintained, would be advantageous for everyone concerned. When Bikle refused this request, the students asked the faculty for permission to publish their own monthly journal. The professors responded by giving the *College Monthly* a vote of confidence. It "was established by the Faculty in the interests of the College," they said, "and has successfully represented these interests for sixteen years." They could not now encourage another journal, but neither could they object to one. With this statement as their license, the students published the first issue of the *College Mercury* in March 1893.[191] "It will be the object of this magazine to give the news of the college and alumni," they announced, "and to discuss the questions relating to the welfare of the institution." They were now joining more than two hundred similar publications, they said, which were entirely in student hands. As far as form and arrangement were concerned, their stated model was the *Swarthmore Phoenix,* but the content of the first issue was very similar to that of the *College Monthly.*

In the March issue of his journal, Bikle did not resist the temptation to belittle the new publication. "Whether the new paper lives or not," he declared, "the *College Monthly* will continue, and, as heretofore, will strive to promote the highest welfare of the College . . . . It had its struggles in its earlier years, and may have again, but all in all it has been well sustained, and we believe can rely on the friends of the College as faithful and loyal patrons." Nevertheless, by the end of the year Editor Bikle, always the professor and now also dean, changed his mind. The last issue of the *College Monthly* was published in December 1893.

The announced purpose of the founders of the *Mercury* to turn it over to the control of the literary societies was quickly realized. Each of the latter severed its connection with the *College Monthly*

---

[191] Their response to the students contained the following standard provision: "If the publication is made, the board of editors shall be held personally responsible to the Faculty for all matters published." The April issue of the new *Mercury* reprinted a letter signed by all members of the faculty except Bikle, denying the charge that its supporters were guilty of insubordination and that the faculty disapproved of their effort.

and assumed its share of responsibility for the new magazine. In June 1893, without breaking its ties with the older publication, the Alumni Association named an associate editor for the *Mercury*. Although the latter continued to include the same variety of College news as had its predecessor, it soon became obvious that the student voice, usually a responsible and mature one, was in firm control. The *Mercury* called the attention of College authorities to the need for improved facilities. It goaded the students into making better use of the library and improving their understanding of what a superior college education entailed. At the same time, it was a faithful booster of Gettysburg College: of school spirit, intramural and intercollegiate athletics, dramatics, musical organizations, debating, the literary societies, and the campus beautiful. In January 1897 it revealed its close kinship with the former *College Monthly* by declaring that "this publication is maintained chiefly in the interest of the Alumni."

On March 9, 1897 the *Mercury* was confronted by a repeat of the coup which had resulted in its own birth four years before. On that day the first issue of the *Gettysburgian* appeared. Ours "is a newspaper," its founders proclaimed, and "hence it is to be issued weekly, for items that are not timely fail to be news." Their stated

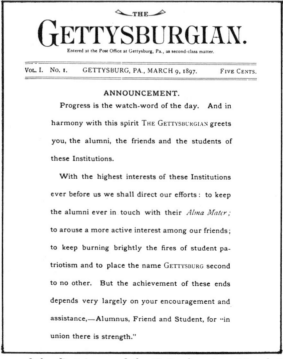

First page of the first issue of the Gettysburgian, March 9, 1897.

purpose closely resembled that of the *Mercury:* "to keep the Alumni ever in touch with their *Alma Mater,* to keep burning brightly the fires of student patriotism, and to place the name Gettysburg second to no other." Their coverage of news equally closely resembled that of the older publication. The editors of the *Mercury* were much less graceful in greeting competition than Philip M. Bikle had been in 1893. It was "a self appointed triumvirate" which had initiated the new venture, one which they considered "an antagonistic upstart." The *Gettysburgian* was "a distinctly private enterprise" whose avowed purpose was the "personal aggrandizement and gain of the aforesaid triumvirate." The editors questioned how an institution of two hundred students could maintain two journals and called upon all subscribers and advertisers to support the *Mercury* as long "as it continues to be the representative and official organ of the institution."

As it turned out, the *Gettysburgian* did survive. By 1899, the *Mercury* became a literary magazine, while its competitor carried on the tradition begun by the *College Monthly.* The *Mercury* is "published monthly in term time under the control of the Literary Societies," the 1904 catalogue stated, and "is a literary journal sustained by the contributions of students and alumni." At the same time, the *Gettysburgian,* "under private control of students, is published weekly and makes a specialty of college and town news."[192]

On four occasions between 1868 and 1882, one of the classes published a booklet with information about the College, its students, and their organizations and activities. The *Ragout* appeared in 1868, *Our Olio* in 1874, *Our Centennial Olio* in 1876, and *Arcana* in 1882. According to its editors, *Our Centennial Olio* was issued in the hope that it would "prove a pleasant reminder of the duties and sports of the 'merry days of College' to those who are now battling with sterner realities," while for present undergraduates it was intended to be "a welcome visitor" which might be cherished in later years. An effort to bring out another *Arcana* in 1885 ended in failure. Then, in February 1891, the *College Monthly* announced that the junior class had decided to issue what it hoped would become an annual publication, to be called the *Spectrum.* The first number appeared in May. This class had set a precedent. The *Spectrum* continued to come out each spring, with one exception. In the depression year of 1895, the number of advance orders and the amount of advertising were so disappointingly low that the junior class decided not to publish. The first *Spectrum* bears the year 1892,

---

[192]A faculty committee on College publications told the trustees in 1899 that the *Mercury* had 268 subscriptions in that year and the *Gettysburgian* had 500.

but it appeared in the spring of 1891 and featured the senior class of that year. This method of dating the volume continued to be used until 1952. The early years of the *Spectrum* were marred by intraclass squabbles and financial troubles. Largely because of the latter, the board of trustees in June 1898 named a faculty committee to exercise general supervision over all College publications. Each succeeding issue of the *Spectrum* quickly became an invaluable photographic and narrative record of one year in the life of the College.

Athletic Activity

From the beginning, the Gettysburg faculty recognized the importance of physical activity in promoting the welfare of their students. The earliest rules and regulations included "hours of recreation" in the detailed daily schedule and set aside a lot "for the purpose of exercise and play." Playing ball in or near the building might get one into serious trouble, but we should attribute this rule to the desire to avoid property damage rather than a hostility to playing games. There are references to several kinds of ball in the 1840s and 1850s, to baseball as early as the 1860s, and to football as early as 1877. The *Ragout* published in March 1868 listed three baseball clubs, named College, Manito, and Star. About the same time a skating rink was constructed for the use of the students.[193]

The McCreary Gymnasium which was dedicated in October 1872, after an effort extending over seven years, was the first major facility on campus designed to encourage students to engage in regular exercise. When the gymnasium was first being discussed, the faculty wanted to require students to use it, under the direction of a qualified faculty member. This being an unrealistic goal for the depressed 1870s, the faculty opted instead for the frequently used method of getting the students to take the responsibility for a College undertaking. On the day before the dedication, the McCreary Gymnasium Association of Pennsylvania College was organized "to receive for use, from the Faculty the 'John B. McCreary Gymnasium' and assume its control." The agreement entered into carefully specified the responsibilities of each of the parties. The faculty agreed to furnish "proper apparatus for gymnastic exercise" and the students to make "ordinary repairs to the building, replacing worn out apparatus, procuring additional apparatus, and furnishing light, etc., etc." Most of the students

[193]For a more detailed account than is presented here, see Robert L. Bloom, *Intercollegiate Athletics at Gettysburg College, 1879-1919* (Gettysburg, 1976).

promptly joined the association, which tried heroically to operate the facility. It proved to be an overwhelming task. Citing "want of interest" and the refusal of the students to pay the charge of twenty-five cents per term which it tried to levy upon them, the association voted in June 1875 to turn the gymnasium back to the faculty.[194] The professors were able to add, first seventy-five cents and then one dollar per year, to the cost of attending College, and to use the proceeds from this charge to maintain the facility. At times many students took advantage of the opportunities which it afforded. "The gymnasium is being used almost constantly," reported the *College Monthly* in April 1882, "and the few moments spent there bring an ample reward." There was considerable vandalism and eventually the faculty placed wire screens over the windows to make it more difficult for town and campus boys to break them.

The construction and early use of the McCreary Gymnasium coincided with the development of intercollegiate athletics in the United States: baseball in 1859, football in 1869, followed by other sports. In September 1869 the Gettysburg students petitioned the faculty for permission to go to Emmitsburg after Saturday morning classes "to play a social game of Base Ball" with Mount St. Mary's students. To make their request more attractive, they asked for a tutor to accompany them. Six years later, the "College 'Base Ball Nine' " asked leave to travel to Hanover to play a game, but not with a College team. In May 1876 fourteen members of the "Penna. College Base Ball Club" sought permission to travel to Chambersburg on one day and return the next, "to play a friendly game of Base Ball with the club of that city," promising that, "if we are favored in this, our humble entreaty, you can rest assured, Gentlemen, that we will rigidly regard all the rules of gentility."[195] In October 1879, after a Dickinson College team played on the campus, students asked the faculty to allow their football team to play a return game in Carlisle.

These four requests, over a ten-year period, ran counter to the spirit, if not the letter, of the long-established rules and regulations of the College. In the decade between 1869 and 1879, the professors saw no valid reason to regard intercollegiate or out-of-town athletic contests as creating a new situation which justified their changing those rules. Nevertheless, after a short time they proved willing to bend, if only slightly.

The 1869 request was denied. The faculty did allow the College Nine to go to Hanover, but its members were required to leave

---

[194]The book containing the agreement, the constitution, and the minutes of the association is in the GCA.

[195]These three student petitions are preserved in the GCA.

following afternoon classes, return before the evening bell rang, and include no one but College students in their party. The first vote on the Chambersburg request ended in a tie. A second tally resulted in permission to go, but only for those who had parental consent.[196] When the faculty first voted on the proposal to allow the football team to visit Carlisle – making a decision viewed by them as one setting no precedent – the result was another tie vote. Summoned to a special meeting the next day, they debated and then passed three resolutions. The first declared that their earlier decision was "in accordance with a fixed principle that such excursions are not in accordance with the objects of College communities and are subversive of the best discipline." The second then granted the students' request, but only because a football game with Dickinson had already been played in Gettysburg and it would be embarrassing not to permit the return match which most assumed would follow. The third resolution was designed to put an end to these requests, once and for all, forever:

> Resolved, That we now enact a standing rule, that, hereafter, no proposition looking to the making or accepting a challenge to play any game or engage in any athletic exercise, away from the College grounds, be entertained at all by the Faculty.

These resolutions were read at all 11 A.M. classes and published in the *College Monthly*.[197]

In an article entitled "The Status of Athletics in American Colleges," which appeared in the *Atlantic Monthly* in July 1890, Albert Bushnell Hart, of the Harvard history faculty, traced the interest in intercollegiate activity which had grown markedly in the previous decade or two, concluding that "no votes of the Faculty or other governing boards can permanently put an end to intercollegiate athletic contests at the present day, because nine tenths of the students and at least seven tenths of the graduates consider them desirable." In Hart's opinion, "athletic sports and competitions and intercollegiate contests are an established part of the life of American colleges." That being the case, he counseled faculties to use their time and energies to best advantage by trying to correct the admitted evils which had arisen. They could do this by "judicious legislation, founded on a few reasonable principles, and by giving to students full freedom within these limitations."[198]

---

[196]After learning that the faculty was displeased because they did not return from Chambersburg by the time agreed upon, the members of the team expressed their formal regret that they had left Chambersburg "after what has been deemed a proper hour, thus necessitating the use of the some of the hours of the Sabbath for our return and also unfitting some of us from the discharge of some of our duties."

[197]The games with Dickinson on September 27 and October 18, 1879 are taken to mark the beginning of intercollegiate football for Gettysburg College.

[198]*Atlantic Monthly* (July 1890), pp. 63-71.

Most people would agree on what at least some of these evils were. Several of the sports, especially football, were still games without widely accepted rules. Each year play resulted in many injuries and several deaths. In April 1877 the *College Monthly* reported that two persons out of twenty-three participants had emerged unhurt from a recent campus football game. The rest had cracked shins and bad bruises. In October 1879 the same publication observed that "several new victims have recently been added to the long list, who seem determined to sacrifice their heads, as well as their shins in their devotion to the game." A Dickinson student died during a football contest in 1886. Another evil, in many minds, was the professionalizing of college sports. Officials of many schools quickly realized that strong and winning teams could bring their institutions much more favorable publicity than any musical organization, debating team, or outstanding faculty member. Newspapers set up sports pages which attracted greater public interest in colleges, or at least in college teams, than ever before in the history of the country. The temptation to purchase strong and winning teams was too great for some administrators to resist. These team members might have little or no interest in a college curriculum or an academic degree. Also, it was widely believed that many people who attended games had too much interest in gambling and drinking while they were there. Finally, intercollegiate athletics were costly. How many colleges could afford to compete and hope to win enough contests to preserve, if not advance, their reputation?

As a leading faculty member, the editor of the *College Monthly* could be counted on to defend the position which a majority of his colleagues took on the subject of intercollegiate athletics at Gettysburg College. In December 1884 Philip M. Bikle argued that students should exercise for their own health and pleasure, not to fit themselves to contest with students in other colleges. At the same time, he was critical of those newspapers which made disparaging remarks about intercollegiate sports even while they gave ever-increasing publicity to them. Three months later he commended Princeton, Harvard, and other schools for beginning to exercise some control over the games, which the public had come to believe "were the main features of the college courses and the studies merely incidental matters."

But it remained for George D. Stahley, who became the alumni editor of the *College Monthly* in June 1882, to develop the most coherent statement of the College position on physical activity and intercollegiate athletics. Speaking to the alumni in June 1887, he proposed "the union in holy wedlock, of mind and body, of brain and brawn, of thought and nerve tissue." Later, he argued that "as

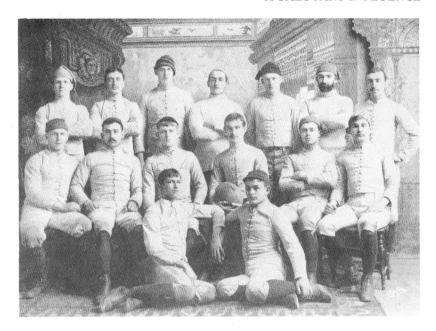

The first College football team, 1890.

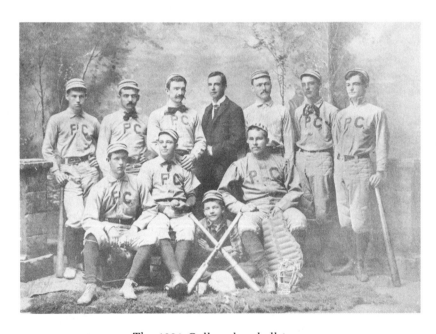

The 1891 College baseball team.

all our worldly activities are manifested through these human bodies which we possess, it follows that the more perfect these bodies are in their development and functions, the greater will be their efficiency in service." Every college should have a medical director to determine the physical condition of each student and prescribe the best exercise for him. None of this would prevent a physically fit student from engaging in those outdoor sports which he enjoys and which benefit him, but colleges should not operate "a system of training for producing professional athletes." In May 1885 Stahley had advocated eliminating "the inter-collegiate baseball, foot-ball and rowing nuisances." A year later, upon learning that a Dickinson student had died during a game, he again condemned football, which was once "interesting and healthful," but was now "brutalizing and dangerous." It should be abolished.[199]

While Bikle and Stahley were stating their cases for sound minds in sound bodies, Gettysburg students were bringing intercollegiate athletics to the campus. In 1881 baseball teams began competing with other schools in two or three games each year, at first with Dickinson and Western Maryland Colleges.[200] In March 1886 the faculty allowed two students who were "regularly attending to their duties" to meet with representatives of other colleges in Harrisburg. Out of their deliberations came the Pennsylvania State Intercollegiate Baseball Association. Gettysburg students joined others from Bucknell, Dickinson, and Franklin and Marshall in agreeing to a set of rules governing how they would compete with each other. By the end of the 1880s intercollegiate baseball games each May and June were an established fact. Comparable football rivalry began in the fall of 1890, when games were played with Millersville Normal School in October and Franklin and Marshall College in November. As happened at other schools, football quickly attracted much more attention than any other sport. After several unsuccessful tries, in 1896 Gettysburg sent its first track team to the recently established relay races at the University of Pennsylvania.[201] As early as 1897 the Mercury began to encourage students to organize a team to play the newly devised game of basketball, but not until February 1901 did intercollegiate competition in this sport begin.

Until long after 1904, the board of trustees provided little staff or financial support for the athletic program, which was considered to be the primary responsibility of the students. In the spring of 1885

[199]Stahley's views were expressed in articles which appeared in the College Monthly for May 1885, December 1886, June 1887, and October 1888.

[200]The game with Dickinson played in Gettysburg in October or November 1881 is taken to mark the beginning of intercollegiate baseball for Gettysburg College.

[201]One student represented Gettysburg in field sports competition at Swarthmore in May 1893.

the latter organized an athletic association, adopted the inevitable constitution, and announced that they were interested in encouraging all sports.[202] Early in 1886 they reorganized, elected Philip M. Bikle as their president, decided to meet once a month, and declared that they were going to make McCreary Gymnasium a much more useful campus facility. Their main object, as announced in the February 1886 issue of the *College Monthly*, was "general physical culture and not, as is the case in so many colleges, the playing of intercollegiate games of football, base-ball, etc." It was this organization which helped to found the intercollegiate baseball association and which was given the proceeds from the gymnasium fee which the College collected to maintain that facility, but within a very short time its most immediate concern was its own survival.[203] For the next four years there are almost no references to it in the *College Monthly*. The ongoing intercollegiate baseball program was operated by a separate baseball club. In October 1887 the faculty delegated the task of maintaining the gymnasium to the Y.M.C.A.[204]

The Athletic Association which was revived in the spring of 1890, when there was a definite quickening of interest in sports generally, had a continuous existence through and beyond 1904. For about a decade it administered the intercollegiate athletic program.[205] This meant electing team managers, hiring coaches, arranging schedules, trying to maintain student interest, and raising money to pay for the program. Sources of income were initiation fees (until they were dropped in 1900); dues; gate receipts at home games (admission was twenty-five cents); appeals to alumni; and proceeds of fund raising events, such as dramatic productions and "phonographic entertainments." One of the first achievements of the association, in April 1890, was persuading the faculty to change the long-established time of the afternoon class from 4 P.M. to 3 P.M., which gave an extra hour of practice time.

---

[202]A baseball association was organized in May 1882.

[203]In the spring of 1886 the association repaired the bowling alley in the gymnasium and purchased new pins and balls.

[204]The question of who should care for the gymnasium was settled once and for all when the College relocated the facility in 1890 and began to require work in physical education and hygiene. Perhaps preoccupation with the building program of 1888-1890 may have had something to do with the lack of interest in the athletic association.

[205]Before that, the faculty always reserved the right to intervene. For example, in 1895 it decreed that no off-campus games could be played without its permission. The members of the Athletic Association wisely created the three-man alumni advisory committee, which beginning in 1891 consisted of George D. Stahley, Charles S. Duncan, and John B. McPherson, all local men.

The students supporting athletics were also successful in persuading the board of trustees and faculty to help them in obtaining a proper place for playing their games. The field west of Washington street and south of Lincoln avenue which they were using had several disadvantages. It was not large enough; it lacked the high fence which made practical charging admission to the games; and, since it was never intended as an intercollegiate field, some teams the students wanted to play at home refused to come to Gettysburg. In 1890 the Athletic Association asked the trustee repair committee for a different site on which to construct a modern field. The latter referred the question to the faculty, which in April 1891 granted the students use of a plot 500 feet by 350 feet west and north of the New Recitation Building. The students were required to raise the money to prepare and maintain the field, which they could use until such time as it might be needed for building purposes. In a financial appeal to the alumni which appeared in the *College Monthly* in November 1892, the association explained what it understood a good athletic field to be:

> We mean a desirable tract of ground, nicely leveled and enclosed by a high board fence; large enough to enable us to fit up a good base ball and foot ball ground; commodious enough to permit us to lay out a sufficient number of lawn tennis courts; capacious enough to make it possible to construct a suitable and creditable running and bicycle track; of sufficient size to allow the erection of a "grand stand" should it be desired.

Nixon Field was completed in 1895 and first used for an intercollegiate contest in the spring of 1896.

Unfortunately, this appeal produced only a small fraction of what was needed to complete the project. In the summer of 1893 a student sent out by the Athletic Association tried his hand at raising money; he met with only limited success. At the end of 1894, which was a depression year, the students were still unable to proceed with their plans, but by this time an important change in location had been agreed upon. The field would be constructed at the old site: more than four acres of land north of Pennsylvania Hall. Only when the board of trustees loaned the association $1,000 could work on the project finally begin, early in 1895. By May of that year the area had been graded, by October grass seed was sown, and by December an eight-and-one-half-foot high board fence was being placed. Although the new field was ready for intramural games in the fall of 1895, it was first used for an intercollegiate contest when Gettysburg entertained the Washington and Jefferson College baseball team on April 17, 1896. In March 1897 the Mercury reported that the students had named the field in honor of Henry B. Nixon who, with his students, furnished the necessary professional direction for its completion.[206] In 1903 the Athletic Association built a large grandstand along the south side of the field to supplement the movable bleachers in use since 1896.

If rigorously enforced, the standing rule which the faculty adopted in 1879, prohibiting off-campus games outside of Gettysburg, would have prevented the College from participating fully in intercollegiate athletics as they were developing. Although it was perhaps not evident in 1879, strict enforcement of the rule would certainly have led to constant and serious bickering between students and faculty, and perhaps as some feared to an eventual loss in enrollment. As early as 1885, the faculty began changing its policy when it adopted an amendment to the standing rule which allowed members of the football and baseball teams one one-day absence each year to play a return game. Permitting the baseball team to enter the intercollegiate baseball association a year later meant eventually granting that team enough absences to play a return game on the campus of each of the other members. In 1891 the faculty began granting fifteen periods each year to the musical organizations for making off-campus trips and, as an afterthought, it extended this privilege to the baseball and football teams.

These gradual changes in policy, however, did not deal with one of the strongest desires of the athletic program's supporters, who believed that it was vital for success that students accompany the teams off campus and cheer them on. In November 1891, after refusing one such request and granting another, the faculty named

---

[206]Only in 1922 did the board of trustees officially name Nixon Field.

Henry B. Nixon and George D. Stahley a committee "to draft a set of rules for the future regulation of athletics."[207] A month later they adopted its report, most of which applied to team members: each was required to present written permission from parent or guardian in order to participate in intercollegiate games; only games "with student teams from regular schools or colleges" could be played; captains had to report to Stahley even the most trivial accidents occurring during practice; and team members had to report to him for examination after every contest game. The last item adopted was a rule that only "those who may be necessary as substitutes" could accompany teams playing away games. When the faculty revised these rules in 1895, they increased the physical requirements and established minimum academic averages for participating in inter-collegiate games, but they did not repeal the prohibition against students following the teams off campus.[208] Later in the same year, the students asked the faculty to make an exception by permitting them to accompany the football team to Harrisburg to participate in a game with Bucknell. Their request was denied. "As a result," the *Mercury* for November 1895 explained, "the team was deprived of the enthusiastic presence of its loyal followers and the game was lost to Bucknell." The faculty began to retreat from its well-established position in November 1901, when it permitted students with permission from parents and who would sign a pledge of good conduct to accompany the football team to the Thanksgiving game in Lancaster. The minutes attribute this decision to the earnest entreaties of the coach and the faculty's confidence in him. Be that as it may, when the request was repeated in 1902 and 1903 it was given the same positive response.

During the very years in which the faculty were trying to develop and refine what was in their opinion a sensible athletic policy for the College, the West Pennsylvania Synod of the Lutheran church embarked upon an unsuccessful attempt to influence it to reverse the direction in which it was moving. In October 1893 the synodical committee on the state of the College reported that it was

> sorry to learn that the authorities of the College permit the students to engage in athletic contests with the students of other institutions, traveling about the country expending time and money. We fear that these contests are not only serious interruptions of study, but also the occasions of great moral evils and will in the end injure the students and the efficiency and good name of the College.

---

[207]As one would expect, the faculty in June 1888 denied permission for the Bicycle Club to attend a week-long convention in Baltimore.

[208]The required academic averages were eliminated in 1898 because they "were not producing the results anticipated at their adoption."

One year later, the same committee, but with different members, repeated its opposition to intercollegiate athletics "on the ground of economy, faithful prosecution of study, and a high standard of morality," while denying any desire to interfere with the "scholastic management" of the College or to oppose athletic activity. Later in its sessions the synod passed a resolution denying its financial aid to any student (he would be one studying for the ministry) engaging in intercollegiate contests and directing its education committee to enforce the rule. "The extremes to which some of the synods have gone," remarked the *Mercury* in November 1894, "drives us to wondering what sort of men they would have their ministers be."

In October 1895 the synodical committee on the state of the College, with its membership changed again, expressed its regret that the "well-meant suggestion of last year" did not appear "to have met with the approval of the management." Nevertheless, it repeated the request, urging the College to bring itself "into harmony with the sober verdict of many of the larger colleges of our land . . ., and placing it in a position to merit and receive solid honor and ever-increasing patronage." Once more the *Mercury* rose to the occasion. In the November 1895 issue, it claimed that intercollegiate athletic contests were "the best way at present to keep our college in touch with our neighboring institutions" and "the *only* interesting diversion for our students." The writer admitted that "members of the teams have not always acted in a manner consistent with the standard of morality set up by the clergy," but argued that if the students "understand that the future of our athletics is conditioned on the suppression of these evils, they will take steps to suppress them." When the board of trustees met in January 1896, as we shall see, they had more pressing matters to deal with than the synod's request.[209]

By the later 1890s, College authorities may have had no intention of curtailing or eliminating the intercollegiate athletic program, but they had decided to alter the way in which it was being operated. In June 1897 the trustees named Edward S. Breidenbaugh, Henry B. Nixon, and George D. Stahley to a committee charged with review-

---

[209]In an article in the *Lutheran Observer* for January 20, 1893, George D. Stahley tried to reassure the church that a college such as Gettysburg would "always keep its enthusiasm and its physical prowess considerably beneath the athletic grade of a university." Brutal, immoral, and sensual were words which did not apply to sports at Gettysburg, he insisted, where the sporting constituency, institutional rivalry, pool of athletic skill, and part-time students simply did not exist. By this time Stahley was defending football as less brutal than many people had thought. In 1890 and again in 1899, the Maryland Synod committee on the College expressed its approval of "athletic contests" as part of the College "stimulus to the student to discover himself, as well as to awaken the powers of self mastery and fraternal contest on the field and platform."

ing proposed athletic expenditures and approving playing commitments. After these three professors presented a lengthy report eighteen months later, the board entrusted its disposition to a committee of its own members. What emerged by June 1899 was an Athletic Council (or Committee) of twelve members: three faculty, two alumni, one seminarian alumnus, the president of the Athletic Association, and one student from each of the four classes and the preparatory department. The board of trustees appointed the faculty and alumni members; the classes elected the student members. This council was authorized to administer the athletic program in conjunction with the Athletic Association.[210] Stahley became ex officio chairman of the council. In announcing this new arrangement, the *Gettysburgian* for June 7, 1899 declared that "it is the method of control in vogue at every institution of prominence." It was, in fact, very similar to that which Albert Bushnell Hart reported Harvard had adopted in 1888.[211]

The 1904 College catalogue informed the public that at Gettysburg

> athletic sports are encouraged, but under such regulations as, it is believed, prevent them from becoming a source of demoralization to the students, or interfering with the legitimate work of the Institution. A student who has not first secured the permission of his parents is not allowed to engage in any public contest.

Of the intercollegiate teams in 1904, the football varsity was the most newsworthy. In the first years of the new century it was playing an average of ten games per season. Usual rivals were Baltimore Medical College, the Carlisle Indian School, Lebanon Valley, Western Maryland, and Franklin and Marshall.[212] A Thanksgiving day game with the latter school in 1900 set the precedent for a practice which continued for more than forty years. The baseball team played an average of sixteen games each season, in most years including Bucknell, Carlisle Indian School, Franklin and Marshall,

---

[210]The regulations promulgated by the trustee committee were published as *Rules Governing Athletic Sports, Pennsylvania College, 1899.*

[211]The *Gettysburgian* for March 15, 1899 saw the Athletic Council as a method of control placing "some responsibility upon the alumni and faculty as well as undergraduates," and not as an unwelcome intrusion upon student rights. The council could mean "better management, better coaching, better finances, teams, and at this period of college life, better athletics will mean a larger Gettysburg."

[212]Athletic relations between Gettysburg and Dickinson students during this period were strained, to say the least. Each thought the other guilty of unfair practices. They did not meet each other in football competition in 1895-1897 or in baseball in 1896-1898. A formal three-year agreement between the two athletic associations in November 1898 reinaugurated play, but between 1901 and 1904 there were only four games played between them in the three intercollegiate sports. The text of the agreement is included in the lead article of the *Gettysburgian* for December 7, 1898.

and Pennsylvania State College. During a southern trip in the spring of 1903, the team took on the Universities of North Carolina, Virginia, and Maryland, defeating the latter. The basketball team, which had its first season in 1901, was playing an average of seven games each year, usually including Bucknell, Dickinson, Franklin and Marshall, and the Steelton Y.M.C.A. After participating in the Penn relays for the first time in 1896, the College was not able thereafter to fjeld a track team every year; interest in this sport waxed and waned. There was a track meet with Dickinson in 1899, but this did not set a precedent. The College sports program in 1904 was not limited to intercollegiate activities. The fifteenth annual tennis tournament was held in the spring of that year. The Sons of Hercules carried on a tradition in gymnastics begun in the new gymnasium in 1891. Finally, there was a considerable amount of intramural activity.

The Sons of Hercules posed for this picture in the gymnasium during the 1900-1901 year.

By 1904 there were unmistakable signs that the College athletic program as described above had gained wide acceptance and support. What was being reported in minor items on the last pages of the *College Monthly* in the 1880s and early 1890s now flourished in lead stories which actually dominated some issues of the *Gettysburgian*. The annual issues of the *Spectrum* gave full coverage to athletics, including photographs of team members, statistics, summaries of the year's activities, and occasional historical accounts. Writers for the *Mercury* and *Gettysburgian* repeatedly claimed that a strong athletic program was essential in attracting more and better students to Gettysburg. "It has become the almost universal custom among students to measure a college's reputation by its athletics," argued the *Mercury* in November 1895, "and no matter whether this is the correct standard or not, we must submit to it, and pay attention to our athletics if we wish to keep in line with other colleges." A small but telling sign of the times was the faculty decision in 1892 to permit the football team of that year to board at, of all places, a local hotel, although Professor Stahley was made responsible for the members' diet and conduct. To meet the objections of other teams, the Athletic Association declared in 1896 that town boys could no longer play on College teams. Whether this prohibition was always honored is another question. In 1900 the Athletic Association devised a system of varsity letters and established the requirements for wearing the soon-coveted G.[213] In 1903 the *Gettysburgian* urged someone in authority to find a place to keep the trophies which College teams were beginning to win.

In 1904 there was evidence that Gettysburg had so far avoided many of the abuses which had been predicted for all intercollegiate athletic programs and which actually existed in some. It would be incorrect to say that sports at Gettysburg had become professionalized or that they were significantly influenced by outside control. With meager funds, the Athletic Association paid the coaches, who came and went with great frequency. The students lost no opportunity to praise their teams if they had a fair season without the services of a coach. By the mid 1890s, however, there was an increasing chorus of calls for a permanent coach who would work throughout the year with all of the teams. Only such a person could insure that team members would engage in the regular and systematic training necessary to turn the all-too-frequent losing seasons into winning ones.[214] It was evident that a continuing effort

---

[213]The varsity letter was a G, not a P.

[214]Writing in the *Gettysburgian* for February 22, 1899, William Arch McClean, a member of the advisory committee, argued that, since winning teams were "the best advertisement that can be had for the outlay of money," the board of trustees should appropriate whatever was needed for a permanent coach.

was still needed to insure that enough students would volunteer for all of the teams, that those who offered themselves would practice the amount of time required for success, and that a sufficient number of students would support them from the sidelines.[215] Some of the publicity in College publications was intended primarily to cultivate student interest in the athletic program. That this state of affairs was not limited to Gettysburg is indicated by the fact that it was not uncommon for a competing team to call off a scheduled game because not enough young men were available to play it.

Gymnasium
Interior view of the former Linnaean Hall, which served as the College gymnasium from 1890 until 1927.

College Spirit

There are evidences from the earliest years of the College of a sentiment among students resulting from their association with each other in an educational community. It took the form of pride in the class of which they were members, in organizations to which they

---

[215]On April 19, 1899 the *Gettysburgian* wondered how thirty or more men could be picked for the track team from fifteen applicants.

belonged, and in the College which sheltered them. This pride continued beyond graduation and helps to explain the vigorous alumni association which maintained a continuous existence from 1835.

After 1868 what came to be called college spirit took new forms in most American colleges. Gettysburg was no exception. In the 1870s classes adopted special hats and their own identifying colors.[216] Random publications such as the *Ragout* and the *Olios* helped in promoting spirit, but not nearly as much as the *College Monthly* and its successors. As early as March 1880, the *Monthly* began urging students to "get up some college songs" to be used on moonlight evenings. When the editors learned early in 1882 that plans were under way to publish a book of songs drawn from many American colleges, they urged the students to rouse themselves and make their contribution to its pages. *The American College Song Book: a Collection of the Songs of Fifty Representative American Colleges* (Chicago, 1882), which was published about six months later, contained four Gettysburg contributions: "Commencement Day," "Banquet Song," "Adoratio," and "Song and Work." Some fifty copies of the new book were sold on campus. "A new impetus has been given to singing among the students," declared the *College Monthly* in June 1882, and "every man in College seems to want a copy." In the same issue, the editors reported that the students had chosen scarlet and deep canary as the College colors. A pennant of these colors flew along with the American flag from the staff atop Pennsylvania Hall during the semicentennial exercises in June 1882.

The choice of the College colors was made by an agency which was itself a manifestation of the spirit of the post-1868 period: what was often described as a mass meeting of students. Undoubtedly, there were such gatherings before 1868, but the faculty were inclined to regard them as subversive of good order and discipline. Gradually, and probably somewhat reluctantly, they now accepted these meetings as part of the evolving polity of the College. The students used them on many occasions and for many different purposes.

The development of intercollegiate athletics greatly intensified the spirit on most college campuses. While songs might still be needed for moonlight nights, they now became indispensable at football and other games. These were also times for showing one's colors. Nor could any self-respecting college be without its distinctive yells. Writing in the December 1888 issue of the *College Monthly*, George D. Stahley observed that "the 'Rah, Rah, Rah' feature of

---

[216]According to the *College Monthly* for June 1881, the seniors wore high white hats for commencement. A year later, the same journal reported that all classes had adopted class hats.

college life seems to be on the increase, and is becoming more and more complicated and luxuriant." As for the yell, "we have learnt it at base-ball and foot-ball contests, in the political parade, at cane rushes, informal jubilations, etc.," he observed, "and we cannot but believe that there is a deep under-lying principle, aesthetic, philosophic or scientific, which asserts its necessary existence in this manner." While he could not clearly see the relationship between the yells and higher education, Stahley was not prepared to say that it did not exist. "Harmony of purpose, unity of action, intense earnestness and a great display of enthusiasm," all elements of success in life, characterize the yells, which also "exercise the vocal and respiratory muscles, empty the lungs most completely of carbon di-oxide, and send the pure arterial blood to the remotest tissue of the body." Stahley could now report proudly to his fellow-alumni that their alma mater was no longer without its very own yell: "Rah, Rah, Rah, Rah, Rah, Rah; Penn-syl-van-yah!!" And, within a few months, a student mass meeting adopted a new set of College colors: orange and navy blue. At its request, the faculty ratified the choice, on April 4, 1889.[217]

The choice of orange and blue as the College colors proved to be a popular one; though not without criticism, they have remained to the time of this writing. It was much more difficult for students to find acceptable yells and songs. In October 1892 the recently revived Athletic Association named a committee of fifteen to select a number of yells from which a mass meeting of students could then choose one or more. In this instance direct democracy appeared not to work. Immediate dissatisfaction with the choice made led more than one hundred students to petition for another mass meeting, which repealed the now-despised yell and ordered the committee to submit more candidates. A third mass meeting in April 1893 adopted two yells. The first was "Rah! Rah! Rah! Rah! Rah! Rah! Rah! Gettysburg." The second was "Hoo-rah, Hoo-rah, Hoo-rah, Get-tys-burg-i-a." A third yell was accepted in 1896-1897:

Brackey Corax, Corix, Coree,
Brackey Corax, Corix, Coree,
Heigh Oh! Umpty Ah!
Hulla Belloo, Bellee, Bellah
Gettysburg, Gettysburg, Gettysburg!

[217]Writing for the 1932 College history, Charles H. Huber (1892) explained that the colors were changed because the students were told that it was either difficult or impossible to buy scarlet and deep canary caps, while orange and blue caps were readily available. *1932 History*, pp. 438-439. The *College Monthly* published the yells of thirty schools in November 1888 and the colors of some forty in October 1892.

> Rah, Rah-Rah, Rah-Rah, Rah, Rah!
> Bing, Bang! S--- s, Boom-Boom!
> Gettysburg, Gettysburg, Gettysburg![218]

In March 1895 the Mercury told the students that the College sorely needed a recognized and popular song of its own. Not only would singing it help the baseball teams, but also it would be much more mannerly "than guying and hooting at our opponents." Two years later, in June 1897, the same publication had to confess that "the fact still stares us in the face, . . . we have no college song." The writer urged one or more students to put forth the effort needed to compose a good song and bring Gettysburg abreast of many of her sister colleges. Before such a production could be written and selected, the Gettysburgian proclaimed that, since many other colleges now had their own song books, Gettysburg students should have one too. Early in 1899 an alumnus, through the Pen and Sword Society, offered a small prize for the best college song written by an undergraduate. In this case, a committee of three, rather than a mass meeting, would conduct the contest and select the winner. The rules were simple: contestants had to be Gettysburg undergraduates, the lyrics had to be "adapted to some appropriate air," the identity of the author could not be known to the judges, and all songs submitted became eligible for inclusion in the proposed College song book. After getting off to a disappointingly slow start, the contest closed in May. The winning entry, "The Orange and the Blue," was written by Louis S. Weaver (1899) and set to the tune of "Annie Laurie." Honorable mention went to Joseph B. Baker (1901) for "Heigh Oh! Heigh Oh!" which incorporated the College yell into its lyrics. The June 7, 1899 issue of the Gettysburgian reprinted what may have been another entry in the contest. It was "Our Alma Mater," written by Joseph N. K. Hickman (1899) and sung to the tune of "America." For some years this last song appears to have served as an unofficial alma mater for the College.[219]

---

[218]The students who returned from the Y.M.C.A. conference in Northfield, Massachusetts, in the summer of 1903 told their fellows that Bracky corax was the only original Gettysburg yell. The others then in use on the campus were all borrowed from some other college or university. Gettysburgian, October 14, 1903.

[219]The rules for the song contest appeared in the Gettysburgian for March 8, 1899. The song book was never published, but these three and several other selections were included in the Spectrum (1901). Some sixty years later, when these songs were played and sung for three members of the class of 1904 (Hamsher, Wentz, and Wolf), they insisted that they did not recognize them at all.

The Orange and the Blue

Tune: "Annie Laurie"   Words: Louis S. Weaver (1899)

ON the far famed field of battle,
Where her sons fought, tried and true,
Stand walls of Alma Mater,
Hail! The Orange and the Blue.
Hail! The Orange and the Blue.
Hail! The Orange and the Blue.
While there's life and strength within us,
We will cheer the colors true.

If we've won renown in learning,
If we've worn the much sought "G,"
If we've gained the college honor
By a scarcely passing "D,"
Yet it's all together boys,
For the Orange and the Blue,
While there's life and strength within us,
We will cheer the colors true.

Whether Fresh. or Soph. or Junior,
Seniors, Grad. with a degree,
We shall strive to keep the colors,
Ever crowned with victory.
Ever crowned with victory.
Ever crowned with victory.
While there's life and strength within us,
They'll be crowned with victory.

When we've faced the great life struggle,
Tried to win success and fame,
Oft' we'll think in recollection
Of dear Gettysburg's fair name.
For it's all together boys,
For the Orange and the Blue,
While there's life and strength within us,
We will cheer the colors true.

'Till our life's thread here is severed,
'Till we rest beneath the dew,
We will stand by Alma Mater,
And the Orange and the Blue.
For it's all together boys,
For the Orange and the Blue,
While there's life and strength within us,
We will cheer the colors true.

That College spirit was more than colors, yells, and songs was something which the *Gettysburgian* tried to establish in its issue for April 19, 1899:

College spirit is a feeling of love and devotion to *Alma Mater* which finds its expression only in words and acts of practical beneficence, a feeling that is born of happy associations and a recognition of favors received. College spirit considers the best interests of *Alma Mater* first, last and always. It is not sour and pessimistic, but bright and hopeful. It encourages every laudable student enterprise, and frowns down all forms of negativism.

Our Alma Mater.

Tune: "America"   Words: Joseph N.K. Hickman (1899)

OUR Alma Mater, dear,
Thy name we love to hear,
  O', Gettysburg!
Bright scenes of happy days,
Vivid and dear, always,
Our hearts are joined in praise
  To Gettysburg.

The brightest years of life,
So free from anxious strife,
  Are spent with thee;
Where friendships true arise,
And bind our hearts with ties
Of love that sanctifies
  Our loyalty.

To God, and Nation, true,
We pledge the Orange and Blue
  Our love sincere.
When doubt and care arise
To dim thy cloudless skies, —
O, then, thy name inspires
  Our hearts with cheer.

And when life's race is o'er,
We near that unknown shore,
  Dear Gettysburg,
Still shall each heart be thine,
Bound by love's cords divine —
A pure and sacred shrine
  For Gettysburg.

Alumni

In 1868 the Alumni Association was one of the strongest institutions within the constituencies of Gettysburg College. Since its founding in 1835, it had met each year during commencement week, except for 1863, when there were no graduation exercises. Martin L. Stoever, the secretary since 1842, used his interest in former students and his position as faculty member to keep in close touch with many, if not most, of the growing body of alumni. The active members of the association demonstrated a commendable interest in supporting their alma mater, perhaps the most potentially valuable instance of which was their commitment made in 1859 to raise enough money to establish an endowed professorship.

The Alumni Association continued meeting without fail during every commencement week between 1868 and 1904. Edward McPherson, first elected president in 1862, was reelected each year and died in office in December 1895. Not only was he a political figure of national importance, but also he was a longtime member of the College board of trustees (1861-1895) and of its executive committee (1872-1895). After his death, Charles S. Duncan (1882), a local attorney, served as president from 1896 to 1902, and Harry M. Clabaugh (1877), a District of Columbia jurist, served from 1902 until 1906. Stoever's successors as secretary were also faculty members: Luther S. Croll (1871-1889) and John A. Himes (1889-1902). Harry C. Picking (1879) became treasurer in 1886 and remained in office until 1917. During most of this period he was also treasurer of the College.

The alumni activities of commencement week were varied. Until 1896 the old tradition of having an alumnus give a public address was observed. Each year several classes held their own reunions, sometimes as few as one or two, at other times as many as six or more. In 1871 and 1872 the returning graduates held a banquet at the Springs Hotel. While this did not immediately become an established annual event, it was revived from time to time, and by 1904 the alumni banquet was an accepted feature of commencement week. Finally, there always had to be a business meeting of the Alumni Association, to admit the graduating class to membership; if possible, collect an initiation fee of one dollar from new members and a signature in the minute book; note the death of fellow-alumni; elect officers; and dispose of any other matters which those present wished to consider and act upon. Six such matters warrant discussion: the right of the Alumni Association to nominate certain members of the board of trustees; alumni representation on the editorial staff of College publications; the encouragement of district alumni associations; responsibility for proper celebration of the fiftieth anniversary of the College; endowment of a professorship; and keeping track of the alumni.

Although by 1873 seventeen of the thirty-six trustees had been students of the College (most had finished the course and received degrees), the newly formed executive committee of the board (of which Edward McPherson was a member) recommended in June of that year amending the charter of the College in order to establish more formal ties between the institution and its Alumni Association. They proposed making trustee terms six years in length and permitting the Alumni Association to fill one of the six vacancies that would be occurring annually. The executive committee repeated this recommendation in 1874 and 1875; the Alumni

Association endorsed it in the former year; but a majority of the trustees were not prepared at that time to institute any such change in the polity of the College. After taking no action in 1873 and rejecting the proposal in the following year, they told the Alumni Association in 1875 that "having given the subject, in all its bearings, a patient and respectful consideration, we reply that we deem it inexpedient at present to make the desired change in the Charter of the College."

Ten years later, a group of influential Philadelphia alumni echoed others who had urged earlier that the matter of alumni representation be reopened. In response, the executive committee of the board of trustees renewed its 1875 recommendation, which the full board now accepted, apparently with little or no opposition. It named a committee of three, all of them alumni, to meet with a committee named by the Alumni Association, to draw up a plan. In June 1886 the trustees approved the committee's proposal, which made possible formal alumni representation on the board, without requiring a change in the charter or instituting terms of specific length. As each alternate vacancy in the board occurred, the trustees agreed, they would call upon the Alumni Association to nominate a candidate until such time as they had elected six members in this fashion, after which the number of alumni-designated trustees would be maintained at six. No alumnus of fewer than ten years was eligible to serve nor was one who was a faculty member in any college. Members present at an annual meeting of the Alumni Association were eligible to vote for nominees. The first alumnus trustee was elected in 1887; the full complement of six was first reached in 1893.[220]

When the faculty established the *College Monthly* in 1876-1877, it accorded the Alumni Association the opportunity to name an alumni editor. Recognizing the importance of this publication to anyone deeply interested in the College and its future, the association took this responsibility seriously. Between 1877 and 1893 it named five persons to serve in this capacity. It also designated an alumni editor for the *Mercury*, who served from 1893 until the position was abolished six years later. The two outstanding alumni editors for the *College Monthly* were George D. Stahley (1882-1889) and Charles R. Trowbridge (1890-1893), the latter a Lutheran pastor

[220]The first eight alumni trustees were John E. Smith (1887-1889), George D. Stahley (1887-1890), Daniel R. Miller (1888-1897), Samuel M. Swope (1890-1931), William H. Dunbar (1890-1920), J. Hay Brown (1892-1899), Thomas C. Billheimer (1892-1923), and John Wagner (1893-1934). With Wagner's election, there were six alumni trustees for the first time. Writing in the May 1890 issue of the *College Monthly,* the alumni editor urged members of the association to attend the annual meetings and elect as trustees strong men who would attend board meetings and "give of their time, interest, influence and means in support of the institution."

and grandson of John G. Morris. Both men regularly contributed articles and editorials on subjects of current interest. Some of Stahley's writings have already been discussed. In his three year tenure, Trowbridge expressed his views on many topics. People in a college town, he thought, had an obligation to support their educational institution. The College needed an experienced, full-time chaplain. Alumni and friends of Gettysburg should do more to attract Lutheran students to the Lutheran schools which they should attend. Faculty members should be chosen because they were qualified teachers, not because they were Lutheran or alumni. Princeton should be praised for its efforts to eliminate hazing. Harvard's president Eliot should be criticized for wanting to shorten the college course to three years. Donors should not make their gifts burdens by attaching conditions to them. Most young men who go to college are looking for a sound education in a progressive environment, and not primarily for instruction in achieving athletic prowess. Through it all, Trowbridge was proud of Gettysburg. "It is the peer of any college of equal age – the superior of very many with greater pretensions." His advice to alumni who do not have a good word to say about their College was to keep quiet.[221]

Writing in one of the earliest numbers of the College Monthly, in May 1877, Philip M. Bikle commended the alumni for the support which they were giving the new magazine and urged them to evidence their interest in the College in an additional way: by forming district alumni associations. He claimed that these would serve two useful purposes. They would create social occasions for alumni and give them the opportunity to "awaken and maintain a deeper interest" in the prosperity of the College. At the annual meeting of the Alumni Association a month later, Bikle reported that the first district association was about to be established. On July 25, 1877, during a major national railroad strike, the Reunion of Alumni and Students of Pennsylvania College, Resident in Maryland and other Southern States was organized in Frederick. Urged on by periodic reminders in the College Monthly, during the next five years alumni established four more district associations: Japan Branch (1877), Central Pennsylvania (1879), Alma Mater District (1879), and Philadelphia (1882). These associations met once or twice a year. Usually some member read a paper on a serious topic related to education and discussion followed. Although the extensive reports of their meetings carried in the College Monthly easily gave the impression that these associations were taking root and thriving, by

---

[221] As alumni editor for the Mercury, David F. Garland (1888) functioned in the Stahley-Trowbridge tradition.

1885 only the one in Philadelphia remained. Its leaders included several of the most useful College trustees (John E. Graeff, William M. Baum, and Frederick W. Conrad) as well as other alumni (Samuel P. Sadtler and George S. Eyster). Milton Valentine and later Harvey W. McKnight, usually in company with a faculty member, regularly attended the annual banquet meetings and reported on the state of the College. The last of these gatherings occurred in 1894.

About the time when the Philadelphia association was becoming inactive, alumni in other parts of the College constituency were beginning to think again about the desirability of district organizations. Within two years three new ones were formed: Harrisburg (1894), Pittsburgh (1895), and Yale (1896).[222] The mortality rate for these ventures remained high. Only the Yale club survived into 1897. The editors of the Mercury and Gettysburgian were as much in favor of district associations as Philip M. Bikle had been. They echoed him in stating the advantages accruing to both alumni and the College from a system of vigorous clubs. In 1898 the Alumni Association named a five-man committee "to devise a scheme for the establishment of district alumni associations." While it is not clear whether its members ever produced the desired scheme, within the next several years six clubs were formed: New York (1898), Harrisburg (1899), York (1899), Maryland (1900), Philadelphia (1901), and Pittsburgh (1903). The five active clubs in 1904 were Yale, New York, Harrisburg, Philadelphia, and Pittsburgh.[223]

In June 1878 Edward S. Breidenbaugh proposed to the annual Alumni Association meeting that a committee be named to draw up a feasible plan for the proper celebration of the fiftieth anniversary,

---

[222]According to the Mercury for November 1896, there were eleven Gettysburgians at Yale in that year. The prime mover in organizing the club was William J. Gies (1872-1956), of the class of 1893. While an undergraduate, he was a member of the baseball team and the Athletic Association, editor of the 1893 Spectrum, an editor of the College Monthly, an organizer of the Philo Debating Club, and one of those urging changing the name of the College to Gettysburg. Entering Yale in the fall of 1893, he studied physiological chemistry and was awarded the Ph.D. degree in 1897. In the following year he began a long career on the chemistry faculty of Columbia University. His interest in his alma mater was demonstrated in many ways, including helping found the Pen and Sword Society, providing the money for prizes in both English composition and debating, and being the prime mover for alumni clubs in New Haven and New York. The Spectrum (1906), pp. 125-148, contains a detailed summary of his career up to that time.

[223]Memories are indeed short. When the Philadelphia club was reorganized in 1901, some of its members did not know that an earlier club had existed less than ten years before. Those who called the meeting, however, did remember and specifically called it a reorganization.

or semicentennial, of the College in 1882.[224] Not surprisingly, he was named chairman of the seven persons to whom this task was delegated. A year later, the association accepted their report, and the committee, increased in size to nine members, began to perfect its plans. Believing that the alumni would find it more convenient if all of the semicentennial exercises were held at one time, they decided to schedule them during commencement week. While they wanted to avoid appealing for money during these exercises, the committee felt obligated to use the anniversary occasion in some way for a major fund raising effort. Finally, they wanted to produce a permanent reminder of the event which would be available to every person who wanted it. In 1880, at Breidenbaugh's request, the trustees named five of their own members to work in an advisory capacity with his committee. Meanwhile, the *College Monthly* ran many stories about the forthcoming celebration in an effort to keep it in the minds of the alumni.

The semicentennial exercises occurred on June 27-29, 1882, interspersed with the usual events of commencement week. They began with a reception in the College church on Tuesday evening, featuring several addresses and replies, as well as a poem composed for the occasion. On Wednesday morning, on the campus, four speakers discussed the beginnings of the College, the Krauth presidency, the Baugher presidency, and the fourteen years of the Valentine administration. A heavy rainstorm forced the social gathering of the Alumni Association, which was scheduled for that evening, from out of doors into the College church. On Thursday morning, again on the campus, five speakers discussed the influence of Gettysburg College upon theology, education, literature, medicine, and science. At noon, upon the conclusion of the annual meeting of the Alumni Association, some five hundred of its members shared a collation prepared by the ladies of Gettysburg and served in front of McCreary Gymnasium. The celebration concluded on Thursday evening with a promenade concert on the campus, attended by an estimated two or three thousand people. According to the *College Monthly,* "hundreds of vari-colored lanterns, the torches, and heaps of blazing fire, made the prospect far and near a brilliant one." Commencement exercises, which began at 8:30 the next morning, must have been an anticlimax. The College buildings were decorated with

---

[224]The College participated in the United States centennial celebration in 1876 by sending an extensive exhibit to the exposition in Philadelphia, as requested by the State Superintendent of Public Instruction. They also praised the exposition commissioners for deciding not to open the exposition on Sunday; "our interests as a Christian nation are greatly imperilled by the proposed opening of the Centennial Exhibition on the Lord's day."

wreaths and banners for the week-long occasion. Campus and other groups presented music at all of the events. The *College Monthly* estimated that almost half of the living alumni attended at least part of the program and concluded that "everybody seemed pleased all the week. We think the Semi-centennial, if voted on, would be elected a fine success."[225]

On February 15, 1882 the semicentennial committee, including the advisory trustee members, addressed their financial appeal to the College constituency. Reminding the readers that no attempt to raise money would be made during the June exercises, they declared that "it would nevertheless be improper and unworthy of us all to permit the occasion to pass by without doing something for the enlargement and greater prosperity of the institution, which will form a fitting memorial of this half-century of its history." Since the most pressing need of the College was increased endowment, the committee had secured the consent of the board of trustees and the Alumni Association to use money raised to endow the professorship which the president occupied and to strengthen science instruction, in an unspecified way. The goal which they set was at least $50,000. The committee appealed to every alumnus, every nongraduate, and every pastor to make his own contribution and to appeal to others to do likewise. "Let no one fail to give because he cannot give much," they advised, " and no one give less than the most liberal gift he can present." Unfortunately, this general appeal to the constituency was woefully inadequate to produce the desired results, and there was no one available to undertake the intense personal solicitation almost certainly required to yield $50,000.

The committee early decided that their permanent reminder of the semicentennial would be what they called a memorial volume. Breidenbaugh agreed to edit what was published in 1882 as *The Pennsylvania College Book, 1832-1882*. Within its 475 pages he included Milton Valentine's history of the College; Beale M. Schmucker's account of its beginnings; sketches of the literary societies, Linnaean Association, Alumni Association, and fraternities; biographical sketches of twenty faculty members of the Gymnasium and College; accounts of eight institutions described as daughters of the College; biographical sketches of former students both graduates and nongraduates; a list of trustees; human interest stories; as well as other information. From beginning to end the text was well-written and historically accurate. A century later the work remained a reliable source well-worth consulting. Not the least of the assets of the book were the many excellent photographs by

---

[225]The *College Monthly* for July 1882 contains an excellent account of the exercises. Attempts to celebrate the sixtieth anniversary were unsuccessful.

William H. Tipton, the Gettysburg photographer, some of which have been reproduced in this book.[226]

As earlier noted, during the abortive endowment campaign of 1859 the Alumni Association voted to raise $15,000 to establish an alumni professorship. By 1868 it had secured more than $7,000 in pledges and about $3,200 of this amount had actually been paid to the College treasurer. Few further efforts were made to complete this undertaking until the board of trustees, during the hard times of the 1870s, attempted to relieve their continuing financial distress by persuading several synods to endow a number of professorships. At the annual meeting in June 1873, the Alumni Association agreed to participate in this campaign by reviving its lapsed efforts. On July 1 its committee on the professorship addressed a letter to all alumni and to other friends of the College, announcing a new goal of $25,000 and asking recipients to contribute at least $100 each, payable at once or by means of interest-bearing notes due in from one to five years. The committee secured an agent for each graduating class to solicit and receive commitments. The 1874 College catalogue devoted two pages to describing the alumni endowment campaign, listed the names and addresses of all the class agents, and expressed the hope that enough money would be secured to conclude the drive by the next commencement. When one considers the depressed times in which this appeal was made, it is remarkable that there were about one hundred donors and that the committee could announce to the Alumni Association in June 1876 a total of $15,475 in pledges and cash thus far secured. However, this was an amount still far short of the goal and the campaign had obviously run its course. Few more gifts came in. The Alumni Association moved on to other things and the endowed professorship was all but forgotten. In 1882 the association made another effort, just described, to complete the undertaking (it now raised the goal to $30,000) and assign the endowment to the professorship which the president held. It was an effort which failed utterly.

After a hiatus of sixteen years, broken by only one reference to the professorship in the minutes, the Alumni Association voted in 1898 to ask a committee to report on the status of the fund and the feasibility of bringing it to completion. The committee brought in the depressing report next year that an "examination of the records of this Association, of the books of the College Treasurer and of

---

[226]The eight institutions described as daughters of the College were Wittenberg, Roanoke, Newberry, North Carolina College, Illinois State University, Muhlenberg, Thiel, and Carthage Colleges. The effort to gather biographical information about all former students began in 1879. Much of it was obtained from the alumni themselves.

records of the Board give no information as to the amounts subscribed or paid on account of this fund." Another committee reported in 1900 that it was unable to learn anything more than had
its predecessor.

The last chapter in this long and somewhat ludicrous story began
when the Alumni Association in June 1902 named still another committee and directed it to take its case to the board of trustees. The
chairman, Frank G. Turner (1893), a young Baltimore attorney, and
his two colleagues lost little time in presenting the president of the
board with five questions to which the association desired an
answer. Philip H. Glatfelter consulted President McKnight and
Treasurer Picking. By early 1903 some startling replies began to
emerge. All of the moneys contributed to the alumni professorship
were deposited in the general endowment fund; there never was a
separate alumni professorship account. Sometimes Treasurer
Buehler would identify the source of these contributions, but on
other occasions he would not. A careful examination of the books
which Picking and Turner made showed 122 entries, between 1865
and 1887, recording gifts to the fund amounting to $12,490.
Obviously there had been more contributions, but no one could be
sure how many more. "If Mr. Buehler the former treasurer had been
living," Picking told Glatfelter, "the question [which the alumni
committee asked] could have been properly answered." But Alexander D. Buehler had been dead for ten years.

The resolutions which the Alumni Association passed in 1859,
when it inaugurated its endowment campaign, specified that all
sums contributed should be paid to the College treasurer. He was to
invest them and add the interest each year to the principal until the
goal was reached and the professorship established. In 1903 the Turner committee reckoned that the Alumni Association was now
entitled to a total of $58,350.79, principal and interest, far more than
it had ever promised the College.[227]

The Alumni Association brought the entire matter to the attention
of the full board of trustees in August 1903 and asked for some equitable settlement. The issues were sufficiently confusing that the
board referred them to a committee, of which one member was president and another treasurer of the Alumni Association. In June 1904
this committee made a lengthy report, in which it carefully presented and evaluated the available records of the alumni professorship

---

[227]The report of the Turner committee, with supporting documents, was copied
into the minute book of the Alumni Association, which is in the GCA. The *Adams
County Independent,* published in Littlestown, in its issues for June 6 and 20, 1903,
gave extensive coverage to the Turner committee's investigation. The editor claimed
that College authorities were preventing local newspapers, including the *Gettysburgian,* from giving the matter proper attention.

effort. The committee concluded that $14,267 had actually been paid into the College treasury from this source. It could find no evidence whatsoever that Buehler, a man of great probity who had never attended College and hence was not a member of the Alumni Association, was ever informed that interest was to be added to the moneys which it entrusted to him. Surely, he could not be held responsible for failing to do something of which he had no knowledge. Taking everything into consideration and wishing at long last to resolve the matter, the committee recommended that the board of trustees establish an Alumni Professorship Fund, allocate to it $25,000, use the proceeds for paying the salary of the Alumni Professor of Mathematics and Astronomy (in 1904 $25,000 yielded a professor's annual salary), and disclaim any further responsibility for money received from the Alumni Association since 1859. The trustees unanimously adopted these recommendations in June 1904 and thus brought to a successful conclusion a genuine effort to help the College which had begun almost half a century earlier.

As late as 1904, the Alumni Association still maintained its earlier interest in all of the graduates and former students of the College. At each annual meeting, the obituary committee read biographical sketches of the graduates known to have died during the preceding year. As already noted, in 1860 and 1870 the association published comprehensive reports on the alumni. The one originally projected for 1880 actually appeared as part of the *Pennsylvania College Book* in 1882. By the next decade, publication of a report similar to those of 1860 and 1870 was more than the Alumni Association wished to undertake. The next such compilation, the *Alumni Directory of Pennsylvania College of Gettysburg, 1832-1918 (Gettysburg, 1918)*, was a project of the College.

Until 1891 (except for five years in the 1870s), the faculty continued its earlier practice of including in each annual catalogue the names and known addresses of all graduates. This was considered a useful form of advertisement, and when it was dropped the faculty promised that "if found desirable, such list, with additional information, may be published every third or fifth year." Obviously it was found desirable, since names and addresses reappeared in the 1895, 1900, and 1905 catalogues. The *Spectrum* was another College publication which usually devoted considerable attention to graduates. Not only did it list the alumni clubs, as they were now called, but also it named their officers and members. Several *Spectrums* also listed all the graduates.

Taking as their text the statement that "a tree is known by its fruits," the editors of the 1904 *Spectrum* undertook the large task of classifying the alumni since 1834 by occupation or profession. "For the college to live and keep abreast with the times it needs both the concrete and abstract service of its friends," they wrote, "and we know of no better way of stimulating such a spirit of loyalty than by keeping before their minds the record of usefulness of the men who have gone out from the institution." Of 1264 graduates included in their report, 616 were classified as ministers, 177 as lawyers, 136 as teachers and administrators in public school systems, 128 as businessmen, 113 as college and seminary professors and presidents, 100 as doctors, and the rest in more than a dozen other categories. "Although but few of her sons have risen to great political prominence," the editors noted, "yet the great good they have been doing in the educational and religious world makes up for any apparent deficiency along other lines of activity."[228]

By 1904 there were at least twelve names to add to the list of alumni who had been college or seminary presidents and who were named in the preceding chapter: J. P. Benjamin Sadtler (1842), Muhlenberg; John A. Kunkelman (1855), Carthage; Louis A. Bikle (1857), North Carolina; Jonathan R. Dimm (1857), Susquehanna; David L. Tressler (1860), Carthage; Henry W. Roth (1861), Thiel; Theodore L. Seip (1864), Muhlenberg; Harvey W. McKnight (1865), Gettysburg; Edward F. Bartholomew (1871), Carthage; John S. Detweiler (1871), Carthage; Holmes Dysinger (1878), Carthage; and Charles W. Heisler (1880), Susquehanna.[229]

Town and Gown

The built-in tensions between persons in the Gettysburg community and those in the College which existed in the first period of the latter's history continued in the years between 1868 and 1904. There were many possibilities for misunderstanding between townspeople who sometimes resented the privileges which collegians enjoyed and students who sometimes believed that townspeople had little respect for either them or their rights. Nevertheless, having said that, one must reiterate that relations between the town and the College were usually good, probably better than those in many other college towns. Such resident trustees as David A. Buehler, Edward McPherson, John M. Krauth, and Harry C. Picking were influential and respected persons in the community,

[228]The report identified but one governor (Conrad Baker, Indiana, 1867-1873), nine members of Congress, and thirty state legislators. Several of these were nongraduates whom the editors nevertheless chose to include. Some persons were listed in several categories in the report.

[229]Other alumni headed educational institutions which were not recognized as four-year colleges during this time. For example, John Jacob Scherer (1852) was associated with Marion College in Virginia for more than forty years.

View of Gettysburg from the Glatfelter Hall tower, about 1890. Courtesy Adams County Historical Society.

and excellent in interpreting each side to the other.

Both the town of Gettysburg and the rest of Adams county continued to contribute a good proportion of the College's student body. For example, more than one-fourth of the freshman class and one-half of the preparatory department in the fall of 1900 were Adams countians. Young women of the town of Gettysburg continued to fascinate students. Every College publication to which students contributed gives testimony to this fact. The "College Locals" section of each recounted, undoubtedly often with tongue in cheek, the endless trials and tribulations of students who were in love, or who thought they were in love, with a towngirl. An article in the *College Monthly* for April 1883 listed twenty-eight collegians who since the beginning of 1877 had actually married Gettysburg women. The *College Monthly, Mercury,* and *Gettysburgian* all had sections on happenings in town for the obvious benefit of alumni readers. The "fantastical" parades on Washington's birthday eventually became community rather than merely student affairs.

Town disasters brought out the collegians, to assist and not merely to look on. The burgess in 1880 thanked seminary and College students for helping to fight a blaze which destroyed several buildings, including the old Gettys family house, in the alley to the north of the first block of York street. Five years later, when they turned out again to help battle a major blaze in the first block of

Chambersburg street, one old citizen exclaimed, according to the December 1885 issue of the *College Monthly*, "I haven't much use for them students, but they're mighty good fellows at a fire." When the Spanish-American War began in April 1898, some 150 students marched through the town behind an American and a Cuban flag, and then listened to patriotic speeches by representatives of town and gown. Several students enlisted and entered the service.[230]

The faculty contribution to the life of the community persisted. Henry Eyster Jacobs succeeded his father as president of the Gettysburg Gas Company, and, when he moved to Philadelphia, passed the mantle along to Edward S. Breidenbaugh, whose "standard thermometer" replaced that of Michael Jacobs in town. Luther H. Croll surveyed some of the newly established streets and served as president of the Gettysburg school board. Philip M. Bikle was one of two local pastors who in 1887 agreed for one year to conduct services for the A.M.E. Zion congregation, in an effort to help it pay a building debt by relieving it of the necessity of supporting a pastor during that period of time. Until the battlefield was turned over to the War Department in 1895, Harvey W. McKnight was a director of the Gettysburg Battlefield Memorial Association, which had maintained it for many years.

The battlefield in and around the town of Gettysburg affected the College in many ways. "On Saturdays the students used to go out with hatchets to cut bullets from trees," George D. Stahley (1871) remembered many years later. "I have some of those bullets yet. Others took spades and dug for bones – several rooms were decorated with cross bones and skulls." William M. Baum, Jr. (1877) recalled that in his day "the popular walk for students and townsfolk alike was up Baltimore street to the National Cemetery and then back again." Many of these promenades occurred on Saturday evening. "As the classes paraded along this way," he wrote, "it certainly made the sensation that was intended."[231]

As the twenty-fifth anniversary of the famous battle approached, the number of visitors to Gettysburg increased. The general revision of the College catalogue in 1887 took cognizance of this fact and attempted to turn it to the advantage of the institution:

> The great battle, of the civil war, fought here July 1-3, 1863, has made Gettysburg historically famous. The preservation of the lines of battle, and the many commemorative monuments erected under the auspices of the Gettysburg Battlefield Memorial Association, bring annually thousands of visitors, and constantly instill lessons

---

[230]*Star and Sentinel,* April 26 and May 10, 1898.
[231]*Gettysburg College Bulletin* (March 1934), p. 7; *Spectrum* (1902), p. 184.

of patriotism. Consequently, there is no better location for a National Institution.[232]

Trustees and faculty were fully aware of the public relations possibilities which were created as many of the visitors to Gettysburg came to the campus. Frequently the editors of the *College Monthly* urged that the grounds be better kept and instructed the students on the proper reception to be accorded all guests. They were told to refrain from their usual practices of guying visitors and throwing water (or worse) upon them from the windows of Pennsylvania Hall.

The campus was extensively used during the twenty-fifth anniversary celebration in June-July 1888, which coincided with commencement, the cornerstone laying for the new Recitation Building, and groundbreaking for Brua Chapel. By 1890 more than three hundred monuments had been erected on the battlefield. The faculty sometimes suspended classes to permit students to attend the inevitable dedication exercises. In 1888 the trustees gave permission to the State of Ohio to erect a monument to Battery K, First Ohio Light Artillery, at the corner of Carlisle street and West Lincoln avenue. Four years later, a monument was erected at the west end of Chambersburg street to Company A, Twenty-sixth Regiment, Pennsylvania Volunteer Militia. The main speakers on the occasion of its dedication, September 1, 1892, were Judge Samuel W. Pennypacker, later governor of Pennsylvania, and Harvey W. McKnight, president of the College.[233]

On October 15, 1890 the Count of Paris, who had fought with the Army of the Potomac during the Civil War, had written a history of the struggle, and was now visiting the battlefield, was given a reception by townspeople and students who filled Brua Chapel to capacity. Among those present to honor the pretender to the French throne were Generals Daniel E. Sickles, Henry W. Slocum, Oliver O. Howard, Daniel Butterfield, John Newton, David M. Gregg, and John P.S. Gobin. David Wills presided. The *College Monthly* for November 1890 claimed that this occasion brought together more

---

[232]This paragraph appears in a new introductory section of the catalogue, headed Location. The section still retained some of the flavor of the earliest days of the College. "The moral tone of the community [of Gettysburg] is unusually good. There are fewer temptations than in most towns of its size and the direct influence on the young men is excellent." This and subsequent catalogues informed the public that direct rail connections between Gettysburg and Harrisburg (1884) and between Gettysburg and Hagerstown (1889) had now been established.

[233]According to the *Gettysburgian* for October 6, 1897, John A. Himes proposed to assign juniors to interview Adams countians, asking them to give their recollections of the Civil War. In this way he could put on record some of "those things which ordinarily do not appear in history." It is regrettable that this oral history, if it was ever gathered, has not survived.

Monument dedicated in 1892 to Company A, Twenty-sixth Regiment, Pennsylvania Volunteer Militia.

corps commanders from the battle of Gettysburg than at any time since the end of the war. The students gave the count a royal sendoff with a yell composed especially for the occasion: "Comte de Paris, Rah! Rah! Rah! Rah! Siss, boom, tiger, Penn-syl-va-ni-yah."[234]

There was another side to the relationship between College and community. Faculty and students had a number of persistent complaints against the government and people of Gettysburg. The faculty still believed that the borough council was derelict in performing its duty to provide sidewalks and street lights near the campus. This became less and less a concern as the area east and southeast of the College property was developed. Both students and faculty were annoyed by town boys who used College facilities, especially McCreary Gymnasium, and sometimes left behind

---

[234]The Count of Paris was but one of a number of visiting lecturers. Among the others were J.H. Wilburn Stuckenberg (1892 and later), Henry Watterson (1895), and Confederate General John B. Gordon (1896).

damaged equipment and broken windows. "Is the Gymnasium for the benefit of the College or the town boys?" asked the *College Monthly* for November 1878. Someone writing in a later issue urged the students to take this matter into their own hands, arguing that it was their tuition money which was being used to keep the gymnasium in repair. After no-trespassing signs were placed on campus, the *College Monthly* for December 1885 explained that they did not mean the College no longer welcomed visitors. The warnings were intended only "to prevent ball-playing on the grounds in front of the buildings and the free and careless use of the gym by which both the building and apparatus had been greatly damaged." The culprits were identified as being "troops of boys, not connected with the College." The faculty remained bitter at those keepers of taverns and hotels who violated the law by selling intoxicating beverages to students who were minors. In January 1886 they asked the county court to reduce the number of liquor licenses granted in the borough. Three years later, as the prohibition movement was reviving in many parts of the country, college and seminary professors and students announced themselves in favor of a state constitutional amendment prohibiting the sales of such beverages.

Occasionally, both faculty and students reacted strongly to what they took to be unfair treatment by townsmen. For example, in 1877 the faculty protested at being assessed at a higher rate than any other occupation or profession in the borough and asked the board of trustees to come to their relief.[235] Perhaps the feeling which during these years was most pervasive was one of not being appreciated. In commenting on a report that the students and faculty at Cornell University spent annually in Ithaca the equivalent of an investment of $6,000,000, the *College Monthly* wondered in February 1881 "whether there are any citizens of Ithaca so blind, as there are here in Gettysburg, as to think that a few machine shops could pay better than a College."[236]

The community sometimes had its own reasons for feelings of bitterness and of not being appreciated. Some countians undoubtedly resented the regular suggestions emanating from the College that those closest geographically to the institution had a special responsibility for supporting it financially. They may have questioned at times whether its removal to some other place would be such a great loss, after all. In June 1887, as the College was about to embark upon its ambitious building program, the board of trustees passed a sense motion that countians should be expected to contribute at least $10,000

---

[235]For similar incidents, see the *Mercury* for November 1894 and May 1896.

[236]In November 1889 the *College Monthly* estimated that the annual College contribution to the local economy amounted to $60,000.

to the project and named a committee consisting of resident trustees to raise the money. In its issue of February 21, 1888, the *Star and Sentinel* went to great pains "to correct some erroneous impressions that are current in our community and county" by explaining the College's immediate and continuing needs and the role the community should play in meeting them. If we can believe the account in the *College Monthly* for November 1889, the county's financial contribution to the building program was a small one.[237]

The College and the Lutheran Church

In the summer of 1873 Milton Valentine wrote the article describing Gettysburg College which was scheduled to appear in the forthcoming *Johnson's New Universal Cyclopaedia*. "It is under the special auspices of the Lutheran Church," he explained, "but as in other American Colleges in such general denominational connection, its management and instruction are carefully guarded from being made sectarian." Then, assuming that one more sentence of explication was needed, he added : "Its design, in this respect, is to give a thoroughly Christian culture." These words, which might have been written by Charles P. Krauth forty years earlier, demonstrate that, as far as its president was concerned, Gettysburg College had not changed its basic relationship to the church with which it was identified since the very beginning. The large majority of trustees, faculty, and students continued to be Lutheran. Whenever it approached the church for money, the College stressed the close spiritual ties binding the two institutions together. Nevertheless, Gettysburg shared with most other American colleges of the time a highly valued freedom from outside control.[238]

The Lutheran church with which the College was identified in this period was that part which remained in the General Synod after the secession in 1863 of what eventually became the United Synod in the South and after the withdrawal in 1867 of several district synods which then formed the General Council.[239] The leading force in the

---

[237]According to a city paper, many observed "how little of the $90,000" cost of the new building "came from Gettysburg."

[238]See also Harold A. Dunkelberger, *Gettysburg College and the Lutheran Connection: . . .* (Gettysburg, 1975).

[239]The southern district synods in 1863 formed the General Synod of the Evangelical Lutheran Church in the Confederate States of America. After the war they changed their name several times. Between 1886 and 1918 it was the United Synod of the Evangelical Lutheran Church in the South. The synods which withdrew from the General Synod in 1867, together with several other bodies, formed the General Council of the Evangelical Lutheran Church in North America.

latter was the Synod of Pennsylvania, which helped to organize the General Synod in 1820, withdrew from that body three years later, and then returned to the fold in 1853. The conservative eastern Pennsylvania churchmen soon began to question the wisdom of their reaffiliation, largely because of the continued unwillingness of the General Synod to commit itself to the Unaltered Augsburg Confession strongly enough to satisfy them. In 1864, three years before the General Council was formed, these conservative Lutherans established their own theological seminary in Philadelphia and called Charles F. Schaeffer, Professor of German Language and Literature at Gettysburg, to join its faculty. Three years later they organized their own college at Allentown and called Frederick A. Muhlenberg, Franklin Professor of Ancient Languages at Gettysburg, to be its president. Both Schaeffer and Muhlenberg had been the first incumbents of their respective chairs at Gettysburg.

According to the agreement between the Pennsylvania Synod and Gettysburg College, the former controlled the endowment from which Schaeffer's salary had been paid and had the right to nominate his successors as German professor. According to the act of April 19, 1850, Gettysburg College held the endowment for the Franklin professorship which Muhlenberg occupied, but the synod had the right to nominate his successors. No sooner had Schaeffer resigned and departed for Philadelphia than it became evident that these arrangements, negotiated in the 1850s when the relations between the Pennsylvania Synod and the General Synod were improving, were not going to work as smoothly as intended.[240]

In April 1865 the Gettysburg trustees, after accepting Schaeffer's resignation and asking the Pennsylvania Synod to nominate his successor, approved a motion offered by Thaddeus Stevens, who was making one of his rare appearances at a board meeting, that they endeavor to gain control of the German professorship endowment, using whatever "ulterior measures might be necessary." Not surprisingly, the synod promptly rejected this proposal and nominated its candidate to succeed Schaeffer. After the trustees voted to defer any action on the nomination until his relationship to the seminary faculty could be clarified (Schaeffer, it should be recalled, taught in both institutions; the synod wanted his successor to devote full time to the College), the candidate withdrew his name from further con-

---

[240]There was ill feeling in Gettysburg over Schaeffer's hasty departure, for which he himself was not responsible. As late as August 10, 1864 he wrote to the College trustees that he did not expect to be called upon to leave his position for months, possibly for several years. Seventeen days later the president of the Synod of Pennsylvania informed the College that Schaeffer was being asked to assume his new duties in Philadelphia in a matter of days, which he did. The letters are in the GCA.

sideration. The synod then nominated John F. Wilken, whom the trustees, sorely in need of a German professor, elected in August 1866. At the same time, the College proposed to the synod referring the question of custodianship of the endowment to the decision of a third party. Not only did the synod reject this overture, but also it now suggested that part of the German endowment should be used to help support a professor at the Philadelphia seminary and that the number of its members in the College board should be increased.

The disputes were far from over. In May 1867 Muhlenberg resigned and the board dutifully asked the synod to nominate his successor. On the grounds that he "would not prove an efficient instructor, and would not meet the demands of this Institution," the board in August 1867 resoundingly rejected the synod's candidate for the Franklin professorship. At the same meeting, it authorized an immediate lawsuit to secure control of the German professorship funds. In 1868 the board rejected a second candidate for the Franklin professorship. Meanwhile the students were making life so miserable for Wilken that, during the summer, he resigned. The synod officers then nominated William Notz to serve in his place for one year. The trustees, again sorely needing a German professor, promptly elected him.

"The relations between the Synod and the Board of Trustees of the college," wrote the synod president in his report for the May 1869 meeting, "instead of being, as the Synod meant them to be, relations of intelligent co-operation and sympathy in a good and noble work, are simply relations of conflict, and that a very unequal conflict." If only because it was the synod which had secured the entire endowment of the German professorship and had used its influence to direct the endowment of the Franklin professorship to Gettysburg, he thought, its nominees for faculty positions were entitled to the "respectful consideration" which they were not receiving. "If we are to judge of the future from the past," he concluded, "there is much reason to fear, that the nominees who, in the deliberate opinion of the Synod, are, by their manners, their talents, their acquirements, fully qualified for the positions, will be exposed to the pain of a mortifying rejection by the Trustees."[241]

---

[241]In a letter written in 1868, the president of the synod stated its case succinctly. The synod had collected the funds for the German professorship with the understanding that it would always retain the principal "as a sacred trust which we are not at liberty, even were we so disposed, to alienate from our Synod." It was committed to using the interest to support the education of young men who will "enter the Lutheran Ministry prepared and qualified to preach in the German language and for no other purpose." The synod was bound "to defend the Fund in the name of the Congregations and in the name of God." A. T. Geissenhainer to Benjamin Sadtler, Bethlehem, May 10, 1868, GCA.

The season of mortification had not yet run its course, since there were now two vacancies at Gettysburg for which the synod was entitled to nominate candidates. In May 1869 it offered the names of Henry Eyster Jacobs for the Franklin and Adam Martin for the German professorships. Three months later the trustees almost unanimously rejected Jacobs and unanimously accepted Martin. When the synod met in 1870, it adopted a report expressing the judgment that the College trustees had "exceeded their just and lawful powers in the rejection, without assigning any reasonable cause, of the nominee of this Synod to the Franklin professorship." Accordingly, the synod presented again the name of Henry Eyster Jacobs, whom the trustees accepted in June 1870.[242]

The election of Martin and Jacobs to the Gettysburg faculty and their continued service therein brought to an end five years of harmful bickering over nominees and endowments, during the course of which the trustees either declined to act upon or rejected candidates five times. Still unanswered was the question of the long-term relationship between the two antagonists. What would happen when the next vacancy occurred? At one time or another both College and synod had sought legal advice as how best to protect what they believed were their rights. The College had named several committees to seek an end to their differences "upon such terms as may be deemed equitable and mutually satisfactory," as the minutes of August 1867 phrased it. Unfortunately, neither side had found acceptable the solutions offered by the other. Occasional efforts at agreement undertaken during the early 1870s got nowhere.

It was only in 1878 that serious negotiations leading to a final settlement at last seemed possible. Committees representing both sides met and reached an agreement by which the synod turned over the German professorship endowment to the College and gave up its right to nominate candidates for the two faculty positions. Apparently believing that the contest was still a very unequal one, as well as one not worth being continued, the synod was now willing to accept the College position in return for a release from any liability arising under either professorship. Both the Pennsylvania Synod and the College trustees approved the agreements in June 1879. With the full cooperation of the synod, on February 20, 1880 the College secured the amendment to its charter which was necessary to perfect these arrangements.[243]

---

[242]The synod was unhappy that the board had changed the Franklin professorship to Greek in 1867 and history in 1868 without first consulting them. Henry Eyster Jacobs attributed his rejection in 1869 to the fact that he was now a General Council pastor. Jacobs, *Memoirs*, p. 130.

Without a doubt, the actions of the Pennsylvania Synod in helping to secure the Franklin professorship for Gettysburg and in endowing the German professorship had been of great value to the College. For more than a quarter of a century the income from these two endowments had paid the salaries of a sizable fraction of the faculty, thus offering major relief to the slender College treasury. Nevertheless, by the time the second incumbents of these chairs were to be chosen, the trustees clearly resented any arrangement which limited their choice of faculty to persons nominated by some other agency. Once free of the agreements with the Pennsylvania Synod, they were careful not to enter into any similar ones.[244]

The election of Adam Martin in 1869 and of Henry Eyster Jacobs in 1870 occurred at the beginning of the financially troubled decade of the 1870s. Plagued by the debt incurred in building Stevens Hall and by recurring annual deficits, the trustees turned for help, as they had in the 1840s, to the Lutheran church. A circular sent to the synods in 1870 put the need at $50,000 and asked them to urge congregations to respond generously to the appeals of a newly appointed financial agent. At the board's request, Milton Valentine attended four synod meetings in the fall of 1872 in order to present the College's case in person. Then, in 1873, the trustees asked the Maryland, West Pennsylvania, and East Pennsylvania Synods each to raise $25,000 for an endowed professorship, and the Allegheny, Pittsburgh, Central Pennsylvania, and Susquehanna Synods together to raise a like amount for a fourth professorship.[245] At their fall meetings, most of these synods, after expressing their confidence in and support of the College, agreed willingly enough to

---

[243]This was the first amendment to the College charter which was approved by the Court of Common Pleas of Adams county. Before the Constitution of 1874 went into effect, an act of the legislature was required to change the organic law of the College. Adams County Deed Book NN, pp. 325-329. The agreement ratified in June 1879 resulted in the synod's transferring mortgages on Philadelphia property amounting to $10,000; title to the house in Gettysburg occupied by the German professor; title to a house and lot in Bethlehem; and a $3,000 claim, with thirteen years' unpaid interest, against Illinois State University. The latter claim proved to be worthless. College Monthly (June 1879), p. 178. With complete control of the Franklin professorship in hand, the trustees in June 1880 transferred its endowment to the general endowment fund.

[244]One can follow this lengthy controversy by reading the minutes of the trustees and of the annual meetings of the synod. By 1880 there were no longer General Council men on the board of trustees.

[245]These seven synods constituted the College's normal Lutheran constituency between 1868 and 1904. The Central Pennsylvania Synod dated from 1855 and the Susquehanna Synod from 1867. The College had its closest ties with the Maryland, West Pennsylvania, East Pennsylvania, and Allegheny Synods.

accept their assigned share, but in the only possible way then available to them.[246] Since synodical treasuries had annual incomes of only several thousand dollars, all these bodies could do was ask their pastors to preach about the needs of the College and to invite its representatives into their parishes to supplement these sermons and to make personal solicitations for contributions.

Late in 1873 the endowment committee of the board of trustees, in an effort to arouse interest in the financial campaign, published a sixteen-page pamphlet entitled *Pennsylvania College and the Lutheran Church*. Colleges, they claimed, "form one of the grandest agencies in the work of the Church and the successes of Christianity." Finding the beginning of the church's educational interest in the three years' experience of the disciples with Jesus, the authors traced that interest over more than eighteen hundred years. In America, they argued,

> the Church's efforts through its Colleges have, without doubt, been among the most successful and fruitful of all its work for Christ's kingdom . . . . Though these Colleges are unsectarian, Christianity, in it essential doctrines, is fully and constantly taught. Its truths are made to pervade and mould all the teaching.

Since these colleges exist, "not to make money, but to do good," they should be within the reach of "almost every earnest young man" who wishes to attend them. Hence the need for an endowment; "no College of high order can be established or carried on without one."

The authors of this pamphlet then discussed the many ways in which since 1832 Gettysburg College had assisted the Lutheran church. "Has any other instrumentality served the Church better?" they asked. Does the Church owe more to any other? Has the money given by it in any other direction, in equal amount, been more fruitful?" In its present hour of need, Gettysburg was calling upon its church to do no more than other churches were already doing for their colleges. "The time has come," they concluded, "when the Lutheran Church, if she means to do her work and maintain her honor, must wake up to the necessity upon her."

Unfortunately, both this fervent appeal for help, the most extensive which the College had yet issued, and the energetic efforts of Milton Valentine and others came during the time of a severe depression. Nevertheless, the college kept trying. As late as 1879 it revised and reissued the pamphlet, which was then sent to a number of potential donors. As noted earlier in this chapter, the results were

---

[246]Neither the Pittsburgh nor the Susquehanna Synod took any action. The Central Pennsylvania Synod had agreed in 1872 to invite representatives of the College into its congregations, but took no action in 1873.

disappointing. Not enough money was ever raised within the territory of any synod to endow even one professorship, let alone four.

Ever since the 1830s the faculty had adjourned classes in late February each year to permit the campus to join in a nationwide observance of a day of prayer for colleges. In 1875 the General Synod recommended that the date be changed to the last Thursday in January and six years later, in the hope that more congregations would observe it, that it be moved to the last Sunday in January. In June 1886, when the College treasury again experienced a deficit, the board of trustees asked the president to expand his recently begun efforts to persuade congregations to take a special collection on the day of prayer, the proceeds to be used to meet the College's incidental expenses. McKnight decided to work through both pastors and synods. In 1886 and 1887 he visited seven synod meetings, asking each to recommend that its congregations receive offerings for a specific purpose: to improve College buildings and grounds. He argued that an increasing number of people were visiting Gettysburg. It would enhance the reputations of both the College and the church if the campus always looked presentable. The synods responded favorably, and the first of many such offerings was received in January 1887. Apparently deciding that this practice was fast becoming an established one, the faculty included a paragraph on what it called the contingent fund in the 1887 catalogue, which reported that about $1,600 had already been contributed. Gifts reported during the next three years brought the total to $4,300. For many years, the synods annually commended this practice to their congregations, and as late as 1904 the catalogue still contained a paragraph describing the contingent fund.

During the 1870s and 1880s the relations between the College and the supporting synods, following the pattern established before the Civil War, were warm and friendly. Both presidents made it their practice to attend many annual synod meetings, meet the delegates, and address them on behalf of the College. Usually the synod president annually named a committee to examine the latest College catalogue and make a report on its findings. The East Pennsylvania Synod had a regular standing committee on the College. Because at least one of the members of these committees could be expected to be an alumnus of the College, the report often went beyond what was on the printed page of the catalogue. Almost without exception, it called attention to the pressing need for increased endowment, either by bequest or immediate gift; praised the quality of the educational program; insisted that the church needed the College; and, noting the small number of students enrolled, lamented the fact that some Lutheran parents were sending their sons to other colleges. In 1888, the Central Pennsylvania Synod declared that it "is the duty of all Lutherans to patronize our Lutheran institutions of learning . . . . they can do no better anywhere in the United States than to education their sons at Pennsylvania College."

The facts that about half of the Gettysburg graduates since 1834 had entered the Lutheran ministry and that they valued the training which they had received help explain the close relations between the synods and the College. "Nearly all the clerical members of this Synod have breathed the invigorating atmosphere created by this institution," declared the Maryland Synod committee in 1882, "and have felt its social, intellectual, moral, and ecclesiastical vitalizing power." By the end of the 1880s it was clear that the synods had developed a high regard for the leadership of Harvey W. McKnight. "What a work this man has done for our college," declared the West Pennsylvania Synod in 1889. "We owe him more than a mere vote of thanks. We owe him an abiding interest in the continued support of the Institution by sending our sons and the sons of our people to her halls for education, and by pecuniary help for the college over which he presides."[247]

Another tie binding the College and the church together was provided by the many trustees and faculty who were active participants in the affairs of district synods and of the General Synod. Between 1868 and 1904 five trustees served two-year terms as president of the latter body. In addition, Harvey W. McKnight was its executive officer in 1889-1891 and H. Louis Baugher in 1895-1897. Still another tie was provided by the close relationship between the two Lutheran institutions in Gettysburg. During the entire period from 1868 to 1904 there were pastors and laymen who served as trustees of both College and seminary. Faculty members of each served from time to time on the staff of the other. All but one of the seven men who joined the seminary faculty during this period were alumni of the College. Eight of the twelve students who entered the seminary in the fall of 1886 and fourteen of the eighteen who entered in the fall of 1904 were Gettysburg College graduates. Although the relations between the two schools were almost always cordial, there were occasions when those who were more concerned with the College looked with some jealousy upon the seminary's better fortune in attracting gifts. From time to time in the 1880s the College Monthly declared that the school which it represented obviously had the greater need at the moment and urged potential donors to respond accordingly.[248] In an attempt to coordinate efforts, the trus-

---

[247]In 1889 the trustees voted to charge sons of Lutheran ministers half tuition, a concession which the West Pennsylvania Synod had asked for some years earlier.
[248]See the College Monthly for July and October 1884.

This picture of the seminary faculty and students, which appeared in the 1905 Spectrum, *illustrates the continuation of the close relationship between that institution and the College.*

tees named a committee in 1899 to confer with seminary officials in an effort "to devise a plan for the raising of money for both Institutions at the beginning of the Twentieth century."

Almost entirely absent from written statements between 1832 and the later 1880s was any complaint on the part of the supporting synods about the lack of formal legal ties between the College and the church. Synodical committees called Gettysburg our college or the oldest Lutheran college, apparently without ever questioning whether the absence of the word Lutheran from the original College charter weakened the force of their claim.[249]

The first indication that opinions on this subject might be changing came in 1889, when the Allegheny Synod, after approving a report filled with high praise for the College, passed the following resolution:

Believing that a closer relation should exist between Pennsylvania College and the Synods in her territory, we urge a proportionate representation of these Synods in the Board of Trustees of said institution. We are of the opinion that as vacancies occur, except those which the alumni are entitled to fill, the Synods

---

[249]The word Lutheran does appear in the 1850 amendment to the charter, but not to describe an ongoing legal relationship between College and church.

should be permitted to nominate candidates for election to membership in the Board, and that the Trustees representing each Synod should present annually written reports of the work, needs and claims of the college.

A few weeks later, the Central Pennsylvania Synod passed a similar resolution, expressing its further belief that College trustees should be elected for a term of years rather than for indefinite terms.[250] Obviously, both of these bodies were calling upon the board to grant to the supporting synods the same privilege which it had extended in 1886 to the Alumni Association. The trustees did not act upon these expressions of synodical opinion.

The incident which initiated a major controversy between the College and the synods occurred in April 1892, when the board of trustees established the Amanda Rupert Strong Professorship of English Bible and chaplaincy of the College. As already noted, the trustees went into more detail in describing the duties of this position and its place in the College than they did with any other endowed professorship. In addition to making the English Bible a required study; offering as electives Hebrew, Septuagint Greek, and New Testament Greek; and assigning exclusive responsibility for chapel services and supervision of the "moral and spiritual interests and welfare" of the students to the chaplain and president, the trustees declared that

the Teaching in the department shall be positively Christian, according to the accepted standards of Evangelical Christendom, but in no sense denominational.

As instructed, the secretary of the board gave every faculty member written notice of this action and impressed upon him that any violation of its terms, by his engaging in denominational instruction in the classroom, would be sufficient grounds for dismissal.

The minutes of the meeting at which this action was taken do not reveal why the trustees felt it necessary, in accepting the new professorship, to define its position in the College in a way certain to be easily misunderstood and highly controversial. Within several weeks of the meeting, a letter purportedly written by a student to a trustee appeared in print, giving one possible answer to the question. The unidentified student, if such he was, charged that Harvey W. McKnight, whom he described as a very shrewd man, had a personal dislike of the Greek professor, H. Louis Baugher; disagreed with him on issues in the Lutheran church; and was trying to secure the dismissal of the man the writer called one of the two best teachers in the College. A few months earlier, Baugher had agreed to

---

[250]In 1887 the Allegheny Synod had recommended that trustees be elected for a term of years. The above and similar quotes in this section can be found in the published minutes of the synods.

Eli Huber
(1834-1911)

First Amanda Rupert Strong professor and first College chaplain.

H. Louis Baugher
(1840-1899)

His differences with President McKnight and other College officials helped precipitate the crisis of the 1890s.

instruct several College and seminary students in Luther's Catechism, a task traditionally performed by the pastor of Christ Lutheran church. McKnight opposed this venture, the student wrote, and did everything he could to stop it, but without success. The new rule would enable the president to take stronger measures against his foe. "Dr. McKnight hates Dr. Baugher, " the student concluded, "and is trying to weave a net around him from reasons in the church."[251]

---

[251]The "reasons in the church" relate to liturgy. In 1885 a joint committee from the General Synod, General Council, and United Synod of the South began working on a liturgy which congregations in all three Lutheran bodies could use. In 1889 the General Synod approved the Common Service which this committee had prepared and directed that it be included, together with the existing General Synod liturgy, in future editions of the Book of Worship. The College church voted in July 1889 not to use the Common Service, a decision which stood until 1923. Robert Fortenbaugh, A History of Christ's (College) Evangelical Lutheran Congregation of Gettysburg, Pennsylvania (1836-1936) (Gettysburg, 1936), pp. 44, 60. Harvey W. McKnight, Milton Valentine (even though he was a member of the committee which prepared it),

When the trustees held their regular meeting in June 1892, they granted Baugher's request to appear before them and received two communications from Lutheran conferences whose members were disturbed by the news of their action two months earlier. By a vote of 20 to 3 the trustees added several sentences of clarification to their April action, so that the pertinent sections now read:

> The teaching in the required work of the department [of English Bible] and of the College shall be positively Christian according to the accepted standards of Evangelical Christendom but in no sense denominational. This not to interfere with the voluntary religious and denominational work in which students may engage under the Chaplain, who shall be in charge of all the religious instruction in it, subject to the approval of the President, nor to disturb the basis on which the College has, in this respect, always been administered by the Board, in compliance with the provisions of its charter.

Trustees also met with each faculty member individually, requiring each to declare that he could accept the directive "as a guide of his action and loyally carry it out." They named John E. Graeff, Milton Valentine, and Harvey W. McKnight to prepare a statement of the Lutheran status of the College which had suddenly been called into question. Finally, they designated certain of their number to appear before synods of which they were members to explain their action to date.[252]

When the supporting synods held their annual meetings in the fall of 1892, they had their first opportunity to respond formally to the developments of the previous six months. A spectrum of opinion resulted. The East Pennsylvania Synod, of which McKnight and Eli Huber, the new Amanda Rupert Strong professor, were members, passed resolutions praising the new arrangements and expressing its confidence in the College. The Pittsburgh Synod, whose meeting McKnight attended, voted to "assure him of our unabating confidence and support." The West Pennsylvania Synod, of which Baugher was a member and on whose territory the College was located, expressed the hope that the trustees "in their wisdom will set forth its Lutheran character in such a way as to remove all

and Charles A. Hay all opposed using the Common Service. H. Louis Baugher strongly favored it as an expression of historic Lutheranism and a step toward eventual union of the several Lutheran bodies in the United States. A copy of the "student" letter, dated May 10, 1892, is in the GCA.

[252]In June 1892 another in the long series of College burlesques appeared. Entitled *The Bloody Lutheran: Gory but in no sense undenominational,* it was attributed by its authors to the Y.M.C.A. It was critical of every person and arrangement of the College which it discussed. "Although the Board has tried to apply the 'gag rule' to some of the Professors," it declared, somewhat beside the point, "we scarcely deem Lutheranism in so tottering a state that it will not bear the test of discussion." As it was, "we have a strictly non-sectarian and anti-common service college."

possibility of misunderstanding" and requested synodical representation, but then specified that "this action of the Synod is in no sense meant to alienate the sympathy and support of the church from the institution, but on the contrary we ask for it the continued confidence and patronage of our people." The members of the Maryland Synod were appreciative of the June efforts of the board "to allay the uneasiness wrought by the action taken in April," but thought that further steps were necessary "to fully restore the confidence of all of our people in the institution as a part of the Church's educational machinery." One such step would be synodical representation in the board of trustees. The Central Pennsylvania Synod readopted its earlier motions in favor of such representation and then, after listening to McKnight's "encouraging remarks on the progress of Pennsylvania College," pronounced itself "not satisfied with the recent action of the Board of Trustees." The Allegheny Synod was the least charitable of all. After considering, but finally voting down, four critical resolutions, one of which threatened to send its preministerial candidates elsewhere if the board did not reverse itself, this synod passed a fifth motion which declared that "the instruction imparted in Pennsylvania College should be in harmony with the doctrine of the Lutheran Church as held by the General Synod."[253]

The report on the Lutheran status of the College which the board commissioned Graeff, Valentine, and McKnight to prepare was published in the *College Monthly* in October 1892 and issued in pamphlet form about the same time. The authors chose to develop five points which they considered essential to a proper understanding of the issues at hand.

First, they insisted that the College always had, and would continue to have, a "positive and well-secured 'Lutheran status.'" It was founded by Lutherans, although with the active help of members of other faiths, in order to promote the interests of the Lutheran church. Thirty-two of the thirty-six trustees in 1892 were Lutheran; the four who were not were alumni of the institution fully committed to its traditions. All of the faculty were Lutheran. "In the sense in which American colleges take denominational names," they insisted, "Pennsylvania College is a Lutheran college . . . . It belongs to the Lutheran church, and is consecrated peculiarly to its interests and prosperity." Calling Abraham Lincoln to their aid, they proclaimed that "it is of the church, by the church and for the Church." Only "a total, immoral, and incredible breach of trust" could change this long-established relationship.

---

[253]The Susquehanna Synod which met in June ignored the developing controversy.

Second, the requirement that teaching in courses within the curriculum be Christian, but not denominational, the authors contended, was merely reaffirmation of a policy established in 1832 and in force ever since. The objection being raised in 1892, it should be remembered, was not to the Christian part of this policy, but to the prohibition of denominational instruction. To establish the soundness of the board position in this regard, the authors first quoted from Schmucker's famous 1831 statement, then referred to the 1873 pamphlet on *The College and the Lutheran Church*, and finally turned to the 1882 history. They also called attention to the language of the charter, which defined the purpose of the College: to educate "youth in the learned languages, the arts, sciences, and useful literature." This, they contended, did not include "Lutheran or denominational theology." But entirely apart from these historical references to justify the board's action, the authors insisted that any college "necessarily surrenders its best chance of strength and prominence as an educational center by cutting itself off, by sectarian teaching, from the patronage of the great general public, and drawing only from a particular denomination or a section of its territory." The best way for Lutheran colleges to serve the Lutheran church and the Christian cause was for them to "offer, as they are doing under the wise rule adopted, diplomas that count for as broad and liberal a culture as the best Colleges of the land afford." Statements solicited from such sister institutions as Wittenberg, Carthage, Roanoke, Dickinson, Bucknell, Franklin and Marshall, Lafayette, Allegheny, and Princeton were introduced at this point to illustrate that the position of Gettysburg was fully consistent with that of many other church-related colleges.

Third, the authors responded to the charge that "distinctive Lutheran teaching" was being eliminated under the new rules by claiming that actually the reverse was the case. In addition to the opportunities for Lutheran studies which had always existed outside the curriculum, there would now be even more, made possible by an additional faculty member who was also chaplain of the College. Thus, there was clear "provision for distinctive Lutheran teaching in its true and proper place." To claim otherwise was a "grotesque absurdity and an intolerable misrepresentation."

Fourth, Graeff, Valentine, and McKnight replied to the charge that the new professor and chaplain would have no independence in carrying on his work because he would be answerable to the president. They observed that, by action of the trustees in 1834, the president was the "head of the whole administration." Historically he had a special responsibility for the religious life of the College. Now he and the chaplain would share that responsibility. It would be "an utter perversion" of the meaning of the trustee action to imply that it was intended to emasculate the chaplain.

The fifth point was a crucial one. What was the real intention of the board of trustees in entirely excluding the rest of the faculty from giving religious instruction in the College and in warning them that violation of this rule would be sufficient reason for dismissal? The answer which the three authors gave was simple and direct: "necessary unity and good order" required it. Every professor is chosen because he is qualified to serve a particular department, and "not for work that belongs to another department or because he may have assumed ministerial obligations." To allow any faculty member free rein in this matter would surely open the College to "all the partisan strifes whose waves of unhappy agitation afflict the church." The several professors simply could not, "at personal impulse or suggestion of others, be at full liberty to take up 'denominational teaching,' whether from the mere fact of ordination vows or because of dissatisfaction, perhaps, with the explanations of the department to which it is assigned." The board was fully justified in insisting upon "strict compliance" with the order it had adopted.[254]

Having developed these five points, Graeff, Valentine, and McKnight rested their case, confident it showed that "there has been no just ground for the opposition that has been raised against" the board and that "the Lutheran interests in Pennsylvania College have been conscientiously and faithfully cared for, and that the Board has a right to look for the fullest confidence, support and cooperation of the Church."[255]

As could be expected, this argumentative document, directed largely against one faculty member and his supporters, did not bring the controversy to an end. When the board met in June 1893, it had to deal with the still unanswered question of synodical representation in its membership. It began doing so by referring the matter to a committee and directing its members to report at the next meeting. Before that occurred, the several synods held their fall 1893

---

[254]In his memoirs, Henry Eyster Jacobs, who was Baugher's faculty colleague for more than a decade, wrote that "he was repeatedly warned not to wander in the Class Room beyond the branches pertaining to his own particular field." He was told to teach Greek, not theology. "This – as one called to the position as a part of his ministry – he declined to accept." Jacobs, Memoirs, p. 385. Certainly, in naming Baugher to the faculty in 1869 and again in 1883, the board of trustees believed that it was choosing a qualified college teacher who was incidentally an ordained Lutheran minister. It was engaging a professor, not calling a pastor.

[255]The Lutheran Status of Pennsylvania College (1892) was a fifteen-page pamphlet. The 1893 catalogue, the first to incorporate information about the new professorship, declared that "whilst instruction in the required work is not strictly sectarian, abundant opportunity is given through catechetical and other classes for thorough training in the teachings and customs of the Lutheran church."

sessions. Those which had expressed their dissatisfactions a year before were not mollified by the explanation contained in *The Lutheran Status of Pennsylvania College.* For example, the West Pennsylvania Synod was grieved that the College "had passed to so large a degree out of the control of the Lutheran church and her ministry" and expressed the conviction that "it would serve the best interests of the College to expunge or modify the prohibition of Lutheran denominational doctrine." This synod repeated its earlier request for synodical representation under conditions similar to those already accorded the Alumni Association.

A special meeting of the board of trustees convened in December 1893 to hear the report of its committee. Early in the meeting the secretary read a letter from Harvey W. McKnight, submitting his resignation as president and giving two reasons for his action. The first was the "serious and irreconcilable differences between Professor H. L. Baugher D.D. and myself on the questions of policy and management, which through his appeals to the church, have awakened unnecessary and unjustifiable opposition to the college and ill-will towards me personally." The second was the embarrassment caused by the unpaid debt incurred during the building and renovation program, a debt which the controversy had made it nearly impossible to reduce. All in all, McKnight wrote, the burden of his office had become "heavier than I ought to bear."[256] The secretary then read a second document, which was a statement adopted by eighty-five students at a mass meeting held two weeks earlier. "Having confidence in his administration and being in sympathy with his policy," the students asked that the trustees refuse McKnight's resignation and "remove all obstacles to his continuance" as president.

Several hours of persuasion and negotiation followed from these developments. Six trustees pledged a total of $1,600 for debt reduction. A committee visited Baugher and once again secured his promise to abide by the regulations of the board. After twice refusing to reconsider his resignation, McKnight took these pledges of support into consideration and finally agreed to remain as president. Meanwhile, the members of the board were also dealing with the question of synodical representation. After prolonged discussion, they passed resolutions which deplored the fact that many had interpreted their action in establishing the Strong professorship as altering the Lutheran status of the College and which unequivocally reaffirmed the prohibition of denominational teaching in degree work. In an effort to respond in some positive manner to the synods,

---

[256]On the advice of his physician, McKnight had taken a trip to Europe in the spring of 1893.

the trustees then declared that, while they could not see their "way clear to grant the request of the Synods . . . in the precise form in which it is made," they were willing to seek an amendment to the College charter which would require that, henceforth, at least three-fourths of the trustees be members of the Lutheran church. Furthermore, they agreed to fill vacancies in the board, as far as possible, in a way which would give those synods according the College their "undivided support" a form of representation which they did not then enjoy. The committee had urged the trustees to adopt their report "as a full and final settlement of the whole question" and, in an effort "to take away all cause for distrust and agitation," to request the faculty to promise in writing that they would support it "in the College and outside of the College." All of the professors agreed to do so.

The Court of Common Pleas of Adams county approved the proposed charter change on May 21, 1894.[257] The amendment was an accomplished fact by the time the synods met in the fall of that year. Although the Central Pennsylvania and West Pennsylvania Synods reiterated their earlier requests for more direct representation, it is apparent that all bodies which took any action at this time were prepared to consider the matter closed. "The action of the Board," declared the Allegheny Synod, should be accepted "as a final settle-ment of the question as to the religious status of the College," which was then commended "to the patronage of the Synod."

Even before these synods met, events in Gettysburg had taken an unexpected turn. At the June 1894 meeting of the trustees, President McKnight reported that a member of the faculty – it was H. Louis Baugher – was stating repeatedly that the academic standards of the College were being lowered, a charge which the president claimed was hurting the institution.[258] He demanded an investigation. The matter was referred to the executive committee, whose resident members conducted their inquiry in September. After interviewing Baugher and several other faculty members, and after examining some of the records, the members concluded that Baugher had not established the validity of his charges. They noted that he had complained about "the changes and development of the curriculum, under the sanction of the Board, in order to meet the educational

---

[257]Adams County Deed Book UU, p. 359.

[258]In June 1894 the faculty voted reluctantly to recommend for the bachelor of arts degree two candidates who had not taken the additional examination in Greek which they had been directed to take. The faculty believed there were extenuating circumstances. Baugher saw this action as a lowering of standards. He believed that admitting students to College on the strength of a preparatory school principal's certificate was also a lowering of standards. It is evident that he associated an increasing student body with a decline in quality of instruction and student performance.

demands of our times, especially in the increased stress laid upon the natural sciences." He was also critical of the lack of college preparatory schools which offered adequate training in Greek and Latin in those areas from which Gettysburg drew many of its students. The full board adopted this report at its next meeting, in June 1895. At the same time, it passed a rule requiring faculty to respect the departments of their colleagues and refrain from criticizing them in the presence of students.

The last acts in this unfortunate drama were yet to occur. Having decided to increase the number of meetings from one a year to two, the trustees assembled for their first winter session in January 1896, only to hear the secretary read yet another letter of resignation from the president. "Owing to the trouble which has existed in the College during the last seven years, growing out of the partisanship in the General Synod," and which continues, preventing "the further and full success of my work through a lack of harmonious cooperation," McKnight informed the trustees that he was leaving office in September.[259] According to the minutes, "this letter was regretfully heard by the Board and its reading was followed by considerable discussion." The members then decided to refer the resignation to a committee which was asked to report no later than the June meeting. They also passed a resolution binding themselves to refrain from commenting to others about their deliberations. At a special meeting in February, the committee proposed that the board give McKnight a vote of confidence, ask him to withhold his resignation, and make certain changes in the administration which were designed to lighten his burdens. When he refused to change his mind about resigning, the board asked the committee to "investigate the troubles and difficulties that apparently prevent harmony and efficiency in the successful working of the College" and to recommend whatever action was deemed necessary to remove them.

The members of the committee presented their lengthy report to the June 1896 meeting of the board. As a result of their investigation, they had reached the conclusion that the president had been subjected "to annoyances which embittered his life, and made it impossible for him to labor with any degree of hopefulness." Most of these annoyances began with the prohibition of denominational teaching in 1892 and came from H. Louis Baugher. After the board "compelled silence" on that issue, the Greek professor had turned his attention to other College policies, charging publicly that academic standards were being lowered and that discipline was "culpably lax." After interviewing several faculty and examining College records,

---

[259]Note that in his letter McKnight traced the trouble in the College to the year in which the General Synod approved the Common Service.

the committee concluded that it could not substantiate Baugher's charges. For example, the members believed that discipline, "if not perfect, compares favorably with the order under other administrations." The committee stated that Baugher had denied the accuracy of most of McKnight's complaints about him, "even though it involved a question of veracity between himself and others." Whatever the truth of the matter might be, it was clear that McKnight would not continue in office under the existing circumstances.

The committee found that both men had many friends. McKnight's pointed to his undeniable major achievements on behalf of the College during the preceding twelve years. They were giving "no uncertain sound" in insisting that, if he could not be retained, then Baugher would also have to be dismissed or their support of the College, financially and otherwise, would be withdrawn. Baugher's friends pointed to his distinguished service to the institution and to the Lutheran church over a period of many years. He had long been active in the General Synod and in 1896 was its president. They insisted that, if he were dismissed, it would in fact be as a result of "personal enmity" and opposition to his religious opinions.

Having been asked by the board to recommend steps to end the dispute, the committee found itself facing what it called a "most painful" dilemma, but it did perform the task assigned. Concluding that Baugher's "injudicious conduct" had brought about McKnight's resignation, which now involved the College in "serious difficulties," and that the latter's remaining in office was "indispensable to its continued success," the committee recommended that the resignation be refused. Further, since Baugher could not be retained "with any degree of comfort to the Board of Trustees or to the harmonious working of the Administration of the College," it recommended that his services be terminated according to the conditions of his contract "without bringing any direct specific charges" against him. The board adopted the first recommendation by a vote of 20 to 2 and the second by a vote of 21 to 3. McKnight remained. Baugher left.[260]

---

[260]In June 1896 the trustees also terminated the services of Franklin Menges, Assistant in Chemistry, who shared Baugher's views and supported him. With one exception, the two local newspapers and the Littlestown *Adams County Independent* reported only briefly and without comment on the five months crisis. The exception was the *Star and Sentinel* treatment (January 28, 1896) of McKnight's resignation. Without mentioning Baugher by name, the story defended the president and stated that he had become weary of the constant annoyances he had to face. All three papers reprinted without comment (June 30 and July 4, 1896) the long letter which Baugher wrote to the trustees after his services were terminated. In it, he tenaciously defended all of his positions. "Whether the position of the late 'Franklin Professor' or that of

It is evident that, in taking each step during the long controversy, the trustees had acted deliberately and with near unanimity in determining their course of action. Whatever Baugher's fellow-professors may have thought about his differences with the president, there is no evidence from either the faculty or trustee minutes that they wanted to go on record with an expression of their own sentiments. Perhaps, in choosing between two colleagues, they too faced a most painful dilemma.[261] Although the students had acted with near unanimity in 1893 to support McKnight, it is clear that they too preferred peace to war. Now "everything is amicably adjusted," the Mercury declared in March 1894, surely in hope but scarcely in realism, "and the Faculty as a Unit is united with the administration. We are now ready for a new campaign of prosperity." During the 1896 phase of the crisis, the Mercury confined itself largely to observing that, although there was a lot of speculation, few people knew very much about what was happening. "For one who is not very familiar with the inner workings of the matter it is by no means easy to see the good which is being done by this division of opinions," wrote the editor in May 1896, "and even less easy to decide who is in the right." One thing seemed certain to him: much harm would come to the College if it were not soon ended. "Our institution is not in a condition at the present to remain uninjured by a conflict which is so fundamental."[262]

The only major results which the events of 1896 produced in the church came from the Maryland Synod in October. Baugher

---

the board and administration is the better for the welfare of the public, the church or the college," he wrote, "we may safely allow intelligent people to decide." Not all intelligent people think alike, but the preponderance of opinion over the years on the issues which the controversy raised is clear. Under the headline, "War in the College," the Baltimore American for June 29, 1896 presented a decidedly slanted view of the controversy and also reprinted Baugher's letter.

[261] In the November 1893 issue of the College Monthly, which was the next-to-the-last one, Philip M. Bikle wrote that the controversy was "a subject we have studiously avoided ourselves, and earnestly desire that no discussion of it shall appear in our pages." It is probable that if Baugher's colleagues had seen the board actions from 1892 on as an infringement upon their duties and rights, they would have protested. Edward S. Breidenbaugh wrote an appreciative obituary of Baugher which appeared in the March 1899 Mercury.

[262] In March 1895 the Mercury published an account of the beginnings of the College which Samuel Simon Schmucker had written in 1863 and which had only recently been found in the seminary library. The editor wrote that the account was "a thorough vindication of the much criticised action" of the board of trustees regarding denominational instruction. "Whatever uncertainty or doubt the friends of the College may have entertained on this question within recent years, it is very evident that no like doubt or uncertainty existed at the time of the founding of the College." The 1892 action, "instead of being a departure from the original intent of the founders was in strictest accord with it."

appeared before that body and presented his case in detail. Speaking for the College trustees who were in attendance, William H. Dunbar explained that, while he and his colleagues were prepared then and there "to go into the full details of the case," it would be preferable for the synod to ask the board itself "for an authoritative statement in explanation of its action." The synod took this advice, and a delegation presented its request to the January 1897 meeting. In reply, the trustees explained that Baugher had not been summarily dismissed; his contract was terminated in a regular way when the College gave him six months' notice that his services were no longer required. This action was made necessary because of the "want of harmony" within the College, which had nothing to do with Baugher's personal religious convictions. In conclusion, the trustees gave the synod a brief lecture on how a college must be run. The detailed administration of such an institution "must be confided to the discretion of its trustees and . . . all that can reasonably be expected or required of them is that they should act in such administration in good faith and according to their best judgment, which is what the Board has done in the present case." What more could be said?[263] Although scars and memories of the bitter contest remained for a long time, the minutes of the supporting synods after 1897 once again conveyed sentiments of full support for the College and praise for those who were managing its affairs.

After the board's decision in June 1896, Harvey W. McKnight continued as president of the College for eight more years. H. Louis Baugher, stunned by the action of the board in terminating his services, declined a call to a Baltimore parish. From his Gettysburg home he edited the *Lutheran World*, a weekly periodical published in York, from December 1896 until February 1898. By then in failing health, he sought relief in a Philadelphia sanitarium, where he died of what was called nervous prostration in February 1899.[264]

---

[263]The same response was sent to the Synod of New York and New Jersey, which had also questioned the board's decision. In October 1897 the Maryland Synod listened to the report of the committee which had visited Gettysburg and then voted, 62 to 39, to lay it on the table. In October 1896 the West Pennsylvania Synod met at St. James Lutheran church, Gettysburg, whose council stated its unwillingness to allow the church to be used for discussing the issues between Baugher and the College. The synod declined to forbid such discussion, but did ask any who might engage in it to proceed with "moderation, toleration and charity," confining themselves "strictly to the principles and facts in the case." There is a copy in the College Archives of a printed address supposedly delivered by Baugher before the synod on October 19. In it he again strongly defends his position. The minutes of the synod do not contain any notation that this address was in fact delivered.

[264]Henry Eyster Jacobs visited Baugher during his last illness in Philadelphia and ministered to him there. The two men had grown up together in Gettysburg, knew

In The World Of Higher Education

There is abundant evidence from the years between 1868 and 1904 that the trustees, faculty, students, alumni, and friends of Gettysburg College were quite aware that this institution was part of a world of American higher education, which included a growing number of colleges and universities, as well as students. Although they learned about this world from a number of different sources, after 1877 there was one which all of them could share in common. No one carefully read the *College Monthly, Mercury,* or *Gettysburgian* without being informed (certainly not always accurately or sufficiently) about major developments occurring in other institutions in all parts of the United States. Many members of the constituency, in advocating a course of action for the College to follow, used the experiences of some of these other institutions as examples of what Gettysburg should or should not do. The common refrain was that Gettysburg must be abreast of the better or best colleges in the land. For a number of reasons, rooted in its history, there was almost no call for it to be in the forefront of curricular or other educational developments. Perhaps most agreed with the alumni editor of the *College Monthly,* who in 1886 took for granted that Gettysburg would not be the first college to institute student government, but who did not want it to be the last.

Both trustees and faculty were interested in more and better advertising of the College, in part because of their desire to attract more students, but also simply because they believed that it needed to be better and more widely known than it had ever been in the past. They took great pains to prepare and send an exhibit to the Centennial Exhibition in 1876. During that financially troubled decade, they allocated what funds they could for advertisements in church and other newspapers and periodicals. Unlike many other college officials, they regularly completed and submitted questionnaires, the information from which was then published in the annual reports of the Pennsylvania Superintendent of Public Instruction (beginning in 1875) and of the United States Commissioner of Education (beginning in 1870). Especially after the mid-1880s, they were careful to identify the location of the College with

---

each other intimately, and were lifelong friends. In his memoirs, Jacobs wrote that Baugher's "entire caste of mind and temperament put him generally in the minority. He was critical by nature, and outspoken." Jacobs considered him "a born agitator . . . not satisfied with protesting, but . . . always determined to force a conflict. His sarcasm was burning; his treatment of opponents brusque and irritating." According to Jacobs, Baugher's assets were "his unquestioned ability as a teacher, and his gifts as a preacher." Jacobs, *Memoirs,* p. 385.

that of a momentous Civil War battle and an increasingly heavily visited battlefield.

In no feature of the College's life was the awareness of the world of higher education more pronounced than in the post-1868 development of the curriculum. Clearly, trustees and faculty wanted to have the best educational program which their always scanty financial resources permitted, one which was nevertheless consistent with the purposes of the institution and their estimate of the needs of the students who came to them. They were willing to seek advice. Thus, in the late 1860s the faculty sent to Amherst for information on what to include in a good gymnasium. The architect who designed the College observatory in the 1870s first visited both existing installations and "eminent astronomers." Before taking up his duties in 1889, the new Professor of Physical Culture and Hygiene drew upon the experience of Harvard University with a similar position. College authorities were also willing to respond to outside initiatives which they deemed worthwhile. Thus, in the early 1880s the trustees acceded promptly to the request of the American Philological Association and the American Association for the Advancement of Science that the honorary doctorate in philosophy be abandoned. About fifteen years later the trustees and faculty responded with equal promptness to changes then occurring in medical education by establishing a program in biology.

By 1904 there were a number of professional societies in existence, to which faculty members could belong. These included the American Chemical Society (1876), the Modern Language Association (1883), and the American Historical Association (1884). There were still no influential national educational associations, such as the American Council on Education, but there were already four regional agencies in existence: in New England (1885), the Middle States (1887), the South (1895), and the North Central States (1895). None had yet assumed the accrediting function for which they eventually became best known. Their main original purpose was to establish closer relations between colleges and universities, on the one hand, and the growing number of high schools and academies, on the other, in an effort to reach agreement on proper standards and procedures for admission to institutions of higher education.

Largely as a result of the efforts of President Edward Hicks Magill of Swarthmore, the College Association of Pennsylvania (which eventually became the Middle States Association of Colleges and Schools) was organized in 1887. Harvey W. McKnight and Edward S. Breidenbaugh attended several of the initial meetings.[265] In 1893

---

[265]McKnight and Breidenbaugh attended the meeting held in Harrisburg on March 1, 1887 and McKnight the one held in Lancaster on July 5 and 6, 1887. Minutes of the

the association adopted guidelines for uniform college entrance examinations in English language and literature. Four years later the Gettysburg faculty and trustees agreed to increase their entrance requirements in accordance with these guidelines.

In an effort to bring Pennsylvania colleges and universities under some measure of public control, the legislature on June 26, 1895 enacted a law which laid down specific requirements for all new institutions of higher learning seeking authority to confer degrees. The act also set the minimum amount of assets needed for existing colleges ($100,000) and universities ($500,000) wishing to continue conferring degrees. Administration of this measure was vested in a College and University Council, whose certification that all of the requirements had been met was needed before a county court could grant a charter of incorporation to any college or university.[266] Among the first twelve members of the council were presidents of three liberal arts colleges: Muhlenberg, Dickinson, and Washington and Jefferson. In 1903 Harvey W. McKnight succeeded the president of Dickinson as the central Pennsylvania representative on the College and University Council.

Toll No More The Bell

In September 1900, at the beginning of the first complete academic year in a new century, the faculty ended a practice which had been introduced during the very earliest days of the College's existence. They decreed that "the ringing of the college bell at noon and evening, shall hereafter be dispensed with." While this silencing of so familiar a sound does not signal any sharp break with the institution's past which occurred about this time, it is a convenient reminder that by 1900 many of the main features of Gettysburg College and of the issues which would confront it in the new century were already clearly in evidence. Because of its long record of limited success in raising money, it had a smaller endowment than most of the colleges with which it was accustomed to comparing itself. At the same time, trustees and faculty were aware of the need to continue adjusting both curriculum and standards if they hoped to remain competitive with these other institutions.

Obviously, by 1900 there had been a retreat from the old notions of order and discipline in the College, enough to accommodate both social fraternities and intercollegiate athletics. Equally obviously,

College Association of Pennsylvania, Middle States Association of Colleges and Schools, Commission on Higher Education, Philadelphia.

[266]Sack, *Higher Education,* pp. 300-303. In 1921 the College and University Council became the State Council of Education.

the retreat was far from total; many of the old rules and regulations still remained on the books and were being enforced, with the usual vigor and the usual results. What must be regarded as the most successful financial effort thus far in the history of the College had yielded three new and three renovated buildings. These structures provided the wider place for the greater work which fulfilled the aspirations of many in the 1880s.

Without a doubt, the most valuable assets which Gettysburg College had in 1900, and in 1904, were not its buildings, but a host of devoted trustees, faculty, students, alumni, and friends. Working together, they had it within their power to determine whether this already venerable institution would exercise an even more salutary influence in advancing the cause of liberal education in the twentieth century than it had in the nineteenth.